Safari Nation

NEW AFRICAN HISTORIES

SERIES EDITORS: JEAN ALLMAN, ALLEN ISAACMAN, AND DEREK R. PETERSON

David William Cohen and E. S. Atieno Odhiambo, *The Risks of Knowledge*

Belinda Bozzoli, *Theatres of Struggle and the End of Apartheid*

Gary Kynoch, *We Are Fighting the World*

Stephanie Newell, *The Forger's Tale*

Jacob A. Tropp, *Natures of Colonial Change*

Jan Bender Shetler, *Imagining Serengeti*

Cheikh Anta Babou, *Fighting the Greater Jihad*

Marc Epprecht, *Heterosexual Africa?*

Marissa J. Moorman, *Intonations*

Karen E. Flint, *Healing Traditions*

Derek R. Peterson and Giacomo Macola, editors, *Recasting the Past*

Moses E. Ochonu, *Colonial Meltdown*

Emily S. Burrill, Richard L. Roberts, and Elizabeth Thornberry, editors, *Domestic Violence and the Law in Colonial and Postcolonial Africa*

Daniel R. Magaziner, *The Law and the Prophets*

Emily Lynn Osborn, *Our New Husbands Are Here*

Robert Trent Vinson, *The Americans Are Coming!*

James R. Brennan, *Taifa*

Benjamin N. Lawrance and Richard L. Roberts, editors, *Trafficking in Slavery's Wake*

David M. Gordon, *Invisible Agents*

Allen F. Isaacman and Barbara S. Isaacman, *Dams, Displacement, and the Delusion of Development*

Stephanie Newell, *The Power to Name*

Gibril R. Cole, *The Krio of West Africa*

Matthew M. Heaton, *Black Skin, White Coats*

Meredith Terretta, *Nation of Outlaws, State of Violence*

Paolo Israel, *In Step with the Times*

Michelle R. Moyd, *Violent Intermediaries*

Abosede A. George, *Making Modern Girls*

Alicia C. Decker, *In Idi Amin's Shadow*

Rachel Jean-Baptiste, *Conjugal Rights*

Shobana Shankar, *Who Shall Enter Paradise?*

Emily S. Burrill, *States of Marriage*

Todd Cleveland, *Diamonds in the Rough*

Carina E. Ray, *Crossing the Color Line*

Sarah Van Beurden, *Authentically African*

Giacomo Macola, *The Gun in Central Africa*

Lynn Schler, *Nation on Board*

Julie MacArthur, *Cartography and the Political Imagination*

Abou B. Bamba, *African Miracle, African Mirage*

Daniel Magaziner, *The Art of Life in South Africa*

Paul Ocobock, *An Uncertain Age*

Keren Weitzberg, *We Do Not Have Borders*

Nuno Domingos, *Football and Colonialism*

Jeffrey S. Ahlman, *Living with Nkrumahism*

Bianca Murillo, *Market Encounters*

Laura Fair, *Reel Pleasures*

Thomas F. McDow, *Buying Time*

Jon Soske, *Internal Frontiers*

Elizabeth W. Giorgis, *Modernist Art in Ethiopia*

Matthew V. Bender, *Water Brings No Harm*

David Morton, *Age of Concrete*

Marissa J. Moorman, *Powerful Frequencies*

Ndubueze L. Mbah, *Emergent Masculinities*

Judith A. Byfield, *The Great Upheaval*

Patricia Hayes and Gary Minkley, editors, *Ambivalent*

Mari K. Webel, *The Politics of Disease Control*

Kara Moskowitz, *Seeing Like a Citizen*

Jacob S. T. Dlamini, *Safari Nation*

Safari Nation

A Social History of the Kruger National Park

⌇

Jacob S. T. Dlamini

OHIO UNIVERSITY PRESS ⌇ ATHENS, OHIO

Ohio University Press, Athens, Ohio 45701
ohioswallow.com
© 2020 by Ohio University Press

To obtain permission to quote, reprint, or otherwise reproduce or distribute
    material from Ohio University Press publications, please contact our
    rights and permissions department at (740) 593-1154 or (740) 593-4536
    (fax).

Printed in the United States of America
Ohio University Press books are printed on acid-free paper ∞ ™

30 29 28 27 26 25 24 23 22 21 20   5 4 3 2 1

Library of Congress Cataloging-in-Publication Data

Names: Dlamini, Jacob, 1973- author.
Title: Safari nation : a social history of the Kruger National Park /
    Jacob S. T. Dlamini.
Other titles: New African histories series.
Description: Athens : Ohio University Press, 2020. | Series: New African
    histories | Includes bibliographical references and index.
Identifiers: LCCN 2019059715 | ISBN 9780821424087 (hardcover) |
    ISBN 9780821424094 (paperback) | ISBN 9780821440889 (adobe pdf)
Subjects: LCSH: National parks and reserves--Social aspects--South Africa. |
    Nature conservation--South Africa--History. | Nature conservation--Social
    aspects--South Africa--History. | Kruger National Park (South Africa)–
    History.
Classification: LCC SB484.S5 D53 2020 | DDC 363.6/80968--dc23
LC record available at https://lccn.loc.gov/2019059715

This book is for Patricia

Now I want to suggest that in the colonial situation presence was the critical question, the crucial word. Its denial was the keynote of colonialist ideology. Question: Were there people there? Answer: Well . . . not really, you know . . . people of sorts perhaps, but not as you and I understand the word.

—Chinua Achebe, 1992

Contents

Illustrations

Acknowledgments

I HAVE incurred so many debts, on at least three continents and in as many languages if not more, in the writing of this book that no words can repay fully what I owe the hundreds of people who helped me along the way. But I must mention some by name or affiliation. A big thank-you to Robert Harms, Michael Mahoney, Paul Sabin, and Daniel Magaziner for their guidance. Bob supervised the dissertation from which this book grew, while Michael, Paul, and Daniel served on the dissertation committee that helped turn a jumble of ideas into a story. Nancy Jacobs, Isabel Hofmeyr, and Jan Bender Shetler gave generously of their experience, time, and wisdom at a crucial moment in the rewriting of that story. Jean Allman, Allen Isaacman, Derek Peterson, and Gillian Berchowitz believed that this story could be turned into a book worth publishing and found anonymous reviewers whose astute readings made the book much better than it might have been otherwise. Ricky Huard, Sally Welch, Beth Pratt, and Nancy Basmajian saw to it that the book was published. William Beinart, Adrian Browne, James T. Campbell, Jacklyn Cock, Harvey Feinberg, Gerhard Maré, Lynn Meskell, Jeanne Penvenne, Stephen Sparks, Ed Teversham, Laura Phillips, Goolam Vahed, and Thembisa Waetjen shared tips and references that helped enrich this book. Nasima Coovadia, Ahmed Bhabha, Coco Cachalia, Ahmed Essop, and Ed February generously let me into their family archives; Jeremy Anderson and Rose Smuts shared their love of the lowveld with me. Joep Stevens, Lazarus Makitla, and Salomon Joubert helped me negotiate my way through the SANParks Archives, and Jacqueline Manche and Murphy Morobe saw to it that I had access to some hard-to-obtain material. Farieda Khan pioneered many of the ideas canvassed in this book and, kindly, shared her work with me. Tlhagiso Molantoa covered ground I could not and helped make this book possible.

Safari Nation would be a fraction of what it is without the stories of the men and women who live with the Kruger National Park in ways that I cannot even begin to imagine. From the Ngomanes, Lukheles, Mthombothis, and Mnisis to many other families for whom the romance of the park is bound up with the reality of elephants and lions that can and do kill, these men and women allowed me into their homes and shared stories whose telling will, I hope, inspire new approaches to conservation.

If the experiences of the above-mentioned communities shape this book, the dedication and expertise of a number of archivists and librarians supplement it in immeasurable ways. Here I must thank the staff of the SANParks archives in Pretoria and at Skukuza, the Transnet Heritage Archives in which Yolanda Meyer labors with passion and professionalism, the National Library in Cape Town, the Parliamentary Library in Cape Town, the National Archives in Pretoria, the Limpopo Archives in Giyani, the National Party Archives at the University of the Free State, the TEBA Archive at the University of Johannesburg, Wits Historical Papers, the Killie Campbell Collections at the University of KwaZulu-Natal, University of Cape Town's Historical Papers Collection, Sterling Memorial Library at Yale University, the Bodleian Library at Oxford University, Widener Library at Harvard University, and Firestone Library at Princeton University. I also benefited from the knowledge of audiences and colleagues at a number of universities, including Johannesburg, Harvard, Michigan, Rhodes, Stanford, Princeton, Wits, and Yale. The Stellenbosch Institute for Advanced Study generously supported the writing of this book, as did the Institute for Advanced Study at Princeton. My eternal gratitude to both institutes.

Princeton University and its History Department have been my intellectual home since 2015, and in that time I have benefited immensely from the collegiality and wisdom of my colleagues. The example of their scholarship and the imprint of their counsel are all over the pages of this book. Vera Candiani, Angela Creager, Sheldon Garon, Tera Hunter, Matthew Karp, Emmanuel Kreike, Michael Laffan, Erika Milam, Philip Nord, Jack Tannous, and Keith Wailoo helped me refine my introduction and sharpen my argument, and the book is better for it. Robert Tignor, Fabian Krautwald, Morgan Robinson, Marcia Schenck, Elisa Prosperetti, and Kim Worthington gave me a hearing and, in the process, helped improve this book. I must thank

Keith, in his capacity as chair of the History Department, together with Judy Hanson and Deborah Macy for everything they did to support the book's publication. I am indebted to Wendy Belcher, Brooke Fitzgerald, Kelly Lin-Kramer, Max Siles, Carla Zimowsk, Sorat Tungkasiri, and Wangyal Tsering for their unstinting support.

I dedicate this book to Patty, for everything she has done to support its writing and publication. This includes running the 2007 Kruger National Park half-marathon. Very few people can claim to have run with warthogs. Patty can. Thank you for that and for everything besides.

Abbreviations

ANC	African National Congress
KNP	Kruger National Park
SAIRR	South African Institute of Race Relations
SANNC	South African Native National Congress
SAR	South African Railways
WENELA	Witwatersrand Native Labor Association

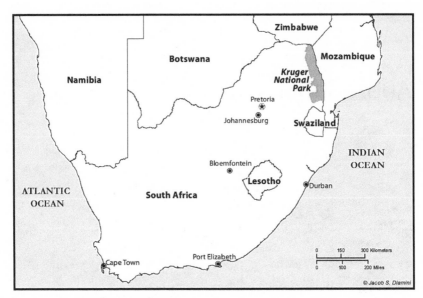

MAP I.1. South Africa showing KNP

Introduction

THE KRUGER National Park (KNP) is one of the most iconic wild-life sanctuaries in the world. Established in May 1926, it is one of the oldest national parks in Africa and, at 2 million hectares, one of the biggest on earth.[1] Situated in the northeastern corner of South Africa, it is home to about 132,000 impala, 37,000 buffaloes, 13,000 elephants, 6,700 giraffes, 1,600 lions, and 1,000 leopards. These are part of an impressive floral and faunal collection that includes 500 bird species, 336 tree species, and about 145 mammal species. But animals have not been the only inhabitants of the park. There were also human be-ings who lived there—thousands of whom were expelled from the park during the course of the twentieth century. The displacement of these Africans did not mean the end of their connection to the park. It only marked the beginning of a new phase in this relationship.

Scholars working in different disciplines have long noted the con-nection between Africans and the KNP. This relationship, however, has typically been described as one of restriction. Jane Carruthers, for instance, noted that "Africans were not permitted to visit the park for recreation," Hector Magome and James Murombedzi argued that "black people were legally restricted from entering Kruger," Jacklyn Cock said that "black South Africans were denied access as visitors," and Lynn Meskell maintained that "many black South Africans . . . [were] long excluded from the park on racial grounds (other than as service workers or guides)," while Lindisizwe Magi claimed that apart-heid barred blacks from South Africa's outdoors *tout court*.[2] By under-standing the relationship between the KNP and Africans primarily as one of restriction, these commentators have reduced this connection to a paradigm in which Africans in the park have been viewed as either laborers or poachers.[3]

FIGURE I.1. Wildebeest and zebras at a watering hole in the KNP, ca. 1930s.
Source: Transnet Heritage Museum Photo Collection

In what follows, my goal will be to challenge this paradigm and to put forward a new understanding of how Africans (and blacks in general) related socially and politically to the KNP during the twentieth century.[4] By retrieving a lost history, I will attempt to offer a richer, alternate paradigm for viewing the relationship between blacks and the KNP. To put it succinctly, *Safari Nation* is about the black history of the KNP. It is about the social and political relations between blacks and the KNP during the twentieth century. These relations were a complex bundle made up of struggles over resources, migrant labor, loss and trauma, the rise of tourism, South Africa's transition from segregation to apartheid to democracy, and the making of the South African state over the long twentieth century. The book's fundamental argument will be that these relations were far more intricate and significantly more varied than conventional accounts of the park's history have allowed. Put another way, *Safari Nation*'s argument is not just that relations between blacks and the KNP were complex but that beyond that complexity lay a universe whose exploration allows the reader to see the multifaceted methods by which blacks gave meaning to their lives, despite colonial and apartheid rule, in twentieth-century South Africa. These methods ranged from accommodation to collaboration, from indifference to resistance. Although some were political, many were not necessarily so. They were the actions of individuals in given contexts. *Safari Nation* shows that complexity is not the end of an argument but only its beginning. This is a significant observation that, when taken beyond the study of relations between blacks and the KNP, should apply to every relationship of domination, especially in colonial and postcolonial settings. By calling attention to the ways in which blacks lived with—as opposed to under—colonial and apartheid rule, *Safari Nation* allows the reader to see when asymmetries of power persist, and when they might be challenged.[5]

A HISTORIOGRAPHIC SAFARI

Scholarly (mis)characterizations notwithstanding, at no stage in its history did the KNP restrict access to blacks, especially when they came as tourists. While the National Parks Board, the state agency responsible for South Africa's national parks, did limit black access to the park's rest camps and restaurants, especially during the high apartheid years of 1948 to 1980, it did not bar blacks from visiting the park itself. In fact, blacks could visit from the very beginning, in 1923, of tourism to the sanctuary. That was three years before it became a national park. As a visitors' guide issued by the National Parks Board in 1938 stated: "The Park may be visited by Asiatics and Natives, but, except at Skukuza, there is as yet no accommodation available for them."[6] Black visitors had to arrange their own shelter and bring their own tents if they planned to stay at camps other than Skukuza. "They are also strongly advised to avoid paying visits during rush periods, such as long weekends, school holidays, etc.," the guide said.[7] The welcome was anything but warm. But it was a welcome, nonetheless.[8]

The KNP has, I will argue, a hidden history. To unveil this forgotten past, I will use the idea of "histories of presence," a conceptual frame that I have derived from the notion of a "politics of presence." This latter concept, suggested independently by James Ferguson and Anne-Maria Makhulu, provides a useful tool for apprehending hidden histories.[9] It does so by directing our historical gaze to places where scholars of the KNP and its history have rarely sought the presence of blacks before. By recuperating, both conceptually and empirically, the histories of black presence in the KNP, I will show how, to para-phrase Makhulu, the sheer presence of black South Africans altered the history of the KNP.[10] As Makhulu points out in her study of squat-ter politics in Cape Town, homeless communities rendered apartheid unworkable and changed the course of South African history simply by being present in that city—in spite of what the government wanted.

By revising the social history of the KNP, I will show how blacks lived with white rule. My goal will be to change our understanding of the black experience in twentieth-century South Africa. This experi-ence, lodged in the colonial and apartheid archives often as fragments and marginalia, is made up in part of the yet-to-be-written story of blacks and conservation in South Africa. Writing that history means acknowledging that the very categories—African, Coloured, Indian—key to its recovery are not natural but themselves products of history. It also requires understanding that calling these diverse individuals black does not presume a commonality of experience. But it does presuppose a shared sense of political solidarity among some of the black individu-als in this story. As *Bantu World*, a black elite newspaper, editorialized in February 1935 in response to yet another government plan to confis-cate African land for the sake of the KNP:

> While the Government is engaged in this gigantic land scheme for the preservation of animal life, thousands of human beings are landless and homeless and are living in a state of abject pov-erty. No black man will grudge the animals for the magnani-mous consideration of their needs by the authorities; but one would have thought that before more land is added to the Game Reserve, the homeless black man, who is drifting to urban areas, only to find he is unwanted, would have been attended to first. The preservation of animals . . . is a noble thing, but nobler still is the preservation of human life, be it white or black.[11]

As the editorial made clear, *Bantu World* objected to the govern-ment's neglect of landless blacks—not to the preservation of animals, which was a "noble thing." *Bantu World* did not oppose conservation as such. It only objected to its use in the service of racial segregation. Richard Victor Selope Thema, a pioneering writer and African nation-alist who edited *Bantu World* from its founding in 1932 to 1952, likely

FIGURE 1.2. KNP ranger Judas Mashele, date unknown. *Source*: SANParks Archive

wrote that editorial. As *Safari Nation* shows, Thema had a lot to say about the KNP. He approached conservation the same way that he thought about his political standing as a black person in colonial and apartheid South Africa—as open to negotiation. He did not see why conservation had to be a winner-take-all struggle between humans and other animals. He thought it possible to preserve both human and nonhuman life. But Thema's voice is not the only one amplified on the pages that follow. Krishna Somers, who visited the park with a group of friends in 1944, recalled: "In stopping in Kruger Park, the only place where accommodation was available for us as non-whites was Skukuza. The building was made of corrugated iron held with wooden supports. There were no facilities. After an overnight stopover, we proceeded to cross the border to Mozambique, where we tasted for the first time freedom from any kind of racial discrimination."[12] It would be easy to focus solely on Somers's confirmation of the racial discrimination to which the park subjected him and other nonwhite visitors. However, *Safari Nation* challenges the reader to see Somers as more than just another victim of colonial racism. Without minimizing the effects of that racism, this book suggests that readers look at what else Somers's story reveals: it proves that he was there; it tells the reader that, four years before the advent of apartheid, Somers and his friends were present in the KNP as paying visitors. It is that kind of presence, not only stories of victimization, that this book recuperates.[13]

Somers and the other black tourists who visited the park were part of a small but mobile and vocal elite drawn from mission-educated African converts to Christianity, aspirant middle-class Coloured communities, and mostly merchant Indian families. These elites saw themselves as modern subjects in control of their time and destiny. They desired tourism because that is what people of their class—some reared on Romanticism in mission schools—were expected to desire. But black tourists were not the only ones present in the park. For many blacks, the colonial boundaries that demarcated native reserve from national park, South Africa from Mozambique, were arbitrary lines that failed to take account of old connections between communities subject through historical accident to Portuguese and Boer/British rule in the lowveld, meaning the northeastern region of southern Africa with a low elevation of between 150 meters and 600 meters above sea level. These communities kept their links despite colonial interdictions that rendered them, in the view of Portuguese and South African authorities, trespassers.

Some of these so-called trespassers were subject to one colonial regime but had relatives under another. As David Bunn points out, until the advent of the park, those living between South Africa and Mozambique were in a sense "citizens of the blurred border, able to live within the very thickness of the line drawn on the map."[14] Members of these communities traveled through the park to visit friends and relatives on either side of the colonial border, sometimes with fatal consequences, as chapter 2 shows. This, after all, was a place teeming with wildlife. As the stories recounted in *Safari Nation* illustrate, the black people who dealt with the park came in many categories. Among them were men from Mozambique and other parts of southeastern Africa who came to South Africa in search of jobs in the country's coal, diamond, and gold mines.[15] These men became part of a migrant labor system that shaped modern South Africa and transformed African polities in southern Africa. Some of these migrants traveled out of their own initiative; many more did so as part of a vast labor recruitment network set up by South Africa's mining industry at the turn of the twentieth century.

Safari Nation not only charts the histories of black presence in the KNP; it also explores the varied reasons behind that presence, as well as the ways that presence changed over time. For the blacks whose stories this book tells, nature was at different times an economic, political, and social resource. But that resource held different meanings for different individuals. That is, nature was not simply the physical environment but the ideas that flowed from that environment—ideas about access, entitlement, and value. Who had access to the natural environment? The Indian holidaymakers who dominated black tourism in the KNP between the 1920s and the 1980s gave their answer. Who was entitled to nature's produce? The traditional doctors who harvested herbs, plants, and animal products from protected areas gave yet another. Who could appropriate the value that came from nature? The poachers who troubled state and park officials had their answer. But these answers were not static; they changed over time. Like the Japanese nationalists studied by Julia Thomas, some blacks also saw nature as a political and ideological concept, a "changing, contested matrix" within which to explore different possibilities of what South Africa was or could become.[16] If Afrikaner nationalists saw their history as a "struggle against nature, the natives and Imperialism," black nationalists like Thema saw theirs as a struggle for a democratic and inclusive South Africa.[17] People like Thema were fascinated by the park and by South Africa's landscapes. But they were also interested in the political nature of South African society. They understood that, as Thomas puts it, "whoever can define nature for a nation defines that nation's polity on a fundamental level."[18] These individuals wanted a South Africa in which blacks, too, had a home, but as a part of the polity and not of nature.

FROM AFRICANS, COLOUREDS, INDIANS TO BLACKS

In what follows, I will treat the category *black* as a political—as opposed to an ethnic or racial—category.[19] At the same time, I will attempt to disaggregate this category in order to show how so-called Africans, Coloureds, and Indians of various backgrounds participated in struggles over resources, in migrant labor, in the rise of tourism, in South Africa's transition from segregation to apartheid to democracy, and in the making of the South African state itself. I will also show how, for some Africans, the park represented both loss and trauma. More importantly, I will argue that social and political relations between blacks and the KNP cannot be reduced to encounters between colonizer and colonized, powerful and powerless, victim and victimizer. To do that would be to miss the density at the center of these relations and to offer a flat rendering of who these people were and why their stories matter. These men and women occupied such a range of subject positions—from migrant laborers, to park residents, to laborers, to park neighbors, to poachers, and to tourists—that we can only make qualified generalizations about them. Some were South African subjects and citizens, some Portuguese, some Rhodesian, and some a mix of all three—if not indifferent to claims of nation and nationalism altogether.

At different times, colonial and apartheid authorities classified these people and their communities as native/African, Coloured, and Asian. Some were Christian, some Muslim, and some followers of indigenous religions; some were women, and many were men.[20] These backgrounds affected how each person related to the park. They also engendered a diversity of experiences that should call into question any attempt to present a uniform account of black life under white rule in South Africa. *Safari Nation* is also careful not to naturalize the African, Coloured, and Indian identities depicted here or to take as a given their existence as coherent—even as it acknowledges that, for some of the black actors in this historical drama, these identities carried political and strategic worth. This book also eschews the easy conflation of blackness with phenotype. Instead, it looks at how individuals interpellated by the colonial and apartheid states as African, Asiatic, Coloured, and native related to political landscapes that made room for them only if they responded to their official interpellation as African, Asiatic, Coloured, or native.[21] If anything united these disparate individuals and communities, it was their political standing in relation to the colonial and apartheid states. That, in fact, is what defined their blackness: their varied but relative standing vis-à-vis political power in colonial and apartheid South Africa. On the whole, these people did not possess political power. But this is not to be confused with a lack of political agency, of which they had a lot. In fact, it is precisely because they had agency and used it widely that these men and women exist in the official archive—even if many come to us as specters whose haunting presence we can discern but not grasp fully. By disaggregating the category black, *Safari Nation* looks also at how black intellectuals such as Thema understood the role of nature in the political constitution of South Africa into a nation-state, and at how they propagated ideas about conservation.[22] It also examines the interplay between the politicization of nature and the naturalization of politics in twentieth-century South Africa. By this I mean, first, the use of racial discrimination by colonial and apartheid authorities to determine who could enter nature and on what terms and, second, the deployment by those authorities of nature to justify racial hierarchies and other asymmetrical forms of power. In other words, *Safari Nation* analyzes the convoluted ways in which colonial and apartheid officials sought to Africanize minority white rule in southern Africa while casting blacks, especially Africans, as nature's denizens—there to be seen and to labor, but not to count as citizens.

FROM RESIDENT NATIVES TO TAXPAYING SUBJECTS

Some of the individuals whose stories are told here came from communities that had long been resident in the reserve when it was founded—first in 1898 as the Sabi Game Reserve and in 1926 as the Kruger National Park—and whose presence park officials sought to naturalize. As park warden James Stevenson-Hamilton claimed on one occasion, "The few residents native [to the park] live still to a great extent under tribal law, unspoiled by contact with civilization."[23] Stevenson-Hamilton sought to cast these men and women as being one with nature—even as he drew extensively on their labor and knew that they were taxpaying subjects of white rule. As he remarked on another occasion, "Natives living in the park have no fear of lions, and visitors may note this for themselves by observing how women accompanied by small children and usually carrying babies on their backs freely use the roads at all times of day and, I may add, frequently at night also."[24] Far from being left out of the reserve's landscape, Africans were in fact written and drawn visually into early depictions of the reserve, as Stevenson-Hamilton above and the numerous pieces of visual evidence presented in *Safari Nation* make clear (see figs. I.3 and I.4).[25] This naturalization of Africans was a political move intended to strip them of political agency and, consequently, to deny their claims for political equality.

This casting of indigenous peoples as premodern subjects was not unique to South Africa. As Susan Sessions Rugh points out, in the United States, Native Americans were often presented in advertisements for national parks as part of the landscape to be consumed and not as consumers in their own right.[26] In South Africa, colonial officials similarly put Africans in the role of native attraction and marketed them extensively both locally and abroad as one of the country's exceptional features. As Deputy Prime Minister Jan Smuts said in a 1934 speech promoting tourism in South Africa, "It is only our shortsightedness that prevents us from seeing what a chance we have here. In every overcrowded town in the overworked countries of the world there are vast numbers of people who want to see Africa, its scenery, its wildness, its flowers, its mountains and rivers, its natives."[27] Contrary to claims by Meskell, the park did not, certainly not in its early days, offer "people-free landscapes with few archaeological sites to remind visitors that this was once a living landscape for indigenous Africans."[28] It made it a point to people its landscapes with a certain kind of human: the so-called native.

FIGURE 1.3. A group of African women with children on their backs walking through the KNP, ca. 1930s–1940s. *Source*: Selby Collection 590.72, used with the permission of MuseumAfrica

FIGURE 1.4. Children in the Crocodile River in the southern section of the KNP, date unknown. *Source*: Ludwig Jindra

If relations between blacks and the KNP were as complex as this book says they were, why do claims of black exclusion persist? Why does the dominant scholarship on the park insist on a black absence that was, in fact, not there? One answer is that scholars have simply neglected the black presence that has animated relations between blacks and the park over time. Rather than look at how blacks made their presence felt in the park, scholars have taken segregation and apartheid at face value, thereby limiting their search to the stock figures of the laborer and the poacher. Jacklyn Cock and Njabulo Ndebele have rightly called attention to how places such as the KNP made black labor invisible, all so they could present themselves as pristine wilderness areas removed from the soiled political economy of southern Africa, while Carruthers and Stanley Trapido have reminded us that poaching is by definition political in that it involves a contest over who gets what part of nature's bounty, when, and how.[29] But there was more to the presence of blacks in the history of the KNP. By taking seriously the histories of presence made visible by, for example, Thema's editorial and Somers's story, we can see blacks in places where scholars have not looked before: the villages inside the park where the KNP drew its staff, the rest camps set aside specifically for blacks, the lodgings provided to black domestics accompanying white families, the opinion pages in which black thinkers debated the leisure question, the government halls in which black politicians drew unfavorable comparisons between their treatment by the apartheid government and the care that the same government took of the wildlife in the KNP, the communities outside the park, and the homelands adjacent to the KNP where Bantustan leaders professed political support for apartheid even as they pointed out that apartheid policies (illustrated by the apartheid signage in fig. I.5) could not work because they undermined the ecological integrity of the KNP.

By putting forth histories of presence as a conceptual frame through which to recover and to understand the hidden history of the KNP, *Safari Nation* undoes the national(ist) casing that surrounds most histories of the KNP. Even though the KNP has been, since 2002, an essential part of the Great Limpopo Transfrontier Park—a transnational initiative that includes Mozambique's Limpopo National Park and Zimbabwe's Gonarezhou National Park—it remains a national institution, South Africa's premier national park par excellence. As Bram Büscher,

FIGURE 1.5. Still from a 1968 documentary titled *The Heart of Apartheid*.
Source: Still image supplied by BBC Studios

Elizabeth Lunstrum, Clapperton Mavhunga, Maano Ramutsindela, Marja Spierenburg, and Harry Wels have shown, despite claims to the contrary, the promise of a borderless zone entailed by the transfrontier initiative has been extended only to the megafauna of the three constituent parks and to the tourists who pay to see these animals—not to the millions of Africans who live on either side of these political borders.[30]

These Africans remain citizens of their respective countries. They remain national subjects whose movement across international boundaries is governed still by protocols that take the nation-state as their starting point. This is despite the fact that, throughout the twentieth century, the region in which the KNP and the other two parks lie was an important corridor for the movement of humans, animals, epizootics, and commodities.[31] If anything defines this corner of southern Africa, it is the fact that it was one of the few places in the region where the nation-state form met its limit. This corner boasts a record of flows, connections, and movements whose historical significance we risk missing unless we look at the histories of presence that include more than the laborers, the poachers, and the crooks who turned the northern corner of the KNP into a hiding place—a no-man's-land—from the weak but searching eyes of three colonial governments.[32]

THE KRUGER NATIONAL PARK IN THEORY

To be sure, *Safari Nation* is not the first book to examine the role of blacks in the history of the KNP. Leslie Dikeni has documented struggles over the park's habitats and shown how Africans forced to live with the park remember its creation.[33] Dikeni combines ethnography and sociology to show how memories of dispossession have colored attempts by the KNP to make itself a postapartheid park for the benefit of all South Africans. Lynn Meskell has examined the ways in which the KNP privileged the heritage of white South Africans over that of their black counterparts by, for example, neglecting the extensive archaeological record that points to a rich prehistory of the area that is now the KNP.[34] David Bunn has pioneered rich ethnographies that illustrate the place of the park in the symbolic economy of white rule in southern Africa.[35] As Bunn makes clear, the KNP was instrumental in the naturalization and staging of racial hierarchies in South Africa (see figs. I.6 and I.7).

Salomon Joubert, the last white warden of the KNP, and Uys de V. Pienaar, arguably the most influential warden of the park after James Stevenson-Hamilton, have each given us official and magisterial accounts that place the KNP within the broader sweep of South African history.[36] Cock has pointed to the much-neglected labor history of the park and shown the ways in which the presence of black laborers in the park has been effaced. Cock has also explored the ways in which an authoritarian form of conservation marginalized black voices and victimized blacks.[37] Carruthers, on whose pioneering shoulders this book stands, was the first historian to challenge the romantic myths that inform the literature on conservation.[38] As Carruthers shows, the establishment of the KNP depended on the active removal of Africans from the land and on their marginalization (except as mute laborers, as fig. I.8 shows) from debates about conservation in South Africa.

The scholarship cited above has certainly enriched our understanding of the park and its history. But narratives of dispossession dominate the historiographic insights of this scholarship.[39] Driven by a commitment to historical redress, scholars have examined the ways in which

FIGURE I.6. Unnamed KNP ranger with photographer Ludwig Jindra at the park's Numbi Gate, date unknown. *Source*: Ludwig Jindra

FIGURE I.7. Unnamed KNP ranger at entrance to a KNP rest camp, date unknown. *Source*: Transnet Heritage Museum Photo Collection

FIGURE 1.8. Color spread of a holiday camp by artist Charles E. Turner. The spread was part of an advertising campaign run by the South African Railways corporation between the 1920s and the 1940s through select publications in Africa, Asia, Europe, and North America. *Source*: Transnet Heritage Museum Photo Collection

protected areas have exploited and victimized Africans through approaches such as "fortress conservation" or by imposing racialized notions of wilderness on Africa.[40] Carruthers and others have rightly challenged the "white romantic myth" whereby enlightened Europeans saved Africa's flora and fauna from savage Africans (see fig. 1.9 for an idealized portrayal of the African wild in which the African figure only appears as a servant).[41] However, the scholars' focus on these narratives has blinded us to dimensions of the black experience of protected areas defined not by dispossession but by *possession*, not by hostility but by ambivalence—if not appropriation.

Carruthers observes, for example, that "there is considerable substance to the African attitude that game reserves and wildlife protectionist legislation have from the start been detrimental to African interests."[42] But, as *Safari Nation* shows, there was no singular African attitude and certainly no uniform African interests. By focusing on the dispossession and marginalization entailed by protected areas, scholars have done well to remind us of the centrality of justice to the postcolonial and postapartheid projects. But their neglect of the stories of possession and the agency implied by that possession has left us with a truncated understanding of the history of black responses to protected areas in Africa. In the process, we have ceded the last word on the

FIGURE 1.9. Color spread by artist Charles E. Turner celebrating the twenty-fifth anniversary of the founding of South Africa. *Source*: Transnet Heritage Museum Photo Collection

matter to Julius Nyerere, Tanzania's first president, who quipped in 1961, "I do not want to spend my holidays watching crocodiles,"[43] or to the Zambian parliamentarian who remarked, when asked in 1982 to support the stiffening of Zambia's laws against poaching, "At no time did rhinoceros or elephants participate in the fight of our independence."[44]

Nyerere might have cared little about crocodiles. Still, he believed that they should be conserved for posterity and for the benefit of Westerners who traveled thousands of miles to satisfy their "strange urge to see these animals."[45] To hear Nyerere and the Zambian MP tell it, Africa's protected areas existed primarily for the benefit of paying Europeans and North Americans. Nyerere and the MP implied that the flora and fauna of these places held no meaning for Africans beyond the economic, cosmological, and utilitarian.[46] But might there be reasons, beyond the economic and the utilitarian, why protected areas not only survived the demise of white rule but thrived in postcolonial Africa?[47] If the creation of these areas was, as Mavhunga says, the most "sadistic colonial act," why do they continue to be such a marked feature of African landscapes?[48] How might we get past Roderick Nash's mythical Maasai, for whom a giraffe holds as much interest as does a yellow taxicab for a New Yorker, and the idealized African conjured up by Gilson Kaweche, for whom the "meaning of conservation has been always in each African's heart"?[49] For both Nash and Kaweche, Africans are such an organic part of nature that they cannot adopt a tourist gaze or cultivate an affective appreciation of wildlife. For Nash, Africans are also not meaningful players in conservation at all. A pioneer of environmental history in the United States, he once said that if Tanzania could not stop poaching in the Serengeti, "we will just have to go in and buy it."[50] In the South African context, narratives of dispossession have led to claims that the reason why blacks in postapartheid South Africa did not visit the KNP in large numbers was because, as one government official put it, blacks had "no history of travel" or because, as Ndebele said, the "black tourist is conditioned to find the political sociology of the game lodge ontologically disturbing."[51] This book tells a different story. It does so by looking for black faces in places other than the "white spaces" — the usual nooks and crannies — of the KNP's history.[52]

THE NATURE OF HISTORY

By recuperating stories that have yet to trouble conventional histories of the park, *Safari Nation* contributes to a growing literature about alternative histories of conservation in Africa. This literature is part of a historiographic trend defined by an interest in how ordinary people, acting as something other than victims, have engaged with conservation. Scholars who have contributed to this trend include Nancy Jacobs, who examines the active role that a number of Africans played in colonial and postcolonial birding networks.[53] There is also Maitseo Bolaane, whose account of the creation of the Moremi Game Reserve in Botswana's Okavango Delta in 1963 places local African elites at the center of Moremi's founding. As Bolaane points out, Moremi is unique among southern Africa's protected areas because African initiative — not European imposition — brought the sanctuary into existence.[54] In fact, influential Europeans opposed Moremi's establishment, but their opposition proved futile when confronted with the house-to-house campaigning that African activists undertook to gain popular support for the park.[55] Most importantly, Bolaane shows that Moremi did not come about because of some supposedly natural connection between Africans and wildlife. Supporters of the park idea, led by the female monarch Pulane Moremi, had to expend considerable political capital to persuade the different ethnic and interest groups that made up the delta region to throw in their lot with the reserve.

Bolaane's story finds echoes in other colonial contexts where, as Edward Teversham points out, "the creation of a national park was a strategic move to maintain access to traditional lands, as happened with the Ngati Tuwharetou Mori in New Zealand."[56] Understanding the discursive power of the idea of wildlife protection, individuals and communities in places such as Botswana and New Zealand took up the idea to secure their interests. Reuben Matheka has also detailed the historical antecedents to wildlife conservation in Kenya, showing the role played by Maasai and other communities in establishing protected areas under colonial rule. Thanks to local activism, Kenya's colonial officials promoted the establishment of "park adjuncts," areas whose creation was premised on the coexistence of humans and wildlife.[57] As Matheka points out, "While formal wildlife conservation in most colonial societies was a foreign imposition based on [a] Western ethos, it was sometimes modified in line with local circumstances of ecology, culture and politics."[58] In a similar vein, Adrian Browne examines the key roles played by Africans in the "Africanization" of conservation in Uganda during the transition to independence. Browne notes that scholars have yet to examine why the decolonization of Africa did not lead to the much-predicted collapse of Africa's national parks.[59] By looking at the transformation of Murchison Falls National Park (Kabalega Falls) and Queen Elizabeth National Park (Rwenzori), Browne shows the "existence or creation of a non-functionalist, non-materialist African constituency for wildlife conservation."[60] In addition, Browne tracks the careers of a number of Africans to show how this constituency developed; from its ranks emerged the men who, come independence in 1962, led Uganda's national parks and transformed them into places for the enjoyment of all.

These men invested in educational programs designed to take national parks to the public. Their efforts paid off, with more Ugandans visiting national parks for vacation and school trips as the 1960s gave way to the 1970s. Tragically, Idi Amin destroyed some of these men together with what they had built. The significance of Browne's account lies not in its detail of the tragedy of Amin's rule but in its documenting of African initiative in the propagation of conservation. Browne's account and studies like it insist that scholars do more than recount stories of marginalization and victimization. While the experience of marginalization and victimization is certainly real and, sadly, an important part of the story of conservation in Africa, it does not account fully for the history of protected areas in Africa. In fact, as Carruthers and others have shown, even the dominant narratives of displacement and victimization need a rethink, given the paucity of research on the topic.[61] We assume more than we know about displacements in protected areas and, in the process, collapse disparate histories into one. Carruthers and others have also warned that conflating displacements from protected areas into a "single generalized universal narrative has polarized diverse perspectives and established a discourse of conflict rather than a dialogue."[62] Scholars can only give a better account of the history of protected areas in Africa and on other continents by moving beyond narratives of displacement.[63] This book does that. But it does not ignore the history of displacement and victimization. In fact, for the vast majority of the black communities that dealt with the KNP over the time period covered by *Safari Nation*, theirs was indeed a story of official neglect, as well as colonial and apartheid violence. As Jimmy Mnisi (who was born inside the KNP and is a descendant of a community expelled from the park in 1969) said, the tourist enjoyment of the park cannot be divorced from a critical appreciation of its history. Mnisi said that his grandfather, who was a KNP ranger, was killed by lions while cycling through the park on his way to work sometime in the 1960s. The only thing left to bury was the old man's intestines. Mnisi recalled:

> Remember, it was during apartheid. They [the family] were given the remains with no compensation. Nothing. That's very traumatic. But it's more traumatic with us because we know our rights. Remember, with the old people exposed to apartheid, illiterates, they did not know their rights. They were not aware that there's supposed to be compensation. The old man was the only source of income. But they were not aware. When our mothers start to relate the story, because we are learned, literate, and know our rights, we feel trauma.[64]

THE KRUGER NATIONAL PARK IN HISTORY

To understand why the KNP would induce feelings of the kind experienced by Mnisi, we need to understand something of the park's creation. The KNP, which sits on South Africa's borders with Mozambique to the east and Zimbabwe to the north, is the flagship of South Africa's nineteen national parks. Paul Kruger's South African Republic established it as the Sabi Game Reserve in 1898. This was a year before the outbreak of the South African War, which sent Kruger into terminal exile in Switzerland, destroyed the two Boer republics (Transvaal and the Orange Free State), and laid the foundations for the creation of the Union of South Africa in 1910. The British reproclaimed the reserve in 1902 after defeating the Boers and bringing South Africa under a single political authority for the first time in its history. The reserve became the Kruger National Park in May 1926 in a flurry of state-making activities that saw South Africa's parliament adopt, in addition to the National Parks Act of 1926, the National Flag Act and, two years later, the National Monuments Act. This was preceded in 1925 by the designation of Afrikaans as one of South Africa's two official languages—a move that signaled the beginning of the political ascendancy of Afrikaner nationalists in South Africa. As figure I.9 shows, colonial officials depicted the development of South Africa as a natural and organic process in which the country's history began in the fifteenth century with the arrival of the Portuguese in southern Africa.

Described as a state within a state, the park certainly enjoys the trappings of a state.[65] It exercises sovereignty over a bounded territory with clearly demarcated borders, it conducts a regular census to keep track of its nonhuman inhabitants, it employs experts (e.g., biologists, ecologists, social scientists, veterinarians), and it has a paramilitary force (with a special forces component) to police its boundaries.[66] Until the 1960s, the region in which the park sits was malarial and had poor soils, low rainfall, and no decent mining prospects.[67] When nineteenth-century European settlers of varying economic means used it, it was mostly for hunting (as seen in fig. I.10) and winter grazing.

Europeans considered the area a white man's grave in the nineteenth and early twentieth centuries, even though it had African economies based on hunting and the ivory trade.[68] The region was one of the last parts of Africa to come under direct European rule.[69] It was also a source of inspiration for the lost-world fiction of Arthur Conan Doyle and Rider Haggard. In fact, in the last decades of the nineteenth century, most lowveld Africans still lived in polities belonging to the Pedi, Tsonga, Swazi, and Venda. Alongside these were isolated Boer

FIGURE I.10. Color spread from 1927 by artist William R. S. Stott depicting a hunting scene in the lowveld. *Source*: Transnet Heritage Museum Photo Collection

settlements. These settlements competed with Africans for land, livestock, and trade in ivory and hides (see figs. I.11–I.14).[70] One of these Boer settlements was the Zoutpansberg Republic, founded in the 1840s as a splinter community from Kruger's republic. It was not until 1879 and, even then, only with the help of the British and the Swazi that Boers defeated the Pedi kingdom. It was not until 1898, the same year in which the Sabi Game Reserve was founded, that the Boers defeated the Venda.

The defeat of African polities had major implications for Africans at the turn of the twentieth century, especially with regard to access to land.[71] Kruger's republic had proclaimed the Sabi Game Reserve to preserve what little game had survived the wanton hunting that had accompanied the mid-nineteenth-century entry of European settlers and guns into the lowveld.[72] Africans and Europeans alike had used guns extensively to drive, for example, the region's rhino to extinction and to bring the elephant to the brink. The proclamation of the reserve sought to reverse that process of extirpation—a mission continued by the KNP when it was founded in 1926. However, as Carruthers has shown, the park did more than preserve South Africa's flora and fauna.

100108/13

Verzameling Zuiderhoek~aannemerslaut No.No. 61.

FIGURE I.11, I.12. Photographs depicting hunting in the lowveld in the 1890s.
Source: Transnet Heritage Museum Photo Collection

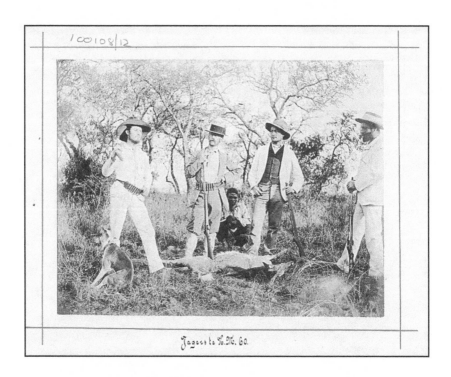

FIGURES I.13, I.14. Photographs depicting hunting in the lowveld in the 1890s. *Source:* Transnet Heritage Museum Photo Collection

It also served a political function.[73] It gave natural expression to the "expedient solidarity" between English- and Afrikaans-speaking white South Africans founded on the political subjection (see fig. I.12) and exclusion of blacks from the realm of citizenship.[74] Colonial authorities used the park to promote a "national feeling" among whites, who were still "groping for a common identity" following the end of the destructive South African War.[75] This was not unique to South Africa. The United States and Australia, for example, also used ideas about the preservation of nature and distinctive landscapes to promote a sense of nationhood built on the exclusion of indigenous peoples. The KNP also helped consolidate the interests of white South Africa in its political conflict with blacks over land and labor.[76] Over time, the park became a commemoration site for South Africa's "white heritage."[77] But the political exclusion of blacks from what the park was intended to commemorate did not mean their physical exclusion from the park itself, as the following story demonstrates.

EDUCATING NATIVES

On November 30, 1926, J. L. de Jager, a white game ranger in the KNP, arrested an African man named Mastulela for trespassing.[78] Mastulela, traveling from Mozambique to the South African side of the border, was carrying 529 hides of wild animals that he had collected from the Portuguese colony. He claimed not to know that his movement through the park violated South African law and the game preservation regulations of the Transvaal. De Jager confiscated the hides, warned Mastulela not to trespass again, and let him go. But the matter did not go away, judging by the flurry of correspondence that ensued between various government officials.

A clerk in the Native Affairs Department in Sibasa, northern Transvaal, told his boss, the sub–native commissioner for Louis Trichardt, "I understand that the natives of this area have in the past made a habit of passing through the Reserve while enroute to and from Portuguese Territory." The clerk said he was "taking steps to put a stop to this, and to advise the natives of the provisions of Act 55 of 1926"—meaning the piece of legislation that had brought about the existence of the KNP in May of that year. In turn, the sub–native commissioner informed his superior, the secretary for native affairs, that "steps are being taken to warn all natives of the consequences of traveling through the park without authority." On February 12, 1927, the Native Affairs Department ordered that Mastulela's hides be returned to him.

Mastulela's professed ignorance of the law may have been genuine. After all, the park was only about six months old at the time of his meeting with de Jager and was in a remote corner of South Africa. In fact, South African surveyors and their Portuguese counterparts had only finished demarcating the border a month before Mastulela's arrest.[79] But it is also possible that he was dissembling because, although new in law, the park was founded on the Sabi Game Reserve, which had been around since 1898. Reserve warden James Stevenson-Hamilton had made his presence felt as early as 1902 by expelling three thousand Africans from the reserve following its reproclamation after the end of the South African War. While we cannot say for certain what Mastulela knew about the park, his presence there, not to mention the bureaucratic anxieties it generated, does serve to illustrate Karl Jacoby's observation that "landscapes do not magically reshape themselves in accordance with the desires expressed in legislation."[80] In fact, colonial authorities had to expend a lot of bureaucratic and political energy teaching people like Mastulela new colonial truths about the actual meaning of the park. They had to do this because there was nothing obvious or natural about the park's political meaning (see fig. I.15) and what it represented.

ECOLOGICAL FICTIONS

The park was founded in part on the idea of territorial integrity. Its founders imagined it as a place with finite boundaries—even if these had to be fixed by law to turn a political desire to preserve South Africa's fauna into the legal fiction of a sovereign sanctuary. The founders said the park must form "one continuous whole" and be large enough particularly for animals that "require plenty of room to move about."[81] The imaginary park thus conceived demanded a fiction of form (a clearly demarcated place with identifiable borders) and content (flora and fauna that existed independently of the world beyond the park's boundaries). But how would this be achieved in a place that was in fact traversed by the likes of Mastulela? A place with a "peopled past?"[82] Minister of Lands Piet Grobler knew that claims of territorial integrity for the park were open to challenge. But he saw the threat as coming from the government itself.

FIGURE I.15. Photograph depicting the unveiling of tablets carved onto a granite boulder in the KNP in honor of Paul Kruger and Piet Grobler. Left to right: Unnamed ranger, Mrs. Hilda Stevenson-Hamilton, Grobler, and National Parks Board chairman W. J. C. Brebner. September 22, 1933. *Source*: SANParks Archive

He told Parliament in 1926, "In the first place we must fix the boundaries by legislation." There were vocal mining and farming lobbies with considerable political support that wanted free reign in the park. Grobler worried that these lobbies might prevail—unless the park's boundaries were cast in law: "As long as the alteration of the boundary is in the hands of the Government the Government will always be exposed to being pressed by supporters to alter the boundary."[83] The boundaries were indeed established by law, thus creating the fiction of territorial integrity. In truth, the boundaries fixed in 1926 were never as stable as the legal fiction made them appear. There were territorial inclusions, excisions, fencing, and de-fencing throughout the park's history. These changes happened as farms were bought, land swapped, and Africans such as Jimmy Mnisi's community removed—to make real the fiction of the park's contiguity.[84] The fiction persisted, despite evidence to the contrary. It rested on myths about the park's locality that downplayed a history of flows.

These flows belied claims that the park was separate from the biological, economic, and political ecosystems around it. They also went against the raison d'être of the National Parks Board, which saw its mission as the defense of South Africa from diseases, Africans, illicit goods, and political insurgents, especially after the decolonization of southern Africa in the 1970s.[85] In fact, by the 1980s, the KNP was one of the most militarized zones in South Africa.[86] Despite this, the flows that defined the lowveld continued; millions of blacks continued to make their presence felt, thereby giving us the histories recuperated here. These histories have a lot to teach us about how blacks lived with white rule. They also have a lot to say about how their presence in the KNP shapes the ways in which many blacks relate to the park in post-apartheid South Africa.

SITUATING HISTORICAL TRAUMA

Take Jimmy Mnisi, the man who lost his grandfather to lions in the KNP in the 1960s. When I interviewed him in November 2009, Mnisi was a local African National Congress (ANC) politician and leading member of the Mahashi community, which had instituted a restitution claim for the community's return to the land taken away by the park in 1969.[87] When I examined the National Parks Board's annual reports about the KNP for the 1960s, I found no account of a park ranger killed by lions during that decade. The only incident mentioned of a ranger killed on the job was in the report for the year 1963–64 and concerned an elephant that "attacked a Native Ranger for no apparent reason and killed him. He was cycling along the road alone."[88] I mention this not to question the veracity of Mnisi's story. I do not believe that the colonial and apartheid archives on which this book draws set the standard for truth against which all claims about the past must be measured. Rather, I mention the apparent dissonance between Mnisi's memory of his grandfather's demise and the archival record in order to show the importance of context.[89]

More than that, I mention the apparent discord to foreground my awareness of the historiographic challenges posed by the archival and oral sources on which I rely, as well as to point out the limitations of the methodological approaches used in this study.[90] This book seeks neither to confirm nor to challenge Mnisi's account. But it does provide the historical context within which his memory of loss and trauma can be understood. When Mnisi told me about the feelings that overcame him—a learned, literate man who knew his rights—each time the elders in his family related the story of how his grandfather died, he was talking as much about the past as he was about the present. He was giving me the setting within which to understand his and his community's claim for the return of their land from the KNP.[91] Mnisi said that, unlike the elders in the family, his generation felt the trauma of the grandfather's death most keenly because "we know our rights." But there was far more to the story than Mnisi let on. Mnisi spoke to me as a citizen of the democratic Republic of South Africa. The difference between him and his elders was not that they "did not know their rights" whereas he and his contemporaries knew theirs. The difference was that when the old man died, Mnisi's family were subjects and not citizens. There was a limit to what they could claim. Mnisi, on the other hand, could not only express personal and collective memories of loss but also make claims for justice that a democratic government committed to redress for historic injustices was bound to honor, even if only on paper.[92] This means that Mnisi's feelings must be understood, first and foremost, politically. His talk of trauma was as much about the "social memories" of what happened in the past—the grandfather's death, the community's expulsion from the park—as it was about his standing in a democratic South Africa.[93] Mnisi's feelings were no doubt sincere and an important source of fuel for his demands for justice. But they could not be divorced from what he was trying to do—that is, stake a claim for compensation in ways that his family could not under apartheid. Here was a vivid illustration of the profound social and political changes that people like Mnisi and institutions like the KNP went through during the twentieth century and the first decade of the twenty-first. This book documents these changes by looking at the context, circumstances, and contingencies that brought them about.

The history presented here does not go in a straight line, with blacks starting out as powerless subjects and then growing into political citizens, and with the KNP as a national playground against which the story unfolds. The story presented here is far too complicated to allow for such plotting. It is a story of absences (of equality, of justice, of rights) and presence (of a range of individuals and communities). Whereas past histories of the park have tended to emphasize the absences, this book asks that we look also at the histories of presence that animate the park and its unsettled pasts.[94] The two go together. They have to go together for the black history of the KNP to claim its place in the world—not as a replacement for the white romantic histories of the park but as both a corrective and supplement to those histories.

THE STRUCTURE OF THE BOOK

The book is divided into two parts. Each part is made up of four chapters. Part 1, titled Movements, is about poachers, migrant laborers, and early histories of black tourism. Chapter 1, "Natural Enemies," looks at struggles over the park's resources between park and state officials, on the one hand, and groups of people labeled poachers, on the other. As this chapter shows, park and state officials sought to present the so-called poaching problem as a law-and-order issue, when it was in fact a political matter involving disputes over who could claim the resources of the park. Displaying a pronounced indifference to borders as markers of national identity, these so-called poachers challenged the colonial state through their sheer presence in the park. Playing the border like a concertina, they moved back and forth as they used their presence to take advantage of the weak and incomplete state's failure to be present in the park. Chapter 2, "Stray Boys," researches the role of migrant labor in the creation of a particular kind of black presence inside the park. This presence helped turn the National Parks Board and the mining industry into strong allies. But, as this chapter shows, it was the presence of these migrant laborers inside the park that brought this alliance about. In other words, black initiative helped bring colonial conservationists and the mining industry together—in ways that did not necessarily benefit the migrant laborers.

Chapter 3, "New Africans," and Chapter 4, "From Roots to Routes," zoom out of the KNP to set the scene for the emergence of black traditions of holidaymaking and tourism in the early twentieth century. Chapter 3 studies the ways in which members of the black elite made themselves present in colonial South Africa by developing a cult of travel designed to make the new country known to them while also making them known to the new country. These elites used the opinion pages of their newspapers to make themselves present in the making of South Africa. They had to do this because they did not enjoy an organic connection to the country. South Africa was not already known to them—it had to be discovered through imaginative and real travel. Chapter 4 documents the struggles that these elites waged for the right to be present wherever their means took them. For them to know South

Africa and to claim it politically as their own, they had to take its rail-ways and highways. Colonial racism made it difficult for them to get around, but, as this chapter shows, they got around. They made their presence felt.

Part 2, titled Homelands, zooms back into the KNP to offer a de-tailed social history of black tourism to the park. Chapter 5, "Civilized Natives," explores how African, Coloured, and Indian visitors made use of the park as a place of leisure and social distinction. The chapter looks especially at how black domestics, ostensibly there to tend to the needs of their white bosses, made their presence felt through surreptitious subversion and by linking the park's employees to wider circles of po-litical struggle beyond the park. Chapter 6, "Black Mobility," examines the paradoxical role of homelands in the expansion of black tourism to the KNP. The chapter shows how, in order to stay faithful to its claim that homelands were indeed independent nations worthy of interna-tional recognition, the apartheid government had to treat the "citizens" of these Bantustans in the park as international citizens no different from those of, say, Italy. However, doing so meant getting rid of petty apartheid in the park—all so the park could avoid international embar-rassment. Part 2 also explores changes over time in relations between the park and the descendants of those expelled from the park over the years. Chapter 7, "Beggar Thy Neighbor," analyzes how these rela-tions continue to inform patterns of engagement between the park and local communities in postapartheid South Africa. The chapter illus-trates this, in part, through oral historical accounts of the worst human tragedy in the history of the park—a 2001 fire that killed twenty-four people and injured many. Chapter 8, "The Road to Kruger," shows how communities adjacent to the KNP use their proximity to the park to make demands on the postapartheid government. That is, the chap-ter assesses the ways in which local communities draw the park into the political calculus of their struggles against the state. Whenever these communities have complaints against the government, they blockade the roads that take tourists to the park, thereby endangering the park's reputation and revenue. But, as the chapter shows, this is not a post-apartheid tactic. It goes back to the days of apartheid. Recuperating this history of protest on the margins of the KNP helps *Safari Nation* challenge assumptions that the rural areas adjacent to the park were either acquiescent or too conservative to challenge injustice during colonial and apartheid rule. They were not. In fact, when communities adjacent to the KNP protested in postapartheid South Africa, they drew on much older traditions of struggle and protest. That, then, is the structure of the book.

SO WHAT?

The KNP is truly one of the most beautiful places on earth. Alan Paton had another part of South Africa in mind when he called it beautiful beyond the singing of it. But he might as well have had the KNP in mind, such is its majesty. The park is beautiful beyond the singing of it. No song, no melody, can do the park justice. But that splendor has a history. That beauty has a past that cannot be divorced from South Africa's ugly history. Above all, *Safari Nation* is about the beauty of the KNP, as well as the ugly side of that beauty. The book will have succeeded if it helps readers already familiar with the park renew their love for the park, and if it drives readers not acquainted with the park to fall in love with it. But, for both sets of readers, that must be critical love. It must be love rooted in history, not some cant about a pristine wilderness or, worse, some unspoiled Africa somewhere. To help preserve the KNP for posterity, we have to come to terms with its past while helping to prepare it for an uncertain future. The future of Africa's national parks depends on our opening our eyes, not on closing them and imagining histories that never were. Hopefully, *Safari Nation* can contribute to this by helping the reader look anew at the Kruger National Park.

PART 1
Movements

1 ✎ Natural Enemies

WHEN JAMES Stevenson-Hamilton entered the Sabi Game Reserve for the first time on August 1, 1902, to assume his duties as warden, he found between two thousand and three thousand African men, women, and children living in the sanctuary. Most of the men had firearms, kept dogs, and hunted game. There was also a military regiment, veterans of the South African War, made up of about 40 white men and 150 African subalterns armed with Martini Henry rifles. The soldiers lived on game meat but prevented the resident Africans from hunting in the vicinity of the regiment's four camps.[1] There were also Boers who hunted mostly buck, especially impala and wildebeest.

But by August 1, 1903, the warden had disarmed and expelled the African families, driven the regiment out, and put a stop to open hunting. "All Natives have left the Game Reserve, which is now uninhabited by human beings except the Warden, three Rangers and Native Police or game watchers. The latter are not allowed firearms, nor are they, the Rangers, permitted to kill buck, unless in the case of the latter under exceptional circumstances," Stevenson-Hamilton said in a report detailing his first year in charge.[2]

The expulsions earned Stevenson-Hamilton the moniker Skukuza, meaning "the destroyer." Although not meant as a compliment, the moniker was appropriated by colonial officials and used later to refer to the reserve's main camp. Skukuza's arrival did not so much mark the coming of a new warden to the bush as signify the enactment of a new social and political order in the lowveld. It meant the introduction of a different regime, one premised as much on the preservation of the reserve's dwindling fauna as on the control of people, especially the Africans who had always lived in and adjacent to the reserve. Not surprisingly, Africans and Boers challenged this new order.

The warden had the colonial state, however weak, behind him. He could employ exemplary violence to make the locals feel his presence. But no amount of strong will on the warden's part could make Africans and Boers readily accept the new order. In his 1903 report, Stevenson-Hamilton complained about several cases of Africans from the Transvaal and Mozambique continuing to hunt in the reserve: "They believed that old conditions still obtained and that no white man would be found willing to travel about after November in the Low Veld, and that they could hunt with impunity, no doubt some were able to do so." But Stevenson-Hamilton was a seasoned colonialist.[3] Not for him were fears of perishing in this white man's grave. He determined to make an example of the Africans he caught hunting in the reserve: two cases, one for killing a zebra and another for killing a warthog and impala, were "severely dealt with."[4]

Stevenson-Hamilton said the "case of a boy from Portuguese Territory who was found hunting with a M.H. Rifle, and who received an exemplary sentence, had the effect of putting a complete stop to depredations on the part of the Natives, and under present conditions they are not likely to give much trouble, although it must be borne in mind that natives are quite able to kill and capture large antelope without guns."[5] Stevenson-Hamilton, a veteran of the British imperial army who had seen action in the Sudan, came highly recommended for the job. He came to his job as warden with knowledge about the bush that rested on an implied perspicacity about Africans and their place in the world. Behind that perspicacity was one essential idea: that to know the African wild was to know the African subject. Stevenson-Hamilton came with what George Steinmetz calls "ethnographic acuity."[6] This is a form of knowledge intrinsic to racially defined social relations, whereby those in power had to know their natives in order to develop effective forms of rule.

Ethnographic acuity, which could also mean "native intelligence" of sorts, was the common currency among colonizers and conservationists. When the British government appointed James Stevenson-Hamilton warden of the Sabi Game Reserve in July 1902, one of the qualities that recommended him (a Scottish aristocrat who had never set foot in the lowveld) for the job was that he understood the "treatment and control of natives."[7] When Jan Smuts plugged Stevenson-Hamilton's book about the lowveld, he, too, remarked on the Scotsman's bureaucratic dexterity in "administering its natives and . . . caring for its wild life."[8] Smuts and other colonial officials understood that official concern with nature conservation was at the same time concern with "native administration," meaning the political control of Africans whose presence could not be ignored. But the so-called native depredations continued unabated.

In fact, the word *depredations* soon became a byword for a conflict involving Africans, Stevenson-Hamilton, the National Parks Board, the Native Affairs Department, and wildlife. When used by the department, *depredations* meant animals from the reserve preying on African crops and livestock; when deployed by the board, the word referred to poaching and trespassing by Africans. Even though Stevenson-Hamilton's arrival in the lowveld had meant the practical expansion of the colonial order to places where that order had had a limited footprint previously, the reserve's mandate to protect wildlife was still being honored more in the breach.[9] In contrast, local Africans felt the warden's presence almost immediately, hence his nickname. By preventing Africans in the area from living off the land, Stevenson-Hamilton and his staff denied the Africans opportunities for independent living, effectively forcing them off the land. The Africans had to find other sources of livelihood. It did not help that Transvaal Africans were the most heavily taxed in South Africa.[10]

Potential sources of income included the mines of Johannesburg, Kimberley, and the lowveld; white farms in the area (an unpopular option); or factories and domestic service in the cities. "Wildlife protection thus played a role in creating a proletariat as the industrialization of the Transvaal began at the turn of the century," Carruthers notes.[11] Stevenson-Hamilton's order meant that, for the first time, many more Africans were exposed directly to the colonial state. "It was this," argues Carruthers, "more than the protectionist measures, which impinged on and altered African life in the area."[12] Stevenson-Hamilton's order also created conflict between Africans and wildlife. Ironically, this conflict confirmed his anti-African prejudices. Stevenson-Hamilton believed that Africans were, by nature, bad for wildlife and that it was only the "natural indolence" of Africans and their lack of the "weapons of civilization" that had prevented the extermination of wildlife in precolonial Africa.[13]

To say that the warden's order created conflict between Africans and wildlife is not to suggest that Africans had positive relations with wildlife before his arrival. It is to say, rather, that Stevenson-Hamilton's order disrupted a social ecosystem hundreds of years in the making. This left Africans exposed to greater depredations by wildlife on crops and livestock as the warden and his men placed limits on how Africans could protect themselves. Africans could not prevent these depredations without running the risk of being labeled poachers. They could not kill wildlife without being criminalized. Thus was created a conflict that would mar relations between local Africans and the reserve for more than a century. The bureaucratic clash between native administration and nature conservation created what we might call, after John Knight, "natural enemies" between Africans, on the one hand, and wild animals and the environment, on the other.[14]

Knight uses the term *natural enemies* to explain conflicts between people and wildlife. One reason why these fights occur is that often "human settlement is predicated on the environmental displacement and territorial expulsion of other larger mammals."[15] On the face of it, the conflict between humans and wildlife that developed in and around the reserve was about disputes over how Africans and wildlife were to share resources.[16] In truth, this was a political fight about the presence of the colonial state in local life. Native depredations only became such when state officials ruled that Africans could not carry firearms, keep dogs, or hunt game; wildlife depredations became such only once the state limited what Africans could do to protect their property. This was not a new problem, to be sure. Africans had hunted before; game had destroyed crops and domestic animals before. But it was made a new problem by a colonial order that criminalized African responses.

Afraid to incur the wrath of the colonial authorities, Africans beat drums to shoo away the elephants that trampled on their crops and to drive away the lions that ate their cattle, and then complained about these depredations after the fact.[17] To its credit, the Native Affairs Department took seriously the complaints of its African wards.[18] It confronted the National Parks Board and sought a range of remedies, including the exemption of chiefs from laws barring Africans from carrying firearms. It also deployed armed officers to some of the most-affected areas. But the National Parks Board also took seriously its mandate to protect wildlife. It fought the department over what Stevenson-Hamilton and others saw as its mollycoddling of Africans. The resulting clash of mandates exposed the bureaucratic inconsistency and ideological incoherence of the colonial state. This was no all-seeing leviathan but a lumbering beast tripping over its own bureaucratic limbs as officials fought over turf.[19]

This did not mean that the men of the Native Affairs Department and the National Parks Board challenged the white supremacist premises of colonial and apartheid rule in South Africa. Neither did it mean that the relationship between the board and the department was always fractious. In fact, Stevenson-Hamilton enjoyed a long but complicated relationship with the department. A strong-willed man, the warden also did not always have good relations with his own board.[20] But he and his superiors were united in their mission to preserve the game reserve, while the Native Affairs Department sought to protect African reserves. This did not stop Africans from complaining bitterly about wildlife receiving preferential treatment from the state. But African complaints were about more than just wildlife. They were also about ownership of and access to land.

The Native Affairs Department understood this. The National Parks Board had no sympathy. Even though the board and the department were government bureaucracies that saw their respective missions as advancing the interests of the state, they differed sharply over how to advance those interests. That is, this was no uniform state acting in concert but a weak and fractious entity. Carruthers says, "Stevenson-Hamilton suffered because the existence of the game reserves impinged upon the interests of numerous government portfolios. The game reserves occasionally bore the brunt of jealousies that sometimes flared up between various departments, particularly Lands, Native Affairs and the Colonial Secretary."[21] But Stevenson-Hamilton was no innocent victim of bureaucratic jealousies. He was in fact a key player in the disputes between the Native Affairs Department and the National Parks Board. Skukuza had a dog in this fight and he was determined to see it win, as I show below. This had material consequences for thousands of Africans.

NATIVE DEPREDATIONS: FROM BOWS AND ARROWS TO TRAPS

On September 4, 1903, Stevenson-Hamilton, with African attendants and pack donkeys in tow, left Sabi Bridge, his base of operations, for a destination about 150 miles north of the Olifants River. The purpose of the trip was to inspect a new sanctuary, the Singwitsi Game Reserve, proclaimed by the Transvaal Administration in May 1903. When he and his entourage arrived in Singwitsi, which was to be incorporated into the KNP in 1926, they found many African homesteads in Singwitsi, "the natives of which trap extensively and hunt with bows and poisoned arrows."[22] They also came across a party of Boer hunters.

Game figures were uneven, some areas showing decent numbers and others none at all. There were no elephants, which had fled to Mozambique during the war. Stevenson-Hamilton and his attendants spent time during his two-month inspection tour examining different parts of the new reserve. They visited a district in which no white hunters had appeared in two years. There they saw different types of buck for a stretch of 15 miles. Africans hunted these using bows and poisoned arrows, "though the damage they do in a year will not equal that done by a few Boers in a week," the warden said.

Still, he went on, "where game is so very scarce is [sic] should be put a stop to."[23] He was pleased with his progress in installing a new order in the lowveld. But he worried about the Boer hunters, for whom the "Game Laws and Ordinances of all kinds are so much waste paper," especially once these hunters were "far away from civilization." Boer hunters had no "sporting instincts and no sense of honor as a rule."[24] Despite his acknowledgment that bows and arrows were a minor threat to game compared to the firearms used by the Boers (as depicted in fig. 1.1), Stevenson-Hamilton still considered Africans the bigger problem for conservation. He held on to this view for his forty-four-year tenure as warden. On October 27, 1922, for example, he wrote to the provincial secretary of the Transvaal to ask that the native commissioner for the Northern Transvaal be ordered to confiscate "these lethal weapons." He said:

> Bows and poisoned arrows cannot be kept for any other purpose than for hunting game, and from their noiselessness render them much safer weapons for natives to use when hunting illegally, than are guns, and they cannot be discovered as can wire snares, the late sites of which may always be identified. Besides this, they are most deadly weapons, and if discharged at a Native Ranger endeavoring to arrest poachers would certainly cause his death without chance of identifying the assailants.[25]

FIGURE 1.1. Group portrait of KNP rangers. *Left to right:* Maksin, Nombolo, Sajine, Watch 1, Watch 2, July 1909. *Source:* SANParks Archive

Stevenson-Hamilton's letter went to the sub–native commissioner for Sibasa in the Northern Transvaal, who said the following in a reply dated November 21, 1922, and addressed to the secretary for native affairs:

> I beg to inform you that it is a common practice for the natives in the wilder parts of the district to carry bow and arrows, but only in rare instances are they poisoned arrows, I also know from experience that natives do at times enter the Game Reserve armed with these weapons but as to whether these are used solely for the purpose of hunting game is questionable, as the natives claim that they use them for protection against attacks from wild beasts, lions, leopards and wild dogs, which have during the last year done considerable damage throughout the district.[26]

The sub–native commissioner went on to tell the secretary for native affairs that Africans had killed four lions outside the game reserve that year alone. In fact, said the official, "one was killed last Saturday within five miles of this camp and since these natives, with the exception of a chosen few, have been deprived of their firearms, it seems only reasonable that they should be allowed to possess some means of protecting themselves and their property against the depredations of these animals." The exchange between Stevenson-Hamilton and the sub–native commissioner brought into sharp relief the terms of the tension between native administration and nature conservation.[27] For the warden, armed Africans meant depredations; for the sub–native commissioner, bows and arrows meant protection. In the eyes of conservation officials, game was at the mercy of unscrupulous Africans; in the view of the Native Affairs Department, Africans had every right to protect themselves and their property from wildlife.

But something else, not stated by either side, was at stake in this bureaucratic kerfuffle. The clash over depredations masked deep-seated colonial anxieties over African autonomy. Hunting offered Africans a chance to pursue livelihoods independent of the colonial state.[28] This posed a challenge to the state, with its need for African land and labor. It is possible that, as the sub–native commissioner conceded, Africans used their bows and arrows to poach. But it was equally true that bows and arrows were the only weapons legally available to them after colonial authorities banned them from carrying firearms and keeping dogs. For Stevenson-Hamilton, however, bows and arrows threatened colonial authority because they allowed Africans to oppose the state by stealth. Africans could fire these rudimentary weapons safe in the knowledge that they would not be found. Stevenson-Hamilton and the sub–native commissioner each claimed to speak for the state—but to different ends.

Even though both men were acting within the law, they were doing so on behalf of a colonial regime that ignored the reality on the ground. As Stevenson-Hamilton had observed in his report for the year 1903, there was a lot of movement between the reserve and the surrounding areas involving Africans.[29] Many traveled for work and leisure across the lowveld. Yet others traveled for purposes at odds with the reserve's mission. The warden had noted in 1903 that among the difficulties "to be contended with" in the reserve were "Portuguese Natives armed with guns who can dodge backwards and forwards over the border."[30] Africans from the Portuguese side constantly undermined colonial control and rendered the park's borders ineffective by moving back and forth at will.[31] This was an old problem dating back to the park's early days. The warden's use of stiff punishment to curb African depredations had not worked.

As early as March 1913, he had submitted a memorandum to the secretary for native affairs detailing the extent of the problem. The warden said that incursions by Mozambicans were a constant problem in part because Transvaal's game laws did not provide for the extradition of poachers who fled beyond its borders. It did not help that Stevenson-Hamilton had insisted that his African rangers be unarmed. The decision was coming back to haunt him. He said of the Mozambicans, "They have the more impunity in that while they are all well-armed our native police have assegais only, and they [the poachers] have let it be known along the border that they will not hesitate to shoot if they cannot otherwise escape."[32] This was no idle threat, as the warden well knew. In 1905, a group of Mozambicans had murdered an African ranger named Mehlwana near the Lebombo Hills in the reserve. Stevenson-Hamilton's dilemma was that, as he conceded in his memorandum, many of the poachers were also "hunting natives" employed by Europeans in Mozambique to supply them with game meat.

The poachers were armed with firearms that ranged from old muzzleloaders to excellent breech-loading Westley Richards and Martini Henry rifles.[33] According to the warden, Africans had obtained these weapons during the war. He asked the Transvaal government to lean on the Portuguese authorities to stop border incursions. Unless this was done, he warned, either the reserve would lose its supervision or his rangers (see fig. 1.2) would be forced to defend themselves more vigorously, leading to loss of life and possibly "serious native unrest especially in Portuguese Territory, but also in the Transvaal since the natives on both sides of the border are closely and intimately connected by blood and marriage ties."[34]

These ties were so close that Stevenson-Hamilton had noted the following in his report for 1911: "In one or two cases where convictions on minor charges were obtained against natives related to the native constable who brought the charge, he himself paid the fine out of his own wages, which I think shows a satisfactory spirit."[35] The border was an artificial line that divided people with deep connections. The poachers and the rangers who encountered one another in the wilds knew each other. Some were even related. Stevenson-Hamilton's 1913

FIGURE 1.2. James Maluleke (born 1919), a ranger at the Punda Maria Gate. Date of photograph unknown. *Source*: SANParks Archive

memorandum included an addendum detailing an episode during which three African rangers were attacked. This was to prove how close the ties were between the people living on either side of the border. The incident took place in December 1912 during a patrol by "Native Corporals" Mpampuni, Breakfast, and Mafuta.[36] The three confronted a group of armed men stalking a wildebeest herd grazing inside the reserve. The poachers fled; the rangers gave chase and arrested an old man who was with the poachers. However, the poachers returned and fired two shots at the rangers, freeing the old man. One bullet passed so close to Ranger Breakfast's ear that he fell to the ground, thinking he had been hit. "After he was fired at Breakfast called out to one of the [poachers] whom he recognized as a relative 'Why do you want to kill me?' This man answered 'Because we want to kill meat and because you have caught my brother Sigodo,'" Stevenson-Hamilton said.[37] (Sigodo was a well-known poacher arrested on November 29, 1912.) Stevenson-Hamilton said he had also sent an African spy into Portuguese territory in May 1912 to buy arms and ammunition—to prove how easy this was. He wanted the Portuguese authorities to follow the lead set by the Transvaal and stop Africans from owning firearms. He wrote:

> It is a serious danger to all Europeans living in the Low Country, but especially to the Portuguese themselves, that such a large number of natives should not only be well provided with firearms and ammunition, but should also have so much opportunity of learning to use them to advantage. In the event of an general [sic] or partial rising in the border districts, it would, I am confident, be quickly discovered that the Portuguese natives are not only adequately equipped but are many of them extremely capable marksmen. Native trouble of a serious nature has before now arisen from causes quite as slight as the present.[38]

The colonial authorities took Stevenson-Hamilton's warning seriously. The relevant government ministers approached South Africa's governor-general, who promised to ask his Portuguese colleagues to put a stop to the incursions. In a letter to the Transvaal provincial secretary dated April 16, 1913, the secretary for native affairs announced that government ministers had asked the governor-general to apply for the extradition of one Malafene, accused of poaching in the reserve and then hiding out across the border.[39]

The problem persisted, however. By 1914, even the Transvaal Game Protection Association, which was made up of white landowners in the Transvaal, got in on the act. In a letter dated June 13, 1914, J. C. V. Roos, secretary of the association, complained to the Transvaal provincial secretary about poaching by Africans living along the borders with Swaziland and Mozambique. The association asked the administrator of the Transvaal to approach the Portuguese authorities "as was done in 1912 when, on representations from the warden . . . Government patrols were sent to disarm such natives on the Portuguese side of the Game Reserve as were illegally in possession of firearms."[40] But the poachers would not let up even though cooperation from the Portuguese side seemed to improve the situation for the reserve authorities.

On July 20, 1914, Stevenson-Hamilton wrote to the Transvaal provincial secretary asking that he approach the Portuguese authorities for help in apprehending a group of poachers who had fled into Portuguese territory. The poachers, eight men and three women, had been discovered by a ranger patrol at a hunting camp inside the reserve. The camp was full of game meat in the process of being dried. The group had killed a hippo, waterbuck, sable antelope, and zebra. The hippo's hide had been cut into whips. The women were caught but the men fled across the border. However, the men ran back to free the women, firing their rifles at the unarmed African rangers. One of the alleged poachers, Makabene, was already on a police wanted list for the alleged killing of a hippo two years earlier.[41] Still, the Africans proved elusive. On July 22, 1915, the secretary for justice wrote to the secretary for native affairs to share a minute from Transvaal's attorney general about a group of alleged poachers wanted in the Transvaal for attempted murder and contravening game laws. The poachers were Portuguese subjects. The secretary for justice wrote:

> As the Portuguese authorities are not bound to surrender their own subjects some difficulty may arise if extradition is applied for. Moreover, the offence more easily provable appears to be one under the Game Laws in respect of which extradition cannot be obtained. The best course would seem to be to await an opportunity to arrest the accused within the Transvaal when

they may be tried both for attempting to commit murder and for contravening the Game Laws.[42]

We should remark on the presence of the three women.[43] They are among scores of females who populate the colonial archive, their presence noted but not acknowledged in official complaints about native depredations. Their presence in the hunting parties that, for colonial authorities, embodied the poaching menace calls for a gendered reading of poaching and of the wild. This is because the women's involvement in the hunt challenges conventional depictions of the African wild as a male domain. Not only are these women involved in the hunt; they are also important enough to the rest of the hunting party to call for rescue from rangers, as the story above illustrates. But these are not damsels in distress. They are participants in a labor process in which the private and the public were neither fixed in place nor separate in time. Drawing on ethnographic work in southeastern Africa, Clapperton Mavhunga describes the hunt as a "transient workspace — an area, site, or space where mechanical work is being performed as and because the body is moving."[44] Mavhunga counterposes the idea of a transient workspace to Marxist understandings of a factory as an institution "tethered to immovable places." Central to Mavhunga's notion of a transient workspace is the idea of mobility. He sees the African as a "spatial traveler whose mobilities are not merely conveyances across geographic space but transient workspaces, with people as engaged in work-in-transit."[45] But Mavhunga implies that only men hunted. We see this in his definition of the "professoriate of the hunt." This is a "spiritually guided institution and practice that educated boys in the chase through doing."[46] Because Mavhunga wants us to read the hunt cosmologically, as part of some African Weltanschauung, he cannot help us account for the presence of women in what is clearly a hunt. Mavhunga calls poaching a "critique of a top-down view of 'benefit'" but leaves women out of that critique.[47] Colonial officials could not afford to be so dismissive. The men and women who gave park authorities and the Transvaal government such headaches gave short shrift to the park's boundaries and the interdictions represented by those borders. For them the borders marked transition points — not end points. These Africans were, to borrow an expression from David Bunn, citizens of a fluid zone of movement. If colonial authorities were "unified in their understanding that the success of any border resides not only in its ability to barricade but also in the way that it is able to naturalize its control," then they were not ready to concede defeat to the Africans who refused to recognize the borders intended to demarcate where they could live, travel, and hunt.[48] To do that would have been to concede on a far more important political point about the legitimacy of colonial rule. Colonial authorities needed borders in order to put Africans in their place. As Bunn says, border control functioned as an "allegory of good governance by whites, over unequal citizenship."[49] Stevenson-Hamilton understood what was at stake in the battle against African depredations, especially those represented by Africans from the Portuguese side. In his view, poaching could not go unchecked because it was only a step away from political resistance by Africans. As he said in his memorandum, Africans with firearms and the skill to use them were a danger to Europeans. They could turn those guns on Europeans. That is why they could not be allowed to keep guns. Poaching was not only against the law; it also provided practice for armed insurrection. The colonial state could not allow that. Stevenson-Hamilton worried that, if left unchecked, poaching could develop into a bigger political threat to white rule in the lowveld. However, poaching was not subversive simply because it was illegal. It also pointed to independent modes of living among Africans, ways of existence not governed by any colonial structure. The Africans who hunted in the park were not premodern subjects living in a timeless place. They were men and women of the here and now. They had guns and knew how to use them. They understood the place of borders in the political ecosystem of their time. But that did not stop them from moving around and eking out an independent existence, manipulating said borders in the process. These men and women treated the border like a concertina, contracting and expanding it at will. The Native Affairs Department knew this. It also understood that this was, at heart, a political and not a law-and-order problem.

"GAME LAWS AND ORDINANCES OF ALL KINDS ARE SO MUCH WASTE PAPER"

For Stevenson-Hamilton, part of the problem was that game laws and ordinances were, as he said, "so much waste paper," especially for Boer hunters.[50] However, the problem with the laws and ordinances was not simply that Africans and Boers alike ignored them. The laws were also confusing, making their implementation by conservation authorities and the courts difficult. This difficulty was brought into sharp relief on March 5, 1923, when the Transvaal Division of the Supreme Court of South Africa quashed the conviction of three men. The case was *Rex v. Chevalo, Falasa and Munyonwse.* The sub–native commissioner of Barberton had convicted the three Africans for contravening the Game Preservation Act of 1905. The men were accused of killing a warthog in the Sabi Game Reserve without the permission of the warden. The sub–native commissioner had convicted the three based on confessions allegedly made to two African rangers. However, the confessions were not written down, as required by law. In his review, Justice Benjamin Tindall said, "The Sub-Native Commissioner evidently overlooked that fact—that the evidence of these confessions was not admissible against the accused. Under those circumstances the conviction and sentence must be set aside."[51] Five years later, the Supreme Court found itself having to review another judgment passed in a poaching case. On October 9, 1928, the Supreme Court heard two cases together: *Rex v. Befula Mabuza and Mgono Mabuza* and *Rex v. Befula Mabuza.* In the first case, the two men were convicted for unlawfully entering the KNP on or about September 28, 1928, armed with a Lee Enfield rifle and intending to poach game. The men had pleaded guilty to the charge, following testimony from the African ranger who had apprehended them just outside the park. They had each been convicted and fined £25 with the alternative of six months' imprisonment with hard labor.

However, the Supreme Court found in its review that the men were convicted under the wrong section of the law. The court ruled that their sentences should be altered to reflect the correct charge. The court said the men should each pay a £9 fine instead. Justice Richard Feetham said, "In fixing the amount of the fine I have had regard to the fact that the accused being native squatters are probably not in a position to pay a heavy fine."[52] By "squatters" he meant that the men lived in the park. In the second case, the judge confirmed Befula Mabuza's conviction for the illegal possession of a rifle but reduced his £15 fine plus a month's hard labor in prison to £8 and a month's hard labor. Feetham said that many cases regarding contraventions of the act relating to trespassing and poaching in the KNP were coming up for review and that "it seems to be a constant trouble that the charge is improperly framed and the case is not dealt with in strict relation to the charge, the evidence given and the provisions of the act." In other words, sub–native commissioners and park rangers were making things up as they went along. Speaking of Act 56 of 1926, the law establishing the KNP, Feetham said, "The Act is rather complicated in its provisions; but care should be taken to instruct the officers concerned how to frame their charges, and the necessary guidance should be afforded to the sub-native commissioners so as to enable them to deal with these cases." Feetham said that the court had complained about these errors before but that the court's remarks "appear to have very little effect in safeguarding against the repetition of the same errors." The judge went on: "Of course the Court has a certain discretion to correct proceedings; but if the same errors are habitually made the Court will be forced to take the course of setting the convictions aside altogether." He asked that his remarks be communicated to the officials concerned "so that they may not make again and again the same mistakes."

It is possible that the mistakes stemmed from the zealotry of the colonial authorities in dealing with poachers. It is far more likely that colonial officials were charging poachers under wrong legal provisions because they themselves did not fully understand what was essentially a new legal order. Empowered by a colonial state that brooked no dissent, especially when it came from alleged poachers, state officials seemed to have thrown the entire book at suspects, in hopes that something might stick. Charges did stick, but only after the Supreme Court cleaned up the legal mess created by state officials. The constant complaints by the Supreme Court about state officials making the same mistakes over and over again suggest that these officials were not particularly concerned about legal niceties. This might have created legal confusion in the courts, but there was no confusion over the meaning of the park for the Africans who lived in its shadow. Viewed from the historian's vantage point, the court's attempt to clear up this confusion does something else. It clears up the condescending fog that has enveloped many of the individuals characterized as poachers. This allows us to follow the advice given by Edward P. Thompson in *Whigs and Hunters*, his magisterial study of the origin of antipoaching laws in eighteenth-century England. As Thompson says, "one cannot read the character of a historical event from a glimpse of the face." One must "attempt a closer acquaintance."[53] So who were these Mozambicans, and can we get close enough to them to say something meaningful about their motivations?

BLOOD RELATIONS

To answer these questions, we have to read the colonial archive against the grain, finding in it evidence that was not meant to be there, locating meaning not intended by the archives, and hearing voices not meant to be heard. Recall the December 1912 incident during which three African rangers were attacked by a well-armed group of Mozambican poachers inside the park. The poachers fired two bullets, narrowly missing a ranger named Breakfast. As Breakfast went down, thinking he was hit, he called out to one of the attackers, whom he recognized as a relative, "Why do you want to kill me?"

The man answered, "Because we want to kill meat and because you have caught my brother Sigodo." We do not know the man's name and his voice comes to us secondhand, but there is no missing the personal stakes between him and Ranger Breakfast. This was no abstract struggle between an impersonal state and faceless resistance. The men and women who did battle in the bush over wildlife knew one another. Nothing illustrates this better than one of the most dramatic episodes in the history of poaching in the KNP.

On November 25, 1927, about forty Mozambicans attacked five park rangers, killing one, Stephanus Mtebuge, and seriously injuring another, Cement Mathlabi. The attack led the National Parks Board, with the approval of the Defense Department, to issue firearms to all African rangers. The decision marked the formal reversal of a policy that had been in place since Stevenson-Hamilton assumed control of the park in 1902. I say "formal" because even though Stevenson-Hamilton had long refused to arm African rangers with guns, white park rangers had long enjoyed the discretion of deciding whether to give African rangers guns. The discretion acknowledged the seriousness of the poaching problem as much as it did the importance of African rangers in the fight against poachers.

African rangers were, after all, the first line of defense against poachers. It was not just that the rangers were on the ground, patrolling great distances on foot and by bicycle. They knew many of the poachers personally and understood the communities from which the poachers came. Some of them had been poachers themselves, hired by Stevenson-Hamilton on the principle of "setting a thief to catch a thief."[54] We get a glimpse of this familiarity through a close inspection of the attack on November 25. The attackers had crossed into the park to rescue a man by the name of Penny, whom the rangers had arrested the day before for poaching two waterbuck and one steenbok.[55] Penny had been part of a three-man gang accompanied by six dogs. His two accomplices, named Shilikana and Government, had fled back to Mozambique. The rangers had destroyed four of the dogs and confiscated the remaining two. According to Cecil E. Kidger, a magistrate ordered by the minister of justice to look into the incident, the attackers sought to "intimidate the rangers from patrolling the border."[56] However, Kidger also found that there was widespread resentment toward the park's rangers and its officials among Mozambicans.

This had been "intensified by the fact that a number of their cattle which had been brought over the Union border for water during the drought, and found in the Park by the native rangers, were destroyed on the instructions of the Department of Agriculture some few months ago, under the East Coast Fever regulations." Kidger also heard rumors that, before Penny's arrest, rangers had killed two poachers from Mozambique. He objected to the decision by the National Parks Board to give African rangers firearms: "I wish to point out that this course is fraught with danger and may lead to international complications if our native game rangers should fire across the border at their 'enemies' the Portuguese natives whose kraals are within easy range of Union Territory. Feeling between the native game rangers of the Reserve and their native neighbors in Portuguese East Africa is very strained."[57]

Rather than give African rangers firearms, Kidger suggested, the South African police should establish posts at intervals along the border "with a view to the preservation of the peace, the checking of raids, and, incidentally, to keep an eye on the native game rangers of the park." This last task was especially important because the African rangers were, "after all, not a disciplined body, but just raw natives."

Meanwhile, state law advisers, who had been asked by Prime Minister J. B. Hertzog to offer an opinion "as to the remedy which the Union Government may have against the Government of Mozambique" regarding the attack, said that the Mozambican government could not be held responsible for the incident. Also, South Africa could not push for the assailants' extradition because it was bound by the terms of an extradition treaty between Great Britain and Portugal, which explicitly barred Portugal or any of its colonies from extraditing "any Portuguese subject."[58]

Even though most of the group were, in a formal sense, Portuguese subjects, in truth they were known to their victims. Rangers Cement Mathlabi and Johannes Mgvemana, for example, were well acquainted with Penny, whose rescue motivated the fight.[59] As Mathlabi told Kidger's inquest: "I know Penny well." Mgvemana also knew his assaulters quite well. "I had known these men before," he said, referring to Penny and the two who fled back to Mozambique to mobilize the attackers. Mathlabi and Mgvemana each knew at least eight of the aggressors by name. As Mathlabi told Kidger, "I knew five of them well." Mathlabi and Mgvemana also knew Batane Ndhlovu, the "petty Chief" who led the group. According to the surviving rangers, Ndhlovu's band did not speak much during the attack, except one man named Mbueni Maseu, who allegedly told Mathlabi, "They say they are going to arrest you and take you to Portuguese Territory. If they do you must agree and let them handcuff you." Mathlabi refused: "I declined and said as they had killed Stephanes they had better kill me." The assailants responded, "You can go as we have given you enough."

Mathlabi and Mgvemana were not the only ones to know the gang. Stevenson-Hamilton also knew at least five of them, including Mahashi Gumbane and Mahashi Matebula, both former park rangers "discharged for ill-conduct."[60] What's more, the five that the warden knew were, in fact, South African "subjects" who "at various times have decamped into Portuguese East Africa, to escape punishment for offences committed while residing in the Game Reserve." Three of the attackers had lived in the reserve until their escape to Mozambique. As for Mahashi Gumbane, one of the former rangers dismissed for "ill-conduct," Stevenson-Hamilton said, "I know from personal knowledge to be a very dangerous character." The warden worried he might not "get justice done without active assistance from the Portuguese authorities."

But he need not have worried. Drawing on personal connections with the Portuguese official in charge of "native immigration" in the border town of Komatipoort, Stevenson-Hamilton lobbied the Portuguese to act. The Portuguese agreed to arrest the attackers and to punish them under Portuguese law, thereby making it unnecessary for

South Africa to go against the treaty between Great Britain and Portugal. The warden's lobbying was informal. As he told the National Parks Board, "This is, of course, entirely unofficial." The Portuguese kept their word. In January 1929, five of the attackers were each sentenced to six years' hard labor, three were each sentenced to seven years' hard labor, and three were each sentenced to two months in jail.

We should hesitate before we pronounce on the appropriateness of these sentences and the extralegal manner in which they were secured. Contra Mavhunga, we should also resist the urge to see the attackers as heroes, going against a foreign authority impinging on their mode of life. But we should see them for what they were: men and women with grievances and material interests. These were not faceless men and women driven by bloodlust into killing wildlife. They were individuals with names, relatives, and interests. They knew what they were doing. But how could the Native Affairs Department address African grievances when the problem was colonial rule itself? Not prepared for the bigger fight about the legitimacy of colonialism itself, colonial administrators and conservationists fought about depredations instead.

On October 24, 1930, the National Parks Board wrote to the secretary for native affairs to protest against plans by the Native Affairs Department to acquire land near a town called Acornhoek, adjacent to the southwestern section of the park, for African settlement. J. S. Potgieter, the secretary of the board, wrote:

> The Board learns with considerable alarm that your department is making enquiries for the purchase of farms near Acornhoek in the vicinity of the Kruger National Park. The Board desires that the danger of having Natives in areas bordering on the park should be pointed out, and it will be glad if you will be so good as to inform it of your Department's policy in this regard.[61]

In his response, dated November 17, 1930, John S. Allison, the secretary for native affairs, did more than simply apprise his National Parks Board colleagues of his department's policy. He reminded them of the department's mandate, which flew out of the 1913 Natives Land Act. In terms of the act, Africans could buy land in "certain areas," so-called released or scheduled lands as laid down by the act. He wrote:

Your department will no doubt fully appreciate that it would be most difficult and invidious for this Department to prohibit Natives, who, it must be remembered prior to the commencement of the Native Lands Act, had an unrestricted right to purchase privately-owned land throughout the Transvaal, from acquiring land within the released areas, the extent of which, it may be added, is limited and by no means adequate. Indeed, it would seem that no object would be achieved by such a prohibition, seeing that under the law as it stands at present it is open to any European owner of a farm adjoining the Park to keep on such farm as many Native families as he pleases under labor conditions.[62]

Allison was of course pointing out the board's hypocrisy in trying to use its power as a government agency to undermine a law that was, from the point of view of Africans and their legal guardians in the Native Affairs Department, already bad enough. However, the board was not deterred. In April 1931 the board again wrote "with great regret" to complain about plans by the Native Affairs Department to find Africans land, in keeping with the provisions of the 1913 Land Act, near the KNP.[63] The board said that such a transaction would be regrettable. It would also go against the interests of the board. The National Parks Board did not want Africans near the park, believing they were responsible for depredations against game.

In a letter dated April 27, 1931, Potgieter, the board secretary, wrote that "it was most desirable in the interests of the Kruger National Park that the farms in question should be continued to be owned by Europeans who favored the protection of wildlife."[64] The farms in question were Sandringham and Birmingham, situated southwest of the park. The Mhlangana tribe, under Chief Shopiana Mnisi, wanted to buy them. Native Affairs Secretary A. L. Barrett, in his response to Potgieter's April 27 letter, wrote, "The properties in question are some considerable distance from the Kruger National Park and . . . their acquisition will not extend native-owned property in that direction."[65] This was neither the first nor the last time the Native Affairs Department would clash with the National Parks Board over land for Africans. The board was also not the only adversary the department had to worry about when it came to finding land for Africans near the park.

In 1939 Oswald Pirow, a cabinet minister, objected to Africans buying land near the park "on the grounds that the Natives would destroy the game."[66] Pirow was persuaded to change his mind, but only on the condition that the Native Affairs Department extend the area of jurisdiction of Stevenson-Hamilton—already an assistant native commissioner for Skukuza, the headquarters of the park—to cover areas bordering the park. Land and access to it were not the only issues over which the Native Affairs Department clashed with the National Parks Board and government ministers. There was also the treatment of Africans and their grievances by the government and the board. On May 22, 1946, the secretary for native affairs wrote the following to the National Parks Board:

> While this Department realizes that the protection of animal life is the primary duty of your Board's officials and servants, it will appreciate your active cooperation in ensuring that, in their zeal to prevent poaching, your Rangers preserve the balance between the exercise of the duties required to attain this object and the interference with the right of Natives to protect their crops and property from the depredations of the animals.[67]

The secretary was talking about different kinds of depredations. But he did not leave it there. He reminded his counterparts of the following: "The National Parks Act of 1926 limits the jurisdiction of the National Parks Board and its officers and servants to within 1 mile beyond the Kruger National Park." This reminder to park officials of the park's territorial reach and the legal obligations that went with that did not sit well with the board or indeed with Stevenson-Hamilton himself. He responded: "No one seeks or has sought to prevent natives from protecting their crops, but hundreds of snares, and hunting with dogs in wild country close to the park border and not in the neighborhood of any lands, can hardly be classed under that head."[68] Stevenson-Hamilton saw himself (through the presence of men such as the ranger and customs official depicted in fig. 1.3) as an extension of colonial authority in the lowveld. On paper, the park might have been concerned only with the preservation of flora and fauna. But in practice, it was about more than that, as the board's disputes with the Native Affairs Department show.

FIGURE 1.3. Unnamed KNP ranger and customs officer stationed at Crooks' Corner, date unknown. *Source*: Ludwig Jindra

The park allowed the state to broadcast its power over vast stretches of the lowveld, especially the troublesome border regions adjacent to Mozambique. As Stevenson-Hamilton said in response to the Native Affairs Department's reminder about the extent of the park's jurisdiction, the park exercised authority in places where "no other adequate control existed." Stevenson-Hamilton's claim confirmed the material effects of the park's creation on African communities.[69] The park did not come alone to the lowveld. It brought with it a portmanteau filled with the onerous demands of a colonial state. On October 31, 1941, the additional native commissioner for Bushbuckridge, a town west of the KNP, wrote to the secretary for native affairs to report that hyenas had killed a donkey belonging to an African and that lions and hyenas had killed six cattle in the kraal of another African.[70] Bushbuckridge seemed to have been the most affected of the communities adjacent to the park. In a letter dated April 2, 1943, the secretary for native affairs reminded the additional native commissioner that, in terms of the Transvaal Game Ordinance of 1935, it was lawful to kill game that was destroying trees, plants, and standing crops. The secretary went on: "If the position in your area is such that the depredations of game on Native crops has reached a stage that it is a question of self-preservation in so far as the natives are concerned, their interests are the primary concern." He said that Africans could set traps because they were not, after all, allowed to bear arms:

> While no doubt there is bound to be abuse, if the damage to crops is so serious that the game must be destroyed, the natives should be allowed to protect their crops, which are their livelihood, in such ways as may be possible to them, especially as the law entitles them to do so.[71]

On May 5, 1944, the additional native commissioner was again complaining about more animal depredations and echoing growing calls for the department to authorize the shooting of animals harassing Africans outside the park. However, the man was quick to add the following: "I do not shoot myself, holding strong views on game protection; but I do agree with the [police] Station Commander that it is necessary to keep the number of big game within reasonable limits."[72] He blamed the depredations visited on African crops on animal overpopulation. The department responded positively to calls for the shooting of game outside the park, using modified .303 sporting rifles bought especially from the South African Defense Force for £610.[73]

However, the plan's slapdash execution angered the native commissioner for Nelspruit. The commissioner complained on May 15, 1944, that the execution was "half-hearted" and that it would "only cause a further distrust by the Natives in the officials." He said:

> It is submitted that it should be obvious to any reasonable person that the killing of only six head of big game which come into the [African] reserve by the hundreds over a border approximately 30 miles long, would have no restraining effect and would only be a waste of time. . . . Unless adequate measures can be taken for the protection of crops against game from the Kruger National Park, and incidentally for the preservation of grazing, it is suggested that consideration be given to the question of reducing or altogether remitting the squatters' rent payable by the Natives affected.[74]

There is no indication in the archives whether the man's recommendation was ever accepted. But his letter is one of many that point to the porous nature of the park's borders. It was telling of the times that while animals from the park were going outside the park and destroying African crops and stock at will, Africans were in some ways frozen in place by the 1913 Land Act. With no freedom to move except to seek employment, Africans could do little but shoo away game from their crops and animals and then complain to the Native Affairs Department afterward. Even seasoned bureaucrats seemed moved by the plight of the Africans. In October 1946, Victor P. Ahrens, the secretary for native affairs, wrote of "long-suffering natives" who "sustained great losses in stock and crops."

Like the native commissioner for Nelspruit, who believed that Africans were entitled to tax breaks because of losses caused by the park's animals, Ahrens thought that Africans were entitled to some form of compensation from the park:

> I do feel that they are entitled to some compensation from the Parks Board, who breed and keep lions and other carnivora besides the game, and which do considerable damage to stock and crops, of lawful rent-paying residents of Trust land. . . . After all, the Parks Board must rake in quite a fair amount of revenue, and I should say, would be in a position to meet these claims, I mean, properly substantiated claims of stock losses or damage to crops. If not, then I suggest that we organize an armed guard on the boundary and shoot and kill off all the lions, etc.[75]

That was strong language indeed coming from a government official talking about another arm of government. We can tell from the exasperated tone of the letters from Native Affairs Department officials that the board's responses were not positive. The National Parks Board does not seem to have been concerned about the Africans who lived on the margins of its borders and the animals that had no regard for the park's much-vaunted territorial integrity. But the National Parks Board was not the only entity with no regard for Africans.

In a letter dated April 17, 1947, the Transvaal Land Owners' Association asked the Native Affairs Department "to consider the question of trekpassing out of the [Pilgrim's Rest] District any Native found guilty of poaching in the area. If this suggestion were brought into effect it would help considerably in checking the destruction of game."[76] Trekpassing was a notorious measure used by the state to regulate the movement of Africans. It functioned like an expulsion order. In a note dated August 6, 1947, the chief native commissioner said, "There is no such thing as a 'trekpass' in any of the laws governing the occupation and control of Trust lands."[77]

"Trust lands" referred to lands set aside for Africans through the Native Trust and Land Act of 1936, which sought to consolidate the land set aside for Africans by the 1913 Land Act. In the same note, the chief native commissioner pointed out that, by law, Africans may be expelled or removed from an area "for specified reasons, but poaching is not one of them." Agitators and troublesome persons could be moved "in the interests of good order and administration." The official answer given to the association by the secretary for native affairs on September 1, 1947, was no less forthright, if more diplomatic. The secretary said that African crops were suffering and that some of the culprits were game belonging to farms owned by members of the association.

The secretary wrote, "The amount of poaching done by Natives, who have no firearms, is small compared with the destruction effected by Europeans, but it is inconceivable that confirmed European poachers should be moved out of the district." The secretary added, "Where there is a conflict between game preservation and Native settlement on Trust land, native settlement must receive paramount consideration."[78] The exchanges between the Native Affairs Department and the National Parks Board and, to a lesser extent, the Transvaal Land Owners' Association alert us to the danger of talking glibly about "the state" as if the state were one thing. The Native Affairs Department and the National Parks Board did not see eye to eye. This was not simply a case of bureaucratic wrangling. It was also a case of different mandates. The park was, in effect, an extension of the state in the lowveld. The Native Affairs Department was responsible for native welfare.

However, even though it was not concerned with native policy as such, the National Parks Board was concerned with the thousands of Africans who lived on the park's borders and had to deal with animals that knew no borders. The colonial and apartheid states always developed wildlife legislation with Africans in mind. In fact, the (absent) presence of Africans in the formulation of wildlife laws was a key feature of South African conservation laws. African presence was a "crucial determinant in shaping wildlife legislation in South Africa."[79] This meant that the KNP was concerned with Africans even when it was not concerned with them. How could it not be? Its actions and policies affected Africans in myriad ways. But what about Africans who, in their own ways, knew no boundaries? They had to be schooled to understand and respect the legal fiction of the KNP's territorial integrity. However, this schooling was not a simple process of transmission. It was a complex process of give-and-take that exposed some of the contradictions within the colonial enterprise between native administration and nature conservation.

2 ⤳ Stray Boys

SOMETIME IN September 1920, an unnamed African from Mozambique was killed and his corpse eaten by hyenas inside the Sabi Game Reserve.[1] According to the findings of a government investigation launched by C. L. Harries, the sub–native commissioner for Sibasa, the man was part of a group of labor recruits traveling from a place called Mpafula on the Portuguese side of the border to Punda Maria, in the northern section of the reserve.

Mafuta Sitoye and Longone Makuleke, "native runners" for the Witwatersrand Native Labor Association, led the group, which included the man's son. Popularly known as Wenela, the association was a labor recruitment agency founded in 1900 by the Chamber of Mines to help the mining industry meet its needs. The runners' job was to accompany recruits from the Portuguese territory through the reserve to a pick-up point in the northern section of the sanctuary, where donkey wagons, trucks, and trains would transport them to the mines in the Transvaal and the Orange Free State.[2]

Every member of the group except the unnamed man was a contracted recruit, meaning each had signed a contract to work on the mines for at least eighteen months. The man had decided to travel with the group in order to visit friends on the South African side of the border. However, while the group was walking through the reserve, the man fell ill. The runners ordered his son to stay and look after him. According to Harries, "This was right in the Game Reserve, miles

"'Stray Boys': The Kruger National Park and Migrant Labor" was originally published in *A Long Way Home: Migrant Worker Worlds, 1800–2014*, edited by Peter Delius, Laura Phillips, and Fiona Rankin-Smith, published by Wits University Press, Johannesburg, and used with permission.

away from any habitation."[3] Father and son slept in the bush, but the next day the runners came back and ordered the son to leave his father behind and proceed with them to Punda Maria because he was a registered recruit and had contractual obligations to meet. The son duly left his father and moved on to Punda Maria.

Meanwhile, the father was abandoned for ten days and "left to suffer and await death at the spot where he first took ill."[4] The two runners passed him often during those ten days as they ferried recruits back and forth through the reserve. In a letter to H. C. Nanth, the magistrate of Louis Trichardt, dated October 5, 1920, Harries said:

> This in itself is bad enough, but when one thinks of runner Mafuta passing by later with other gangs of recruits and making no attempt to get the suffering old man to some place where he could get shelter and attention, the matter leaves a very deplorable impression on one's mind.[5]

Harries wanted the case investigated and action taken against "those who have acted in this inhumane manner." He also wanted the magistrate to complain formally to Wenela in order to prevent a recurrence. His letter contained a sworn statement from a constable named Jim Shifango, who said that when he arrived at the scene of the man's death on October 2, 1920, the man's corpse "was more than half-eaten by hyenas." The spot was about 24 miles from Punda Maria and 15 miles from Wenela's camp in Mpafula. It was also "right in the middle of the Game Reserve with no habitation of any sort." Shifango said the dead man was on his way to a place called Shikundu to visit friends. The police constable confirmed that the Wenela runners and their recruits passed the stricken man frequently in the ten days before he died but made no attempt to take him to a safe place. "It is a shame the way deceased was left to die out in the wilds with no shelter of any sort over him and no one to look after him. At least his son might have been allowed to remain with him," said Shifango.

Magistrate Nanth duly took up the matter with Wenela. But the association disputed the charges of neglect and inhumane conduct leveled at its runners. It produced a sworn statement by runner Mafuta Sitoye dated October 2, 1920. Sitoye said he had given the stricken man some food and water and had reported him to his "baas." Nanth, apparently finding Sitoye's explanation unsatisfactory, again took the matter up with Wenela. He also referred it to the Transvaal attorney general for an official probe. Wenela responded in a letter dated October 28, 1920. In his response, Wenela's manager and secretary effectively blamed the dead man for bringing his fate upon himself:

> A certain number of natives, some with friends amongst the contracted natives and others having no connection whatever with them, for protection and company join the parties of contracted natives proceeding in charge of the Association's Conductors from the Portuguese border to Louis Trichardt. No advantage of any kind of course accrues to the Association through these *stray boys* [my emphasis] — rather the reverse but it is the Association's policy to assist outside natives in such circumstances where it can conveniently do so.[6]

The secretary's reference to "stray boys," with its evocation of stray animals, was telling. It suggested that the dead man had been without an owner: domesticated perhaps but under no one's control. The secretary said that one of the runners did in fact ask the recruits he was transporting to help him carry the stricken man to a place of safety, "but the boys in the gang refused, perhaps not unnaturally, to carry him." The secretary also blamed his runners for the man's death. He said they could have done more,

> but it is, I am afraid, asking too much to expect natives, whether in the employ of the Association, or anyone else, to evince the same initiative and sense of humanity in such circumstances as would be expected from a European, and it is difficult to see in what way the Association can possibly give instructions to their native servants which will provide for every contingency.[7]

The secretary said that while Wenela wished to assist so-called stray Africans passing through the reserve, it was not responsible for them. He suggested that, in the future, stray Africans who fell ill in the reserve be made the wards of the warden. "The responsibility of attending to the native will then lie with the Ranger as a Government official, and also as the representative of the Native Affairs Department," said the secretary. It is not clear from the archives whether anyone was punished for the man's death.

However, the tragedy brings to light aspects of the park's complex social history. The dead man's fate highlights three facets of the relationship between Africans and the park: the matter of Africans for whom the park was, despite the inherent dangers, a zone of movement; the lives of the Africans who lived in the park; and, more importantly, the lives of the thousands of Africans for whom the park was a transit point between their homes and the mines in South Africa's burgeoning cities. The dead man was a stray because he had no master. He did not come in any of the categories that would have been immediately understood by park officials and those in Wenela's head office in Johannesburg.

He was neither a poacher nor a laborer. But he was clearly not the only one to see the park as a zone of movement. As reserve warden James Stevenson-Hamilton had observed in 1903, there was a lot of movement by Africans between the reserve and its outsides. He noted: "There is a good deal of native traffic between the Crocodile and Sabi [Rivers], Natives going from working in Komati Poort and Barberton chiefly, or people on the Crocodile [River] visiting their friends north of the Sabi or at Kraals under the Drakensberg, and vice versa."[8] The Africans Stevenson-Hamilton saw moving through the reserve were part of a historical network of flows and paths stretching over great distances.

The founders of the reserve might have prided themselves on their creation of a pristine wildlife sanctuary that would go back to being untouched by human influence once cleansed of human agents. But the reserve was in a place where wildlife history was in effect human history. The reserve also happened to straddle one of the most significant corridors for southern Africa's migrant labor system, with Rhodesia to the north and Mozambique to the east. Through this corridor moved animals and people, especially migrant laborers.

The migrant labor system had been in place since the discovery of diamonds in Kimberley in 1868, Mozambique proving to be one of the most fertile recruiting grounds for the mining industry.[9] Young men from Mozambique's southern provinces came to South Africa in droves to work on the diamond, gold, and coal mines of South Africa. The popularity of migrant labor in southern Mozambique was connected to ecological, social, and political factors in African polities in the area.[10] These factors included political warring within the Gaza kingdom, ecological crises, generational and gender disputes over resources, and the resultant need by young men to earn money independently of the senior men who held chiefly and political authority. These migrants were pioneers of southern Africa's industrial working class. They were among the builders of a modern South Africa. As the Transvaal Chamber of Mines acknowledged in 1961:

> The first Natives to be attracted to the mines came from the Portuguese territory of Mozambique. These men had already had some experience of industrial employment as a result of the earlier discoveries of minerals elsewhere in the Transvaal and at Kimberley. They came to the mines with the object of earning money which would enable them to return to their homes and enjoy the fruits of their labors in pursuit of the ordinary round of simple tribal activities until the need to earn money again obliged them to seek work.[11]

Working in the mines offered these migrants a chance to start their own families and to free themselves from the clutches of their fathers and uncles, who controlled such resources as the cattle needed to pay the bridewealth necessary to get married. Another important driver of the men's migrancy was Portuguese colonialism itself, particularly the harsh demands it placed on its African subjects. Migrant laborers sought to avoid a system of forced labor known as *xibalo* that, like wage labor in the Portuguese colony, paid less than work on the mines.[12] Even though mine work was difficult and dangerous, it was still considered better than forced labor[13]—so much so that, between 1886 and 1936, the majority of the Africans working on South Africa's mines came from Mozambique.

RUNNING RISKS

By 1906 Wenela had built an "extensive recruiting network" in Mozambique, with recruiters and their runners leading recruits by every available means of transportation, including the sea.[14] But this was not oscillating migration, with migrants moving back and forth between their homes and the mines.[15] Migrants in the Witbank collieries, for example, set up homes near their new places of employment and started families. What their nationality was depended on where they were at any given time. They were not national subjects rooted in place. And they did not necessarily oscillate between Mozambique and South Africa. Peter Alexander found that by 1924 there were 2,303 African women living on the Witbank collieries and that 90 percent of these were described as "Portuguese," meaning they came from Mozambique.[16]

A range of motivations that cannot be reduced to a uniform consciousness drove migrant laborers.[17] This means we must reject assumptions of a "singular migrant worker consciousness" and focus instead on the diversity of identities and motivations.[18] The journey of a migrant laborer was filled with peril. It was not taken lightly. We know about the dead man's fate because his case was exceptional. But what about cases that, while they might have been harrowing ordeals, did not draw the attention of colonial officials because they were not exceptional? In fact, C. L. Harries, the sub–native commissioner for Sibasa, complained about the tragedy because he understood that migrant labor was crucial to the development of the mining industry in South Africa and that the reserve was an important part of the recruitment network. But what was it like to be a part of this network?

Mining was unpleasant business.[19] The heat in the mines was intense and the stopes from which the ore was mined so narrow that workers had to crouch to get to it. Yet migrants kept coming. Wenela employed an army of recruiters called mine labor agents to find workers. The mining industry needed cheap labor because, with the price of gold fixed by the gold standard, there was little that mine owners could control by way of costs.[20] But they could control what they paid their workers, especially Africans. African workers tried to improve their lot by going on strike in the early years of the industry. Their struggles failed. For not only were they going against the owners; they were also challenging white workers who insisted, often violently, on a white monopoly on skilled work.[21] Recruiting workers was highly competitive and difficult, especially in the first decades of the gold-mining industry.

It also involved a range of actors, from chiefs to fathers to white criminals. "Fathers were induced to contract their children; chiefs to mobilize their followers, storekeepers to dispatch their debtor customers; white brigands connived with the mines to hijack workers bound for other employment."[22] Having found and signed up their recruits, labor agents had to move them quickly and efficiently to the mines and avoid, in the process, having the workers kidnapped by rival recruiters. That is where runners such as Mafuta Sitoye and Longone Makuleke came in.[23] A runner's job was to deliver recruits on time to depots, where recruits would be put on trains and sent to the mines. Runners worked under pressure for relatively little pay. In 1918, a runner earned two pounds and ten shillings a month.[24] Sitoye and Makuleke abandoned the old man because they had to deliver their recruits. They could not let the man's son stay with his ailing father because the son had been contracted. He had to go.

Until 1900, when Wenela was founded, recruitment was a "scandalously wasteful and expensive system."[25] By 1910, the mining industry needed about 200,000 recruits a year.[26] Every healthy recruit counted. But labor agents would sometimes dupe recruits into signing contracts they did not understand, or agents would poach recruits from one another. Wenela introduced order to the system. But traveling to the mines was still a perilous journey for migrants. As Alan Jeeves says, traveling to the mines meant running a gauntlet filled with all sorts of peril.[27]

CONSERVATION AND MINING: AN ODD COUPLE?

Where did the KNP fit in this story of movement and peril? To ask this is to raise, in effect, a question about the relationship between the park and the mining industry, between the National Parks Board and the Chamber of Mines.[28] Simply put, the relationship between the park and the mining industry was characterized by what one mining industry official called "the most friendly co-operation."[29] While Stevenson-Hamilton was, on the whole, opposed to industry and what he saw as industry's grubby designs on the park, he was generally friendly toward the mining industry.[30]

In fact, Wenela built some of the first roads in the park.[31] These, many in the northern section of the park, were intended to improve the transportation of recruits from Portuguese territory. They proved so useful that Wenela offered the National Parks Board an annual subsidy of £500 "in consideration of the wear and tear caused by their heavy busses traveling in all weathers and several times a week."[32] Furthermore, the government granted the association permission in the 1920s to set up recruitment and processing camps (as seen in figs. 2.1 and 2.2) in the park.[33]

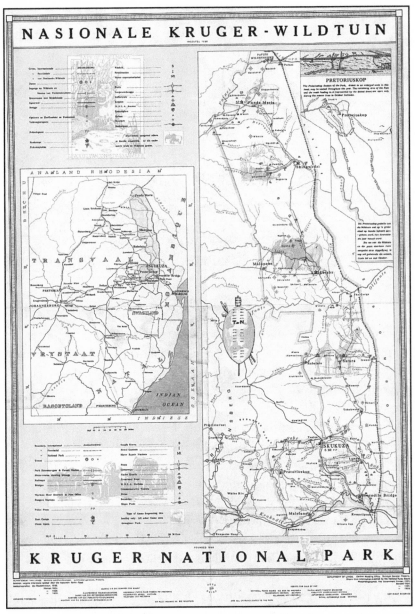

FIGURE 2.1. A 1938 map of the KNP showing extensive African homesteads as well as Wenela camps for migrant laborers passing through the park. *Source*: TEBA Archive, University of Johannesburg

FIGURE 2.2. Photograph of migrant laborers outside a Thornycraft bus used to transport them, ca. 1928. *Source*: SANParks Archive

Wenela set up its main camp in Pafuri in the north, with five rest camps set up at 25-mile intervals between Pafuri and a town northwest of the reserve called Louis Trichardt.[34] A wagon transport service was established in April 1921. The service covered the 130 miles between Pafuri and Louis Trichardt. A journey cost £12, but the sick traveled for free.[35] By June 1922, the Pafuri road was handling 3,500 recruits a year. About 600 recruits came from Massengeri, a recruitment depot on the Mozambican side of the border, while a route that connected Maplanguene in Mozambique to Acornhoek and Zoekmekaar, two major towns on the South African side of the border, handled 3,000 recruits a year. All three routes traversed the park. As W. Gemmill, Wenela's manager and secretary, said in a letter to the Wenela board dated June 9, 1922, "Half of these boys would be lost to the Industry if those routes did not exist."[36]

In 1941 the association donated one of its camps, Isweni, to the KNP. The park converted it to a ranger station. But roads in the park transported more than recruits. They were also key to the development of the reserve as a tourist destination. The National Parks Board first decided to develop roads in the park on September 16, 1926. This followed suggestions that the park construct "a main road with secondary branch roads to make traveling in the Park easier."[37] However, the park did not have enough money to build roads. In June 1927, it asked the government and the South African Railways and Harbours corporation for support. But it was not until 1928, when the park was proving popular as a tourist destination, that tracks were cleared south of the park.[38] By 1929 the park had 377 miles of roads. In fact, Stevenson-Hamilton made road building a part of the responsibilities of rangers. It was not until 1949 that the National Parks Board relieved rangers of road construction duties.

However, one downside of the roads was that they seemed to help increase tree damage by elephants, which was found to be highest near roads.[39] In the 1940s, during the Second World War, Wenela's camps in the park lost their purpose after the Portuguese authorities took over the processing of recruits on their side of the border, as part of their efforts to control movement in their territories. As a result, Wenela reduced its road subsidy to the National Parks Board to £250 a year. In terms of a convention between South Africa and Portuguese authorities signed in 1928, there were four points of entry for labor recruits from Mozambique into South Africa: Pafuri, Messengeri, Maplanguene, and Goba, and all cut through the KNP. By 1941 the Portuguese state was no longer keen on maintaining Pafuri as a port of entry.

However, in 1949, after an eight-year lapse, the National Parks Board gave Wenela permission to reopen its recruitment camps inside the park. In thanks, Wenela immediately restored its annual road subsidy to £500. "An immediate additional road grant of 1000 pounds sterling was also made for the consolidation . . . of the roads to be brought back into use again by the WNLA."[40] The camps were crucial to the recruitment of labor. In 1918, for example, when Wenela set up camp at Pafuri, about two thousand recruits were sourced from the park's northern area by unregistered labor recruiters alone. The park and the Chamber of Mines did not see themselves as simply friendly organizations. They also saw themselves as extensions of the state in territorial South Africa. Their mutual interests extended beyond recruiting laborers and seeing to their passage to the mines. They included also a political investment in making white power visible in the remotest corner of the country.

Wenela and the park saw their roles as being important for the "demonstration of white authority over Africans."[41] The creation of the KNP cemented laws imposed by the South African Republic banning

Africans from hunting, owning firearms, and keeping hunting dogs. "Wildlife protection . . . played a role in creating a proletariat as the industrialization of the Transvaal began at the turn of the century," says Carruthers, by limiting African access to land and independent livelihoods within the borders of the Transvaal.[42]

MAKING DO WITH MODERN CHOICES

Having been pushed off their land, many African men had limited choices except to turn to the mining industry and white-controlled agriculture for wages. But agriculture was not popular. The pay was poor and the conditions akin to serfdom.[43] More important, the mining industry's need for labor benefited the park because it attracted migrants from Mozambique. Migrants who went through the park would work briefly for the park to earn their pass and then move on to the mines. Wenela used the park to transport its recruits. In this sense, Wenela and the reserve benefited each other. This does not mean, however, that the KNP and the mining industry worked in concert, one churning out proletarians and the other gobbling them up as soon as they were produced. That was not the case. If there was any similarity, it was in the ways in which both the KNP and the Chamber of Mines saw their operations as allowing for the projection and broadcasting of colonial power in places where it had only existed on paper before. Officials of the KNP and Wenela believed that their existence took colonial authority into remote corners of the African hinterland.[44]

A. J. Limebeer, secretary of the Gold Producers' Committee of the Chamber of Mines, said in a memorandum dated January 20, 1943:

> The opening up of the Pafuri area is an example of the exploratory work carried out by the WNLA. Before the association's advent, Pafuri was accessible from the Union [of South Africa] only at certain times of the year, and always with difficulty. From the Portuguese side it was practically inaccessible. The nearest Portuguese officials, at Massengena, Secualacuola and Mapao would often not meet another European in six months.[45]

In the words of Limebeer, European power and control were measured by the presence of white bodies on the ground. Not meeting another European in six months was too great a distance, too big a gap. In that gap could emerge habits and actions that pointed to subversive African agency. The colonial state could not allow that. So Wenela came into the breach. It made Pafuri accessible and European power visible. This was not the only instance in which Wenela saw its presence in explicitly political terms. In the 1940s Wenela recalled the role it played in the taming of remote corners of northern South Africa and the KNP. The association said that until it moved into the northern section of the country, the area was a "hotbed for illicit labor recruiting, poaching, robbery, and every kind of illegality on the part of various undesirables, who had for long haunted that part of the country beyond the reach of any police."[46] This was an explicit acknowledgment of how Wenela saw itself in relation to state power, on the one hand, and "undesirables," on the other. That this statement echoed Stevenson-Hamilton's claim that the park controlled a place where "no other adequate control existed" is testament to the similarity between the KNP and Chamber of Mines.[47] Needless to say, this does not mean there was a common purpose between the two or even a conspiracy against Africans. But it is striking that there was a similarity in the ways in which park officials and Wenela saw themselves in relation to the projection of colonial power. In the same letter dated January 20, 1943, Limebeer said:

> It was the advent of the WNLA and the stationing of their agents at Pafuri and in the neighboring parts of Portuguese East Africa with the establishment of a regular transport service by donkey wagon from Pafuri to Zoekmekaar, which proved the main factor in putting the undesirables out of business, and within a year or two they had all faded away.[48]

Limebeer's letter celebrated a "20-year connection" between Wenela and the park. He said this connection had "been characterized throughout by the most friendly co-operation, free from the slightest suggestion of any difficulty or dispute." The connection was so strong that Wenela and park officials expressed happiness with how each party behaved toward the other. Limebeer said the following about the thousands of recruits transported through the park:

> There have been practically no complaints in regard to the behavior of any natives in charge of the WNLA. Its vehicles have

for years carried gratis the posts and parcels—often quite heavy consignments—of the Board and of the Rangers of all sections . . . between their various stations and the railway at Rubbervale and Zoekmekaar.[49]

The connection, Limebeer added, had "proved a very great convenience and saving to us." The arrangement was also of benefit to the park. When Wenela donated the Isweni camp to the park in 1941 as a "mark of appreciation of the facilities and privileges accorded to the association over a long period," this proved "a source of profit to the park," especially its staff. The camp, which came complete with "two single-roomed bungalows, mosquito-proofed, and was built of brick and concrete," cost £226 and had a book value of £119. The park promptly turned the gift into a ranger station for use by rangers during patrols. There is no indication from the archives how park authorities understood the relationship between the park's bounded nature and Wenela's use of the park to ferry migrants to the mines. All we know is that Stevenson-Hamilton did not see any necessary contradiction in this relationship.

CLANDESTINE EMIGRANTS

There is a gap between how agencies such as the KNP and the Chamber of Mines viewed themselves and how Africans formally under the control of these agencies saw themselves. In other words, the projection of colonial power represented by the park and Wenela did not mean that the Africans over whom that power was exercised were helpless. We see displays of their agency in official reports complaining about poaching and trespassing by Portuguese Africans. We see it also in perennial complaints by Wenela officials about Africans making their way through the park to the mines and other places of employment without Wenela's sanction. W. J. C. Brebner, chairman of the National Parks Board, said in a 1928 report that "considerable difficulty is being experienced with natives traveling from Portuguese East Africa through the park to the Union in search of employment."[50]

Wenela archives are also full of letters between officials in the Johannesburg head office and the men on the ground around the KNP and Portuguese territory. The correspondence details complaints about Africans looking for work without Wenela's help. In a letter dated

May 27, 1943, a Portuguese official named Luis Costa alerted a senior official named Dr. Ferrao to "an ever increasing flow of clandestine emigration" from the Portuguese side to South Africa.[51] By July 1943 complaints about "clandestine emigration" or "clandestine natives" were getting so common that A. J. Limebeer, the same secretary of the Gold Producers' Committee, felt moved to write to his officials to explain that "clandestine emigrant" was in fact a technical term used by the Portuguese "and should not be taken necessarily to imply the ordinary meaning of the word clandestine, which is something underhand, hidden or secret." The Portuguese used the term to define those of their subjects who went to South Africa's mines outside the official channels set up by the labor conventions between Portugal and South Africa. Limebeer went on to explain that far from being subversive, "the flow of voluntary labor from Portuguese territory to adjoining countries is a normal, open proceeding throughout the whole of Portuguese East and West Africa." However, Limebeer's explanation did nothing to put his colleagues at ease. In June 1948 a Wenela official named Chapman wrote:

> There is very little new in the situation and the natives continue to cross over without restraint. The Chef de Posto [Portuguese official in charge of an area], Massingir, complained bitterly that he had repeatedly sent more than two reports to headquarters over the past three years drawing the attention of the Authorities to the increasing number of natives crossing the border. . . . I met a number of small parties of natives obviously making their way across the border. The composition of these parties never varied—one or two adults, usually experienced mine natives, and two or three youths between 15 and 17 years of age. In no case did they admit to me that they intended to cross the border.[52]

Chapman certainly knew why so many Africans were crossing the border without restraint. As he said in the same letter quoted above, the majority of clandestine natives "have found avenues of employment where wages are as high or higher than on the mines, and what is of more importance on their return they are not deprived of their earnings . . . by deductions on account of fares, customs etc." Africans making their way to South Africa did not, it was true, have to pay Wenela transportation costs. They could also avoid the collection of taxes at the border post. This meant they could hold on to all of their earnings. No wonder clandestine emigration was common.

In July 1948 G. O. Lovett, general manager of Wenela, wrote the following note to his district manager in Lourenço Marques: "There is no doubt that the clandestine movement has grown considerably on account of the freedom of action the Natives enjoy by leaving the territory in this manner."[53] The freedom of action enjoyed by Africans on the border between the park and Mozambique should not have come as a surprise to Wenela. Flows, connections, and movements had always defined the border area. In fact, even Stevenson-Hamilton was forced to concede in the early days of the park that there were strong connections, blood ties even, between Africans who lived on either side of the border. So-called Portuguese natives could move back and forth over the park's border because they lived within the blurred border between South Africa and Mozambique.

The border was a zone of transition. The so-called clandestine natives existed because they had jobs to go to, friends to visit. But the permeability of the border and the freedom of action should not be taken to mean that Africans could exist outside the colony, as it were. They might have lived in and on the border, but they still needed passes to get from where they lived to the South African towns where the jobs were. They still needed to work in order to meet the obligations imposed on them by the state. But their employment options were not limited to the Transvaal and the Orange Free State. In a letter dated January 12, 1960, a Wenela district manager spoke of a "vast labor force desiring employment along the [Kruger] Park boundaries." The manager urged his bosses to lobby South Africa's minister of labor to speak to his Portuguese counterpart about regularizing the status of this vast source of labor:

> This will ensure the continuance of these industrial and mining enterprises which are dependent on Portuguese clandestine labor for their existence. . . . The WNLA would, in no way, be losers if this formality becomes legalized as the labor force concerned wish to have a short period near home where their wives can visit them between the longer contracts on the Free State mines.[54]

Africans who moved between borders and found their own way to workplaces did not act in a vacuum. They acted based on intelligence that traveled with people as they moved back and forth. Through this intelligence, they knew where the jobs were, which job paid what, and when it made sense to sign up with Wenela. Many even knew that one of the best ways to acquire the much sought-after pass was to travel through the park, get yourself arrested, and then provide unpaid labor for about two weeks before being sent on your way with the necessary pass. This does not mean the problem of clandestine emigration did not matter anymore. It continued to be a serious issue for Wenela and state officials, whose primary concern was the management and regulation of African labor and the control of African movement. In fact, the issue continued to be such a problem that in November 1959 a Wenela official reacted angrily to a newspaper report about clandestine emigration to South Africa, writing:

> This thoughtless report has virtually made the Park, as a whole, the scapegoat of a position that the Bantu Affairs Department could not handle, and had no idea how to approach it. The illegal practice of obtaining unpaid labor has been in existence since time immemorial, willingly accepted by natives who don't possess the ready cash to pay (five shillings) to pass through the park in search of work.[55]

He listed steps taken by the park to contain the problem. There was no longer work for fourteen-day laborers, men needed passports to go through the park, and African women were no longer allowed to pass through the park under any circumstances.[56] But the official was not happy with this last injunction:

> This has created great hardship on those Portuguese native females living adjacent to the border who wish to have medical attention, or hospitalization, or who wish to visit husbands working at Consolidated Murchison or Fosker [two mines close to the KNP]. This means the Natives will be forced to be dishonest with our organization, for which they really cannot be blamed.[57]

To understand why the Wenela official reacted angrily to the report, one must first understand how so-called clandestine emigration benefitted both the KNP and Wenela. The connection between the park and the mining industry did not provide the park with labor directly. Illegal immigrants were arrested or voluntarily gave themselves up to the warden, who was also a special justice of the peace. The immigrants were arrested and put to work in the park during their imprisonment. At the end of their term in jail, they were granted a pass that allowed them to seek employment in the mines and elsewhere. This casual system of labor was not without fault. Park staff did not keep criminal records, for one. In 1924 the park responded to complaints about this by introducing mobile prisons that moved around the park to where labor was needed. The institution ended in 1926 when South Africa and Portugal signed a new labor convention.[58] By the 1950s the situation was such that Wenela's district manager for Zoekmekaar was able to report the following in November 1953:

> All natives found within the Park boundaries are closely interrogated as to their reason for being in the Park. If they state that they are proceeding to the mines they proceed to Zoekmekaar. If they state their object is to reach Lowveld farmers or mines along the Escarpment they are automatically charged a fee to pass through the Park. If they have no money to pay for their permits they are automatically charged and convicted as trespassers, the punishment being a period of labor.[59]

The official added that he was unaware how arrested natives were distributed by the park to serve their sentences. The official's point apparently came in response to suggestions that park officials might have set themselves up as labor recruiters. "I cannot imagine the Park Authorities becoming involved in recruiting natives for sundry employers," he said. The official was correct: the park did not become a labor recruitment agency. But its actions came close to blurring distinctions between it and Wenela.

FROM KRAAL NATIVES TO SQUATTERS TO RESIDENT NATIVES

The Sabi Game Reserve was founded in part on the assumption that Africans were inherently bad for wildlife. Africans were considered primitives who knew nothing of the sporting codes followed by European, but not Boer, hunters. So when Stevenson-Hamilton came upon African homesteads in September and October 1903 during his inspection tour of the Singwitsi Game Reserve, proclaimed by the Transvaal Administration in May 1903, his inclination was to expel them from their lands. He had, after all, got rid of more than two thousand Africans living in the Sabi Game Reserve between August 1902 and August 1903.

However, by the time Stevenson-Hamilton toured the Singwitsi Game Reserve in 1903, colonial authorities had realized that these so-called squatters were more valuable staying in the reserve and providing labor.[60] In 1905, colonial authorities came to an even more important realization, namely that the Africans were tenants on Crown lands and as such were obligated to pay tax and rent. Thus the Africans whose communities predated the founding of the reserve by generations came to be resident natives and squatters on state land (see fig. 2.3). The change in their status had significant material effects on the Africans. They were allowed to stay in the reserve but on terms that altered fundamentally their relationship with their land. Stevenson-Hamilton convinced the government to let him collect rent

FIGURE 2.3. Photograph showing an African homestead inside the park, date unknown. *Source:* Ludwig Jindra

on behalf of the Native Affairs Department. But this was no straight-forward bureaucratic matter. To whom did the Africans belong? Were they the responsibility of the National Parks Board, with its mandate to preserve everything in the reserves? Were they the issue of the Native Affairs Department, whose focus was the welfare of Africans, especially in the so-called native reserves? But these Africans were also taxpaying subjects. So to whom were they answerable? These questions do not mean that there was strict separation between the different branches of the state dealing with Africans. The reserve was on Crown land, to be sure, but from which branch of the government did the Africans rent their land? Matters came to a head in 1931 when a dispute broke out between the commissioner for inland revenue, the secretary for justice, and the secretary of lands, under whom the national park fell, over the rent paid by the Africans as tenants on state land. The dispute began when the commissioner for inland revenue ruled that the collection of rent by the National Parks Board was illegal.

This prompted the secretary for justice to fire back in a letter dated December 14, 1931, in which he sought to cast the rents as some-thing else:

> The annual payments made by natives in the Kruger National Park can hardly be regarded as rentals, because no particular area has been let to them. Those payments must rather be re-garded as a consideration for the permission to reside in the park and to cultivate lands which are probably not defined, but are tilled first in one locality when the soil there is exhausted, in another locality, as is customary with natives.[61]

Keeping Africans inside the reserve as squatters and resident na-tives served another purpose. It made Africans part of the tourist ex-perience of visiting the reserve. The Africans in the reserve enjoyed a paternalistic and semifeudal relationship with the reserve. In deference to African customary law as understood by colonial authorities, the Af-ricans were treated as patriarchal households led by men. They were accorded limited but informal tenure. The tenure expired when the male head of the family died or stopped working for the reserve. The Africans were allowed to grow crops and keep domesticated herds for subsistence. In fact, until 1926, domesticated herds shared watering holes with wild animals inside the reserve. It was only after 1926, with the growth of "Afrikaner segregationist sentiment," that reserve officials barred African-owned animals from using the reserve's watering holes.[62] By 1928, the park reported four hundred so-called taxpaying squatters within the park. "Great care is taken to keep their numbers and also the stock owned by them, within limited bounds," said the National Parks Board in its 1928 report.[63]

Still, the presence of Africans inside the park helped cement what David Bunn calls the "image of an apparently pastoral, contented African village in harmony with nature in the game reserve."[64] The Africans projected the image of loyal subjects to the colonial state. Their presence among the flora and fauna of the reserve turned the sanctuary into a "political museum of sorts."[65] The presence of these Africans in the reserve did not so much signal the preservation of Africans as such (an idea first proposed in 1935) as it did the conservation of a particular type of relationship between Africans and the colonial state (see fig 2.4 for an illustration of the paternalism of this relationship). Bunn says, "For white tourists to the Kruger National Park between 1939 and

FIGURE 2.4. KNP officers Dirk Swart and Nic de Beer giving ranger John Mnisi antimalarial tablets, August 1974. *Source*: SANParks Archive

1960, it was this fixed and posed aspect of African identity that was most memorable."[66]

But I read the relevant archives differently. I see the presence of the resident natives as going beyond the symbolic. It is clear from the archives that the Africans resident in the park were indispensable to the reserve in real material ways. As the National Parks Board itself said in its report for 1928, the so-called squatters were an "essential source of rangers and laborers for us."[67] The so-called squatters, especially the rangers, proved so valuable to the park that even Stevenson-Hamilton commented on their "remarkable" loyalty and sense of duty. He said in his report for 1945: "There is no system of bonuses for good work; and no provision for old age or disability." He said it was "indeed remarkable considering their low pay, how strong a sense of duty generally speaking is found among the native ranger staff."[68] In contrast, white rangers had had insurance and pension policies put in place for them since 1932, when the National Parks Board bought policies for white staff from the Southern Life Association of Africa. In terms of these policies, white rangers were entitled to £10 a month upon retirement or a lump sum of money.[69]

The park and the National Parks Board sought to limit the numbers of Africans within the park. In 1937, following the passage of the Native Trust and Land Act of 1936, the park pushed some out to "released" land to the west of the park.[70] The government had released the land in question to increase the amount of land made available to Africans in terms of the 1913 Land Act.[71] The 1913 act had set aside 7.8 percent of South Africa for Africans; the 1936 act extended that to 13 percent.[72] However, the presence of the so-called squatters within the boundaries of the park served a purpose that went beyond the ideological. That is, their residence in the park was not simply to display a particular political settlement in colonial South Africa. As the archival evidence cited above and in the following pages shows, they also offered the park, in practical terms, cheap labor and a relatively easy source of revenue. This did not mean, however, that the Africans' settlement in the reserve was permanent.

In October 1926, five months after the passage of the National Parks Act and the establishment of the KNP as South Africa's first national park, a subcommittee of the National Parks Board met to consider the fate of the Africans living in the park. The committee noted that the board had no power to expel the Africans from the park. Committee members said it "could not have been the intention of the Act that all these natives should be removed, as they are indispensable to the Board."[73] However, the park wanted their numbers kept under control. Committee members were reminded that, in terms of the resolution permitting the Africans to reside in the reserve, the Africans had the right to cultivate crops, harvest firewood, and draw water sufficient for domestic needs and that their leases were subject to three months' notice. But by November 1926, the National Parks Board was complaining about the dilemma posed by the Africans.

Board secretary J. A. de Ridder wrote the following in a letter to the secretary for native affairs dated November 15, 1926:

> Now it appears there are a considerable number of natives residing in the Park. These natives should really now be removed, but as it is realized that it would be most difficulty [*sic*] to do so and, moreover, as they are extremely useful to the Rangers employed in the Park, my Board has decided to allow them to remain in the Park.[74]

In a minute to the auditor general dated February 14, 1927, Ridder gave an indication of the ways in which the Africans were valuable to the reserve. Ridder said that, in 1926, there were 181 native squatters in the reserve liable for rent and that £271 was collected that year, with £130 outstanding. The unpaid rent was perhaps a sign of the Africans' resistance to colonial control. Africans resident in the reserve resented colonial impositions and showed this, in part, by shirking their labor obligations and failing to pay rent on time or at all.[75] The rents paid by the Africans were collected in terms of resolutions taken by the Transvaal Administration on November 7, 1906, and in 1923. The 1906 resolution said that every adult male African who was an approved resident or cultivator of Crown land was liable for a £1 annual tax. This was a fixed tariff based on the number of livestock herds that grazed on Crown lands. In 1923, annual rent was set at 30 shillings for each adult male, and each male was granted the right to graze ten head of great stock or twenty head of small stock, plus a grazing rent of 10 shillings for each extra head of great stock and £2 and 6 pence for ten extra head of small stock.[76]

At first, officials of the Native Affairs Department collected the rent. But this proved cumbersome. Besides, this system created dual control over the Africans. Stevenson-Hamilton, who was suspicious of the Native Affairs Department at the best of times, disliked having to share responsibility over Africans with other government officials. He believed that dual authority confused Africans and allowed them to play off one official against another.[77] The warden said that Africans needed undivided authority. It was not easy living in the park. Too close to reserve authorities to challenge them overtly, and too afraid to break the law without risking expulsion from the reserve and certain loss of land, Africans resident in the park lived at the mercy of their overlords. They were under constant surveillance and subject to the caprice of their masters. When a white ranger named Tim Healy lost his dog, a greyhound, to heat exhaustion—the dog died after Healy ordered one of his African underlings to take it from one camp to another—Healy summoned all the African workers from their compound in Skukuza and "drove them to weep and lament at the death of the dog."[78] Healy ordered the Africans to conduct themselves as if they were at the funeral of a human being.

POLITICAL GUINEA PIGS?

Being resident natives also meant that Africans in the park were always the first to be subjected to whatever rule or practice the reserve and colonial authorities decided to introduce at any given time. This could be seen, for example, in the manner in which the reserve and colonial authorities responded to the outbreak of diseases in and near the reserve.[79] In July 1938 an epidemic of foot-and-mouth disease appeared in the park. The disease, a highly contagious viral infection that affects cloven-hoofed domestic animals such as cattle, pigs, and sheep and cloven-hoofed wild animals such as buffalo and wildebeest, was first detected in cattle belonging to one of the park's rangers.[80] The cattle had not been in contact with other animals, leading Stevenson-Hamilton to conclude that it was brought to the park either by "natives from Portuguese East Africa . . . or by motor car from the infected districts of Zululand." The park responded by killing the infected cattle, introducing carbolic dips for cars entering and exiting the park, and tightening controls over human cross-border flows. With the foot-and-mouth disease scare still fresh in the minds of many, the park's veterinary authorities decided in December 1938 to destroy all cattle in the park as a precautionary measure.[81] This might have made sense for the park, but it was an unmitigated disaster for the Africans living inside and around the park. The wholesale killing began in January 1939. About one thousand cattle were destroyed, in an orgy of killing whose efficacy even Stevenson-Hamilton questioned. He challenged claims that cattle were a source of infection:

> If, on the other hand, the game was suspected, as has from time to time been indicated, it would on the face of it appear as a waste of money and energy to kill all the cattle in the area without also killing all the game, in which case not only the Park but a belt of from 30 to 40 miles in width to the west of it would also have had to be cleared of both cattle and game.[82]

However, his complaints fell on deaf ears, even after he sarcastically pointed out that the KNP "was practically the only portion of the Lowveld which escaped East Coast fever [which hit the area in 1923], a fact due entirely to the strict regulation of entry and traveling."[83] Veterinary authorities, who belonged to a separate state department, were not well disposed toward the KNP, believing it to be a source of disease.[84] The cattle killings were a disaster for the Africans. The Africans, for whom cattle constituted life's savings, were left so helpless and destitute even Stevenson-Hamilton felt moved to record their plight. He wrote in his annual report for 1940:

> Since the outbreak of foot and mouth disease in 1939 the lot of the resident native has not been an easy one. With the money they received as compensation for their cattle which was destroyed, they purchased donkeys, but ploughing with donkeys was not so successful as with oxen, and crops were generally a failure.[85]

The warden said the Africans had to buy food from outside the reserve and used their donkeys to transport their purchases. However, foot-and-mouth regulations in place at the time said that any equine leaving an infected area must have its hooves disinfected by a veterinary officer at the point of exit. Stevenson-Hamilton said:

In practice this works out as follows. In order to fetch by donkey a bag of meal, from a store three miles outside the Park, the native has first to go and ask the Ranger to forward an application to the district Veterinary Officer. . . . And as the native may live anything up to 20 miles from the Ranger, this means a whole day's trek. At least a week elapses before a reply enclosing the permit can be expected, and if the Veterinary Officer happens to be away which is often the case, the delay is considerably longer. The arrival of the permit does not entitle the native to fetch his meal, because the Ranger must now ask the Stock Inspector of White River, 25 miles away, to come down at his convenience and wash the donkey's feet.[86]

The warden said that this might result in Africans having to wait for weeks on end at the reserve's gate in Pretoriuskop, "without adequate protection against lions." He called the system futile, saying wildebeest, zebra, and large numbers of other cloven-hoofed animals roamed freely between the game reserve and the African reserves where the stores were located. What's more, cattle owned by Africans living outside the game reserve also grazed close to and sometimes beyond the boundaries of the reserve, "yet a donkey in charge of a native cannot leave the Park without having its feet washed under the supervision of a Stock inspector."

But sympathy for the plight of the Africans did not necessarily mean reserve officials made any efforts to improve their lot. The Africans continued to be subject to the disciplining gaze of the authorities. The 1949 annual report recorded what it called a marked improvement in the conduct of African employees, many of whom were drawn from the so-called squatters. The report said that "wherever there have been cases of unsatisfactory conduct the delinquents were dealt with firmly, and wherever the action was justified, the culprit concerned was put out of the Park permanently."[87] The report said the reserve had also got rid of most of its "malcontents and chronic drunks." Even though the reports did not record directly the voices of the Africans in the reserve, there are numerous signs that these Africans were not mute but rather connected to wider worlds and discourses about political struggle. The 1956–57 annual report, for example, noted that while the conduct of the park's reserve was generally good, there was a noticeable decrease in the sense of loyalty and discipline among the younger generation of Natives. There are also indications that Natives from outside taking up employment in the Park, concern themselves to an increasing degree with foreign ideological agitations which are spreading more and more even among the permanent Native staff.[88]

The number of Africans in the park, as well as their land and livestock, decreased markedly between 1938 and 1958. In 1938 there were 2,317 Africans. By 1958 there were 473. In 1948, there were 1,638 Africans with 234 animals (cattle, goats, pigs, donkeys) and 369 morgen of land under cultivation. By 1956 there were 525 with about 93 animals and 126 morgen under cultivation. Between 1957 and 1958, the number dropped to 473. About 63 of these were men and 51 of them were employees of the park.[89] The drop was connected to efforts by the park to make the position of the Africans in the park impermanent. But these Africans stayed in the park—at least until the first decade of the twenty-first century. They made their presence felt in ways both covert and overt. But, as the following chapters show, they were not the only black actors to leave imprints of their presence on the history of the park.

3 ⤳ New Africans

To UNDERSTAND the histories of black presence in the KNP, one must first understand the history of black mobility, specifically tourism, in colonial South Africa.[1] In fact, there was a tradition of independent modern black travel going back at least to the start of the twentieth century.[2] As early as 1902, *Koranta ea Becoana*, a newspaper founded by Sol Plaatje in 1901, was reporting on excursions to the countryside and other parts of the country.[3] On November 22, 1902, for example, *Koranta ea Becoana* reported on a picnic in Bechuanaland during which one of the participants "proposed a vote of thanks to the King for being born at this time of year." King Edward VII was the monarch in question. *Koranta*, which reported mainly on politics in South Africa and the world, served as a mouthpiece for members of Plaatje's class.[4] It articulated their political aspirations as loyal British subjects while reporting on their social activities as a leisured class.[5]

On September 30, 1911, *Tsala ea Becoana*, a successor to *Koranta*, carried an article by Plaatje about a trip he had taken recently to the eastern Cape. A shorter piece in which Plaatje extolled the attractions of a "picturesque" town he had visited accompanied the report. A visit to Basutoland in the same period saw Plaatje drawing on the Swiss Alps to describe the mountain kingdom of Basutoland.[6] On August 9, 1924, *Umteteli wa Bantu*, a newspaper founded in 1920 by the Chamber of Mines to counter the spread of radical ideas among urbanized blacks in South Africa, ran an editorial headlined "The Natives' Leisure." The newspaper urged missionaries to allow "recreation to share the honors with religion." The editorial writer complained that "much conscientious mission work is too dolorous to be successful." The writer said missionaries must spice up their proselytizing with recreational activities such as sports if they wanted to attract and retain black interest in Christianity.[7]

"The pastor who is overzealous is wearisome, and he often repels the people's advance by his ardent solicitude for their spiritual need and comfort. He is dull, and dullness in the teacher always provokes indifference in the pupil."[8] This was one of the first snippets to illustrate the systematic ways in which Christianized black elites, inspired by Romanticism, thought about leisure.[9] However, it was in the 1930s, as South Africa's tourism industry was growing, that these elites started to write regularly about leisure and, significantly, to do so in ways not connected to the profession of their faith. This was secular leisure in the making, part of a social and political development connected to the birth of what Umteteli wa Bantu called, in a July 1928 editorial, the "New African."[10]

The New African was part of a historical stirring: "The awakening of the African is not only seen in the field of learning nor in the professions which are being invaded by Africans. It is seen in the ordinary occupations of life." These occupations included travel and tourism. New Africans saw themselves as modern subjects.[11] They valued the educational aspects of tourism. Writing in July 1930 in Umteteli wa Bantu, journalist and poet Herbert Dhlomo detailed a series of "hurried trips" he had recently taken through the Orange Free State, the Cape Province, and Natal.[12] Reflecting critically on the trips, Dhlomo said:

> Traveling offers a variety of experiences. It is education, change, inspiration, health and amusement. . . . My tour offered a unique opportunity to study the mind, character, habits, inclinations, customs, cultures and tastes of national, racial, local and personal units. Both in the train and out in the veldt I found people dancing to gramophone music and others absorbed in indoor games. These people miss the beauty, romance and thrill of being alone with nature and their thoughts.[13]

Dhlomo was no native stuck in place. Travel for him meant contemplation. But he despaired over how others were using their travels. He favored forms of leisure that allowed one to connect with one's thoughts. Picnics and tours were spoiled, he said, when turned into a modern jazz hall. No jazz tune could rival the melody of a bird; no artificial sound could best the whispers of a tree.[14] Dhlomo chided members of his class for failing to use the opportunity to travel to reflect on the life around them and for turning picnics and trips into festivals of loud music. "No wonder some of our talks and writings are shallow, dull and commonplace," he said. Dhlomo knew about the difficulties that confronted Africans who wanted to travel around the country, especially the absence of respectable eating and sleeping places. "Many a night have I spent walking up and down railway platforms," he said.

However, the absence of a travel and tourism infrastructure geared toward Africans of Dhlomo's class did not mean that Africans did not and could not travel. As Dhlomo's example shows, the Africans for whom the South African landscape was supposedly always already known did not have a natural, organic connection to this landscape. They discovered it as they went about evolving new identities. Travel was central to this process of discovery. But travel varied according to one's social positioning in colonial South Africa. Dhlomo knew that, compared to most Africans, he was privileged.[15] He was an exempted African for whom the pass laws did not apply. He could and did travel in ways not available to most Africans. He acknowledged the differences between Africans of his class and the rest when he declared in August 1931 that leisure had become—for the first time—a viable option for many more Africans. He made the declaration in an opinion piece titled "The Bantu and Leisure": "The Bantu have now reached the stage where the question of leisure enters into their life."[16]

It seems strange that Dhlomo, who had been writing only a year earlier about his hurried trips around South Africa, should be declaring a year later the beginning of something already underway. However, Dhlomo's piece is best understood when seen in the context of the social, economic, and political changes taking place in the 1930s. His article came at a time of rapid change in South Africa: the state founded in 1910 had consolidated itself politically; the country's industrialization, driven by mining, was continuing apace; and South Africa's urban population was growing.[17]

Also growing was the small but vocal class to which Dhlomo belonged. He believed that the social development of his class and other strata of black society had progressed sufficiently for leisure to become a real option. Leisure was fun, he said. "It is enjoyment, a tonic, education, and a means of keeping us fit for life. That is, it should develop our mental, artistic and physical faculties." But leisure depended on temperament and was governed by a person's occupation, time, health, and financial status. "Of course, certain aspects of leisure—holidaying, motoring, hunting, etc.—are out of the question at this stage of their development," he said. Dhlomo's class might have been growing, but in truth, it was relatively small still and its members had limited professional opportunities available to them.

As journalist and intellectual Richard Victor Selope Thema had said in August 1929 in a rather candid opinion piece titled "The Duty of Bantu Intellectuals": "We have about a half dozen doctors, a half dozen lawyers, a half dozen men with university degrees and a half dozen journalists and writers."[18] This was a small group of people, by any measure. But their aspirations and voices carried farther than their numbers. It was largely from their ranks that the people with the means to pursue holidaying, motoring, and hunting were to be drawn. In fact, even among these elites, very few of them had the means to go holidaying, motoring, or hunting. For one, cars were expensive.[19] But the number of cars on South African roads was growing. Between 1923 and 1928, for example, the number of licensed cars and taxis in South Africa grew from 38,815 to 113,002. In the same period, the number of buses, vans, and lorries increased fivefold, from 1,989 to 11,672.[20] It might seem odd, then, to suggest that there was a tradition of African travel and tourism that developed in the first four decades of the twentieth century when Dhlomo, a pioneer of that tradition, was suggesting in 1931 that people of his class did not yet have the means to do things like go on holiday. However, Dhlomo was writing in his time. He was too caught up in his immediate historical moment to see all the changes taking place under his nose. As I show below, some Africans were holidaying, motoring, hunting, and going to places such as the KNP in the same decade as Dhlomo was saying they did not yet have the means to do so.

In fact, such was the pace of social and economic change that barely a year after Dhlomo wrote his 1931 article about Africans and leisure, the *Bantu World* was reporting in its inaugural edition on April 9, 1932, on dramatic social transformations in South Africa: "The Native's standard of living is rising, his wants are multiplying and commodities, but a short time back considered luxuries, are today in demand as necessities." Luxuries turned necessities included tea, coffee, cocoa, sugar, jam, tinned foodstuffs, fruit drinks, paraffin oil, and candles. Reflecting its aspirational bias, the paper said Africans were following Europeans in matters of "clothing, food, sports, music and transport." Africans were also taking up other activities. Johannesburg alone boasted eighty-nine soccer and rugby clubs, fifteen cricket teams, twelve tennis clubs with about six hundred members, thirteen hockey teams, and about ten thousand cyclists. But the change was most dramatic in the area of mobility: "In the matter of transport, the segregation policy of municipal authorities has led to the adoption of European methods of locomotion," with hundreds of Africans driving their own cars. As the newspaper said, "every commodity from mousetraps to motor cars" had its African purchaser. It was one of the many ironies of the history of capitalism in South Africa that, for blacks, the struggle for freedom and political equality was also a struggle for the right to consume. As Thema told the Natives Representative Council in December 1937:

> I think we have passed the stage where we are only an asset to South Africa as laborers. Today we have become consumers and I think as consumers we should be treated differently to those forefathers who were perhaps just an asset as laborers and not consumers. . . . As I say, some people do not know, if we are paid well we would all have motorcars and the motorcar indus-try would expand and the Europeans would get more employ-ment and the poor white problem would be solved. . . . As a race we are really an uncultivated home market to which European people should turn their eyes.[21]

Thema demanded that the African worker be paid a "wage that will enable him to live comfortably and be in a position to save for rainy days."[22] As more and more Africans entered the wage economy and moved to cities, their wants and consumer habits changed.[23] Afri-can newspapers reflected these developments. *Umteteli wa Bantu* ran editorials throughout the 1930s claiming that leisure and recreation were necessary for African progress. On August 9, 1930, the newspaper said, "The Native is by nature a sport lover." On June 18, 1932, the newspaper's editorial praised the Native Economic Commission, set up by government in 1930, for making organized recreation a part of its mandate.[24] *Umteteli wa Bantu* concluded the editorial by saying, "There is no better way to hasten Native development than along the lines of organized recreation." But members of the elite did not wait for the government to organize recreation for them. They pursued their own forms of leisure. They developed their own travel and tourism infrastructure. This included the publication, starting in 1930, of the *African Who's Who*, a collective biography of the black elite in colonial Africa.[25]

This biography could be read like the *Negro Motorist Green Book*, a travel guide for black Americans published in 1936 by black travel agent Victor Green.[26] The guide, which listed black-owned or black-friendly tourist businesses around the United States, was designed to give the black traveler "information that will keep him from running into difficulties, embarrassments and to make his trips more enjoyable."[27] The *Negro Green Book* was necessary because of the perils of Jim Crow racism in America. As Susan Sessions Rugh reminds us, "Discrimination against black travelers meant that vacationing was a fundamentally different experience for them than it was for white families in . . . America."[28] However, bigotry did not stop black Americans from traveling. It inspired the development of a tourist infrastructure geared to their needs. The *Negro Green Book* told black travelers where they could stay, eat, and swim—without humiliation. The *African Who's Who* was not intended to serve as a guidebook. But it too told black travelers in colonial South Africa where they could stay and eat. The *African Who's Who* listed six owners of hotels and boarding houses. Among these was Orange Free State businessman Thomas Mtobi Mapikela. He owned a "first-class boarding house" in Bloemfontein. Eleanor Xiniwe, matriarch of a prominent African elite family in the Cape Province, owned a hotel in King Williamstown. Charles Dube, brother of ANC founder-president John L. Dube, owned the Dube Hotel in Durban.[29] These elites were, however, doing more than creating an infrastructure to ease their own travel around colonial South Africa. They were also enacting modern ways of engaging with the land and its landscapes. They were trying to realize the words of Mr. G. Radase, one of the entries in the *African Who's Who*, who believed that the "salvation of the black man in South Africa is in acquiring land."[30] The elites did this at the same time that colonial authorities were trying to disenfranchise them through the Hertzog bills, to curtail African land ownership, and to turn Africans into what British colonial official Godfrey Lagden had called "profitable citizens" governed only by the needs of capitalism and the colonial state.[31] The elites endeavored to carve out autonomous spaces that, while under the nominal control of Europeans in the colonial order, still allowed them a measure of freedom to explore the modernizing South Africa (see fig. 3.1).[32]

But they had to struggle for this limited freedom. Out of their struggles over time and space emerged a complex relationship between Africans (urbanites especially) and the landscapes they inhabited.[33] These elites took to heart the discursive promises of their new world. But they also took part in leisure for the same reasons that their European counterparts did: to drop out now and again of the rat race fast overtaking South Africa early in the twentieth century. Simply put, they, too, wanted holidays. They went on holiday to recharge their batteries by slowing down the pace of their lives. Travel was but one of the many leisure options available to them. They also organized dances, staged choral and classical musical concerts, formed book-reading clubs and

Introducing!

The only Non-European Modern
Residential Hotel, in the heart
of Durban's business centre.

HOTEL COSMO

71 Beatrice St., DURBAN

Phone 20070

Stay at the COSMO when in Durban.

FIGURE 3.1. Newspaper advertisement, date unknown. The Communist Party of South Africa ran the newspaper, the *Guardian*. *Source*: Amy Thornton Collection BC930, Special Collections, UCT Libraries

debating societies, and went to the bioscope. They started soccer clubs, cricket societies, rugby tournaments, and cycling races. There were also drinking parties whose liquor depended on the class status of their participants.

Scholars such as Peter Alegi, David Coplan, Tim Couzens, and Andre Odendaal have given us excellent studies of these activities.[34] These scholars have helped us understand how urban Africans, both the elite and the poor, occupied their time in colonial South Africa. This has laid the groundwork for my examination of the ways in which black leisure activities helped blacks develop new relations with the land. While travel involved developing a relationship with the land that was different from, say, staging a soccer match or starting a reading club, the social and political struggles for that were the same and often involved the same individuals. Travel involved movement at a time when colonial control made such movement difficult for most blacks. Travel also entailed a process of discovery and visits to places of interest. The blacks who went on holiday and engaged in tourism did so in part because they also wanted to discover the new country called South Africa. These elites did not leave us swashbuckling accounts of their adventures, unlike some of their European counterparts. But they wrote extensively for their newspapers, leaving us with a treasure trove of journalistic accounts to examine. These accounts point to the varied ways in which these elites saw leisure as indeed a modern concept of time that involved a unique use of space.[35] These pioneering elites thought broadly about the notion of leisure, as we see below.

THE QUESTION OF LEISURE

On January 5, 1935, the *Bantu World* published an opinion piece titled "The Question of Holidays" by a writer who used the nom de plume Lady Porcupine. This writer said that the "primary object of a holiday is the refreshment of body and mind by change of air and scene." There were many "utterly mistaken methods of holiday-making" about, said Lady Porcupine, and she wanted to correct them. "I assure you that this subject is an important one, because the more we enjoy and are benefitted by our holidays, the better in trim shall we be when we return to the collar-work of everyday life." Lady Porcupine said a holiday was simply an "endeavor to return for a time to the natural artless life of man." A holiday gave a person a chance to be carefree. "His time is entirely his own, to do with it precisely what he chooses, or to do nothing at all," she said. Time was of the essence in holidaymaking, Lady Porcupine argued. So was the chance to get away from it all, especially the collar work of everyday life:

> Wrapped during the rest of the year in the swaddling clothes of civilization, his holiday should give him the liberty of his primeval ancestor—a wandering in the woods, and enable him to revel in the mere joy of existence like a child knowing and caring for nothing except this . . . that he or she is alive, and that the sun is shining.

Lady Porcupine was critical of repetitive forms of holidaymaking:

> The habit of going always to the same place, and doing the same things in the same way, cuts at the very vitals of the hungry mind that seeks an expanding circle of interest. Sure! It costs no more to go to another place or to choose some fresh center each year, so that we may get the chance and at the same time increase our knowledge of our own country, in which we are lamentably deficient.

Black elites saw South Africa as theirs, too—not just a country for the white man. That, in fact, was the basis of their struggle against colonial racism. However, as Lady Porcupine argued, these were not natives to whom South Africa was always already known. If anything, their knowledge of South Africa was "lamentably deficient." They had to discover the country through leisurely travel. Lady Porcupine suggested that African elites undertake excursions to various places of interest. These were to include beautiful scenery, have ancient associations, or be fashionable resorts. Lady Porcupine's essay was no isolated piece of journalism.

Throughout the 1930s the *Bantu World* published a column titled Who's Who in the News This Week. The column kept track of the comings and goings of its readers. It offered what we might call an imaginative map of black mobility in South Africa. Thus we learn in the November 18, 1933, edition that Mr. S. Mekgoe of the Native Affairs Department in Rosettenville passed through Johannesburg "on his return from the Eastern Transvaal where he spent his holidays," while Mrs. R. Mavela of Idutywa in the Transkei left Johannesburg by train to return home after spending a month's holiday with relatives in the city. On December 16, 1933, the newspaper reported that Mr. B. B. Ndika, principal of Nzozo School in Port St. John's in Pondoland East, "left on December 11 on a Crown Roadster push-bike for Willowvale where he will spend the Christmas holidays and intends visiting various places of interest in the Transkei," while Mrs. B. J. Ngele of Braamfontein was spending a month's holiday in Meyerton for health reasons.

On December 23, 1933, the paper announced that Dr. Roseberry T. Bokwe had finished medical school at Edinburgh University and was visiting continental Europe ahead of his return to South Africa. Bokwe was the son of Rev. John Knox Bokwe, regarded by his contemporaries as the father of African choral music. We learn in the same edition that Mr. M. B. Bulunga of Mbabane, Swaziland, passed through Johannesburg en route to a holiday in Durban, and that Miss Irenah Nagona of the Wesleyan School in Boksburg was vacationing with her parents in Western Native Township. We learn from the January 12, 1935, edition that Mr. B. Wallet Vilakazi "returned to Natal on Wednesday by car" after taking part in a training course in Johannesburg. On February 2, 1935, the paper reported that Miss E. Sixaba "of Grahamstown fame" spent the 1934 Christmas holidays with family in Cape Town. While in Cape Town, Sixaba visited bioscopes, docks, Muizenberg beach, Claremont, Rosebank, the Rhodes Memorial Garden, and the Cape Zoo. The unnamed correspondent who wrote about Sixaba said, "There are two reasons why I wrote this article, the first is that this young lady is a real good spot [sic] and has a very good character. . . . The second is to arouse emulation. Our young ladies should be encouraged to travel so that their knowledge be widened."

On March 16, 1935, the *Bantu World* announced, "Mr. and Mrs. B. Dingake have returned from their vacation and are preparing to send an interesting article to *The Bantu World* on their experiences and the various places they visited." There is no evidence to show that the Dingakes submitted their article. But there is plenty of archival material to show that members of the African elite were thinking systematically about leisure, taking holidays, and writing about them in order to, as the correspondent who told the world about Sixaba's holiday said, arouse emulation. For members of this small elite, the idea was to lead by example.

The *Bantu World* did more than report on the activities of its readers, however. It also sought actively to encourage a tradition of holidaymaking among urban Africans.[36] For example, on December 23, 1933, the paper announced an essay-writing competition open to all African schools from Randfontein to Springs, that is, from the west to the east of Johannesburg. The newspaper wanted readers to suggest ways of improving its sales. The deadline was February 28, 1934, and essays had to be between 250 and 500 words in length and could be written in English, Zulu, Xhosa, or Sotho. Writers of the ten best essays would win a seven-day holiday in Durban. "This free holiday will be in the nature of an educational trip and every effort will be made to ensure the scholars visit as many places of interest as possible." The competition was only for boys aged twelve to eighteen. Girls would get their chance the following year, the newspaper said.[37]

For black elites, leisure was a broad term that included "visiting friends and relatives" and going to places of interest.[38] These were seemingly disparate activities, but they were united by the fact that they displayed a use of time by black elites not governed by the colonial authorities. This does not mean that these actors were free from European control. But, as the following story shows, black elites negotiated for themselves spaces of leisure within the colonial order. The story, which concerns John Dube, reinforces the argument that colonialism was an arena of negotiation in which dichotomies of tradition versus modernity or resistance versus collaboration did not always apply.[39] The story shows how the creation of an independent tradition of travel by African elites in early twentieth-century South Africa took place inside the colonial state itself and not outside it. The episode complicates some of Dhlomo's claims about what was and was not possible for black tourists in the 1930s.

THE EXEMPLARY NATIVE

In January 1936, Dube wrote to the native commissioner for Inanda District in Natal to request exemption from the Natal Firearms Act of 1906,[40] which barred Africans from owning firearms and ammunition. The act allowed for exemptions in certain cases, however, and that is what Dube was asking the native commissioner to arrange. Dube was a prominent African. In addition to having led the ANC from 1912 to 1917, he was the scion of one of the most famous African Christian families in Natal. Dube said, "I make this application not because I have a desire to arm myself, but on principle." He prayed that the governor-general, who had the final say, "may be pleased to grant me this privilege, which would be appreciated not only by me, but by my people for whose upliftment I labor." Dube need not have worried. The native commissioner was only too happy to support his bid. In a letter to Harry C. Lugg, the acting chief native commissioner for Natal, the native commissioner wrote: "Dube is a highly respected Native of this District and is not likely to abuse the privilege if granted to him." Lugg also gladly supported Dube's application. Lugg said the exemption would allow Dube, the legal owner of a .303 rifle and a 12-bore shotgun, to buy himself sufficient gunpowder.[41] Lugg said:

> I may remark that I happen to know that John L. Dube finds considerable relaxation from his onerous work by hunting when he is able, and that for this purpose he has on occasion gone on hunting trips beyond the borders of the Union Territory.[42]

As an "exempted native," Dube enjoyed a freedom of movement that most of his fellow Africans could only dream of. But he still had to jump through all sorts of colonial hoops to get his ammunition. The secretary for native affairs supported his application but first wanted it run by the Department of Defense. The secretary for defense supported it as well. Dube's application eventually made it to J. B. Hertzog, the prime minister. Hertzog wrote to Lord Clarendon, the governor-general, on March 12, 1936, recommending that Dube be granted his exemption. The state granted the exemption that same day in a "letter of exemption" signed by Clarendon and Piet Grobler, the native affairs minister. When Dube was informed of his exemption, he was effusive in his gratitude, thanking all the involved colonial officials by name and asking his magistrate "to let me have kindly a certified copy, so that I may frame the original." There is an explanation for Dube's excitement. This was not his first application for exemption.

In fact, the defense department had opposed an application he had submitted in 1929, despite the support of his local magistrate and the native commissioner for Verulam. The chief of the defense force had said that "the policy followed by the Department [of Defense] in the

Cape, Transvaal and Orange Free State, in so far as natives are concerned, other than chiefs, is to refuse all applications to acquire rifles or revolvers." However, the defense department did allow for exceptions in cases involving shotguns, as long as the applicant was supported by his magistrate and the local police, and "the firearm is required by the applicant for the destruction of vermin on land leased or owned by him." The defense force chief wanted the issuing of exemptions standardized across South Africa and for Natal to follow the example of the other three provinces:

> It is suggested that applications for firearms by natives in Natal should be dealt with similarly as apart from any other considerations it would appear to be desirable that in the matter of control pending the promulgation of a Union Act consolidating the pre-Union laws there should as far as possible be uniformity of practice in all four provinces of the Union.[43]

The secretary for native affairs decided, based on these comments, to reject Dube's application. We do not find another application from Dube in the archives until the successful one he makes in 1936. The effusiveness of his thanks is explained, therefore, by the fact that it came against the backdrop of previous failures to gain exemption. But Dube did not see the exemption in personal terms. As he said in his letter of thanks from April 1936, "This is more for my people than for myself." It is not clear, however, how Dube's exemption would have benefited his people. Did he mean that his hunting (see fig. 3.2) benefited his people? Was he saying that the prestige that came with his being an exempted native benefited his people? The closing lines in Dube's letter of thanks suggest that he saw his prestige as being by definition of benefit to fellow Africans: "These are the words, written in sincerity, of one who all his life has struggled for Light in Darkness."

Dube saw himself as a pioneer trying to bring civilization to his people. Not only was he American-educated, a reverend, and politically connected to the colonial state; he was also the elder statesman of the African elite behind the formation of the ANC. He saw everything he did as reflecting positively on the Africans he wanted to draw out of darkness and into a Christian light. Dube's sense of exceptionalism extended to his leisure activities. He saw his hunting as part of the

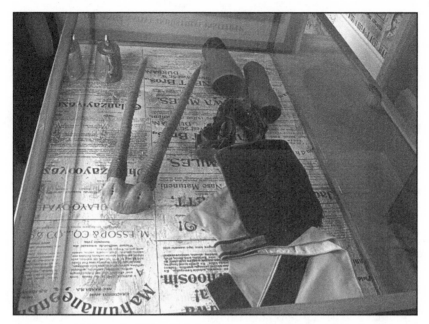

FIGURE 3.2. Photograph of John Dube's hunting trophies, taken at Dube home/museum in 2007.

civilizing mission. Dube was not, of course, the only elite African in his day. He was part of a class that, although small, was growing both vocally and numerically.

THE REAL NATIVE PROBLEM

Through his application for exemption, Dube alerted us to a world of leisure activities inhabited by members of the African elite. Dube's hunting might come across as derivative of Victorian and Edwardian leisure activities. But we cannot ignore the fact that here was an African taking part in hunting and traversing colonial boundaries to do so. Dube's case allows us to ask broader questions about Africans and leisure. It gives us an opening into the history of tourism in South Africa. This is the history that Dhlomo was perhaps too enmeshed in his own time to understand. The African leisure tradition pioneered by the likes of Dube, Plaatje, and Dhlomo—not to mention the scores of Africans whose social life appeared in the *Bantu World*'s Who's Who in the News This Week as well as in *Umteteli wa Bantu*'s own Town and Country gossip column—emerged in the context of debates about the new meanings of space and time in colonial Africa.

These debates pitted various members of the colonial state against members of the black elite and concerned questions about the shape of South African society. What kind of society was developing in the early twentieth century and what was the role of black elites in that society? Members of the black elite did not want to rush their integration into colonial society, but they wanted to know that their hope for equality was real. As *Umteteli wa Bantu* editorialized in October 1921, "The educated and thinking tenth of the Native population will share our belief that the political evolution of the Native will be speedier if he hastens slowly."[44] This talented tenth did not mind waiting for gradual political evolution. But it wanted colonial authorities to show that they understood that African elites were in fact the real "native problem" that needed solving.[45]

Members of the African elite believed that all the colonial authorities had to do was bring educated Africans into the colonial regime as equal partners and South Africa's race problem would be solved. Colonial authorities had failed at the time of union in 1910 to live up to their promise to reward "civilized natives" with certain privileges. If the authorities wanted these elites to stop complaining, they had to recognize these elites and their claims. *Umteteli wa Bantu* said on June 9, 1923: "The problem will be solved by white understanding and by the conferment of privilege upon native men according to their individual merit." According to the African elite, African intellectuals were the "native problem" only because colonial authorities refused to acknowledge the social distinctions between educated Africans and the majority of Africans who were, as *Umteteli wa Bantu* said on June 9, 1923, "ignorant and uncaring, unconscious of repression or hardship and content to live and die as their fathers did."

This view was as old as the Christianized elites themselves. The elites saw themselves as a class apart. But they still opposed the stereotypical view of rural Africans as a people in danger of being overwhelmed by Western civilization. These "out-of-category" elites opposed the two-dimensional characterization of Africans as either hopelessly corrupted by modernity or idyllically traditional.[46] But they did not see Africans as one mass. In fact, members of the elite went to great lengths to distinguish themselves from the great mass of Africans. Writing on September 19, 1925, in *Umteteli wa Bantu*, H. Selby Msimang took Prime Minister Hertzog to task for saying the following: "I have seen two distinct classes [of Africans]—the tribal native, with a strong sense of obedience to his chief and respect for the whites; and the intellectual we know so well—the man of the big towns."

The African elites objected to Hertzog's caricature of Africans because he denied them a stake in modern society. They considered Hertzog's disregard an affront. As *Umteteli wa Bantu* editorialized on May 14, 1921:

> We are convinced that there is no psychological justification for the popular European belief in the inferiority of the Bantu race, and we are inclined to think that the general prejudice is founded on the tendency of the human mind to merge the individual in the class to which he belongs, and to ascribe to him all the characteristics of his class. . . . That there should be Natives of a higher caste physically and mentally than the blanket native is inconceivable to the hide-bound European who revels in the superiority vested in him by 2000 years of progress.

The elites drew a distinction between a "worthy native" and the "uncultured natives" preferred by segregationists like Hertzog.[47] This distinction is worth keeping in mind because it suggests that activities such as tourism, which only a few members of the elite had the means to pursue in the first half of the twentieth century, were one way in which the elites distinguished themselves from the rest of the African population. Members of the elite took for granted claims that, when it came to civilization, Europeans had a two-thousand-year head start on them. But they believed that, given time, they too could become "civilized." As *Umteteli wa Bantu* had said on May 1, 1920: "Let us [Africans] be content to climb the ladder of progress step by step, and not endanger our ascent by reaching for a higher rung until our feet have been firmly planted on the one below it." This did not mean, however, that Africans were to be treated like beasts of burden or confined to a national park. As Thema put it in a column titled "Let the African Dance and Sing":

> The African has sufficient sense to know that in this changed Africa his salvation lies in the assimilation of western civilization. He will refuse steadfastly to be herded like Africa's animals into National Parks and Zoos for the benefit of the white race.[48]

The *Bantu World* said, in a distinctly Kantian vein, "In God's scheme of things, no human is created for the benefit of another, but to make its contribution to the prosperity and progress of all. If black men and women are today servants, it is not by Divine ordination but by force of circumstances."[49] While some colonial officials looked with disdain at social distinction within African communities, members of the elite took seriously the question of differentiation. They wanted recognition as mobile elites and as a social category separate from the mass of Africans. These elites did not want to be confused with Africans who moved because of land hunger caused by state-led dispossession and expulsion. The marginalization against which the elites railed substantiates the argument by scholars such as Jane Carruthers and Njabulo Ndebele that, when it came to conservation, Africans were at best considered irrelevant to matters of "aesthetics, tourism and scientific investigation" and at worst seen as detrimental to conservation unless, of course, they were being paraded for the amusement of tourists (see figs. 3.3 and 3.4).[50]

Ndebele says the marginalization of Africans from conservation left Africans with no "intuitive familiarity" with the world of tourism, making them feel that "perhaps they should be out there with the animals, being viewed."[51] The relevant authorities certainly saw Africans as marginal to tourism except as part of the tourist attraction. But Ndebele's statement is too strong a claim to make about what was in effect a more complicated history of tourism. Africans might have been seen in some circles as irrelevant to conservation and the tourism industry it inspired. But that does not mean that Africans, especially the elites, saw themselves in similar terms. African elites understood the right to free movement not as a subset of a bigger bundle of rights in which the political dominated. They saw the right to free movement as important in and of itself. This is not to say that the right to free movement was not political; it was that and more. Neither does it mean that the elites did not care about the fate of the majority of Africans. When General J. G. G. Kemp, the minister of lands, published a bill in 1935 making allowance for the extension of the KNP, the *Bantu World* said in response that while it supported the "preservation of animals" in principle, it did not want this done at the expense of Africans:

There can be no doubt that the farms which are to be added to the Kruger National Park are at present occupied mostly by Africans who will naturally be evicted when the bill becomes law to give room for animals which are being preserved solely for the amusement and entertainment of tourists.[52]

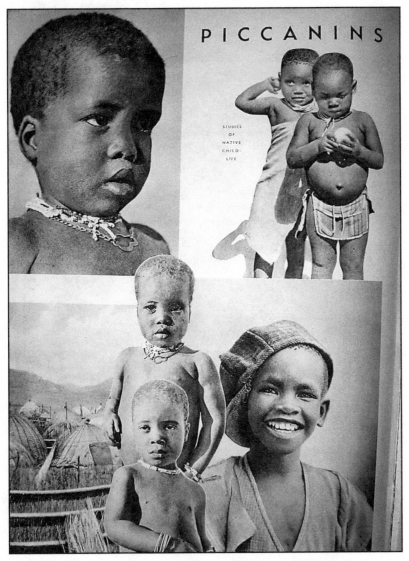

FIGURE 3.3. Photograph depicting so-called native life in South Africa, date unknown. *Source*: Transnet Heritage Museum Photo Collection

FIGURE 3.4. Scenes of so-called native life, ca. 1920s–1930s. *Source*: Transnet Heritage Museum Photo Collection

The editorial called on the government to show the same "magnanimous spirit in dealing with the problem of Native land" that it had displayed toward the denizens of the park. But the expulsion of Africans to make way for the KNP was, of course, the story of the park's history. Indeed, James Stevenson-Hamilton owed his nickname "Skukuza" to it. However, it would be a mistake to conclude that these expulsions resulted in a uniformly hostile attitude by Africans toward the park and conservation. As the *Bantu World*'s editorial made clear, nature preservation was a noble deed. But it needed to be balanced alongside the needs of Africans desperate for land. The newspaper did not see the park as necessarily detrimental to the interests of Africans living inside and beside it. The park and conservation only became detrimental to African livelihoods when the well-being of Africans was ignored. In fact, while some Africans were losing their land and live-stock to the park, others were visiting the park. This distinction lies at the heart of the varied African experiences of the park. Jane Carruthers says that Stevenson-Hamilton would not have objected to the presence of African tourists in the park.[53] But what happens when the historian poses this not as a hypothetical but as a real question? Carruthers does not pursue the import of her observation about Stevenson-Hamilton's attitude toward African tourists. There were many more Africans who engaged with the park than the squatter, poacher, and impoverished African. Members of the black elite enjoyed exemptions that allowed them to engage in tourism. This did not mean, however, that this privi-lege was without inconvenience; black elites had to fight constantly for it. They could never take it for granted. The next chapter describes how these elites traveled to the KNP and other places of interest.

4 ❧ From Roots to Routes

On March 19, 1912, three men called on Jacobus Sauer, the minister of railways in the Union of South Africa.[1] Sefako Makgatho, Thomas Mapikela, and Sol Plaatje were leaders of the South African Native National Congress (SANNC), founded six weeks earlier following calls by Pixley ka Isaka Seme for a "Native Union" to help Africans fight for their political rights in the new state.[2] The men were there to protest against the ill-treatment of Africans by officials of the state-owned South African Railways and Harbours corporation (SAR).[3] William Hoy, the SAR general manager, accompanied Sauer.

This was the second meeting between a government minister and officials of the new organization. The first meeting had taken place in early March 1912 when a delegation led by SANNC president John Dube met Henry Burton, the minister for native affairs, to object to a draft squatters bill that threatened to curtail the already limited rights of Africans to land. We could say, after James Clifford, that these two meetings between the SANNC and the government were about roots and routes: roots concerned the right of Africans to land; routes meant their right to travel.[4]

Roots and routes spoke directly to two of the primary concerns of elite and nonelite blacks in South Africa in the early twentieth century. However, historians have ignored the fact that these two meetings took place within weeks of each other. They have tended instead to focus on the land question and to neglect the equally important struggles by Africans in colonial South Africa over the right to free travel.[5] This privileging of roots over routes has blinded scholars to the complex nature of the black experience of the birth of modern South Africa.[6] It has also made it difficult for scholars to comprehend fully the significance of events such as the meeting that took place in Cape Town on March 19, 1912.

The neglect of the historical significance of that meeting has also made it harder to understand, on Africans' own terms, African grievances about their treatment on the trains. These grievances—a constant of the twentieth century—point to a tangled relationship between Africans of different classes and the land. The three men who met Sauer claimed to speak for Africans. In truth, they spoke for mission-educated elites who wanted to enjoy the trappings of the modern world—such as travel by train—without interference. These elites constituted a small community for whom travel fell outside the dictates of the colonial state and its nascent industrial economy.

They traveled because they could, not out of compulsion by a European master. Their struggles against poor treatment by railway officials shed light on broader disputes about the role of race in the making of South Africa. The railways were key to the political and social creation of South Africa (not to mention the opening of the KNP as a tourist destination). But railways were about more than mobility. They were also about modes of being in the world. They not only symbolized what it meant to be modern; they made it possible for people to be modern.[7]

As Tony Judt says, "More than any other technical design or social institution, the railway stands for modernity."[8] The advent of the railways brought profound change: from the penetration of hitherto unreachable parts of the world to the introduction of the train timetable. Trains changed the way people related to space and time. "No competing form of transport, no subsequent technological innovation, no other industry has wrought or facilitated change on the scale that has been brought about by the invention and adoption of the railway," says Judt.[9] Railways were also key to the making and expansion of countries such as the United States.[10]

In South Africa, the railways transformed four political entities—the Cape, Natal, the Orange Free State, and the Transvaal—into one national entity. In the process, they helped make South Africans out of a disparate collection of peoples. The railways bred new understandings of territory and identity. They inspired what Jeremy Foster calls an "imaginary geography of emergent nationhood."[11] This racialized and politically hierarchical geography included the KNP, whose creation and existence allowed South Africa to present itself as the world's trustee in conservation.

Foster argues that the railways determined how whites perceived the country's landscapes and had a powerful impact on how they encountered the "imaginary territory" of the nation. In fact, says Foster, the "apparatus of the train itself"—from the way the rail network was laid out to "the speed, duration, frequency and cost of the journey; the design of the carriages in which travelers journeyed; and those with whom they traveled"—framed the South African landscape in particular ways (see fig. 4.2).[12] But how was this landscape framed for the likes of Makgatho, Mapikela, and Plaatje?

These men were, after all, widely traveled. It is not clear that Foster can help us answer this question. There is little indication in his argument that he appreciates that, despite the segregation that existed on the trains in South Africa, the railways were not only for white South Africans. To be fair to Foster, he is concerned solely with the "imaginary geography of white South African nationhood." But holding such a narrow conception of the role of the railways in South Africa involves the same problem that bedevils Jane Carruthers's otherwise well-intentioned argument about the Africans' supposedly peculiar

FIGURE 4.1. Scenes of so-called native life, ca. 1920s–1930s. *Source*: Transnet Heritage Museum Photo Collection

FIGURE 4.2. Color spread showing luxury train journey in South Africa, date unknown. SAR commissioned artist Charles E. Turner to paint the spread, which appeared in the British newspaper the *Sketch* on October 3, 1928. *Source*: Transnet Heritage Museum Photo Collection

experience of modernization. That is, Foster's account simplifies what is in fact a complex history of race and the railways in South Africa.

Africans were among the most widely traveled South Africans in the first half of the twentieth century. For the elites represented by Makgatho, Mapikela, and Plaatje, mobility was essential. Their struggle for equal treatment on the railways was also a struggle for a politically inclusive South Africa. These men wanted a South Africa founded on political equality and on the unfettered right to move around.

The South African Railways and Harbours corporation was founded in 1909, a year before South Africa came formally into being.[13] By the 1920s, SAR was the "most powerful single corporation in the sub-continent, and the second largest state-owned railway and harbors system in the world."[14] It employed 7 percent of the white workforce and accounted for the livelihoods of 10 percent of the country's white population. As Foster says, "In many respects, the Railways were the ideal means for bringing about the modernization of South Africa, because their apparently objective workings transcended the cross-currents of ethnically-based politics which the colonial national state wished to overcome." In remote parts of South Africa, the railways were often the "sole evidence of modernity."[15]

African elites wanted recognition as members of the modern world represented by trains. In some ways, they were already recognized members of colonial society. At least until the late 1940s, the SANNC (which changed its name to the African National Congress in 1923) and members of the African elite enjoyed cordial relations with the colonial state. Until 1948, government ministers regularly met the organization's delegations and white mayors hosted its meetings in their town halls. But that recognition did not go far enough. The organization's founders saw themselves as loyal British subjects and expected to be treated as such. They did not always receive treatment in accord with their status.

Makgatho, Mapikela, and Plaatje had supported the British in the South African War precisely because they were loyal British subjects. By the time these men met with Sauer, however, the British had long sacrificed their class at the altar of a racially exclusive white nationalism—a nationalism that sought to build in South Africa a white man's country on the backs of millions of black inhabitants. Deciding that the future of South Africa depended on white supremacy, the British turned their backs on the class from which the three men came.[16] But these elites insisted on their right to travel.

As Thema said, "Like any other member of the human race he [the African] is entitled to free movement and free intercourse with the outside world."[17] How, then, did Makgatho, Mapikela, and Plaatje frame this entitlement to free travel in their meeting with Sauer and Hoy? The grievances detailed by Makgatho, Mapikela, and Plaatje included the following: SAR officials constantly abused African passengers and sometimes threw them off trains for no reason, and Africans were charged fares that did not accord with the services they received. Plaatje told Sauer about a "peculiar system" in two of South Africa's four provinces that, he said, was likely to lead to violent clashes between railway officials and African passengers. Plaatje said that officials in the Transvaal and the Orange Free State were refusing to issue rail tickets to Africans traveling without the government-issued passes that regulated the movement of Africans.[18]

Plaatje said he had "sometimes been forced to take the train without a ticket, and when he complained of this, the GM [Hoy] wrote stating that those who refused to give [Plaatje] the ticket were acting in order, and that those who supplied him with tickets when he had no pass, were exceeding their authority."[19] When Sauer asked for an explanation of this "peculiar system," Hoy said it was the law in the Transvaal and the Orange Free State. The law was driven by fears that Africans would desert their white masters easily if allowed to travel without passes. Makgatho, Mapikela, and Plaatje were, as "civilized natives," exempt from the pass laws. "Yet," Plaatje told Sauer, "when you produced documentary proof to the satisfaction of [SAR] booking officers that you were your own master, traveling in the interest of your work and not deserting it, they refused to issue the ticket." That was not all. The men said that African passengers were not allowed to eat in the dining saloons of trains but were charged extra for eating in their compartments.

Sauer asked Hoy if the last complaint was true. Hoy answered, "Yes, that is the rule." Sauer: "You refuse a man permission to eat in the dining saloon, and you charge him for not eating there? That is putting him between the devil and the deep blue sea." Sauer turned to the three men: "The best thing, in the circumstances, seems [to be] not to eat at all. I will go into the matter and communicate the result to you." This was a less than satisfactory solution considering the vast distances covered by trains.

Sauer was not the only one to promise to address and then fail to act on African grievances. When Makgatho related the story of a group of delegates kicked off a train while on their way to the ANC's founding conference, held in January 1912 outside Bloemfontein, Hoy promised to look into the matter. According to Plaatje's newspaper *Tsala ea Becoana*, nothing came of Hoy's promise. But Hoy's failure to keep his promise did not deter Africans from voicing their complaints. In fact, Africans had been complaining about their treatment by railway officials since the beginning of the twentieth century. As early as October 11, 1902, a correspondent to *Koranta ea Becoana* was complaining about poor service on the trains. The correspondent said, "The return received by this kind of customer [meaning Africans], for the value of his money, is, in many instances, very poor."

It was "no uncommon occurrence," said the correspondent, for Africans with third-class tickets to be "herded into cattle-trucks," with "no allowance being made for the inconvenience." The correspondent said that while each third-class compartment was supposed to take only eight passengers, it was common to see sixteen Africans stuffed into a compartment, "like so many locusts in a boiling pot." The writer wondered how such practices escaped the attention of sanitary inspectors. In the same edition, another correspondent, writing under the moniker Black Ebony, took issue with a white passenger who objected to sharing a train compartment with Africans.

Black Ebony said that the white passenger wished "to give out that it is a cheek on the part of the black man to say that his money was as good as that of anybody else. Now, is that not true?" He challenged the passenger's claim that Africans were unsanitary in their travel habits: "I have been a constant traveler over the railways on the Eastern, Middle and Rhodesian systems and I have very often [seen] the shoe in the other foot. It would be better for these chaps—if they simply agitated for an improvement of the railways, and left alone repeating the time-worn bogey that their coin is more legal tender than ours."

This was not an abstract struggle. Black Ebony drew on personal experience to debunk the racism he encountered on the trains. Alas, the attitude displayed by the white passenger seems to have been common. In February 1903, a *Koranta ea Becoana* correspondent writing under the name Tlhakanchuke related an incident involving a "tall slender white thing, which for want of a proper appellation, I will call a fellow." Tlhakanchuke was traveling from East London to Mafeking. The fellow boarded in Vryburg and, finding Tlhakanchuke already on the train, asked a couple of white men standing nearby, "Has that nigger been traveling in that train with that [white] lady?" The men answered, "Yes, but she did not seem to object."

The woman and her brother, traveling with a sickly boy, had joined the train in Kimberley. Tlhakanchuke had offered the woman milk for the boy. The fellow heard the story but was still unhappy about Tlhakanchuke's presence. "That's why they think they're our equals," he said. Tlhakanchuke wanted to rip off the fellow's nose to bring him to the "limits of reason" but thought better of it. "Such are some of the creatures you meet with under the white skin. They are not merely stupid—but they are base enough to make foolish exhibitions of themselves at a public place, and they claim to be our superiors," said Tlhakanchuke.

But the struggle for the better treatment of African passengers was not always a losing battle. On August 12, 1903, *Koranta ea Becoana* reported on a successful meeting between the general manager of the

Cape government's railways service and Chalmers Nyombolo, the acting general secretary of the Cape National Congress. Following the meeting, the manager instructed his officials on the "proper treatment of Natives while traveling in different parts of the country." He asked Nyombolo to bring cases of abuse to his attention, saying "if the charge is substantiated, the official responsible will be punished."[20]

However, the changes promised by the manager do not seem to have had any lasting effect because on December 2, 1903, *Koranta ea Becoana* was still complaining about the poor treatment of Africans. The paper demanded the reduction of the third-class fare from one penny a mile to half a penny a mile irrespective of distance. The paper also called for a ban on the conveyance of third-class passengers in cattle trucks without the consent of passengers. Even then, the paper said, the passengers must be charged the goods rate.[21]

Given that the men who led the campaign for the better treatment of African passengers on trains were the same men behind the ANC and its struggle for the political rights of Africans, it is no stretch to say that for members of the African elite—some of whom had the vote—the struggle for the right to travel without hindrance was as important as the battle for political recognition. As *Umteteli wa Bantu* put it in its inaugural editorial on May 1, 1920: "The franchise is a valuable gift, and no less to be desired is the right to own property, the right to walk freely in our land untrammeled by pass law restrictions and annoyances, and the right to self-government." The elites understood these rights to be connected. The right to vote could not exist without the right to travel and to own property, especially because of the qualified franchise in the Cape that used property to determine whether a man could vote.

However, we should not ascribe the ill-treatment of black passengers on the trains simply to the stupidity of white bigots. To do that would be to assign too much power to racism. There was more to the story. There was, as Plaatje told Sauer and Hoy, the white fear of black desertions. Railway clerks in the Transvaal and the Orange Free State worried that blacks traveling without passes were deserters. These clerks understood the importance of trains to the mobilization of black labor. But they also knew that neither they nor the colonial state could control how blacks used the trains. Something else was also at play in this "peculiar system." Even though blacks constituted the majority of train passengers throughout the twentieth century, they were not the railways' intended customers. From the physical layout of the railways to their marketing, the railways systematically undermined black patronage. As William M. Macmillan noted wryly, "to locate the native reserves it is no bad rule to look for areas circumvented or entirely missed by even branch lines."[22]

One explanation for this circumvention was no doubt the fact that the rail network was, as Gordon Pirie points out, "built for other purposes."[23] The network was designed to move minerals and produce from the agricultural heartland to the seaports. It was also meant for "settlers, government officials, business [and] tourism."[24] It was not set up for the express purpose of moving elite Africans or thousands of migrant workers between the mines and their homes. The railways skirted African areas because colonial officials considered these reserves to be located in the realm of the traditional as opposed to the modern.

BUILDING A TOURIST PARADISE

Nothing illustrated this idea better than the advent of tourism in South Africa in the first half of the twentieth century. Tourism complicated SAR's official and rather poor understanding of black people as customers in their own right. As far as SAR publicity officials were concerned, blacks should not have been on the trains in the first place (unless they were migrant laborers in cattle trucks); they should have been outside being viewed through the window by local and overseas white passengers as the train went by. But, as I show below, this is not to say the railways completely ignored black people. They could not.

For the record, the Union of South Africa did not inaugurate tourism to the region. John Thompson Rennie is reported to have set up in 1849 as the region's first booking agent, handling passenger and cargo shipping between the Cape and Britain. In 1858 he founded Rennie's Travel.[25] In 1901 Thomas Cook organized tours to the battlefields of the South African War.[26] But these were isolated ventures.[27] They were not part of a uniform tourism campaign. Besides, there was no country called South Africa then. That and the marketing of South Africa as such would come much later, driven—as was the case in many other countries—by the railways.

As Jeremy Foster reminds us, railways were "far more influential in shaping the discursive landscape of the new nation than the work of any individual writer, artist, or even photographer."[28] Trains not only opened up the new country but also fashioned a "new subjectivity toward the landscape that was reflexive, collective and national."[29] But all that took effort—work that began with the unification of South Africa. As governor-general Lord Selborne put it, the mineral revolution, which began with the discovery of diamonds in Kimberly in 1868, turned South Africa from a "country of the ox-wagon" to a "country of the railway." But it took war to bring about the "nationalization of its railways."[30] This, in turn, made possible the development of a national subjectivity, a shared but tentative sense of South Africanness that emerged despite the best efforts of Afrikaner nationalists and colonial leaders such as Jan Smuts to turn South Africa into a white man's country.[31] But before South Africa could market itself as a tourist destination, it had to resolve questions about what it was and who its people were.[32] The country had to know itself first as a nation before it could project itself as a tourist destination. But the country never did settle these questions, meaning that it sold itself to the world without resolving its basic political contradictions.

The advertising of South Africa proper as a tourist destination began in 1914 when the government gave a £25,000 grant for a "publicity scheme" targeting Europe.[33] However, the scheme was abandoned when the First World War broke out. SAR, which had had nominal control of tourism to South Africa since 1911, revived the plan at the war's end. In November 1919, Hoy hosted a two-day "overseas advertising conference" in Johannesburg. This led to the establishment of the South African National Publicity Association, the first body devoted to the promotion of South Africa as a tourist destination. The organization began meeting annually in 1920. SAR opened its first overseas publicity office in London in 1920, followed by a publicity bureau in New York in 1925. Such was the success of the New York office, led by an "officer of enormous energy" named George Oettle, that in 1926 South Africa welcomed its first tourist cruise ship, carrying 350 passengers, from the United States.[34] In 1927 two steamers called; the following year six steamers visited.[35] This was a remarkable marketing success considering that it took twenty-eight days' sea voyage each way to travel between South Africa and the United States. The association believed it had found a way around the obstacles preventing Americans from visiting South Africa: "Many people have the leisure but little capital;

many have the capital, but grudge the time involved. Hence, our plan of attack is to interest the woman, for if she decides to go, the husband invariably follows."[36]

The success of the first steamship visit in 1926 led to the establishment in 1927 of SAR's Publicity and Travel Department. This is the department that sold South Africa to the world, framing it as a place of unique flora, unsurpassed sunshine, exotic animals, and picturesque native life. The department ran the publicity association. Department officers served as the association's secretariat, provided day-to-day management, produced the publicity material distributed around the world, and controlled South Africa's advertising budget. In 1931 the association issued its first policy statement, setting out its objectives and modus operandi.[37] It divided the country into nine regions, with an elected Publicity Advisory Committee to serve as its executive body between annual meetings. The Reuter's Press Agency, as well as the directors of publicity for Johannesburg, Durban, and the Cape, served ex officio on the committee. Each municipality was expected to contribute to an overseas publicity fund, the Publicity and Travel Department matching those contributions on a pound-for-pound basis.

RAW MATERIALS

Only 49 of the 276 municipalities in South Africa made any contributions. Of the 49, Johannesburg gave £1,000, Durban £500, Cape Town £400, and Pretoria and Port Elizabeth £250 each, while the United Castle Steamship Company gave £2,000.[38] Explaining his city's contribution, Cape Town mayor A. J. S Lewis said it was a "sound business investment to put our goods in the window and display them as much as possible."[39] The annual advertising budget was £41,000, of which £25,000 came each year from SAR and £10,000 from government. As the policy statement said, "In its propaganda campaign, the Publicity and Travel Department disseminates to all parts of the world information relating to the tourist attractions, distinctive features and general potentialities of South Africa . . . while sound films are specially called into service for the portrayal of the different aspects of life and conditions in the country, particularly in regard to natives, industries, and scenic attractions."[40]

These were the raw materials key to the development of South Africa's tourism industry. As the association said: "If once the general public could be made to realize the fact that tourism is as much an industry as the more generally-accepted enterprises, such as mining and manufacture, and entails the same demand for raw materials, while influencing the activities of all sections of the populace, then the present-day lack of appreciation of the responsibility for the fostering of this national undertaking would automatically disappear."[41] The idea propounded by the association, of Africans as raw materials, was different from that put forward by Hannah Arendt, who, in her examination of the Boer use of Africans as slaves, described Africans as "the only 'raw material' which Africa provided in abundance." Arendt claimed that Boers "treated the natives as raw material and lived on them as one might live on the fruits of wild trees."[42]

The association had something else in mind. As the association saw it, Africans were raw material in the sense that—like industry and scenic attractions—they were the basic stuff from which South Africa could be made known to the world. They were attractions that South Africa could sell to "practically every civilized country on the globe." As Hoy told delegates at a meeting of the Publicity Advisory Committee in Cape Town in May 1927:

> It is the business of this Executive to preach the gospel, particularly to the peoples of overseas countries that travel, and especially travel abroad, to new lands, among people different in habits, customs, costumes, and national characteristics, puts joy into life, invigorates the intellectual faculties, furnishes material for diversity of thought and gives edge and intensity to the perceptions. It rounds out the functions of the school room and library. It enlarges life, enriches the mind, removes prejudices. It is a boon to the weary and the sick, and to the nerve-racked professional and businessman.[43]

Earlier that year, Hoy said that "if we have only will and imagination enough the next few years should see South Africa firmly established as one of the favored touring countries of the world."[44] He believed that nature had endowed South Africa with features that, if harnessed properly, could make the country a destination of choice for discerning travelers. Hoy had to say this because South Africa always struggled to draw sufficient white settlers or travelers to the country.[45]

He told a meeting in June 1926: "Qualified world-travelers are agreed that for climate, scenic grandeur, agricultural and mineral features and for native life interest and novelty South Africa is unsurpassed. These resources, given by nature, if rightly used, can be made a source of national income and private profit as other countries have clearly proved."[46] To the charge that Africa was the "Dark Continent," Hoy countered that it was, in fact, the "continent of sunshine."[47] South Africa was a country of "exceptional possibility and there was less darkness here than anywhere else in the world, both in intelligence and the possibilities of the future." Even though South Africa was seeing a steady increase in overseas tourism—from 5,538 in the years 1924–25 to 6,234 in 1925–26, 6,356 in 1926–27, 7,678 in 1927–28, and 7,743 in 1928–29—Hoy wanted South Africa to aim for 25,000 overseas tourists a year, "on the principle that if you aim at the moon you will hit something higher than a haystack."[48]

Aiming for the moon meant flooding the overseas market with advertising. In 1927, for example, the Publicity and Travel Department distributed 171,000 publications, thousands of photographs, and hundreds of lantern slides and films around the world. The publications included 27,000 tourist brochures, 51,000 municipal booklets, and 66,000 pamphlets about farming in South Africa. The farming pamphlets remind us that the marketing of South Africa to the world was not solely about turning the country into a tourist destination. It was also about advertising South Africa as a country fit for white settlement.[49] We see this in the distribution pattern of the advertising material. While most of it targeted Europe and North America, a big number was also sent to white settler colonies such as Australia and New Zealand and to places with white settler communities, such as the Belgian Congo, India, Java, and Kenya. Hoy wanted to draw white settlers from these places to South Africa. People like Hoy struggled, without always being explicit about this, with the fact that South Africa's white population was relatively small and did not show any signs of growing sufficiently to make South Africa truly a white man's country, with whites exercising full mastery over nature.

He was not alone. In 1923, T. Ericsen, who represented Kimberley in the publicity association, urged the association to extend its advertising to northern Europe in order to recruit immigrants from Denmark, Sweden, and Norway. Ericsen worried that the association was not

FIGURE 4.3. Color spread showing whites domesticating the wild, ca. 1920s–1930s. *Source:* Transnet Heritage Museum Photo Collection

doing enough to attract the right sort of white settler to South Africa. He said Scandinavians were the "very best settlers" and that their expertise in canning would be good for South Africa's fishing industry.[50] In 1925, P. Finlayson, the publicity officer for Pietermaritzburg, complained about South Africa's stagnating white population. "The fact that South Africa's white population is not increasing is a very serious matter, and although various associations are bringing out settlers, it is felt that if we want the country to really progress, a new movement should be started to induce fresh settlers to come to Africa," he said.[51] Although the association controlled the advertising message and distribution, it could not control the message's reception.

In 1926, for example, an Indian prince visited South Africa on a hunting expedition, drawn no doubt by the publicity material shown in India. At a time when South Africa was in the grip of hysteria about so-called Asiatic migration, the prince brought along a large retinue of fellow Indians. This included ten people who traveled first-class on the trains, twenty who traveled second-class, and twenty-five servants overall.[52] However, no amount of overseas advertising could mask the fact that South Africans themselves were not getting to know their own country. As the *Graaff-Reinet Advertiser* put it in 1929, "It is of little avail to spend thousands on advertising, whilst the goods offered are stored away in a back room in their original wrappings. . . . We can 'deliver the goods,' but in many instances our goods are still stored away in our back store in the original wrappings."[53] This was because many South Africans simply did not know their own country.

They did not know what their country had to offer the tourist. As it turned out, this was a perennial complaint. Hoy had told his colleagues in 1923 that he was "surprised how comparatively few people in South Africa had really seen their country."[54] In 1927 Sir Llewellyn Andersson, representing Johannesburg, said, "We in South Africa do not know our own country."[55] The *Cape Times* knew exactly whom to blame for this state of affairs. The paper said that "modern ideas" were taking too long to penetrate certain parts of the country and that it was not "surprising to find many Afrikanders who still have the very vaguest ideas about the value of intelligent and well-planned national propaganda."[56] The *Cape Times* was playing on anti-Boer prejudices and stereotypes that had lived beyond the South African War. It went without saying that the editorial was not addressed to black South Africans. The kind of ignorance identified by the *Cape Times* was not deplorable simply because it existed. It was bad because it hampered state-led efforts to make the country known to itself and to the world. As the *Natal Mercury* said, many South Africans were "poor advertisers" of South Africa because they were so "woefully ignorant of the land" they lived in.[57]

THE GEOGRAPHICAL IMAGINATION

From the very beginning, South Africa's tourism authorities took an expansive—or what we might call a transnational—view of South Africa in their marketing.[58] That is, the destination they sold as South Africa in their advertising material did not map onto the physical entity called the Union of South Africa. It included the beaches of Lourenço Marques in Portuguese-led Mozambique and the Victoria Falls in the British-controlled Rhodesias. Addressing the association's annual meeting in 1932—held in Lourenço Marques—SAR general manager J. R. More reminded delegates that the association's mission was to "reawaken the ardent desire of our fellow inhabitants of southern Africa to the fact that the advantages we possess in climate, scenery, fauna, and flora should be more widely advertised and brought home to the people of Europe."[59] In August 1933, SAR general manager T. H. Watermeyer said that "in the sphere of publicity and its relation to tourist traffic, the colony of Mozambique, Rhodesia, and the Union of South Africa, all are united in the common aim of attracting visitors from other parts of the world to this sub-continent."[60] Watermeyer and his colleagues had to do this because the falls and Lourenço Marques were especially popular with tourists. As H. J. Crocker, director of the Johannesburg Publicity Association, said, the falls were "undoubtedly the supreme attraction" in the region.[61] The authorities understood that, between the Victoria Falls, the Cango Caves in Oudsthoorn in the Cape, and the KNP, they had "national assets." But these assets could not market themselves. They had to be developed and sold as places of interest.

As Hoy said, "Caves cannot stand by themselves, but associated with such scenic places as the Swartberg [Mountains] and Seven-Weeks-Poort they become a resort to which we could send South Africans in trains loads [sic] as well as people from oversea."[62] Even the KNP, to which SAR started taking tourists in 1923 when it was still the Sabi Game Reserve, had to be advertised. Its charms, however natural they might have been, had to be made known to the world. And SAR had art and photography at hand to package the park for the world. As A. H. Tartlow, manager of the Publicity and Travel Department, said in 1925, SAR made the reserve "better known to the traveling and holiday-making public through the issue of a pictorial poster and a booklet drawing attention to the locality."[63]

A NATIONAL/NATURAL ASSET

As the park gained popularity, the publicity association paid more attention to it (see fig. 4.5). In January 1927, P. G. Louw, a delegate from Pietersburg, told the annual meeting of the Publicity Advisory Committee that the park would "prove [to be] one of the greatest, if not *the* greatest attraction we have to offer in South Africa." Louw said that the park, the "biggest natural zoo in the world," had to be advertised widely. "It is the one thing we possess which cannot be imitated by any other country."[64] By 1931 the association was praising itself and the park's founders for giving this "zoological wonder" to the world. "As a national asset, viewed from all angles, its existence, usefulness and natural beauty, are a tribute to the prescience of those who originally segregated the area as a wild animal sanctuary for all time."[65] At a time when the Union of South Africa had yet to settle the question of what it was, the association dared to describe the Kruger as a national asset.

FIGURE 4.4. Some of the first visitors to the park, ca. 1920s. *Source*: Transnet Heritage Museum Photo Collection

FIGURE 4.5. Scene of so-called native life, ca. 1920s–1930s. *Source*: Transnet Heritage Museum Photo Collection

It might look like black South Africans did not feature at all in the deliberations of the publicity association, except maybe as an abstract category called native.[66] But in fact, blacks figured in a range of discussions. At the association's annual meeting in 1935, delegates complained about the quality of statistics concerning tourist traffic to South Africa. The problem lay with railway clerks who only counted "Europeans and Coloured persons (other than Asiatics)" in possession of one-way tickets when they left South Africa through the east, as well as passengers (excluding Africans) leaving or entering South Africa via the west.[67] When the SAR general manager refused to order his clerks to enumerate every person, regardless of race, entering or leaving South Africa, E. W. Mowbray, a delegate for Kimberley, suggested that perhaps too much was being made of the "Bantu business," meaning that the job of enumerating tourists would not be so difficult if the clerks simply stopped counting black travelers. "Of course if you are going to record every native I can see quite a big job," Mowbray said.[68] That was not the only item on the agenda concerning Africans that year. H. J. Crocker said that members of the Transvaal Publicity Conference were concerned that "visitors to South Africa do not find it easy to see native life under its true conditions, and in some of the kraals they do see, the natives are either partly or wholly Europeanized."[69] This was not what tourists came to South Africa to see. They wanted the authentic experience of Africans in their "true conditions." Crocker suggested that "wherever it is reasonably possible the natives should be encouraged in their kraals near the travel routes, such as between the Rand and the Kruger National Park, in their picturesque customs, dances, dress and industries."[70] When Crocker's proposal was presented to the secretary for native affairs, he rejected it.

The secretary said that "while fully appreciating the advantages of a sound tourist trade," he did not believe the "best interests of the native people would be served by their being exploited for publicity or exhibition purposes." Crocker was not satisfied with the response. He said, "All we want is that the natives should be seen in the same way as the Maoris in New Zealand. They are not exploited, but probably gain something from it."[71] J. H. Farrant, a delegate from Pietermaritzburg, explained the department's response thus: When overseas tourists were encouraged to visit African homesteads in Natal, this led to begging. Durban delegate A. C. D. Williams said that begging became so acute that the government barred tourists from visiting African areas in Natal. However, Williams was still critical of the Native Affairs Department. "After all, our three major attractions are the Kruger National Park, the Victoria Falls, and the native life. We do not want exploitation of the native. We want the tourist to see the native under his natural conditions."[72]

AFRICAN RESPONSES TO NATURE TALK

As for what Africans themselves wanted, Crocker and Williams did not bother to ask. But we know how members of the black elite felt about their suggestion. In its report on the proposal, the *Bantu World* said that the Transvaal Publicity Conference was essentially asking Africans to shun Western-style education and Christianity and "to continue living as their forefathers had done" in order to satisfy the curiosity of tourists who wanted "to see Africa as it was before the white man came."[73] The conference was asking Africans to go back in time and to pretend to be living in some timeless place. This was wrong, said the paper. The *Bantu World* welcomed government's rejection of this "monstrous proposal," saying the plan would mean keeping Africans like animals "in this National Zoo," meaning the KNP (see fig. 4.6). The paper condemned the Transvaal Publicity Conference and "those who, in this enlightened age, still think that black men and women were created for the purpose of serving and amusing the white race."

As the editorial writers of the *Bantu World* well knew, there were of course Africans already living in the park—not as specimen, however, but as real human beings with interests and wants. These people paid rent, provided labor to the park, and needed land on which to subsist. The editorial writers also knew that Crocker's proposal was neither random nor isolated. In the eyes of Crocker and his colleagues in the Transvaal Publicity Conference, Africans were tied to the land and, being native to it, could not become tourists in their own right. Stripped of all signs of their existence in the present, they could become a tourist attraction. As one state official named C. J. Uys put it in a 1936 tourist publication on "native life in South Africa," Africans were there only to be viewed. They were a natural part of South Africa's tourism package. "In this respect alone," Uys said, "and apart from its wealth in other novel allures, South Africa today is a veritable tourist paradise. Here the traveler encounters a remarkable conglomerate of

FIGURE 4.6. Ngutu Sambu, a long-term resident of the Pretoriuskop section of the park. Sambu was allegedly one-hundred when he posed for this photograph in 1927. *Source:* SANParks Archive

races, varying from the most backward and primitive to the most virile and intelligent of the dark-skinned tribes."[74]

Uys said that while South Africa's native life was interesting to the savant, the student, and the dilettante, it would not last. "It may also be safely asserted," he said, "that Bantu culture will not be strong enough to hold its own against the onslaughts of western civilization, and that it is doomed to disappear ultimately."[75] Tourists had to see this quaint African life before it went extinct. They had to come to South Africa quickly before there was nothing left to remind them of what premodern man looked like.

For Uys, the extinction of native life did not necessarily mean that Africans were going the way of the dinosaur. Rather, it meant the collapse of traditional African societies and the urbanization of Africans, many of whom were being transformed fast into an industrial working class. But, as another official said in a publication put out by the Publicity and Travel Department in the 1930s, urbanized Africans were not as exciting an attraction as their rural counterparts:

> Interesting, however, as is the native by virtue of his quaint and ingenuous idiosyncrasies in adapting himself to urban occupations and customs, he is a far more absorbing subject of study when seen in his natural and primitive environment or when, for a few fleeting hours perhaps, he reverts to one or other of the customs of his forebears, and panders to his primitive instincts, as in the thrill of a war dance.[76]

Officials such as Crocker and Uys understood Africans only in terms of stock figures: the urbanized African corrupted by Western civilization or the traditional African living merrily in a primitive environment. The urban African was impure, the rural African pure. As James Stevenson-Hamilton himself said in an article about the Sabi Game Reserve published in the December 1926 edition of SAR *Magazine*, "The few residents native [in the reserve] live still to a great extent under tribal law, unspoiled by contact with civilization."[77] In fact, the Africans living in the park were anything but specimen of premodern man. These were people, after all, with a long history in the park. They had relatives and friends who had become "Portuguese natives" or "South African natives" only through the advent of colonial rule.

An accident of history—not nature—had made different nationalities out of them. Their knowledge of the lowveld was such that they were kept resident in the park so that the park authorities could call on their métis, taxes, and labor.[78]

In fact, it was not until the year 2000 that the last of these "resident natives" left the park—after the family patriarch, who had worked for years as a ranger, died (see fig. 4.7).[79] For David Bunn, the Africans resident in the park offered park officials such as Stevenson-Hamilton more than their knowledge of the lowveld. They also served as "specimens of native loyalty" that were "rooted and grounded in a special form of the heritage landscape that provided an important educative function for white tourists."[80] In addition to being native police, rangers, squatters, and laborers, these Africans also helped park authorities present a set image of African landscapes. Bunn says, "For white tourists to the KNP between 1939 and 1960, it was this fixed and posed aspect of African identity that was most memorable."[81] So Crocker's proposal was not as novel as it might have sounded when he first presented it. It also did not come from nowhere.

To show how mainstream it was, in 1936, a year after Crocker presented his proposal, Alfred Norval, an academic from the University

FIGURE 4.7. Tombstone for long-term park ranger Samuel Nkayinkayi Mavundla, who died in 2000. Mavundla and his family were the last Africans allowed to live in the park. The park moved his family after he died. *Source:* Gareth Roocroft

of Pretoria, published a national and international survey on tourism. The survey, commissioned by SAR and the government, listed rural Africans as one of the unbeatable attractions that South Africa offered. "Native life and culture in its primitive form," Norval said, "is one of the most colorful phases of the many-sided aspects of national life to be observed in South Africa."[82] Like Crocker before him, Norval proposed that stops in African reserves be included alongside visits to the KNP. He suggested that visitors be taken to mining compounds of the Witwatersrand to see Africans performing war dances. He warned, however, that care must be taken to shield Africans from the harmful effects of exposure to "superior" western cultures: "The organizing of tours to native kraals where natives in semi-naked state crowd around a number of tourists, should in the interests of the natives themselves, as well as in the interests of South Africa of the future, be definitely prohibited."[83]

Norval's racialized paternalism was by no means an isolated view, as shown earlier. He also said that Africans could benefit from tourism by making handicraft for the amusement of tourists. Norval did not, of course, invent the idea of making Africans a part of the tourist attraction. An advert run by SAR's New York office in the late 1920s offered visits to "quaint kaffir kraals."[84] The advert asked potential visitors to imagine being introduced to a "dignified Zulu chief and his retinue of dusky wives." The office presented Africans alongside amenities such as luxurious hotels, superb roads, and pastimes such as golf. That was South Africa's tourism package. In the imagination of those who devised the advertisements, the combination of dusky natives and a first-class infrastructure gave South Africa its edge as a tourist destination.

The campaign worked because American and British tourists (the latter made up 80 percent of all overseas visitors in the first half of the twentieth century) came to expect both the tribal and the modern in their experience of South Africa. They demanded to see natives in their supposed element. However, the overseas advertising campaign took a hit in 1930 when cases of malaria among returning tourists generated bad publicity for South Africa in the American and British media.[85] The bad press grew after 4 tourists, who were part of a group of 350 that had arrived in South Africa in 1929 aboard the cruise ship *Duchess of Atholl*, died of malaria. The four (two New Yorkers, one Californian, and one Jamaican) had visited the KNP and Victoria Falls.[86]

SAR knew about the dangers of malaria, which is why its excursions to the park were only offered during the South African winter. As SAR general manager J. R. More said, "The question of malaria is one that requires constantly to be kept in mind, and unfortunately most oversea visitors arrive in South Africa during the period of the year when it is inadvisable to send them into the Reserve."[87] But More's colleagues were no less defensive and dismissive about the impact of malaria because of this. As J. S. Dunn, representing Cape Town, said in response to More, malaria was rampant in India and the Far East, but this had not deterred American tourists. "When one thinks of the American tours to Bombay at the worst time of the year, it seems ridiculous that the London papers should make a fuss over a few cases of malaria contracted at the Victoria Falls," said Dunn.[88]

MINING SPECTACLES

A glaring contradiction of the SAR-led advertising campaign is that those responsible for it were not satisfied with depicting Africans as modernity's foil.[89] They looked for Africans even in South Africa's urban areas, including the mines, and compelled them to perform their being native—all for the benefit of tourists (see fig. 4.8). In fact, from the

FIGURE 4.8. Color spread depicting white tourists observing a change of shift at a mine in Johannesburg. *Source*: Transnet Heritage Museum Photo Collection

beginning of twentieth-century tourism in South Africa, the country's gold mines were considered one of the main attractions. Tourists could travel along the coast, venture into the lowveld, and then end up in Johannesburg, where they would be taken down a mine shaft. SAR arranged this with the support of the Chamber of Mines and Wenela, the chamber's labor recruitment agency. In addition to visiting the mines underground, visitors would go to the compounds where mineworkers lived to watch performances of so-called tribal dances. But the chamber was not always keen on this spectacular use of mine labor. In May 1927 Crocker complained about the chamber's reluctance "to allow tourists to inspect the gold mines." Crocker said the publicity association should write a memorandum to the chamber "thanking them for the sympathy shown so far, and tactfully reminding them it was desirous that the practice of allowing visitors over the mines should be continued."[90]

The entreaty seems to have worked because by November 1927 the association counted sixteen mines, including Brakpan Mines and City Deep, where tourists could visit. However, the chamber changed its mind again a few years after this. In 1931 it turned down a SAR request to let tourists visit and to host native dances (see fig. 4.9). According to the chamber, "Arranging such performances . . . was a 'nuisance:'

FIGURE 4.9. Color spread depicting white tourists observing a so-called native dance at a mine in Johannesburg. SAR commissioned artist William R. S. Stott to paint the spread in 1926. *Source*: Transnet Heritage Museum Photo Collection

it took a 'great deal of work without commensurate advantage.'"[91] But SAR was not deterred. In 1934 it asked the chamber to organize "sight-seeing tours, including 'native dances'" for a group of mostly American tourists who had come to South Africa on the cruise liner *Resolute*.[92] In principle, the chamber was not averse to hosting visitors. It only wanted to do so, however, if there was a clear advantage to be gained. In fact, we see this in a little-advertised bit of political tourism that the chamber indulged in during the first half of the twentieth century.

The chamber began hosting African chiefs at its mines early in the twentieth century as part of a campaign to ensure a steady supply of labor. As G. O. Lovett, acting general manager of Wenela, said, the chamber brought chiefs to its mines "in order that they may gain some knowledge of working conditions on the Rand and would, on their return home, exercise their influence and spread useful propaganda on behalf of the [mining] industry."[93] But chiefs who took advantage of these all-expenses-paid safaris did not always do Wenela's bidding, as shown by Chief Moremi, head of the Batawana community in Ngamiland, northwestern Botswana. Wenela cultivated Moremi in the late 1930s while trying to recruit from Ngamiland. It hosted Moremi and some of his advisers a number of times between December 1937 and December 1946. In December 1937 and January 1938, Moremi and four of his councilors visited the chamber's mines in the Witwatersrand. Wenela paid the men's second-class return tickets, housed the men on its mines, offered them £3 to cover expenses, and gave Moremi four new Goodyear tires for his Jeep as a wedding gift.

Wenela knew exactly what it was doing by extending such largess to Moremi; he did as well, and he was more than happy to play along.[94] S. H. Davies, a Wenela representative in Ngamiland, said, "In an unofficial conversation the Chief informed me that everything possible would be done to encourage natives to go to the mines."[95] But the Batawana were democratic, and Moremi, young and an alcoholic, could not exert his will. Moremi had no influence and was, as one Wenela official commented, "unable to bring any pressure upon the councilors. All matters of business are discussed in the kghotla [*sic*] and nothing can be done without the full consent of the tribal councilors."[96] This did not stop Moremi from using Wenela, however. In 1941 he bought a car on installment from Williams, Hunt & Company, a Johannesburg dealership, after Wenela vouched for him.

He promptly fell into arrears. In November 1946 he asked Wenela for a £20 loan but died in a car accident a month later without having settled his debt.[97] Moremi was not the only chief to play the system. Many chiefs would accept Wenela's invitation to visit their subjects on the mines but then use such visits to collect tribal levies from said subjects. As Lovett conceded, the original intention of the chamber's plan to bring chiefs to the mines had been "largely overshadowed by the desire of Chiefs to make use of them for the purpose of collecting money from their tribesmen—such visits now carry little or no propaganda value."[98] Unlike regular tourists, chiefs were not allowed to go underground. In fact, the Chamber of Mines had an informal rule barring blacks from going underground—unless they were workers. Wenela suspended the chiefs' mine safaris when the Second World War started but made exceptions on occasion "in favor of applicants of distinction, service men, and others."[99] In February 1943, for example, Max Gluckman, the famous anthropologist, asked for permission to visit Van Dyck Consolidated Mines, east of Johannesburg.[100]

In July 1954 Ray Phillips, chairman of the Transvaal Missionary Association, asked the chamber for permission for a group of twelve "American missionaries, plus two negroes" to visit the mines during a tour of Africa.[101] Phillips assured the chamber that the two black members of the delegation were upstanding citizens and that one, Dr. James H. Robinson, was a "well-known contributor to *The New York Times.*" While the chamber fretted over what to do with these two negroes and its informal policy of not allowing black tourists underground, the government came to the rescue by refusing to give the U.S. delegation visas. This might have spared the chamber the embarrassment of splitting the delegation by race, but it also pointed to the need for the chamber's Gold Producers' Council to examine its policy regarding the "question of visits to mines by non-Europeans."[102]

More importantly, the near embarrassment also demonstrated that the Chamber of Mines urgently needed to sort out its relationship with the apartheid government, which had been in power for four years when Phillips made his request. The National Party government had come to power on the back of promises to keep the African in his place and to send the Indian back to India. More than that, it had promised white South Africa that its program of apartheid, which, as Saul Dubow cogently puts it, was "born in fear, nurtured in hubris, and sustained through obfuscation," would keep blacks out of white South Africa unless, of course, they were there to administer to the needs of the white man.[103] The government likely rejected the visa applications of Phillips's delegation—part of a U.S. National Council of Churches mission to Africa—for fear that the delegates would criticize its policies. Despite the challenges posed by apartheid, the Chamber of Mines did not abandon its program of visits to the mines.

WINDS OF CHANGE

In 1960, shortly before he delivered the address that would go down as the "Winds of Change" speech, U.K. prime minister Harold Macmillan visited a mine in Johannesburg. Macmillan was on a six-week safari to Africa that began on January 5 in Ghana. Macmillan's visit was intended to express the United Kingdom's commitment to decolonization. He also visited Nigeria, Rhodesia, and Nyasaland before arriving in South Africa and hitting the tourist sites. In addition to visiting a mine in Johannesburg, Macmillan accepted an appointment as honorary chief of the tribes of the Northern Transvaal (see figs. 4.10 and 4.11).[104] By visiting the mine and taking on the role of chief, Macmillan helped illustrate the twin pillars of an advertising strategy that went back to the first half of the twentieth century. Although Macmillan certainly did not intend it, his outing showed just how successful SAR and its publicity department had been in selling South Africa as a place where the modern (mines) lived side by side with the traditional (chiefs).

The National Publicity Association ceased operation after 1959, its mission having been superseded by the South African Tourism Corporation, founded in 1948. It had given South Africa a marketing template marked by the assumption of a dual temporality: blacks living in some backward time and whites in a progressive time. Africans challenged this poor depiction of their lives and worlds. In the case of the elites, their challenge came in the form of questions about roots and routes; in the case of elites and nonelites alike, it came in the form of travel and insistent struggles for the right to travel. These challenges were not a straightforward case of resistance. The railways did not mean the same thing to all blacks. Indeed, as the grievances listed above show, even the poor treatment about which Africans complained manifested itself differently. But, however varied the complaints were, they were

FIGURE 4.10. British prime minister Harold Macmillan accepting his appointment from chief Frank Maseremule as a chief of "all the Bantu of the Northern Transvaal," January 1960. *Source: South African Scope*

significant because they questioned assumptions about what it meant to call South Africa a modern country.

The complainants took to task colonial assumptions about the place of Africans in the modern world. They challenged, in other words, standard depictions of Africans as modernity's foil. In the case of SAR, this was no easy challenge because, as Albert Grundlingh says, "deeply embedded and enduring in the ethos of marketing South Africa as a tourist destination was the juxtaposition of the 'primitive' and the 'modern.'"[105] In fact, as late as 1963, South Africa's secretary for tourism was still calling the juxtaposition a "romantic theme" that should be at the heart of the country's tourist promotions. "Here is an exhilarating land

FIGURE 4.11. British prime minister Harold Macmillan (*center*) underground at West Driefontein Mines, west of Johannesburg, January 1960. *Source: South African Scope*

lying under a warm beneficial sun," the secretary said. "Cities, alive with prosperity and confidence, form a contrast to picturesque Bantu Villages where ancient tribal rites and traditions are still to be seen."[106] The secretary was using tourism to create what Jeanne van Eeden calls "topographies of power and exclusion" and to market Africans as "stereotypical commodities" from a time before modernity.[107] The man could not be accused of originality.

He was merely reflecting the long history detailed above. As we know, from the very beginning of tourism in South Africa, Africans—together with their supposed picturesque lives—were must-sees on any trip to southern Africa. South African tourist packages for the overseas market were considered incomplete unless they had what one overseas official called the "'five cardinal points of interest' . . . diamond mines, gold mines, the Victoria Falls, the Kruger National Park, and 'picturesque native life.'"[108] The question to ask is not why this persisted but how those blacks with the means to travel and who, in Sol Plaatje's words, were their own masters developed an independent tradition of tourism in colonial South Africa. The following chapter answers that question.

PART 2
Homelands

5 ⌒ Civilized Natives

ON JUNE 15, 1938, John David Rheinhallt Jones, a senator representing Africans from the Transvaal and the Orange Free State in South Africa's whites-only parliament, wrote to James Stevenson-Hamilton, the warden of the KNP, to inquire about the accommodation of African visitors in the sanctuary.[1] Jones sent the letter, which he gave the subject heading "Accommodation for Civilized Natives," on behalf of a group of African teachers who wanted to visit the park during the coming winter holidays but had been "given to understand that there is no accommodation for Native tourists in the Rest Camps."

The teachers had their own car, had their own linen, and were "quite willing to pay the ordinary charges, but they naturally wish to rest in safety at night," Jones said. "If no such accommodation is as yet arranged, is it possible for you to indicate to me any camps at which a temporary arrangement could be made. I have, for instance, addressed your employees in the compound at Skukuza. Could any arrangement be made there and at, say at least, one of the further north camps?"[2] Stevenson-Hamilton's reply was not long in coming. He replied on June 18, 1938: "I have to advise you that the only accommodation in the park which can be made available to the group of Native teachers is in the Indian camp at Skukuza," the park's main camp. Stevenson-Hamilton asked Jones for advance notice of the teachers' arrival so he could make the necessary arrangements. He added, "There is at present practically no demand for accommodation in the park by Native tourists and expenditure on [the] erection of huts and fences at any of the other rest camps is not considered to be justified."

Jones replied to Stevenson-Hamilton two days later, saying he would let the warden know as soon as the teachers gave him their travel dates. I have found no evidence of further correspondence about the matter between Jones and Stevenson-Hamilton after Jones's letter of June 20th. Thus we lose our trail of the teachers and cannot say whether they did make it to the KNP in the end. This chapter follows the teachers' trail, as faint as it is, to see what it might tell us about the interplay between class, gender, and tourism by blacks in the first half of the twentieth century in South Africa. The teachers' story offers clues that, when viewed in a wider context, allow for the historical and imaginative reconstruction of the world of leisure-making to which the teachers belonged. These clues fly in the face of conventional wisdom that, when it came to black tourists in colonial and apartheid South Africa, the KNP was off-limits (see fig. 5.1). Scholars such as Jacklyn Cock, Lindisizwe Magi, Hector Magome, and Lynn Meskell have taken it as an article of faith that, as Jane Carruthers claims, "Africans were not permitted to visit the park for recreation."[3] But the teachers' story hints at a different history. It speaks to the existence of a relationship between blacks and the KNP that was in fact richer than the dominant trend in the historiography of conservation in South Africa suggests.

The tendency in the historiography has been to see relations between blacks—especially Africans—and the sanctuary in utilitarian terms, with scholars taking it as a given that blacks were excluded from the park unless they were there as "service workers or guides."[4] I do not intend to take away from the powerful insights that these scholars have given us or, indeed, to downplay the important fact that, as Cock says, "for many black South Africans, dispossession was the other side of conservation."[5] This is true. But my intention here is to use the opening created by Cock's use of the adjective "many" to examine the connection between the KNP and those blacks who did visit the park for recreation or who at least considered the possibility, as did our unnamed teachers, of doing so. Such an examination yields at least two historical insights: the first is into the existence, even in colonial societies, of spaces for autonomous action by colonial subjects; the second insight is into the material difference that gender and social stratification among black South Africans made regarding who could do what for leisure, where, when, and how.[6] By themselves, these are not novel insights. But applied to the KNP, they allow for a more complex history of the park, one that helps us see, through the park, why South Africa was and is a safari nation.

FIGURE 5.1. Still from a 1968 documentary titled *The Heart of Apartheid*.
Source: Still image supplied by BBC Studios

FIGURE 5.2. Still from a 1968 documentary titled *The Heart of Apartheid*.
Source: Still image supplied by BBC Studios

TAKING LEISURE SERIOUSLY

The study of black leisure pursuits in South Africa has been dominated by what we might call the usual suspects: the theater, sports, and music. Scholars such as Peter Alegi, Tim Couzens, David Coplan, Tyler Fleming, Albert Grundlingh, Paul La Hausse, Andre Odendaal, and Bheki Peterson have explored the history of boxing, beer-drinking, cricket, music, rugby, the theater, and soccer in order to shed light on the spaces of autonomy created by blacks within the interstices of (and despite) colonial and apartheid rule.[7] These pathbreaking explorations have given us a fuller and more nuanced understanding of the social and cultural history of South Africa, especially in the first half of the twentieth century. However, important as the focus on the usual suspects has been, it has left us with some lacunae in our understanding of the history of black leisure pursuits in South Africa. Blacks did more than act, sing, dance, play sports, and host beer parties for leisure. This is not to downplay the historical significance of these pursuits. But blacks also took holidays.

They visited friends and relatives and went to what the tourism literature of the 1930s referred to as places of interest. This use of leisure called for a particular valuation of space. It meant the use of time in ways that, while subject to the overall demands of a market economy, went beyond the strictures of that economy. Tourism depended on an individual's capacity to travel across a given space and to have the time to undertake such travel. This does not mean that tourism was uniquely a modern phenomenon. As any perusal of the literature on religious pilgrimages will confirm, tourism is an age-old undertaking. However, the kind of tourism explored here was a modern phenomenon. It grew out of South Africa's transformation into a modern state. The tourists whose history is recuperated here saw themselves as modern subjects entitled to two of the promises of the modern world: autonomy and mobility.

As seen in the previous chapter, SAR did not consider blacks to be tourists in their own right when it developed South Africa's tourism industry in the first half of the twentieth century. SAR saw Africans instead as quaintly attractive elements of the South African landscape: there to be advertised as a part of the country's attractions. SAR officials and the writers contracted by the corporation to promote South Africa understood Africans to be natives rooted in tradition, which these officials saw as separate from the modern world fast coming into being in South Africa.

As O. Zachariah said in his SAR-sponsored book, "Most natives . . . never leave home, [and] know the outer world only by repute."[8] SAR looked at Africans, regardless of their social and economic status, as devoid of the aesthetic sensibility supposedly needed in a tourist. But the strivings of black elites to develop an independent tradition of modern travel gave a lie to the colonial assumption that Africans were rooted sons and daughters of the soil. These elites believed in the value of leisure and the need to discover the country they called their own—even if that country denied them the full rights of citizenship. They developed a tradition of tourism that undermined two colonial commonplaces: the first, as already stated, was the assumption that so-called natives enjoyed an organic connection to the land and could not become tourists in a place that they were naturally a part of; the second commonplace was the old Christian missionary idea that the only way to stop leisure from turning into idleness was to moralize it, that is, to turn leisure into communion with God.

Many of these elites were mission educated, schooled in the idea that there was a fine line between leisure and idleness and that the only way to keep that line was to moralize leisure time. However, that moralizing conviction was absent from the elites' considerations when they fought colonial authorities for the right to move freely around South Africa.

For these elites, the right to seek leisure where and when they desired was linked to their self-regard as modern subjects—not necessarily to their being as God's children. They saw their ability to travel as linked to their standing as individuals in control of their time and with the means to travel. That they were in control of their time did not mean they were in control of the space over which they sought to travel. They were, after all, colonial subjects. But we should not read too much into their subjection to colonial rule. As Phyllis Martin says, colonialism was a process of "negotiation in which all kinds of political, cultural and social transformations were worked out."[9] These transformations included the creation of new notions of time and space. Colonial authorities sought to impose on their African subjects ideas about time that were driven by the different and sometimes contradictory needs of the church, the colonial state, and capitalist markets.

But, as Martin shows, urban Africans in Brazzaville fought for a measure of freedom in which they could literally have some time to themselves—free from the demands of the church, the colonial state, and capitalism. This was the context in which disputes arose over the treatment of Africans, especially the elites, by various branches of the colonial state. In the case of South Africa, these branches of the colonial state ranged from SAR to the Native Affairs Department to the National Parks Board. These were by no means uniform bureaucracies. Still, as government agencies closely connected to the welfare of Africans, the management of the KNP, and the movement of people over vast distances, they were among the most active participants in debates about the relationship between Africans and the modern world. The white men who staffed these bureaucracies refused to see the existence of blacks as temporally coeval with their own.[10] They saw blacks as historic laggards, always playing catch-up to whites. SAR, for example, interpreted the use of trains by Africans as an adaptation to the habits and conditions of Europeans, while officials of the Native Affairs Department saw it as their mission to monitor "progress in civilization" among Africans.

In the department's annual report for 1909, for example, the native commissioner for the Northern Division said, "Progress, if any, was infinitesimal."[11] The commissioner noted that African "requirements as regards clothing, food, vehicles, shelter, and furniture," had increased, "thereby involving a correspondingly larger outlay, and also demanding a closer, regular, and more systematic application to labor than prevailed hitherto."[12] In the same report, the sub–native commissioner for Haenetsburg noted, "The advent of the railway will probably have a healthy effect upon the progress in civilization in the eastern and at present most remote part of this district."[13] For his part, the sub–native commissioner for Nylstroom said, "Luxurious furniture and utensils are often to be met with, and I have heard a gramophone at a native kraal, if such an instrument can be classed a civilizing agency."[14] Colonial concerns over whether Africans could become truly modern drove the disputes between black elites and the three state agencies mentioned above.

For the black elite, the onset of the modern world meant abandoning old customs for new ways; converting to Christianity in place of traditional African belief systems; acquiring Western-style education;

FIGURE 5.3. Group photograph taken in the KNP, ca. 1930s–1940s. *Source:* Nasima Coovadia's family archive. Image used with permission

and appropriating European clothing, mores, and forms of conduct. But they did not see any of this as an act of mimicry.[15] They saw the adoption of modern ways as a sign of their active presence in the birth of the modern world. As Thema said, "It is my firm belief that we can be Christianized without necessarily being Europeanized. And it is essential that it should be so; for we have qualities which are indispensable to human progress and happiness."[16]

Thema's argument was not unique to the British colonial world, as Frederick Cooper shows in his study of struggles over citizenship in French West Africa. In fact, Leopold Senghor made arguments uncannily similar to Thema's, arguing that Africans could become French citizens without becoming Frenchmen.[17] Writing in January 1930, Thema said, "The jungle has been cleared, and railway trains and motor cars travel over hill and dale, through forests and deserts, disturbing the lives of the most benighted of Africa's children." Africans wanted meaningful parts in this modern drama, said Thema:

> The African has sufficient sense to know that in this changed
> Africa his salvation lies in the assimilation of western civiliza-
> tion. He will refuse steadfastly to be herded like Africa's animals

into National Parks and Zoos for the benefit of the white race. Africa is his, and while he has no objection to alien races making Africa their home, he will not agree to be isolated in reserves for purposes of exploitation. Like any other member of the human race he is entitled to free movement and free intercourse with the outside world.[18]

Thema (1886–1955) is one of the key figures in the black history of the park. Although we have no record that he ever visited the park, we know that, for him, the sanctuary was good to think with. He invoked the park in three different contexts over three decades—all in the service of a claim for political citizenship for blacks. In 1933 Thema wrote with tongue firmly in cheek about visiting the Johannesburg Zoo to see explorer David Livingstone's darkest Africa: "Nowhere can one get a glimpse of that Africa except in the zoological gardens of our big cities and in the Kruger National Park."[19] In 1941 Thema complained about the quality of black housing in Johannesburg, saying, "I think when we ask Americans to come here, they are not shown Orlando. They are kept carefully away from the Native locations—they go to the Kruger

FIGURE 5.4. Group photograph taken in the KNP, ca. 1930s–1940s. *Source:* Nasima Coovadia's family archive. Image used with permission

FIGURES 5.5, 5.6. Group photographs taken in the KNP, ca. 1930s–1940s. *Source:* Nasima Coovadia's family archive. Image used with permission

National Park and there it ends."[20] In 1950 he compared how the apartheid government treated Africans to how it treated the park's wildlife: "At least the animals in the Kruger National Park have more space than I have—those animals have more land than I have, and they are better looked after than I am looked after."[21]

Each reference spoke directly to a particular political context. Each time Thema invoked the park, he did it to argue about the political standing of blacks in South Africa. Such was the force of Thema's argument that the African Wildlife Protection Society of South Africa felt moved to reach out to blacks. "The Native mind needs to be instilled with knowledge of the mutual benefits to be derived from a striving to preserve instead of destroy nature, even if this means setting aside land in which settled encroachment by white or black is debarred," said the society in response to Thema, missing completely his point about land hunger among blacks, especially Africans.[22] But the society took up Thema's challenge and began offering environmental education to young black South Africans. In 1964 it established the African Wildlife Society, whose membership was exclusively black.[23]

Thema and members of his class did not want social equality. As *Koranta ea Becoana* had editorialized as early as September 13, 1902, "We do not hanker after social equality with the white man. . . . We do not care for your parlor nor is it our wish to lounge on couches in your drawing room. . . . All we claim is our just dues: we ask for our recognition as loyal British subjects." Thema opposed segregation in principle. But he was prepared to accept it, provided it was true to its own tenets. As he said to the Natives' Representative Council in December 1937, "I am against this division of the people, but this [segregation] having been forced upon us, I think we have to follow it to its logical conclusion."[24] Thema was objecting to the racist rule that Africans could not represent themselves in South Africa's parliament. In 1949 he said, "And if we say that we want freedom, surely that does not mean that we want to have the right to go to your homes. I don't want to go into a white man's home . . . but the right we want is the right to be able to live our life . . . without let or hindrance."[25] Thema wanted blacks recognized as political subjects in their own right (see fig. 5.3). That recognition had to include the right to travel and to buy property in their own names. Elites such as Thema were products of mission schools. They had been raised on Shakespeare and on the

Romantics.[26] They used their education to develop a secular tradition of travel, a tradition that depended on their exemption from the pass laws that regulated African mobility. Among those exempted from the pass laws were chiefs, headmen, police constables, church ministers, and teachers. They earned their exemptions by satisfying officials of the Native Affairs Department that they were "civilized," people of good character and of clean repute. Exemptions were a privilege, and the elites had to prove themselves worthy of it. Our teachers came from this class. They did not have to worry about passes. But they did have to worry about whether the KNP would accept their patronage.

THE EARLY DAYS

The Sabi Game Reserve began accepting tourists in 1923 when SAR inaugurated the "Round in Nine" service, which took, as the name suggests, nine days.[27]

A popular feature of the Round in Nine excursion was an "impromptu campfire soiree, held in the veld alongside the train in the middle of the Sabi Nature [*sic*] Reserve, complete with piano."[28] This was in fact the second package tour offered by SAR in 1923. Earlier that year SAR promoted a Round in Seven tour, but that did not include stops in the reserve. Harold Trollope, one of the first white rangers hired by Stevenson-Hamilton and also one of the first to accompany tourists through the Sabi Game Reserve during a Round in

FIGURE 5.7. Scene depicting a Round in Nine campfire in KNP, ca. 1938. *Source:* Transnet Heritage Museum Photo Collection

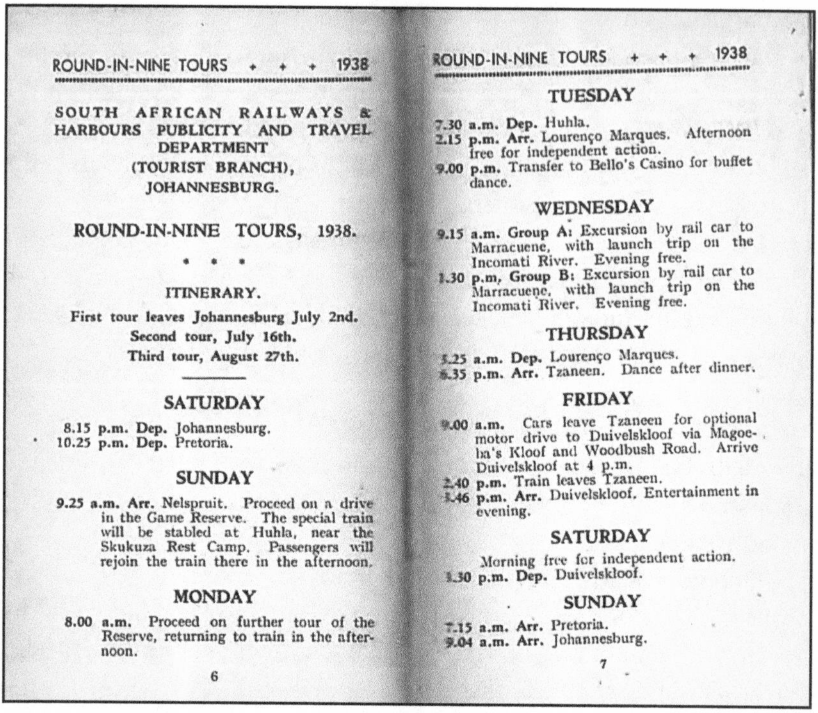

SOUTH AFRICAN RAILWAYS &
HARBOURS PUBLICITY AND TRAVEL
DEPARTMENT
(TOURIST BRANCH),
JOHANNESBURG.

ROUND-IN-NINE TOURS, 1938.

✦ ✦ ✦

ITINERARY.

First tour leaves Johannesburg July 2nd.
Second tour, July 16th.
Third tour, August 27th.

SATURDAY

8.15 p.m. Dep. Johannesburg.
10.25 p.m. Dep. Pretoria.

SUNDAY

9.25 a.m. Arr. Nelspruit. Proceed on a drive
in the Game Reserve. The special train
will be stabled at Huhla, near the
Skukuza Rest Camp. Passengers will
rejoin the train there in the afternoon.

MONDAY

8.00 a.m. Proceed on further tour of the
Reserve, returning to train in the afternoon.

6

TUESDAY

7.30 a.m. Dep. Huhla.
2.15 p.m. Arr. Lourenço Marques. Afternoon
free for independent action.
9.00 p.m. Transfer to Bello's Casino for buffet
dance.

WEDNESDAY

9.15 a.m. Group A: Excursion by rail car to
Marracuene, with launch trip on the
Incomati River. Evening free.
1.30 p.m. Group B: Excursion by rail car to
Marracuene, with launch trip on the
Incomati River. Evening free.

THURSDAY

5.25 a.m. Dep. Lourenço Marques.
8.35 p.m. Arr. Tzaneen. Dance after dinner.

FRIDAY

9.00 a.m. Cars leave Tzaneen for optional
motor drive to Duivelskloof via Magoe-
ba's Kloof and Woodbush Road. Arrive
Duivelskloof at 4 p.m.
2.40 p.m. Train leaves Tzaneen.
5.46 p.m. Arr. Duivelskloof. Entertainment in
evening.

SATURDAY

Morning free for independent action.
3.30 p.m. Dep. Duivelskloof.

SUNDAY

7.15 a.m. Arr. Pretoria.
9.04 a.m. Arr. Johannesburg.

7

FIGURE 5.8. Itinerary from 1938 Round in Nine trip. *Source:* Transnet Heritage Museum Photo Collection

Nine outing, remembered one evening from the jaunt in the following words: "That night we had a big bonfire and an open-air concert, piano, electric lights and the head lamp from the [train] engine."[29]

Trollope enjoyed the experience of looking after tourists: "I think I rather like tourist trains; it was nice seeing a happy crowd of carefree young people together, laughing and talking."[30] By 1925, SAR's tourism service was drawing tourists from as far afield as the United Kingdom and the United States to the reserve.

But Stevenson-Hamilton seems to have been ambivalent about the transformation of the reserve into a tourist destination, if a letter by Harry Stratford Caldecott, a Paris-trained artist whose paintings helped popularize the reserve as a tourist destination, is anything to go by. Writing to the warden in June 1926, that is, a month after the reserve became the KNP, Caldecott said, "I understand that you have no stomach to see the place full of rubberneck wagons and tourists, but it was vulgarization or abolition, I suppose, and it was at that price only that the animals could be saved."[31] Stevenson-Hamilton saw tourism

FIGURE 5.9. Tourists in the park, ca. 1940s–1950s. *Source:* Transnet Heritage Museum Photo Collection

as a necessary evil, a price worth paying for the conservation of the lowveld's fauna.

Although the place is associated in the academic and public mind with the exclusion of blacks, the KNP did not bar blacks from visiting. In 1932 the National Parks Board created a camp called Balule for the exclusive use of Africans and Indians. But the camp's facilities were so basic that, five decades later, it still had a "spartan atmosphere" and none of the modern conveniences found in the other camps.[32] The board considered frequently the question of black tourists, but it never came to any firm conclusion.

When Gustav Preller, a board member and staunch Afrikaner nationalist, complained in 1932 about Indians using the same camp as whites, Stevenson-Hamilton said that he thought the Indians were Portuguese.[33] In 1948 Jacobus G. Strijdom, the minister of lands in the newly elected apartheid government, expressed opposition to different races sharing the park's camps and roads. He proposed that the park be broken up, with a portion set aside for blacks.[34] The board ignored him. But the board's concerns about black tourists and their fluctuating numbers show that it was aware of the existence of blacks who could and did travel to the park, even if their numbers were small compared to those of white visitors.

In fact, the board cited the instability of black visitor numbers often in its debates about what to do with Balule: whether to keep it for the exclusive use of African visitors, set it aside for sole Indian use, or declassify it and hand it over to white visitors.[35] A visitors' guide issued by

FIGURE 5.10. Balule, the first rest camp set aside for blacks, opened in 1932. *Source:* SANParks Archive

FIGURE 5.11. Afrikaner nationalist Gustav Preller, in the middle, visiting the park, ca. 1930s. *Source:* SANParks Archive

the National Parks Board in 1938 said, "The Park may be visited by Asiatics and Natives, but, except at Skukuza, there is as yet no accommodation available for them." African, Coloured, and Indian visitors had to arrange their own shelter and bring their own tents if they planned to stay at camps other than Skukuza. "They are also strongly advised to avoid paying visits during rush periods, such as long weekends, school holidays, etc."[36] They were clearly not the park's priority.

It is a testament to the ambitiousness—not to say stubbornness—of the class to which our teachers belonged that they were able to consider a holiday to the KNP in the first place. For theirs was a "grossly deformed 'elite,' certainly not a power elite."[37] If anything defined them as a class, it was their aspirations—not their economic status. In the 1920s, qualified but low-level African teachers received between £3 and £9 a month; uncertified teachers made £3. This was higher than the £2 and 18 shillings that mine workers earned a month, and the £2 and 15 shillings that rail and dockworkers earned—but not by much. On the mines, only 92 of the 200,000 African employees earned more than £6 a month. In the 1920s, African wages "generally averaged less than one-eighth of white wages." In the 1930s, low-level African primary school teachers earned £6 a month. Hyman Basner, a communist activist who would defeat Rheinhallt Jones as a native senator in the 1942 elections, described African primary school teachers in the 1930s as "near-poverty stricken."[38]

Such was the situation of African teachers that salary increments agreed to by the government in 1928 were not introduced until 1946. Mineworkers fared much worse, their salaries remaining unchanged for the first three decades of the twentieth century.[39] According to the 1936 census, there were 8,199 teachers (4,758 of whom were men and 3,441 women), 1,950 shop assistants, 7 lawyers, and 1 lecturer. This was the core of the modern African elite. As Peter Limb describes it, this was "not only a miniscule but also an impoverished class."[40] Yet there were members of this impoverished class considering a holiday in the KNP. As we know from Rheinhallt Jones, the teachers had not only their own car but also their own linen and the money to pay the necessary charges. But that is not what set these "civilized natives" apart. What set them apart was that they saw themselves as an elite and interacted with all sections of colonial society (black and white) as a self-conscious elite. Caught in a colonial net in which color coincided with class, they developed markers of distinction to set themselves apart from the rest of black society. Their existence as a class rested initially on what we might call, after Michael West, a missionary scaffold.[41] The scaffold seemed firm and promising enough when European missionaries put it in place in the mid-nineteenth century, giving the Christianized African elite a perch atop which they could widen the horizons of their expectations. But once the British had set their sights on the control of South Africa's diamonds and gold, they no longer needed a class of educated natives. West suggests that the "rise of an African middle class simply was not part of the scheme of the European colonizers."[42] But the black elite would not disappear simply because colonial officials no longer needed their type.

They set about developing themselves into a "singular corporate entity," a self-perpetuating class.[43] They intermarried, sent their offspring to local and overseas schools, established newspapers, founded organizations, and fought in ways big and small for a place under the colonial and apartheid sun. They also created literary events, developed a social infrastructure made up of hotels, and adopted modes of living intended specifically to identify them as new Africans. For this new elite, how one lived at home was connected to how one comported oneself in public. One did not have to be educated or Christian to become civilized. It was enough that one lived a civilized life. For these elites, the private was not the zone of colonial difference.[44] The domestic was the domain of experience where one could work out questions of civic standing. As James T. Campbell reminds us, these elites had a self-awareness defined by a "devotion to education . . . pre-occupation with respectability . . . [and] ambivalent feelings of duty and disdain toward their 'uncivilized' cousins."[45] Not for nothing were members of this class called "school people." They were in a literal sense people of the book. That was their corporate identity, and their social activities buttressed that identity.

MAKING IT TO THE KRUGER NATIONAL PARK

If the teachers made it to the KNP in the winter of 1938, they would have been among the thirty-eight thousand tourists who visited the park in some ten thousand cars and trucks that year.[46] Given that the teachers had their own car, it would have cost them £1 to drive into the park.

If there were more than four people in the car, the extra people would have paid 5 shillings each. Cars with trailers or caravans paid £5 per entry, while children under sixteen went in for free. The park charged each visitor 3 shillings a night for accommodation in a rest hut or a tent. But because the teachers (being natives) could only be accommodated in the Indian camp in Skukuza, which came with mattresses, they would have had to pay 3 shillings and 6 pence a night each.[47]

If they chose to sleep within the precinct of a rest camp without using the huts or tents provided, they would have had to pay 1 shilling and 6 pence each a night (9 pence for children). This was for the use of campfires, water, and (native) attendants. Because they would have brought their own linen, they would not have had to pay the 6 pence per item a night that the park charged for blankets, mattresses, and pillows. Given the absence of hotels open to black patrons along the 250 miles that covered the distance between Johannesburg and the park (assuming the teachers came from Johannesburg), the teachers likely would have slept in their car along the way and would have had *padkos*.[48]

Upon arrival at the park, they would have supplemented their provisions with items such as bread, butter, eggs, tea, coffee, and drinks—but not fresh meat—easily obtainable at the park's gates. The park sold petrol and oil at all of its eleven rest camps and had a garage at Skukuza, where motorists could have their cars examined in the event of a mechanical problem. This would have been an expensive undertaking involving a substantial outlay in money and time by the teachers.

There was, of course, the Round in Nine train service to ferry tourists from Johannesburg to the park and back. But, as I show above and below, it was dear and, more importantly, not open to blacks. In 1938 the Round in Nine excursion, which did more than any other promotion to sell the park to domestic and international tourists, cost £15 and 15 shillings a trip. This covered fares, meals, bedding, car transport, permits, catering, and the park's entrance fee. The excursion began with a fourteen-hour train journey from Johannesburg to Komatipoort in the eastern Transvaal.

From there, tourists took SAR buses to Zoekmekaar, about 40 miles west of the park, whence they went into the park in SAR cars. There was also a weekend option through which tourists could catch a 9:10 p.m. train on a Friday or Saturday in Johannesburg, arrive in the eastern Transvaal town of Nelspruit the next morning, have breakfast at a local hotel, and then drive to Pretoriuskop, the park's original camp. Typically, guests would spend two days in the park before going on to Lourenço Marques, famous for its beaches and the relative absence of racial segregation. (Those driving their own cars through the park to Lourenço Marques had to pay a special £5 fee to use the Punda Maria–Pafuri road.) As the National Parks Board publication *Unspoilt Africa* offered, tourists could also visit the "native reserves" to the northwest of the park, "where the Northern Transvaal tribes may be studied in all the fascinating simplicity of their primitive forebears."[49] *Unspoilt Africa* was aimed at white tourists. It was intended for people who saw blacks as representatives of some exotic species—not fellow citizens endowed with rights. So were the luxury trains and buses that ferried tourists to the park. They were not open to Africans, Coloureds, or Indians. Blacks could visit the park, but they had to make their own way. If this was meant to discourage black visitors, it did not work. If anything, their numbers grew exponentially as the twentieth century developed. Blacks kept coming. Some also established facilities to make the park a welcoming place. They did this as part of their travels around a country that they, too, claimed as their own. They understood that to know their country, they had to travel its many paths.

AT HOME IN THE WILD

The Indian camp that Stevenson-Hamilton offered our unnamed teachers was in fact made up of two huts built in 1932 by an Indian merchant named Mohammed Gardee.[50] This must not have been an isolated gesture because in 1934 the Transvaal Indian Congress offered to pay for the construction of more huts for Indian use. Blacks could visit the KNP so long as they did not get in the way of the park's primary target market: whites. Once in the park, whites were guaranteed service by the park's African employees. Visitors had to take on an African guide at the cost of "five shillings per day" plus food during their stay in the reserve. There were also Africans in the camps "to make fires, carry water, etc."[51] That was a key part of the Kruger experience. Visitors could spend the day viewing game and retire in the evenings to campfires and beds prepared by African attendants. Visitors could also bring their African servants along.

A visitors' guide said, "Except for bedding, non-European servants accompanying visitors can be suitably accommodated" at seven of the camps, but this had to be booked in advance.[52] Of the 886,891 people who visited the park between 1946 and 1958, about 19,629 were so-called non-European servants. In the same period, 4,692 Indians and 681 African and Coloured visitors accounted for all the black tourists.[53] In fact, until the 1970s, more Africans visited the park as domestic servants than as regular tourists.

Between January 1961 and October 1962, 104,899 "adults," 46,582 children under sixteen, and 2,416 African servants visited the park. According to the National Parks Board's annual report for the year April 1962 to October 1962, the park had 2,354 beds for white visitors, 54 for black tourists, and 42 for African servants accompanying whites.

According to the report for the year November 1962 to October 1963, the tourist figures for that period were 120,126 adults, 52 children under 16, and 2,757 African servants. The report does not specify the race of the adults, but we can tell that "adults" means "whites" because the same report lists the number of "Asiatics, Bantu and Coloureds" who visited the park in the same period. Between November 1962 and October 1963, 691 so-called Asiatics and 849 Bantu and

FIGURE 5.12. White families in the park. *Source:* Transnet Heritage Museum Photo Collection

Coloureds visited; between November 1963 and October 1964, 656 Asiatics and 944 Bantu and Coloureds came.

The annual reports from 1964 to the 1977–78 financial year do not give a racial breakdown. The report for 1976–77 mentions a slight decrease in the number of white campers. But the report does not provide any context, making it difficult to evaluate the significance of this claim. The National Parks Board takes up the racial breakdown of the park's visitors again in the annual report for 1977–78. According to the report, 344,088 whites and 13,385 Africans, Coloureds, and Indians visited the park in the 1976–77 period. In 1977–78, 357,750 whites and 15,238 Africans, Coloureds, and Indians visited.[54]

DOMESTICATING THE BUSH

Taken together, the figures show that Indians constituted, over time, the single biggest group of black tourists to the park from the 1940s to the 1970s. They also show that African domestics were a dominant segment of black tourism to the park (see fig. 5.13). We do not know what these domestics thought about the park or what they made of their "holidays" to the park. After all, they were not visitors in the strict sense of the term. But we can guess safely that their feelings would not have been too different from those of the domestic worker who said the following in Jacklyn Cock's classic study of domestics in apartheid South Africa: "Every December I accompany the family I work for on their annual holiday by the sea. They think that being away from the city is a holiday for me, but I still have to cook, iron, wash and look after the kids." The informant was pointing out the incongruity of having a place devoted to leisure set aside places for domestic workers as domestic workers.[55]

That is not, of course, how white employers saw it. As one white informant who regularly took her domestic worker along on holiday told Cock, "She does get an hour or so on the beach in the afternoons."[56] The difference in perceptions reflects the power differential between white employers and black domestics in colonial and apartheid South Africa. It also echoes Paul Gilroy's suggestion that gender is the modality in which race is lived. Except, in the case of black domestics accompanying white bosses to the KNP, it was not masculinity but whiteness that was the "boastful centerpiece of a culture of compensation."[57] This culture, promoted by Afrikaner nationalists and white segregationists in the first

FIGURE 5.13. Unnamed domestic worker and her white employer in the park. Still from a 1968 documentary titled *The Heart of Apartheid*. *Source:* Still image supplied by BBC Studios

FIGURE 5.14. A nonwhite camp in the park. Still from a 1968 documentary titled *The Heart of Apartheid*. *Source:* Still image supplied by BBC Studios

FIGURE 5.15. Sign showing apartheid restrictions inside the park. Still from a 1968 documentary titled *The Heart of Apartheid. Source:* Still image supplied by BBC Studios

two decades of the Union of South Africa, sought to compensate for the supposed fragility of so-called white civilization in southern Africa by insisting that a "fair wage" for "civilized workers"—meaning whites— include the expense of hiring black domestics. In other words, white workers had to earn "civilized" wages in order to allow them to employ domestics. This idea had found expression in a report issued by the Economic and Wage Commission, set up by the government in 1925 to look at labor policies needed to determine wages "compatible with a civilized standard of life." Employing a domestic servant was not just a question of having someone perform household chores; it was also about maintaining one's standing as a white person.[58] It was not because these domestics had tasks to perform that they came to the park. They did that and more. Their presence served as affirmation of the social and political standing of their employers as white and, therefore, civilized. This is the context within which we must understand the constant references of the KNP's founders and supporters to what the park and South Africa's other conservationist measures meant for white civilization as such.

As the South African National Publicity Association said in 1928, South Africa's fauna was a "national asset of unique and exceptional interest and value, not only to the scientists and sportsmen of South Africa, but also of the entire civilized world."[59] Rudolph Bigalke, a zoologist and the first professional scientist to serve on the National Parks Board, saw the park as representative of the way wildlife lived before the "standard-bearers of our western civilization landed at the Cape."[60] Bigalke believed that "South Africa's honor" depended on the country keeping its national parks intact.[61] So not only did the park represent life before the onset of white civilization; it also stood for white South Africa's obligations to the so-called civilized world. By taking their domestics along, white tourists used the park as an arena in which to enact, through leisure, the meaning of whiteness. David Bunn leaves domestics out of his account of the significance of the park's resident natives to whites.

But domestics, too, served as "specimens of native loyalty," there to confirm the apparent resolution of the so-called native question.[62] To leave matters here, however, would be to leave untroubled conventional histories of the park. The fact that thousands of blacks visited the park each year as domestics should not blind us to the reality that these domestics were women. In fact, their presence reflected the profound social and economic changes that took place in South Africa early in the twentieth century. As Shireen Ally reminds us, "Domestic service in South Africa began as a project of colonial servitude."[63] In the Cape Colony in the eighteenth century, the first domestics were slave women and immigrant women from Europe; in the new mining town of Johannesburg in the late nineteenth century, the first domestics were white women and African men. By the early 1900s, African men—especially Zulu speakers—had cornered the market.[64]

This was due to the collapse of African polities and to attempts by African patriarchs and colonial officials to suppress African female urbanization. The colonial state used its power to ensure a steady supply of black men to work in white households while holding black women back. These efforts failed.[65] As Teresa Barnes says, African women were present in the making of southern Africa's colonial cities from the very beginning.[66] Urbanization was not a distinctly male phenomenon because women were present in places like Johannesburg from early on. Denied opportunities to seek employment in sectors such as domestic service, they carved niches within the interstices of the colonial state, some brewing beer to sell, some providing the men of the new cities with what Luise White calls the comforts of home, and many doing all this and many things besides to make these cities theirs too.[67] However, the composition of domestic service began to change after the end of the South African War in 1902.

Godfrey Lagden, whose South African Native Affairs Commission sat from 1903 to 1905, recommended that the colonial state encourage the employment of African women as domestics. Lagden explained his reasoning thus: "The employment of Native women for domestic purposes would, particularly in Natal and the Transvaal, release large numbers of men and boys for employment in occupations more suited to them."[68] He had mining in mind. By 1936, African women constituted the majority of domestics in South Africa.[69] This was not a sign of women's late arrival in southern Africa's urban spaces but recognition of their presence as "economic agents, with motivations and experiences either similar to or different from those of their male counterparts."[70] The women from whose ranks the domestics were drawn were not "passive rural widows" confined to "mass immobility."[71] Neither were they natives "rooted in the earth."[72]

But it was not solely the doings of Lagden and the colonial state that brought black women to the colonial cities. Mobility was a key part of this transformation. By the first half of the twentieth century, African women constituted 19 percent of the African urban population in South Africa; by the 1940s, African women were urbanizing at much faster rates than their male counterparts.[73] Like the millions of black actors whose stories are at the heart of this book, the domestics who visited the KNP with their employers were not natives tethered organically to the land. They were actors on the move, fashioning new identities and new worlds as they did so. They were "subjects with sight."[74] Sometimes, they saw more than they—as black females—were supposed to see. We know from the colonial and apartheid archive that these domestics made their presence felt in the park and that some did so in the most political way possible. In its 1949 annual report, the National Parks Board registered the following complaint:

> Trouble is still being caused by native servants of tourists, many of whom act as recruiting agents for their European employers.

Grandiose offers of employment up-country at times induce some of our best natives to leave the park. A very sharp look-out is being kept for any propaganda which might raise discontent amongst natives, who are at present happy and content.

The picture that emerges from this complaint is of domestics who knew the worth of their labor. These domestics moved between different places, in the process gathering and sharing intelligence about what it meant to be a modern worker. They were clearly not "insensate units of labor."[75] They acted, observed, and spoke—as self-conscious modern subjects. The National Parks Board was right to worry about their subversive influence because, as it acknowledged at various times during the twentieth century, it paid its African workers poorly. In 1928, when the board agreed to a wage increase for "native staff" to £2 a month, Stevenson-Hamilton noted that it was "not possible to procure the best type of natives if they were paid the same wages as those employed out of and adjoining the park," meaning the white-owned farms nearby.[76] In its 1951 annual report, the board said that while a "comparatively low wage was being paid [in comparison to wages paid outside the park], no difficulty was experienced in recruiting sufficient labor for work in the rest camps; due to the liberal tipping by visitors." It is not clear from the annual reports how park authorities hoped to combat the propaganda of the domestics without paying their staff a competitive wage. Still, the board objected to "liberal tipping" and "excessive tipping by visitors" because this contradicted its view of "happy and content" natives.[77]

ENTER THE BLACK TOURIST

But what about the black tourists? Can we attempt a closer acquaintance with them as individuals and as members of a class? In fact, we can.[78] In 1944 Krishna Somers, Mohammed Mia, Moosa Lorgat, and Ismail Mayet visited the KNP en route to Lourenço Marques. The four friends were classified as Indian, and all but Somers were from the Transvaal. Somers, at the time a medical student at the University of the Witwatersrand in Johannesburg, was born in Durban. Mia, who had proposed the trip, came from a prominent business and religious family. Traveling in Mia's car, the four friends made their way from the highveld to the lowveld, staying with friends along the 250-mile-long journey. To retrace their itinerary is to map alternative histories of travel and tourism in segregationist South Africa. It is to understand how black South Africans traveled despite the many obstacles placed before them by the colonial state and ordinary members of white society.

Because no hotels between Johannesburg and the park would accept them, the four stayed with friends along the way. In Nelspruit, they lodged with the Mintys, an Indian merchant family long resident in the lowveld. Their next stop was White River, the last major town before the KNP. There they stayed with the Gardee family, another Indian merchant family with business and family connections to the Mias. This was the same family whose wealth paid for two huts in the Indian camp at Skukuza. Recalling the 1944 trip seventy years later, Somers said: "In stopping in the Kruger park, the only place where accommodation was available for us as non-whites was Skukuza. The building was made of corrugated iron held with wooden supports. There were no facilities."[79] Somers and his friends spent a night in the park and then crossed the following day into Mozambique, "where we tasted for the first time freedom from any kind of racial discrimination."

Somers graduated from Wits University in 1949 and then worked in mission hospitals around South Africa before moving first to India and then to England to get away from apartheid and to further his studies. In 1957 he moved to Makerere University in Uganda, where he helped develop the training of doctors. He left Uganda in 1974 after dictator Idi Amin expelled Asians from the East African country. Despite this, Somers had better memories of East Africa than of southern Africa: "I cannot remember being impressed by the game that we saw in the Kruger park. I saw more game in Uganda, Kenya and Tanzania during my years at Makerere University. Indeed, the game parks of East African countries are superior in variety of game and also facilities than anywhere in South Africa."[80] Somers's views about South Africa and East Africa were colored by his experiences in South Africa, which, unlike East Africa, would not be free politically until 1994.

Zuleikha Mayat, a famous journalist and community activist, visited the Kruger National Park on a delayed honeymoon sometime between 1948 and 1949.[81] Mayat, born in 1926 in the western Transvaal, married Durban-born Mahomed Mayat in 1947, shortly after his graduation from the medical school of the University of the Witwatersrand.

Her father Mohammed was a keen traveler who would visit the park during winter holidays, which is how Mayat came to know about the sanctuary. Mayat recalled:

> So we knew about the Kruger National Park . . . and so on and when I got married, my husband wanted to take me also for a honeymoon or somewhere. So there were no hotels where we could really go to so in those days you just landed yourselves on your friends or your friends' [friends] or your family's friends and so on and it was open doors. So my brother, my sister, myself and my husband, we went from Potchefstroom then loaded the car with blankets, my father said take blankets it's very cold there and you won't get any joy from what you have there.[82]

Like Somers and his friends four years earlier, Mayat's party stayed in Nelspruit with the Mintys and in White River with the Gardees, who were good family friends:

> So we arrive, "welcome, welcome, don't worry, you are travelers." So we stayed with the Gardees for the night; next morning they gave us a bag of oranges and a hamper of food that we could have at the park and when we got to the park there was this one tent to the one side and in the morning, somebody brought you some hot water in a basin with which you could now wash. And that was it, there was no bath or anything. And the food too—we carried a lot of food. We could get coffee and we could get *phutu* or something there, that was it. The park itself was very lovely. We saw lions, we saw everything.[83]

However, only a few Indians took the kinds of holiday described above. As Somers, who went on to become a world-famous cardiologist, put it, "Indian South Africans were much too occupied with survival against racial legislation [and] a visit to a game park would have been exceptional luxury."[84] Mayat said that most Indians did not take holidays. "The outings were at a wedding or at a funeral or some family gathering. That is how you socialized." What made holidaying possible for those who did travel were precisely those networks of solidarity that helped Indian travelers avoid the petty humiliations of racism.

These networks—which were primarily mercantile and religious—not only spared Indians the racism but also subsidized their holidays. As Mayat said:

> Always when you go, you would go to an Indian home, and you know that you get at least food and you get a resting place and so on. When I was in Potchefstroom, at our house, I don't think there was a week when we didn't have visitors coming home, either going to a funeral or to a wedding or passing through. So if it is lunchtime, they got lunch; if it was supper, then it was supper and you had to get beds ready for them, you know, *ubuntu*. It was all *ubuntu*.[85]

Somers said there was "never any advertising in the Indian media for inbound tourism in South Africa" before the end of apartheid.[86] So Indian travelers came to know about the KNP through word of mouth. Mayat credits the Gardees with publicizing the park among Indians:

> There were lots of ships, lots of people, lots of immigrants coming from India. [They] used to get off in Lourenço Marques and . . . they would then come to Johannesburg. So if you knew the Gardees, you stopped there for a day or two to get used to the place and then you went to the Mintys in Nelspruit and you stayed for a day or two, before coming to Johannesburg where you knew other people. You stayed a few days and then you would set up your own little whatever you wanted to do.[87]

Mayat said it was possibly through this traffic that people came to know about the park. "Maybe coming through from India via the Gardees and so on, they would hear of this park here," she said. "They all knew about the park, I don't know how. We all knew that there is a Kruger National Park and that there are wild animals. Before I went there, I knew a lot about the park."[88] That knowledge could not always protect her from the indignities of petty apartheid. Mayat remembered an incident involving her husband Mahomed and the park.

In April 1964 Derk Crichton, an obstetrics professor at the University of Natal, invited Mahomed to a congress of the South African Society of Obstetricians and Gynecologists, in Skukuza. Mahomed, who could pass for white with his light skin and blue eyes, asked Mayat to come along. She said: "I couldn't go. . . . He was very fair looking . . . and people would think he was a white man. He could go with his white colleagues to the conference but if I go, that was a give-away. So you can come, your wife can't come. And I said, 'I'm not coming then.'"[89] For the Gardees, the family's relationship with the KNP is inscribed in the park's landscape itself. Mohamed Gardee, whose grandfather Mohamed Ismail Gardee built the Indian camp at Skukuza, said: "At one station during the depression, the animals were dying of starvation. There was a drought. My grandfather very willingly paid for boreholes and waterholes. The apartheid government never acknowledged his contribution. A borehole is still functional, still providing water for the animals."[90]

Mohamed Gardee, born in 1952, said the family would visit the park every week when he was growing up. "We love nature, we love conservation. It's a link, a spiritual link between us and our maker. We don't go there just for fun, to feed the baboons, make merry and get drunk, like the others. It's a spiritual journey."[91] Asked to explain how the Gardee home came to be such an important stop in Indian itineraries to the park, Gardee said: "White River was the only place where Indians could stay on their way to the park." Because there were no hotels open to Indians, the Gardees, as a family of some means, opened their doors to family, friends, strangers, and acquaintances.

COLONIAL NATIVES?

However, not every Indian visitor saw his or her engagement with the park through a religious lens.[92] There is a series of photographs showing a group of Indian men in the KNP. The photographs, taken sometime between the 1940s and 1950s, come from the family album of Nasima Coovadia. In one, two of the men (one of whom is pointing a spear to the left of the photographer) pose with two Africans (fig. 5.6).

In another, five men stare excitedly at the camera while an African woman standing in the middle of the group and holding what looks like a *dabba* (tiffin carrier) stares intently at the camera (fig. 5.5). Yet another photograph shows six men sitting and standing around a fire, each one holding a white tin mug (fig. 5.3). To their right stands an African man in a khaki coat that identifies him as a park attendant. In the background, we can see one of the tourist huts in the park. In another picture, the men and their car are shown crossing a river on a pontoon. In yet another of the photographs, four of the men are on their haunches, posing with two rifles (fig. 5.4). Standing to their right are two men (half visible) in Kruger park uniforms.

The photographs do not simply give us faces behind the "Asiatic" numbers recorded by the park; they also give us a sense of how some of these tourists comported themselves while in the park. A remarkable feature of the photographs is that the men are all dressed in what we can only describe as colonial khaki. "This is absolutely bizarre," said Nasima Coovadia. "Safari-suit get-ups and men in suits."[93] Coovadia's father, who regularly visited the park, is not in any of the photographs, leading Coovadia to think that these men were friends of his. "My family were small-time traders. They were comfortable but not wealthy at all. They valued travel [but] the whole value that was put on education was absolutely key. They valued education as a tool for social mobility. It does not surprise me that they valued going to the Kruger."[94] Coovadia herself first visited the park as a young child. "I have very vague memories of the trip. I would have been four or five at the time. . . . I don't recall us having any camping paraphernalia. We must have."[95] One of Coovadia's vague memories of the park concerns the distance between the Indian and the white camp at Skukuza. She thought the two were very far apart, but her brother recalled the distance being only half a kilometer.

Ahmed Essop grew up in Johannesburg but had family in the lowveld. He said:

> We had family, we used to go to Badplaas. Badplaas, Nelspruit and all that is very close by so I recollect very clearly going in the early 1960s because I was quite young. We often did day trips not to the Kruger park but going around parts of the Eastern Transvaal.[96]

Essop remembered a family holiday sometime in the 1960s during which the family (between twenty and thirty people) took over the entire Indian camp, which was "made of tin, corrugated iron, I suppose, and it was dormitory-style, bunk beds." The Indian camp was in Skukuza but separate from the main—meaning white—camp. Essop said:

It was in [Skukuza] but it was separate. I think it was part of it. . . . It was corrugated iron and there was a fence. So there were the dormitories and there was a bit of land in front and then there was a fence. I presume it was for the animals and the other thing that fascinated me at the time that I recollect is seeing the communities that lived in the park coming past. Some of them were obviously workers, but they were walking. As a kid you were wondering how could they be walking on the other side of the fence because the other side of the fence was danger because that's where the animals were. But we were told they lived near the park, they were working in the park but they were not in the camp. You could see people walking around, up and down. Why would people be on that side of the fence because we couldn't leave other than in the car? But they were walking day and night. At night we also saw people walking around.[97]

Essop's recollection gives us a sense of what the park looked like from the Indian camp looking out. His memories help us see outside the camp from a visitor's perspective. They flesh out the meaning of the park as a zone of labor and, more importantly, a peopled place. For Essop, class was an important part of the reason for who went to the park and why. Essop said people went to the park,

but it wasn't because of affinity with animals. It was something to go and see. It may not have been prestigious but it was the thing to do. It was something to do with a middle class family and there were limited opportunities under apartheid to do anything. I don't think we went there because there was environmental consciousness. I think it was a novelty, you know, more than anything. And then it was also partly a bit of a contradiction because my father wouldn't go to the Rand Easter Show once it was segregated, but we went to this segregated camp.[98]

The visits to the KNP had a communal dimension to them, allowing families, friends, and relatives to commune over food and a shared experience of the wild. We see this clearly in a series of photographs—one dating from 1965 and another from 1981—taken by

Ahmed Essop's uncle Ahmed Bhabha, showing the extended Bhabha family in the KNP (figs. 5.16–5.18). Ahmed Bhabha was a traveling salesman and a keen photographer who documented his family's visits to the park.

A CLASS IN ITSELF

As Somers and Mayat remind us, we should be careful not to assume that the option of going to the KNP was available to every Indian person or every member of the Indian middle class. It would appear that those who did visit the park tended, like Ahmed Essop, to have relatives in the lowveld or to have connections that allowed for ease of travel. The Bismillahs, Coovadias, Essops, Gardees, and Mias tended to traverse the same mercantile and religious networks, whereas Somers got to know the Mias through Mohammed Mia, whom he befriended when he lodged with the family during his first six months of medical school.

We should also be careful not to naturalize the category of Indian and to assume that to be classified Indian in colonial and apartheid South Africa was to share a commonality of interests. As Goolam Vahed and Thembisa Waetjen remind us, the label of Indian masked a lot of differences.[99] What the faces behind the figures of Indian tourists to the KNP tell us is that Indians, like other black communities, did not wait

FIGURE 5.16. Ahmed Bhabha's family in the Indian camp in the park in 1965. *Source:* Ahmed Bhabha's family archive. Image used with permission

FIGURE 5.17. Ahmed Bhabha's family in the park in 1984. *Source:* Ahmed Bhabha's family archive. Image used with permission

FIGURE 5.18. Ahmed Bhabha's family in the park in 1984. *Source:* Ahmed Bhabha's family archive. Image used with permission

for the state to extend to them the privileges of citizenship. They laid claim to the country and its landscapes in ways that defied government attempts to cast them as the ultimate other. Those with the means to do so explored the country despite the Jim Crow–style laws that made leisure a serious undertaking for Indian people. The Orange Free State, for example, had laws barring Indians from spending the night anywhere in the province. Coovadia recalled the stress induced by the thought of having to drive through the Orange Free State, which was necessary to travel between Johannesburg and Durban. "I recall the huge amounts of preparation for going to Natal. I recall my father's anxieties that we not get stuck anywhere in the Orange Free State."[100] Coovadia said her family had to get a permit to visit her grandparents in Natal. They could not simply get into the car and drive. Yet many Indian families asserted their claims to the privileges of national belonging—and they did this in ways banal and big. Mayat's father and in-laws, for example, hunted for sport. So did Essop's family. On its own, this means nothing. However, in the context of the colonial and apartheid governments' systematic refusal to accept the bona fides of Indians as South African, these practices acquire new meaning.

After all, it was not until 1961 that South Africa finally accepted Indians as South Africans, thereby removing the threat of deportation that had hovered over Indians from the moment of their arrival in Natal in 1860. The 1961 concession did not make Indians citizens automatically—that would take years of struggle—but it amounted to a de facto acknowledgment of South Africa's cosmopolitan mix and of the status of Indians as South Africans.[101] South African Indians were a key factor in the development of an inclusive African nationalism in South Africa, as Jon Soske argues.[102] Drawing on the example of India's independence struggle, African intellectuals sought to pay due regard to the cosmopolitan character of South Africa by taking account of the presence and meaning of Indians in South Africa. It was this, argues Soske, that pushed African intellectuals such as Anton Lembede and Albert Luthuli to develop a conception of nationalism that shunned autochthony and nativism. They did this in opposition to colonial and apartheid race thinking.

To show how bureaucratically and ideologically incoherent apartheid was, even as apartheid ideologues fulminated about sending Indians back to India and said that Indians could not and would not become citizens of South Africa, people like Mayat and Essop still traveled on passports that identified each as a "South African citizen." The only difference was that the Department of Indian Affairs—not the Department of the Interior—issued their passports.[103]

It was just as challenging for those classified as Coloured to visit the KNP. Yet we know from the figures cited above that Coloured people also visited the park and that they did so in growing numbers, especially in the second half of the twentieth century. Edmund February is among the Coloured people who visited the park under apartheid. February, one of South Africa's top savanna ecologists and leading rock climbers, first visited the park with his family sometime between 1969 and 1974. February, who was fifteen or sixteen at the time of the visit, remembered little of the trip when I interviewed him in 2017, almost fifty years after it took place:

> I remember there was one, may have been Berg-en-dal because that is the name that keeps coming to mind, was the one camp that we could go to. We couldn't go to any others. So there was one camp we could go to. I remember us going there and I have very clear memories of seeing elephants and how excited my mother was at seeing elephants. My mother got very excited. It was quite amusing and we, the whole car, were very happy about that. . . . And then I have a very clear memory of us driving through the park and coming out at Komatipoort in the south because we then went through into Mozambique and stayed on the beach in Maputo. There was a campsite on the beach and I thought that was all very exotic. That is why I remember it very clearly.[104]

The Februarys were an outdoors family. Edmund's father, Ronald Austin February, and mother, Helen Florence, were avid hikers and some of the earliest members of the Cape Province Mountain Club, founded in Cape Town in 1931 and the oldest black mountain club in Africa. The family were also keen campers, so they camped along the way during their drive from Cape Town to the KNP. February did not return to the park until 1994, when he went there as a PhD student at the University of Cape Town to study the relationship between wood anatomy and rainfall. "I wanted a gradient of rainfall using the same species along the rainfall gradient in a natural system."[105] He chose the KNP because it had good rainfall records and two sites where he could conduct his research. But it was not easy. Park officials ignored

FIGURE 5.19. The February family posing with a park ranger by the park's hippo pool, ca. 1974. *Source:* Edmund February's family archive. Image used with permission

his written requests for permission to do his research in the park. It was only when his master's supervisor wrote to the park that he was told he could come. But park officials would not let him stay in the park's research camp:

> No, I wouldn't have been allowed anywhere near the research camp. I had to pay for tourist accommodation. . . . I had to make an appointment to see [the head of research] in the park. I had to bow, grovel and scrape to get like 20 samples of wood in the Kruger, ten samples of each place. He then did give me permission and then I had to go to these two places that I had to collect in . . . and I had to stand outside the ranger's office. I had to be outside the ranger's office at seven when they opened and I had to wait for him. I can still remember standing there as everybody walked past me and ignored me completely until he had dealt

FIGURE 5.20. The February family outside their cottage in the Lower Sabie Rest Camp, ca. 1974. *Source:* Edmund February's family archive. Image used with permission

with everything. Then he dealt with me. And it was like "hi, I need permission to do this." . . . "Yes, I heard about you. No, I don't have any game guard to go with you. Just don't get killed. Bye. And don't let anyone see you getting out of your car" . . . and that was it.[106]

Twenty years after this experience, February, who became a professor at the University of Cape Town, was back in the KNP running a research project on savannah ecology funded by the U.S.-based Mellon Foundation. The project produced a number of master's students and a PhD graduate (Corli Wigley-Coetsee) who became head of ecology in the KNP. It would be a typical South African move to end this chapter here, showing how black South Africans triumphed over adversity. But that would be too easy. It would tempt the reader to forget the

FIGURE 5.21. An elephant picture taken by the Februarys, ca. 1974. *Source:* Edmund February's family archive. Image used with permission

humiliations and struggles (not necessarily nationalist in orientation or character) of those who fought for a place in the sun. As February said:

> Through the 70s when I first started doing things on my own, it was really, really hard. It wasn't easy. But we didn't think about it. We didn't think about the difficulties of doing it. We didn't think that we weren't allowed to go into campsites, we weren't allowed into certain places. We worked around it. So what does it tell you? It's like people always find a way. If you are interested in something, you will manage to do.[107]

That is exactly what those blacks who took holidays and engaged with nature in various ways did—they managed. They made their lives the best way they could. They could not choose the circumstances under which they acted. But act they did. Rather than see the stories recounted above as well as the story of the unnamed teachers with which we began as either a tragedy of apartheid or a romance of nationalist becoming, I suggest we see these stories for what they are: tales of strivings by a small and largely impoverished elite to have some time to themselves, unencumbered by gender and race.

DISSONANT HISTORIES

Some of the accounts rendered above strike a number of dissonant notes. Zuleikha Mayat recalled the 1964 doctors' conference in the KNP to which she could not go because, unlike her husband Mohamed, she was too dark-skinned to gain entry into the park. Nasima Coovadia and her brother could not agree about the distance between the white and Indian camps. Ahmed Essop remembered the presence of people walking up and down outside his rest camp, while Edmund February remembered Berg-en-dal being the only rest camp in which black people could lodge in 1969–70.

I call these reminiscences dissonant because we know that blacks could certainly visit the KNP in 1964, meaning that Mayat would not have been barred from entering; we know that, pace Coovadia, the distance between the Indian and white camps in Skukuza must not have been that great because when the Department of Indian Affairs complained in 1974 about the lack of toilets for Indians, the National Parks Board responded by cutting open a hole in the fence dividing the Indian and white camps so Indians could use the "white" toilets.[108]

Essop's memories of seeing people walking outside his camp strike us as dissonant because, even though we know about the Africans living in the park, the people Essop saw went against scholarly claims that they provided invisible labor to the park; we also know that, with respect to February, it was Skukuza and not Berg-en-dal that was open to black people. We also know that it would not be until 1974 that the National Parks Board resolved that only the National Parks Act (and not other pieces of apartheid legislation) should apply to the KNP, and only until 1980 that the board would move to get rid of apartheid signage from the park and allow blacks in its shops and restaurants.

I highlight these dissonances to show that I do not have a positivist appreciation of oral history. As Justin Willis reminds us, dissonances illustrate the complex ways in which individuals "structure and understand the past."[109] Drawing on his work in Uganda, Willis says that dissonance shows how people rationalize historical change and the tensions associated with that change. It also reveals how people understand and order social difference.[110] In the case of the KNP, the dissonance I have highlighted is not about whether people are remembering accurately. This is not about the veracity of their memories. It is, rather, about the dissonance "between a historical reality of social mobility (albeit limited and difficult) and a historical presentation of immobility and fixed categories."[111]

Here are black people who enjoyed a degree of mobility trying to recall that mobility in the light of popular renderings of the colonial and apartheid past in which blackness is defined by "immobility and fixed categories." In trying to make sense of their lives under colonial and apartheid rule, my informants have to grapple with memories of what they were able to do while also responding to historical accounts that suggest that black people could do very little under colonialism and apartheid. Faced with the dissonance such as the one struck above, the historian must avoid not only the temptation to "set the record straight"—to show, in other words, how it really was—but also the mistake of assuming that dissonance equals contradiction. There is nothing contradictory about what Mayat, Coovadia, Essop, and February remember. The dissonance in their accounts is, in fact, helpful, for it calls into question a key theoretical assumption of oral history, namely that the older an account of the past is, the more structured it is.

"This approach implies that information on the recent past is relatively unstructured and straightforward, and that the further back in time an account claims to reach, the more structured and difficult of interpretation (and the more homogeneous) it becomes," says Willis.[112] Mayat, Coovadia, Essop, and February give us accounts that show that individuals are constantly "turning their knowledge of the recent past into an argument about the past—that is, into history."[113] Memories—not to mention history—are not pristine reserves to be accessed as and when people need them. The stories by Mayat, Coovadia, Essop, and February show that memories are constantly made and remade, in the process helping the historian understand the myriad ways in which histories of presence impinge on the present.

6 ⇜ Black Mobility

IN JUNE 1962, the South African Institute of Race Relations published *Holiday and Travel Facilities for Non-Whites in South Africa*, a booklet intended to help black South Africans in pursuit of leisure find their way through the maze of apartheid restrictions (see fig. 6.1).[1] The institute, founded in 1929 to promote good race relations through research and advocacy, was opposed to apartheid, which had been the law of the land since 1948. Its mandate included the study of South Africa's socioeconomic conditions as well as the provision of information such as that contained in the 1962 booklet. The pamphlet listed hotels, beaches, cinemas, theaters, sports fields, public gardens, camping sites, picnic resorts, community halls, and parks open to blacks in South Africa's four provinces. The KNP was among the places on the list. The park had one rest camp called Olifants set aside for the use of blacks. It was the only national park with such facilities mentioned in the booklet.

Olifants, originally known by the African name Balule, was in fact one of the oldest camps in the park, having been established in 1932 — during South Africa's segregation era but long before the advent of apartheid — for the use of black tourists. If Olifants was a symbol of the complex accommodation between race thinking and conservation thinking in modern South Africa, then it was also, in a practical sense, proof of a tradition of tourism among blacks that existed despite colonial segregation and apartheid. Olifants served as a home away from home for the park's black visitors. It was a segregated space, to be sure, but that does not mean that segregation determined in total how blacks viewed the KNP and the nature it sought to represent.[2] Whereas the onset of European conquest and colonial rule in southern Africa marked the introduction of racialized ways of relating to time

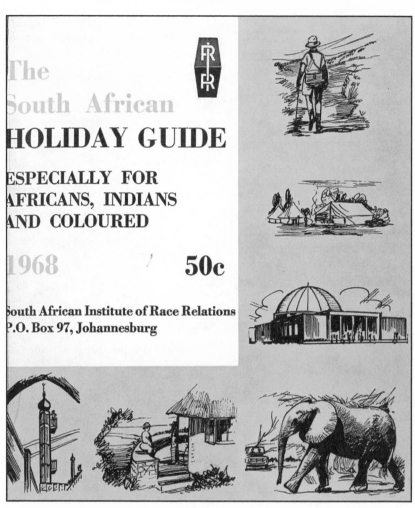

The
South African
HOLIDAY GUIDE

ESPECIALLY FOR
AFRICANS, INDIANS
AND COLOURED

1968   50c

South African Institute of Race Relations
P.O. Box 97, Johannesburg

FIGURE 6.1. Holiday guide for black South Africans, 1968. *Source*: SAIRR

and space, apartheid sought to elaborate these ways both bureaucratically and ideologically.[3] As Deborah Posel has shown, apartheid did
not begin life as an ideologically coherent political project. In fact,
even the Afrikaner nationalist alliance behind the National Party's narrow election victory in 1948 was divided, among other issues, between
those who saw apartheid as "total segregation" and those who wanted
it to be a "practical project."[4] Despite its incoherence, apartheid refined South Africa's systems of racial segregation and altered relations
between blacks and the land in ways that made the 1962 booklet both
relevant and necessary.[5]

Between 1948 and 1962, when the booklet was published, the National Party introduced the following legislation: the Prohibition of Mixed Marriages Act of 1949, the Immorality Amendment Act of 1950, the Population Registration Act of 1950, the Group Areas Act of 1950, the Bantu Authorities Act of 1951, the Bantu Education Act of 1953, and the Reservation of Separate Amenities Act of 1953. These laws covered the whole gamut of black life: from whom black people could marry or sleep with to where they could live and where they could go on holiday. Some of these laws extended legislation that had been in place before 1948; others were altogether new in that they turned into law, complete with the greater use of "Europeans Only" and "Non-Europeans Only" signs, what had previously been more customary segregation than legislative injunction.[6]

When the 1962 booklet was published, the places in which Africans could play and to which they could travel were fast shrinking. There were, for example, only two residential hotels for Africans in all of Johannesburg. In terms of the Native Urban Areas Consolidation Act of 1945, Africans could not stay in a white or urban area in which they were not employed for more than seventy-two hours without a visitor's permit. If they needed to stay for longer than seventy-two hours, they had to obtain permission from the relevant authorities. However, this did not necessarily mean, at least on paper, that black people could not take holidays. As the booklet said, "Except for the necessity of obtaining a visitor's permit, the African is under no restriction, and may move around from one area to another while on holiday or travel, as he pleases."[7] But matters were more complicated than that. To cite one example: travel agents did not offer organized tours for African tourists because of "accommodation difficulties." The booklet said, "They [travel agents] find themselves at a loss as far as arranging accommodation is concerned, partly because of the inadequacy of these facilities and partly because of the ignorance of their whereabouts." The booklet sought to do away with this ignorance. It tried to shield black travelers and travel agents alike from potential embarrassment.

It did this by making information available to the four travel agencies in South Africa that catered to the needs of "travel-conscious" blacks in the 1960s. The booklet was similar to *The Negro Motorist Green Book*, the travel guide produced by black American travel agent Victor Green to help black Americans travel without humiliation.

Black travelers needed it. As Jane Carruthers recounts, shortly after the National Party's election victory in 1948, Jacobus. G. Strijdom, the minister of lands, spoke to the National Parks Board about the introduction of apartheid in the KNP. He "expressed his deep regret not only that different race groups shared camps, but that they even shared the roads."[8] Strijdom suggested that the park be broken up and a portion set aside for sole nonwhite use. The board demurred. But the park did adopt other apartheid practices, such as the use of signs demarcating places for "whites only" and "non-whites only" (see fig. 6.2). For example, a 1963 map of the park shows the "Ngonyamene Resting Spot for Non-Whites" (see fig. 6.3).

The launch of petty apartheid in the park was part of the "Afrikaner nationalization of wildlife conservation" dating back to the late 1940s.[9] As early as 1953, the National Parks Board was reporting positively on the "application of apartheid" in the park:

> Separate rest camps for the use of non-European visitors were provided at Pretoriuskop, Skukuza and Letaba before the start of the winter season. The available accommodation is limited to the provision of tents. Prior to this, portions of the European rest camps had been set apart for non-Europeans, but this arrangement had elicited considerable criticism, as it was difficult to prevent the non-Europeans from wandering around between the European huts and tents at night.[10]

How did the black tourists who visited the park under apartheid—that is, after 1948—experience it? Even though we know that blacks visited the park under colonial and apartheid rule, gaps still remain in our understanding of the social history of the park. We do not know enough, beyond a few texts by swashbuckling European tourists, about how ordinary people (black and white) experienced the park (see fig. 6.4).[11] What did the park mean to the thousands of blacks who visited throughout the latter half of the twentieth century? What did they see and how did they see it? The existence of black tourism under white rule shows that relations between blacks and the park were complex—contrary to suggestions that Africans engaged with the park as an undifferentiated mass of "impoverished Africans."[12] The existence of black tourism under colonial and apartheid rule also calls

FIGURE 6.2. Apartheid signage showing picnic spot for black visitors. *Source:* SANParks

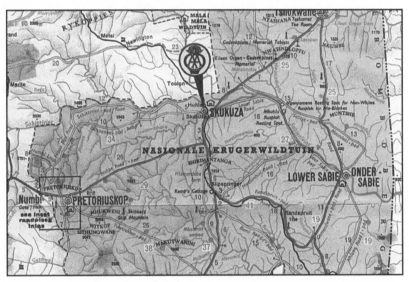

FIGURE 6.3. Map from 1963 showing picnic spot for black visitors. *Source:* SANParks Archive

into question claims that, as one postapartheid South African tourism official put it, Africans "have no history of travel," or that, as Njabulo Ndebele said, the "entire world of contemporary tourism carries no intuitive familiarity" for Africans.[13]

On the contrary, the history of black tourism in South Africa brings to light at least two phenomena: the first is the complexity of black

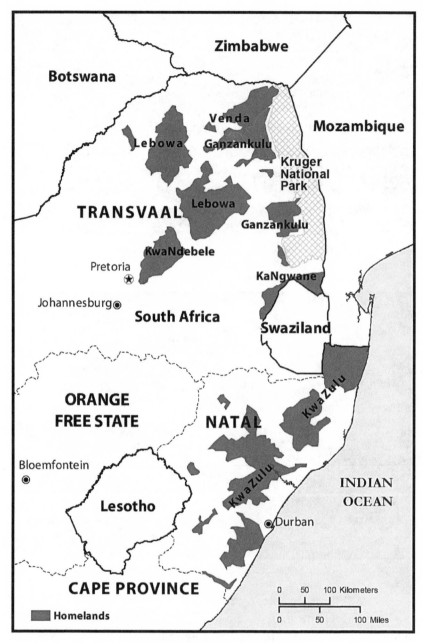

FIGURE 6.4. Map showing South Africa's Bantustans.

responses to white rule; the second is the role of class in determining those responses. In 1946, two years before the advent of apartheid, 37,166 people visited the KNP. Of these, 968 were "natives." The National Parks Board's annual report for 1947 does not say who these "natives" were. It also does not disaggregate the category "native."[14] But it is fair to assume that the majority would have been domestics brought to the park by the 26,755 documented white adults who visited along with their 9,443 children that year. The park did, after all, allow white visitors to bring their domestics along. As the 1946 official guide to the park put it, "Accommodation but no bedding is provided at all camps for native chauffeurs or servants accompanying visitors."[15] In 1953, about 90,000 people visited the park. Of these, 1,678 were domestics, 760 Indian, and 53 Africans and Coloureds.

Throughout the 1950s, the figure for domestics visiting the park stayed constant at about 2 percent of the total number of visitors. In 1954, for example, the park had 824 Indians and 120 African and Coloured tourists.[16] While the number of white visitors to the park ran in the thousands from the earliest days of tourism, the number of African, Coloured, and Indian visitors stayed low. But they started rising in the late 1950s. By the 1970s, they were in the low thousands. In the period 1976–77, 344,088 whites and 13,385 Africans, Coloureds, and Indians visited the park. In 1977–78, 357,750 whites and 15,238 Africans, Coloureds, and Indians visited the park. It is clear from the figures that the number of black visitors to the park was rising.[17] Why was the number going up? After all, apartheid was, so it seemed in the 1960s and 1970s, only getting consolidated and entrenched.

FROM NATIVE RESERVES TO BANTU HOMELANDS

The answer lies in the political changes that took place in the 1950s as the apartheid state sought to anticipate the decolonization wave that would overtake Africa in the 1960s. Prime Minister D. F. Malan's government cast whites as one "African volk" among many and used this to claim anticolonial sovereignty for a white South Africa while severing political links between blacks and apartheid South Africa.[18] It introduced laws designed to deprive blacks of grounds for citizenship. In 1951, the South African Parliament passed the Bantu Authorities Act. According to Hendrik Verwoerd, the minister of native affairs, "The fundamental idea throughout is Bantu control over Bantu areas as and when it becomes possible for them to exercise that control efficiently and properly."[19] In truth, the act sought to bolster chiefly authority by retribalizing Africans. The act provided for the establishment of a three-tier form of so-called native government.

At the lowest level, this new form of government was made up of Tribal Authorities. Chiefs, headmen, and councilors staffed these. The next level up was made up of Regional Authorities, which were constituted by two or more Tribal Authorities. The highest level was the Territorial Authority, constituted by two or more Regional Authorities. These authorities administered so-called native customs, controlled grass burning, sought to combat soil erosion, supervised water supplies, provided sanitation and education, and built dams and roads. They could also levy local taxes.[20] Verwoerd presented these authorities as traditional sites of power for Africans. In fact, these institutions were nothing more than instruments for the indirect rule of Africans and their political removal from so-called white South Africa. The authorities represented an attempt by the apartheid government to use existing traditional leaders to govern Africans outside South Africa "proper." Verwoerd himself acknowledged this point when he said:

> I think the Mau-Mau rising in Kenya has been one of the events from which we can learn a lesson in favor of the tribal system. There we saw that generally it was the chiefs with their authorities who took sides with the forces of law and order and who assisted European authority. In other words, the tribal system is the natural ally of the government of the country.[21]

The 1951 act was followed by the Promotion of Bantu Self-Government Act of 1959, which laid the political foundations for the creation of so-called Bantu homelands.[22] While some traditional African leaders saw through the sham of African political independence offered by Verwoerd and his government through the creation of homelands, many others supported the creation of tribal authorities. Transkei was the first homeland to accept independence, becoming a "free country" in October 1976, with Kaizer Matanzima as prime minister. Matanzima, a cousin of Nelson Mandela's, believed that the homeland system offered an opportunity for African advancement.[23] He said homeland independence would create an atmosphere in which it is possible for whites to accept the leaders of these new black political entities . . . as equals in the same way as blacks from other parts of the world are when they enter white South Africa as distinguished visitors and make use of facilities hitherto reserved for whites.[24]

Matanzima might have been a self-serving politician. But he was definitely on to something when he talked about the political effects of the creation of homelands on white South Africa. Between 1972 and 1981, South Africa granted ten homelands self-rule or independence. Among these, four neighbored the KNP: Lebowa, granted self-rule in 1972; Gazankulu, given self-rule in 1973; Venda, declared independent in 1977; and KaNgwane, which became a self-governing state in 1981.

However, for all their compromised political histories, these homelands were more than make-believe states recognized only by apartheid South Africa. They were also producers of "citizens" who traveled and expected, as Matanzima said, to be treated as "distinguished visitors" in places such as the KNP. The fiction of apartheid's racialized geography was that the ten homelands were independent states. This meant, among other things, that apartheid South Africa had to respect the travel documents issued by these homelands. This had serious implications for the administration of apartheid and the maintenance of its spatial geography.

For one, none of the homelands, except for the Transkei, was territorially contiguous. Bophuthatswana was famously made up of thirteen different patches, many of which were great distances apart, while Gazankulu was made up of four. Second, the history of migrant labor, a key feature of colonial and apartheid South Africa, meant that most of the homelands' citizens had "South African" relatives. So there were Africans who, even though related, were exposed in different ways to apartheid, depending on where they were in time and space. The KNP was alive to these contradictions. It responded to them in two ways.[25] First, the government and the National Parks Board resolved in March 1974 to exempt the KNP and other national parks from the segregationist Group Areas Act. Second, the board resolved in September 1980 to make most of rest camps in the park "international," thereby exempting them from apartheid. This meant that black visitors from the homelands could be accommodated in the park without embarrassment. Tellingly, these concessions did not extend to the park's black employees. They continued to contend with discriminatory employment practices, such as being the only park employees subjected to fingerprint checks and being barred from the park's staff swimming pools and shops. It would take labor struggles and the formal end of apartheid in 1994 for this to change. Salomon Joubert, the last white warden of the park, acknowledged the complications produced by the creation of homelands. He said:

> A growing stream of visitors was being attracted from the Republic of Venda, an independent black state which had been proclaimed next to the Kruger Park, as well as from three self-governing homelands, Gazankulu, KaNgwane and Lebowa. Mixed race groups also visited the Park from neighboring states such as Swaziland.[26]

This was not surprising, considering the proximity of the park to the homelands. The closeness meant that the park was affected by the development of apartheid policy regarding homelands, whether park officials liked it or not. Apartheid ideologues such as Malan and Verwoerd presented homelands and the conferment of self-government on them as a part of Africa's decolonization, a process that had got underway in 1957 with the independence of Ghana. This was a cynical ploy, to be sure, but it could only work if the South African government took these homelands seriously. That meant, among other things, allowing these homelands to set up embassies and consular offices in South Africa "proper," recognizing travel documents issued by the homelands, and providing adequate facilities for visitors from these homelands to places such as the KNP. The idea behind the homeland system was negative on a number of levels. But there is no doubt that homelands helped hasten the demise of apartheid by making it difficult for the KNP, for example, to maintain petty apartheid.

This did not necessarily make homelands a good idea. It did, however, illustrate the law of unintended consequences in operation. Apartheid-era authorities did not intend to use homelands to end apartheid, but that is what they inadvertently helped bring about because of their anxieties about the "diplomatic" embarrassment caused by apartheid. According to Joubert, "Only in 1946 did the Board . . . approve in principle that accommodation would be provided for other race groups at rest camps once funds were available."[27] In 1962, the park hosted a meeting of the International Union for the Conservation of Nature. The National Parks Board, anticipating that African countries participating in the meeting would send black officials, sought guidance from the government about what to do.

One solution was to build guest cottages exempt from the normal management of the park. These were indeed built in 1970. The board also noted in the 1970s that although facilities for black visitors were of a poor standard, demand from blacks was still too low to justify the outlay of money to fix the problem. The board said that the park would have to provide separate facilities for whites, Indians, and Africans. But there were too few Coloureds visiting the park to justify separate camps for them, so the few that came were housed with Indians—an odd move considering that park statistics always lumped African and Coloured visitors together. In March 1974 the board resolved that its "director should compile a priority list for submission to the Board of the facilities for non-Europeans on the basis of temporary facilities within European rest camps as a transitional stage until such time that separate rest camps could eventually be erected."[28] If the National Parks Board thought that it could take its time dealing with the problem of black visitors, it had not bargained on pressure from black groups themselves, even if these were groups operating within government structures. In November 1974, the Department for Indian Affairs complained to the National Parks Board about the lack of toilets in the Indian section of the Skukuza rest camp. The department said Indians were "forced to use the toilets for Bantu servants there, which are invariably in an unsatisfactory condition." The department added:

> As Indians experience difficulty in obtaining reservations, representations should be made for the building of additional cottages for Indians as the existing accommodation is totally inadequate, and for the provision of better facilities such as kitchen and dining room facilities.[29]

The complaint by the Department of Indian Affairs illustrates the danger of reading the history of black tourism in South Africa in simplistic terms. To say that there were black tourists does not mean that the Africans, Coloureds, and Indians who constituted these tourists thought alike. In fact, even their modes of getting to the park were racially separated. In response to the complaint from the Department of Indian Affairs, the National Parks Board cut a hole through the fence separating the Indian from the white section of Skukuza. That way, Indians could use the facilities in the white section—and avoid having to use "Bantu" facilities.

Despite concessions such as this one, the question of what to do with black visitors would not go away. By 1980 more blacks were visiting the park, and many of them came from the homelands adjacent to the park. The park abandoned petty apartheid in 1981, but only as it affected black tourists—not park staff. The abandonment of apartheid, which included the removal of "whites only" and "non-whites only" signs from the park, meant that the park's front office staff could do their jobs without fear of embarrassment. As the National Parks Board said in September 1980, before the park's rejection of outward apartheid:

> In the present situation, it happens at most almost daily during peak periods that visitors of other race groups have to be denied the hitherto accepted white facilities in the Park. It not only causes acute embarrassment to the staff who have to cope with such situations, but also causes grave offence to the citizens of other countries who demand the internationally accepted standards of courtesy applicable to inter-state tourist traffic.[30]

This is not surprising when we consider that the National Parks Board, in conjunction with South Africa's prime minister and the minister of agriculture—under whom national parks fell at the time—had already resolved in 1974 that national parks were meant for the enjoyment of all regardless of race and that only the National Parks Act should apply to the park.[31] If anything, the 1980 resolution calls into question claims by Roger Southall that apartheid South Africa's homelands policy was "devoid of all progressive political potentialities."[32] The policy might have been driven by cynical calculations, but the fact is that when it came to places such as the KNP, the policy effectively forced apartheid officials and their conservation counterparts to abandon petty racial discrimination.

It is worth mentioning that most homeland leaders were self-declared conservationists.[33] As Mangosuthu Buthelezi, chief minister of Kwa-Zulu, told delegates to the first World Wilderness Congress in 1977, "Contrary to the expectations of many, I am a wilderness enthusiast."[34] In fact, for homeland leaders—denied the international recognition that they and their South African overlords craved—conservation provided the international exposure they might not have had otherwise (see fig. 6.5). Enos Mabuza, chief minister of KaNgwane and the first black person to serve on the National Parks Board, was an active member of the World Wilderness Congress (see fig. 6.6). Addressing the inaugural congress in Johannesburg in 1977, Mabuza spoke of the challenges facing black conservationists in apartheid South Africa: "One cannot speak on the need for the conservation of wilderness of a black homeland in South Africa without substantiating such a need as opposed to other pressing needs of the black people concerned."[35] Mabuza said that, because of land hunger and poverty in his homeland, bread-and-butter issues counted for more; there was no quicker way to make oneself "irrelevant to the issues of the day" than to talk to his subjects about conservation.[36] In a speech delivered at the second World Wilderness Congress in Australia in 1980, Mabuza called for a formula "whereby the African, young and old, can participate in the re-creation of game sanctuaries."[37] Buthelezi and Mabuza shared a cosmological approach to conservation. Buthelezi said that Africans supported conservation because "the wilderness is our natural habitat for it is where we were forged as a people."[38] Mabuza described African responses to the wilderness as "instinctive and mystic."[39] Despite this, however, these Bantustan leaders used conservation to issue veiled challenges against apartheid. As Buthelezi said, "Wilderness conservation is as vulnerable to a policy of segregation as everything else in South Africa."[40] So he opposed segregation.

To understand why the story of the demise of apartheid in the KNP was inextricably linked to relations between the park and the homelands, one must understand the geography of South Africa. About 19 percent of South Africa is set aside for national parks, game reserves, and privately owned places of conservation.[41] Most conservation places are situated in rural South Africa, which also happens to be where most homelands were until their formal demise in 1994. Some of these homelands—KaNgwane, Gazankulu, and Venda—were so close to the

FIGURE 6.5. Park warden Uys de V. "Tol" Pienaar handing KwaZulu leader
Mangosuthu Buthelezi an award, date unknown. *Source*: SANParks Archive

park that the park's gates cut through their territories.[42] They could
not help but influence one another's operations. What's more, the
park drew its employees from Mozambique and from the neighboring homelands. These employees performed the labor that made the
tourist experience special. But, as Jacklyn Cock and Karl Jacoby argue,
that labor had to remain "off-stage" to preserve the fiction of pristine
nature.[43] How, then, did homeland citizens and tourists experience the

FIGURE 6.6. Portrait of KaNgwane leader Enos Mabuza, who became the first black person to join the National Parks Board. *Source*: SANParks Archive

KNP? How did these citizens of countries recognized only by apartheid South Africa relate to the park?

To ask these questions is to inquire into the materiality of homelands as institutions and places of experience. It is, in other words, to take us away from the Marxist-inspired unidimensional renderings of homelands from the 1970s that failed to see homelands for what they were: places in which millions of people—with ambitions and interiority—lived.[44] As Audie Klotz reminds us, the creation of homelands "cannot be explained solely in functional terms as a way to preserve segregation. Why opt for an inefficient and costly policy of faux-states that shifted the ontological status of Africans from objects to subjects with rights?"[45] In fact, says Klotz, by establishing homelands, South Africa created an "irresolvable dilemma." The KNP proves that.

HIDDEN HISTORIES OF TRAVEL

Asked about his first visit to the park, Sick Winlight Mdluli said, "It used to be difficult to go to Skukuza."[46] At the time of our interview, Mdluli was a headman, a shopkeeper, and a former member of the legislature of the KaNgwane homeland. He was, in this sense, triply elite, yet he claimed not to have visited the park until after the end of apartheid. But he recalled that there was no barrier between the park and his birthplace Shabalala, a township situated west of the park: "There was no fence when we were growing up. You knew where your road ended and theirs began. We lived OK. There were no problems." Mdluli's story of not having visited the park was made all the more remarkable by the fact that both his father and a brother had worked for the park. But Mdluli was not the only one with a complex relationship with the park.

Simon Fakude, a waiter at the park when I interviewed him in 2009, joined the park's employ in 1980, following his father and other relatives in doing so.[47] But, in the beginning, he hardly knew the park. His father lived in the staff compound, and Fakude said that, even though wives and children could visit the men in the compounds, they needed permission to do so. Even then, they were not allowed to move around the park. They could only stay in the compound. By 2009, Fakude was a regular visitor and a self-taught guide who gave friends guided tours into the park when off duty.

Jimmy Mnisi, a local councilor and one of the leaders of the ANC in Shabalala, was one of Fakude's regular guests. Asked about blacks visiting the park in the colonial and apartheid eras, Mnisi said: "It was very strange. Only few blacks were able to go to the park as tourists— business owners, people with money, the educated, very few were able to go there as tourists."[48] Mnisi said that although he had relatives working in the park during the apartheid era, the first time he visited the park was to play soccer with park employees. A group of women (teachers, business owners, and church leaders) said, when interviewed in 2009, that they had no relationship with the park. "The Kruger park is there," said one, pointing in the distance to indicate the gulf between the park and her community.[49] But, as Mnisi's comments show, there were blacks who visited the park while many more were shunning it or being prevented from visiting it. We can only speculate about who many of them were. However, there is something about the existence of these ghostly tourists that allows us to examine the ways in which apartheid was spooked by its own contradictions.

Apartheid officials, with their insistence on a racially and ethnically balkanized map, could not be true to their own claims without tripping over themselves. Apartheid needed homelands to make itself real. However, it could not have these homelands without hastening its own demise, as its end in the KNP in the 1980s shows. South Africa could not have so-called black self-government without letting the logic of such a commitment run its course. This does not mean that homelands were antiapartheid by definition. But it does point to the paradoxes of South African history. In the following section, I turn to the archives of one of these homelands to show how the paradoxes mentioned above manifested themselves. The homeland in question was Gazankulu and the archival material examined here came from the office of Hudson Ntsanwisi, an educationist and linguist who ran Gazankulu as chief minister and minister of economic affairs from 1969 to 1993, a year before its formal demise. Like many members of the black elite that led the antiapartheid struggle or (like Ntsanwisi) staffed the bureaucracies that made apartheid function, Ntsanwisi came from a mission background.[50]

He was born in 1920 at the Shiluvane Mission Station, founded in 1886 in the Northern Transvaal by Swiss missionaries.[51] He schooled at Shiluvane and at the Lemana teacher training college, founded in 1906, also by Swiss missionaries. Ntsanwisi read for a BA, first by correspondence and then at the University of Fort Hare, the alma mater of many members of the black elite, especially in the first half of the twentieth century. He founded the Shiluvane Secondary School in 1949 and became a school inspector in 1956, assuming one of the most senior positions available to black educationists in the apartheid education system. In 1960 the apartheid state seconded Ntsanwisi to the Department of Bantu Languages at the University of the North, founded in 1959 in keeping with the dictates of the Bantu Education Act that Africans only enroll at universities set aside for their ethnic groups.

The government intended the University of the North, popularly known as Turfloop, for Pedis, Vendas, and the Tsonga, Ntsanwisi's supposed ethnic group. Turfloop was among a number of ethnic universities founded in the late 1950s and early 1960s to train leaders and bureaucrats for the homeland system. These included the University of Zululand (founded in 1960 for Zulus), the University of Western Cape (1959, for Coloureds), and the University of Durban-Westville (1961, for Indians). Because of a shortage of people with the skills to staff and run these institutions—not to mention the homeland bureaucracies they were meant to serve—educated individuals like Ntsanwisi found themselves in demand by these institutions and bureaucracies. Ntsanwisi rose to the top of the university's Department of Bantu Languages, becoming chair of African languages. In 1969 he won election as the first chief minister of the Legislative Assembly of the Machangana Territorial Authority, established in 1962. In 1973 the authority became Gazankulu, with Ntsanwisi as chief minister and minister of economic affairs, with a brief that included conservation.

The Tsonga were invented as an ethnic group by, first, Swiss missionaries and ethnic entrepreneurs like Ntsanwisi and, second, the apartheid state. The Tsonga did not exist as a separate ethnic group until missionaries, apartheid bureaucrats, and mission-educated elites made them such. In fact, when the apartheid government first introduced the Bantu Authorities Act in 1951, its plan was to split Tsonga-speakers between the Pedi and the Venda. However, by the time the government introduced the Promotion of Bantu Self-Government Act in 1959, it had decided that the Tsonga were in fact a separate national unit and deserved a homeland of their own. But the invention of the Tsonga as a "national unit" needed more than legislative fiat. This was because the Tsonga were a "disparate peoples who spoke Tsonga-related dialects" but exhibited no ethnic consciousness as such until encouraged to do so by missionaries, the apartheid government, and ethnic entrepreneurs, many of whom had links to the missions in the area.[52]

The Tsonga also happened to live in areas marked by cultural and linguistic diversity, as well as by fluid political boundaries. They were not unique in this regard. Political subjection in a traditional sense in the lowveld rested on whom one chose to align with—not on ethnicity, language, tribe, or even territory. As government ethnologist Nicolaas van Warmelo said in 1959, the African communities in the lowveld lived in a "remarkable state of ethnological confusion," meaning that the Native Affairs Department had to "sort the people out in such a way that the greatest number of each chief's subjects will belong to the same clan as himself."[53] Van Warmelo was in fact complaining about the slow pace of the introduction of so-called Bantu authorities in the northern regions of South Africa, in keeping with the prescripts of the Promotion of Bantu Self-Government Act of 1959. Van Warmelo knew that, contrary to segregationist and apartheid assumptions about the cultural and political integrity of ethnic groups in the lowveld, a high degree of ethnic mixing defined the region. Many so-called Tsonga had come to the lowveld as refugees from a number of places in southeastern Africa, especially Mozambique. Van Warmelo himself had observed in 1937 that the

> Tsonga-speaking refugees came over the border in small parties and settled down wherever they could. Very often they became the subjects of Sotho and Venda chiefs and, though the tendency to reassemble and live together was there, they usually failed to muster sufficient strength to form tribes of any importance.[54]

It was because of views such as van Warmelo's—influential in the elaboration of apartheid conceptions of ethnicity, tribes, and national units—that the apartheid government initially wanted to divide people identified as Tsonga regionally between Pedi and Venda authorities. Using the Bantu Authorities Act of 1951, the government wanted to bolster traditional leadership in order to

> restore tribal life as far as possible by seeing to it that the chiefs and the whole tribal government adapt themselves to the exigencies of our times and thereby automatically regain the position of authority which they forfeited to a large extent through their backwardness.[55]

So while Verwoerd, who served as prime minister from 1958 until his assassination in 1966, was saying that the "natives of this country do not all belong to the same tribe or race" and that "they have different languages and customs," he did not seem too eager at first to recognize the Tsonga as a standalone group.[56] It did not matter much to Verwoerd whether the Tsonga were a separate group or not, so long as they were under a government-recognized chief (Pedi or Venda) who could levy tax and impose order. However, the government's position regarding the ethnic status of the Tsonga changed after the Tomlinson Commission, appointed by the government in 1954 to look into the economic viability of African reserves, signaled a policy shift away from spatial to ethnic segregation, with nation replacing tribe as the marker of group cohesiveness. Of course, a key influence here was decolonization and its promise of a move away from tribe to nation in colonial Africa. With the government insisting that "the Bantu people of South Africa do not constitute a homogeneous people, but form separate national units on the basis of language and culture," mission-educated elites like Ntsanwisi, who had been calling for the awakening of a national spirit among the Tsonga, could begin agitating for a Tsonga homeland.[57]

Ntsanwisi's election in 1969 to the position of chief minister presaged the realization of his dream. The conferment of self-government status on Gazankulu in 1973 helped him realize that dream. Being chief minister meant that Ntsanwisi had to act like a head of state and attend to all the trappings of statecraft. This meant South Africa was "mimicking the decolonization process in an effort to preserve its international legitimacy."[58] It also meant that the apartheid government had to treat him like a head of state, despite the cynicism and the fictions that both Ntsanwisi and his apartheid allies had to tell themselves about the extent and meaning of his self-government. Gazankulu, with its citizens and bureaucracies, might have been nothing more than a "proletarian dormitory," but it was material enough and the effects of its existence real enough that South Africa had to reckon with it.[59]

POTEMKIN VILLAGES?

As Shireen Ally points out in her reading of the discarded archives of the former homeland of KaNgwane, the mere existence of these archives should give pause to those all too quick to dismiss homelands as toy telephones. To read these archives—along and against the grain— is to enter a world not of make-believe but of human actions with consequences for many human beings. Recorded in the archives of

Gazankulu is not pantomime but real action that took place in a given place and time.[60]

It says something about the smallness of Gazankulu that nothing seemed to escape Ntsanwisi's attention—from the employment of staff in Gazankulu's game reserve, to the cost of a plate of pap and vleis in the reserve, to the conduct of teachers in the homeland's schools.[61] Or it might be an indication of Ntsanwisi's jumped-up ambitions as an omniscient leader that he found time for all these concerns in his role as head of state. In January 1985, Ntsanwisi chastised the principal of Giyani High School for uprooting seven indigenous trees from the schoolyard in order to make a seed bed for a cornfield. In an irate letter directed to the homeland's secretary of education, Ntsanwisi said:

> This wanton destruction of indigenous trees is greatly deplored by the Nature Conservation Section of this Government. The school campus is in no way meant to be a maize field. Application for a maize field should follow normal channels. This irresponsible and senseless invasion of the school campus is viewed in a very serious light and should be placed on record against the official responsible.[62]

Ntsanwisi's ire might have been drawn, in fact, not by the "wanton destruction" of indigenous trees but by the fear that, among the uprooted trees, was a tree that he, as chief minister, had planted in the schoolyard during an official ceremony. However, when the secretary of education looked into the matter, he found that

> the tree in question, i.e., the special tree whose botanical nor traditional name is unknown to us, and which was planted at Giyani High School in a special ceremony through the kind agency of the Honorable Professor H.W.E. Ntsanwisi, Chief Minister of Gazankulu, was found to be alive and intact.[63]

But the tree looked stunted, showed signs of neglect, and had been invaded by termites. The secretary ordered the school principal to "start giving special care to this tree, nursing and nurturing it to bloom, as was the intention of the donors."[64] The secretary also instructed the principal to plant more trees. "At a subsequent visit," said the presumably relieved secretary to the chief minister's office, "the tree was luxuriant (although the lower parts of its trunk still showed invasion by termites), thanks to the recent rains."[65]

For opponents of the homeland system, the story of a head of state getting worked up over trees from a schoolyard might be proof of the parody that was Bantustan rule. However, to do that would be to reduce Ntsanwisi to a caricature and to miss the beliefs animating his actions. He, in fact, considered himself a conservationist. He believed that the survival of Gazankulu's natural resources needed a "philosophy which makes conservation relevant to all interest groups, in all circumstances, within its borders."[66] Speaking in March 1985 at a ceremony marking the official handover of Manyeleti Game Reserve (see fig. 6.7) from South Africa to Gazankulu, Ntsanwisi said:

> With the ongoing and *extensive* [his emphasis] damage wrought on the biosphere by [population] growth and [economic] development, it makes little sense to approach conservation as an *intensive* [his emphasis] activity, as has in the past been the main thrust of the conservation effort both within South Africa and elsewhere in the world.[67]

Ntsanwisi decried conservation efforts directed solely at tourists, saying:

> If conservation efforts, which are in themselves consuming increasing volumes of resources, are to have more than the effect of merely delaying the inevitable, fresh approaches are required. Environmental conservation cannot be viewed, particularly in the context of developing countries, as a bottomless pit of expenditure to serve the *aesthetic objectives* [his emphasis] of a privileged few.[68]

For a traditionalist committed to the homeland system, Ntsanwisi offered a radical conception of conservation. He proposed a philosophy of "extensive conservation" premised on the idea that the "natural boundaries of ecosystems do not necessarily coincide with political boundaries," and that Gazankulu's environment could only be managed meaningfully and constructively "in the context of the total ecological

FIGURE 6.7. Brochure advertising the Manyeleti Game Reserve in Gazankulu.
Source: National Archives and Records Service of South Africa

systems of which it forms part, thus necessitating constructive and on-going interaction with its ecological neighbors at all levels."[69] Here was an apartheid puppet, as many of his opponents called Ntsanwisi, using the idea of nature to undermine apartheid's raison d'être and ideo-logical commitment to separation. Ntsanwisi accepted Manyeleti as a "National Asset for the Shangaan/Tsonga people" but then proceeded to argue why this national asset could be managed not nationally but transnationally.[70]

Although, at a cultural and political level, Ntsanwisi accepted the idea of a Tsonga nation as a separate entity, his idea of conservation un-dermined the idea of nature as something that could be managed na-tionally. Ntsanwisi's philosophy of extensive conservation destabilized Afrikaner nationalist assumptions about nations being natural entities.

If apartheid ideologues like Verwoerd thought they could legitimize homelands by naturalizing them and their inhabitants, Ntsanwisi sought to make Gazankulu part of a bigger transnational ecosystem.

His philosophy was that conservation had to be a "multiple land-use concept, which accommodates the balanced spatial and resource requirements of all aspects of its national life."[71] We should be careful, however, not to romanticize Ntsanwisi's philosophy. His pragmatism was in fact a product of his social and political circumstances. It was an attempt to make virtue out of necessity. Gazankulu lived in the shadow of the KNP, which Ntsanwisi called "our 'big brother' to the East."[72] He understood that, with no serious economic base to speak of, Gazankulu had to take advantage of its proximity to the KNP in hopes of drawing economic benefits to the homeland (see fig. 6.8). As Ntsanwisi put it, Gazankulu had to strengthen its ties to the "big brother" in order to "harmonize our ecological management interests with theirs within the concept of a broader *conservancy* [his emphasis] which recognizes

FIGURE 6.8. Taking charge: (*left to right*) John Seton, a South African Breweries (SAB) executive; Cedric Phatudi, chief minister of Lebowa; Hudson Ntsanwisi, chief minister of Gazankulu; and, in the driver's seat, Andries Treunicht, deputy minister of Bantu Administration. The four men are celebrating SAB's donation of the pictured minivan to Manyeleti, a "Bantu-only" game reserve in Gazankulu. *Source: Rand Daily Mail*, July 7, 1976. Image used courtesy of Gallo Images

the ecological artificiality of the border that separates Gazankulu and the Kruger National Park."[73]

Again, here was a homeland leader expressing political support for the balkanization of South Africa while pointing out the "ecological artificiality" of the boundary between Gazankulu and apartheid South Africa. Scholars who insist on denouncing homelands as "the greatest single fraud ever invented by white officials" run the risk of missing the opportunity to tease out what the paradoxes in Ntsanwisi's ideas tell us about how the homeland system functioned in practice.[74] Ntsanwisi was not unique in his regard for conservation. Mangosuthu Buthelezi, chief minister of KwaZulu, took an active interest in the preservation of the rhino in the Hluhluwe-Umfolozi Game Reserve; Lucas Mangope, president of the Republic of Bophuthatswana, actively supported the establishment of the Pilanesberg National Park in 1977.

Enos Mabuza, the chief minister of KaNgwane and also a committed conservationist, was appointed to the National Parks Board in 1991, becoming the first black member of the board.[75] No two homelands were the same, however, and no other homeland enjoyed such proximity to the KNP as did Gazankulu. As Ntsanwisi said:

> As a most important neighbor of Gazankulu, the possibility of close and practical cooperation . . . with the Kruger National Park is both exciting and compelling. I believe that we can hammer out a formula for such cooperation apropos of Manyeleti [Game Reserve] which will not only set the tone for further cooperation elsewhere along our common border, but will also establish [a] notable precedent in Southern Africa.[76]

Gazankulu needed this close cooperation because Manyeleti was in fact the KNP. The South African government proclaimed the Manyeleti Game Reserve, situated below the midpoint of the western boundary of the KNP, in 1967 as a conservation resort for the exclusive use of Africans.[77] The proclamation might have been in keeping with the early wishes of Jacobus G. Strijdom, apartheid's first minister of lands, for the racial dismemberment of the KNP so whites would not have to share roads and camps with blacks. The original Manyeleti Game Reserve covered 17,000 hectares, but this was extended in 1977 to 23,000 hectares with the purchase of two farms, Albatross and Buffelshoek.[78]

Edward Teversham says that Manyeleti "existed both as a resort for the enjoyment of its visitors and as a conservation space with an ecological and educational goal."[79] However, it is also likely, given the context of its founding, that the resort was a product of the hubris that defined apartheid in the late 1960s, following an economic boom that inspired ever more grandiose separatist schemes. The Department of Bantu Administration and Development—one of the many names that the old Native Affairs Department assumed under apartheid—ran Manyeleti until 1981, when it was incorporated into Gazankulu but managed by a South African government official named Harald Hamburger. In March 1985, Gazankulu took full control of Manyeleti.[80]

But the trouble with living with the "big brother" to the east was that Manyeleti could not avoid comparison with the KNP. In 1983, for example, while the Kruger enjoyed an 80.3 percent occupancy rate, Manyeleti only had 23 percent. Because Manyeleti had been "cast in an essentially educational role" at its founding, 72 percent of its visitors were schoolchildren, with an average length of stay of 1.7 days.[81] The corresponding number for the KNP was 3.2 days, and the vast majority of these were adults.

HUNTING FOR DEVELOPMENT

Being a so-called black resort, Manyeleti charged tariffs that could not be "decoupled from Black consumer spending patterns."[82] Even though the Orpen Gate connected Manyeleti to the KNP, Manyeleti's designation as a black resort meant it could not attract the white tourists who constituted the majority of visitors to the park. What's more, those who did visit Manyeleti placed viewing game as the last thing on their to-do lists.[83] To call Ntsanwisi a pragmatic conservationist, then, is to say that, even though he saw conservation as a good in itself, that good only had real value for him if harnessed to economic development. So for more than a decade Gazankulu ran the only hunting concession right next door to the KNP. The Letaba Ranch, to the west of the KNP, began trophy hunting in April 1981. By the end of that year, 98 percent of the ranch's clients came from abroad. The ranch charged R2,000 for an elephant, R1,500 for a lion, R800 for a buffalo, and R500 for a hippo.[84]

However, as a reminder of who called the shots in the relationship between Gazankulu and South Africa, the South African military kept a base in the ranch. The South African military prided itself on its commitment to conservation, but as Stephen Ellis showed, the South African Defense Force was among the worst poachers in southern Africa.[85] The presence of the military in Letaba created a "major hindrance" as the base came with a road whose traffic interfered with the movement of animals between the park and the ranch. This was just one of the many problems between Gazankulu and the park. In April 1985—a month after Gazankulu assumed full control of Manyeleti—Chief Samuel Dickenson Nxumalo, the minister of justice in Gazankulu, complained to Ntsanwisi about the harassment of his subjects ("my people," he called them) by rangers from the KNP.[86]

Nxumalo detailed cases of arbitrary arrests, brutal assaults, and at least one disappearance of Gazankulu citizens. "Could he be dead or in prison?" Nxumalo asked about a man named Thomas who had been arrested by park rangers on April 7, 1985, tortured, detained illegally for two months, and then dumped in the Louis Trichardt jail, where he may have died. Nxumalo said that Thomas's arrest was related to the poaching of a buffalo in the park in 1984. He objected to the failure of the park rangers to consult the Gazankulu police or the homeland's conservation section, and to the rangers' disregard for Gazankulu's jails and courts, "so that if there are fines they should be channeled to Gazankulu revenue as Gazankulu citizens are involved."[87]

Nxumalo and his subjects were among the communities expelled from the park to an adjacent place called Shangoni in the 1960s. His complaint brought to light the fact that the apartheid government used the homelands to give effect to indirect rule over Africans. It used homelands to outsource matters that had been the preserve of the Native Affairs Department, such as so-called native depredations. However, this outsourcing could not hide the fact that a key source of the depredations was political. As Nxumalo said:

> Gazankulu citizens were not placed at this place of their own liking but were forced by circumstances which came as a result of central Government Policy. The people would be much happier if a buffer zone would be there so that they cannot be accused of killing wild animals in the Kruger National Park.[88]

As Nxumalo's complaint made clear, Gazankulu and the KNP did not enjoy an organic relationship. They had to work at it, despite the existence of what some officials took to be natural affinities between the two. As a secretary for planning put it in a memorandum about how to improve relations between Gazankulu and the park:

> The land area which is now the Kruger National Park has partic-ularly strong significance for the Shangaan people — particularly the area north of Skukuza and up to Pafuri. Shangaan groups such as Makhuva and others once resided in the Park and were moved out of the Park by its first Warden, the celebrated Lieutenant-Colonel James Stevenson-Hamilton, not long after the turn of the century. The Park forms a wedge between the two Shangaan-Tsonga groups and is thus a natural part of the Shangaan/Tsonga interest zone. A large percentage of the Park's personnel are Shangaan/Tsonga people. Gazankulu also has a long common boundary with the Kruger National Park.[89]

The secretary said these elements pointed to a "natural requirement for closer and more constructive interaction" between the park and Ga-zankulu. But, since Gazankulu's founding in 1973 as a self-governing territory, that had not been the case. Park officials complained, for ex-ample, about the conduct of visitors from Gazankulu who went to the park "for other reasons than of game viewing. This occurred over week ends, and the making of music sometimes caused irritation to other vis-itors." Park warden Uys de V. Pienaar put this down to culture, saying the park "understood that there were differences in people's enjoyment of nature, but to obviate all cause of friction they were considering isolated picnic areas for day visitors."[90]

There were other "unfortunate incidents" — including the arrest of professional hunters in Letaba Ranch by park rangers — that had also bedeviled relations between Gazankulu and the park. Park officials were wary of Letaba Ranch because professional hunters would often lure animals from the park or take advantage of fences damaged by elephants to shoot animals from the park. This was jeopardizing the fu-ture of Letaba and the KNP. As the secretary said in his memorandum calling for cooperation between Gazankulu and the park:

> It is my opinion . . . that the various hunting operations along the Kruger Park boundary . . . whilst ostensibly money spinners,

are approaching the end of the bonanza with looming ecological crisis on the horizon. In order to be realistic we should not exclude [from the proposed joint management plan] Letaba Ranch where the situation is aggravated by the presence of the Army, potentially Manyeleti, and very definitely the whole strip of Gazankulu abutting on the Kruger Park's western boundary from this general observation. Not only are all these areas under-utilized at present from . . . the economic viewpoint of Gazankulu, but they represent areas with considerable potential for Gazankulu which have to be responsibly developed and managed with a view both to the present and the future.[91]

For Gazankulu, the problem with the South African military's occupation of the Letaba Ranch was that army officers had turned the ranch into their playground, hunting at will. Gazankulu officials wanted the military out of the ranch but had no way of making that happen. The secretary for planning suggested that by working closely with the National Parks Board, Gazankulu could use the "not inconsiderable" influence of the board to dislodge the army from the ranch. Gazankulu could also use the park, which was sourcing the majority of the curios sold in its shops from abroad, as a marketing outlet for local artists. These were not the only plans floated to improve relations between Gazankulu and the park.[92] In 1984 Ian MacFadyen, head of nature conservation in Gazankulu, approached the KNP with a proposal that the park organize an essay competition about the park for Gazankulu schoolchildren. The idea was for prize winners to visit the park for a wilderness trail experience. The park gave MacFadyen's idea its "wholehearted support." As park warden Uys de V. Pienaar said: "We will ensure that one of out [sic] best trail rangers accompany the group of children and that they get maximum wilderness exposure and conservation education during their stay."[93] In 1987 the National Parks Board proposed a joint educational project involving the park and Gazankulu. The board said the future of the lowveld depended on the educational awareness of the children in the region:

It is in this context that the National Parks Board considers a comprehensive educational program for all the children of the region as one of the soundest investments for the maintenance of the qualities of life and the qualities of the environment for this, and future, generations. It is also this responsibility which the National Parks Board wishes to honor and envisages one of the potentially most rewarding co-operative projects of its nature with the Gazankulu authorities.[94]

In practice, what the board wanted was to offload its educational activities on Gazankulu by turning Manyeleti into one of the "prime environmental education centers in the country." The board needed this because, while the KNP was drawing large numbers of tourists, Manyeleti was struggling to attract them. With the park attracting increasing numbers of schoolchildren, the board worried that it might not have enough room for them. As the board said, the park faced the "challenge of accommodating the increasing number of schoolchildren and young people wishing to visit the area and who constitute one of the prime target groups in terms of environmental conservation."[95]

The joint venture would be open to schoolchildren and to young people of all racial groups, in hopes of promoting "racial harmony." School groups taking part in the educational program would have access to the park while Gazankulu would reap all the financial rewards. Gazankulu supported the board's proposal but wanted to know whether this would mean the construction of a new camp in Manyeleti, whether the camp would be "multiracial," and whether the board would bear the costs of the new camp. Pienaar said the board would bear the cost. He went on:

> The first aim was to provide for Black children, and it was up to Gazankulu to decide whether White children were to use the facility. Multiracial children's attendance could become one of its major attractions and develop it into one of the greatest centers in the country.[96]

The proposal was part of a flurry of collaborative ventures, especially as apartheid neared its end. In October 1991, Gazankulu, Lebowa, and the Transvaal agreed to form a joint political and administrative authority to manage the lowveld's environment.[97] The agreement essentially endorsed Ntsanwisi's 1985 statement that the lowveld consisted of one ecosystem and had to be managed as such. The agreement allowed for joint decision-making over environmental matters affecting the three entities. It paved the way for the reintegration of Gazankulu and Lebowa into South Africa and the creation of a uniform conservation regime for the greater Transvaal after the end of apartheid.

However, there were other less salutary signs that change was afoot and that Ntsanwisi was perhaps losing his grip on Gazankulu. In June 1990, Ian MacFadyen wrote to Ntsanwisi's chief of staff to complain about poaching involving members of the Gazankulu government.[98] MacFadyen said that, in May 1990, Gazankulu rangers caught Chief Hlakene, a member of the homeland legislature, poaching in the government-owned Mbaula Ranch; Hlakene had killed an impala and a duiker. In June 1990, Gazankulu rangers at the Letaba Ranch arrested five men for poaching in the Mbaula Ranch. One of the men, F. Risenga, was Ntsanwisi's driver while another, Josef Maluleke, drove for Gazankulu's minister of health. "Because of the serious nature of the offences," MacFadyen said to his superior,

> I find myself in a very difficult position. Normally I would have directed my findings direct to the Gazankulu police. Due to the present sensitive political situation and as two of the officials are close to the Honorable Chief Minister I believed it necessary to refer the illegal hunting to yourself. Because of implications in the future to myself I believe it necessary to place on record that I have been told by yourself that I am not to proceed further with the legal proceedings as the Honorable Chief Minister will handle the matter.[99]

There the archival trace stops. We cannot say whether Ntsanwisi did act against Risenga and Risenga's accomplices. Ntsanwisi died of cancer in March 1993, and a year later, Gazankulu itself would be no more. In the 1990s the Mnisi, one of the Tsonga-speaking groups expelled from the Kruger area in the 1960s, lodged a claim for the return of Manyeleti Game Reserve to members of the group. The Mnisi won their claim and turned Manyeleti into a private game reserve. Gazankulu disappeared from the map, but Manyeleti lived on into postapartheid South Africa as an instance of what the Comaroffs call Ethnicity, Inc., a political project profiting from ethnic identities.[100]

7 ⤸ Beggar Thy Neighbor

ON JANUARY 21, 1954, *Advance,* a left-wing newspaper based in Johannesburg, ran a story headlined "I Am Not Prepared to Move."[1] Lugedlana Ngomane, a Swazi chief in Tenbosch, an African reserve to south of the KNP, was the man not prepared to move. The government had recently announced plans to move Ngomane and his people, known as the Ngomanes, from Tenbosch to a strip of land on the Lebombo flats, southeast of the park. The government wanted Ngomane and his people out of the way of the railway line that would connect Komatipoort to the Mozambican capital Maputo. The line, which linked the Transvaal to the Indian Ocean, ran through Ngomane's lands. Removal was a potent weapon in the arsenal of the National Party, in power since 1948. The party had used this weapon to make South Africa's map conform to the apartheid vision of racial separation.[2] The Ngomanes themselves were no strangers to removals. They were among the first Africans to be expelled from the KNP by Stevenson-Hamilton after 1902. As *Advance* reported:

> The tribe originally occupied the land now known as Skukuza, which is now part of the game reserve. They were removed at the beginning of the century in order to make place for the animals, and settled in the area from which they are now threatened with removal to the equivalent of Meadowlands, on the dry Lebombo Flats.[3]

Having been forced to make way for animals at the start of the twentieth century, Ngomane and his people were being compelled fifty years later to make way for the train, that potent symbol of modernity

212

and mechanical sign of the government's reach into the farthest corners of the country. Considered neither conservationists nor modern subjects by the government but pawns that could be moved at will to suit the whims of a modernizing state, Ngomane and his people appeared in the eyes of government officials to have been suspended in some legal and political limbo. But Ngomane challenged such a depiction. He spoke to *Advance* as a modern subject—voteless but not voiceless. "I personally am not prepared to move," Ngomane told *Advance.* "If the Government wants to sell the ground let it sell it to me."

Ngomane offered to buy because he believed that his land was Crown property, meaning it belonged to the government, and would be sold to European settlers and farmers after the Ngomanes' expulsion. However, in terms of Ngomane's letter of appointment as a government-recognized chief, Tenbosch was not on Crown land.[4] It was, in fact, owned by the South African Native Trust, a state agency set up by the 1936 Native Trust and Land Act to find and allocate land to Africans.[5] In terms of the act, so-called trust land could not be sold to Europeans. It could only be sold to Africans and held for them by the Native Trust. The place where the government wanted to move the Ngomanes was a dry tract with the nearest water about 10 miles away.

A councilor sent by Ngomane to reconnoiter the place had reported that the place was so dry that cattle only had water about once a week. The community had already moved once to make way for the KNP. It did not want to move again. But what choice did it have? The South African Institute of Race Relations, an outfit founded in part by John David Rheinhallt-Jones to bring about understanding between the races, took up the Ngomanes' case. In February 1954, institute director Quintin Whyte wrote to the secretary for native affairs to ask for the secretary's comments on Ngomane's interview with *Advance.*[6] When there was no response from the secretary to his initial letter, Whyte wrote again in March 1954, demanding a response.

The department finally responded on April 2, 1954, with what T. S. van Rooyen, the "chief journalist" of the department, called a "short historical survey which proves that the statement made in [*Advance*] are [*sic*] substantially incorrect."[7] Van Rooyen's survey bears quoting at length because it illustrates the ways in which officials of the Native Affairs Department used history to construct narratives of belonging and ownership that effectively delegitimized the Ngomanes' claims:

Certain Natives who originally lived in what is now the Kruger National Park and in Swaziland moved many years ago on to a piece of land called Tenbosch adjoining Komatipoort in the district of Barberton. Tenbosch at that time belonged to a European private land co. (Scrutton's Grant)

After the boundary between Swaziland and the Z.A.R. [South African Republic] was defined under article 1 of the Convention of Pretoria on the 3rd August 1881, the Republican Government allowed the Swazies [*sic*], together with the Shangaans, to live there. No provision for locations was made for them and their sojourn was therefore regarded as *temporary* [my emphasis] as the location act of 1885 prohibited more than five families per farm.

As a result of the war intervening, no further provision was made for them and their stay was kept in abeyance till 1936. When the Natives Trust and Land Act was passed in 1936 the aforementioned farm Tenbosch was included in a released area—i.e. an area which could be acquired by the South African Native Trust for Natives.[8]

Van Rooyen said the Native Trust expropriated Tenbosch in 1944 from its European owner. He added:

> The situation of this property is, however, such that it formed an isolated Native area within a European area, whereas on the other hand the other Native areas in the Barberton district formed one compact block. This Native area is about 30 miles south of Tenbosch. It was accordingly decided in the interests of the Natives as well as Europeans to consolidate the Native areas in one block. Compensating land comprising 20 farms of approximately 31,500 morgen adjoining the main Native area was provided by the Government as quid pro quo for the farm Tenbosch and which now has been excised from the Native area.[9]

Van Rooyen said that, by law, the compensating land had to be of equivalent pastoral and agricultural value as the land being taken away. He said each of the families making up Ngomane's community would receive about 31 morgen of arable, pastoral land. These plots were bigger than those currently occupied by the Africans already resident in the area where Ngomane and his people were being moved. "Furthermore," van Rooyen said, "the department has provided the necessary thatch and timber to enable those Natives removed to build their huts while the officials of the land department have been instructed to sink sufficient boreholes" to serve the families and their cattle.

Van Rooyen said that while it was true, as Ngomane had said in his *Advance* interview, that the Native Trust owned Tenbosch, it was untrue that Ngomane and his people were being moved to an arid piece of land to make way for a railway line. Van Rooyen concluded his letter thus:

> We can further state that this land [where the Ngomanes lived] in view of the above survey may neither be regarded as the traditional land of these Natives. Many of the Swazi still own [*sic*] allegiance to the Swazi king. Their sojourn can therefore never have been regarded as permanent and depended entirely on a final decision of the Minister. It is regarded as being in their own interest that they be moved to the new land where their stay would be regarded as permanent in the future.[10]

It is not clear from the archives whether the institute responded to van Rooyen's survey, but it is obvious how institute officials felt, judging by the marginalia they scribbled in their copy of van Rooyen's letter. One official wrote the following note for Whyte's attention: "Whether we agree with them or not, I think we should thank them cordially for this long and comprehensive reply." Just how much institute officials disagreed with van Rooyen can be gleaned from the notes scribbled by one official on the pages making up the correspondence between the institute and the Native Affairs Department.

The notes disputed van Rooyen's claims, especially the statement that the Ngomanes were temporary sojourners on the land in dispute. The official said that by van Rooyen's own calculations, the Ngomanes had been living on the land in question since 1881, meaning they had been there for seventy-three years at the time. "It is difficult to believe that settlement on a piece of land for this period can be regarded as temporary." The official also disputed van Rooyen's claim that Tenbosch was an isolated black spot in a white area, as the area had twice (in 1936 and 1944) been defined as a released area, meaning it had been set aside by the Native Trust and Land Act of 1936 for African settlement. Responding to van Rooyen's claim that the Ngomanes were foreigners who owed loyalty to the Swazi king and therefore not residents of South Africa, the official wrote: "These people may owe allegiance to the Swazi king but they are Union nationals and have been paying Union taxes all the time."[11]

It is also not clear whether these views made it into the institute's response to van Rooyen. Whatever the institute's response, it was not enough to prevent the removal. In the eyes of department officials, only bureaucrats such as van Rooyen had the expertise to know what was good for the Ngomanes. Despite Ngomane's protest, he and his people were indeed moved. In August 1954, government trucks took about seven thousand people to their new sites in the Lebombo flats, a place so arid "all you could grow was jugo beans."[12]

Charlie Mather says, "The trauma for this community was not unlike that experienced by millions of other dispossessed people in the South African countryside."[13] The removal forced the community to abandon its "houses, grain storage huts, agricultural plots, and ancestral grave sites." In the Lebombo flats, the Ngomanes occupied smaller plots, meaning they had to reduce their animal holdings. They also had to live on "brackish" borehole water. The result was "large, poverty-stricken rural villages."

However, like any community, the Ngomanes were not an undifferentiated mass. In fact, not every member of the community moved. Many poorer members remained on what had been their lands "to face new conditions as labor tenants or as fulltime laborers" on what had suddenly become white-owned farms.[14] This meant that the new (white) landowners gained both land and people in one bureaucratic move. But even here, the new tenants faced varying working conditions. Some worked for a wage while others entered into tenancy agreements with the new owners of their old lands. The owners actively sought to redefine the relationship between their African tenants and the land. Although "ownership did not necessarily mean control" for the new owners, some were in fact able to impose their command by "redefining the space of the farm by restricting practices on the land."[15]

They discouraged, for example, tenants' relatives and friends from visiting. They also restricted hunting, trapping, and certain farming practices. However, Mather cautions against seeing the Ngomanes' removal as simply the work of a "barbarous government," even if the National Party government was politically responsible for the act: "The squeezing of the Ngomane has far deeper roots and requires an explanation that is sensitive to the role of white farmers and different sections of the state bureaucracy."[16] More than the complexity noted by Mather, there is another fact worth noting: the removal of the Ngomanes from their land did not mean their removal from history. Descendants of Ngomane and his people continue to live in uneasy tension with the KNP. They have a relationship with the park marked by mistrust, rancor, and that old staple of relations between the park and its neighbors, depredations.

The formal end of apartheid and white rule in 1994 meant that the Africans whose villages abutted the park were citizens and no longer colonial subjects. But their history as colonial subjects haunted attempts by the park to slay the ghosts of the past in order to become a truly "national" park. As the stories of Ngomane's descendants below show, even after the end of apartheid, the KNP remained an "ambiguous symbol" for many of its neighbors.[17] The park might have tried to market itself as a truly national institution, but memories of the past, as well as official and social habits developed over a century, meant it was easier for conservation authorities in postapartheid South Africa to declare the park national than to make it such. The difficulty of transforming the park into a national institution stemmed from the legacy of the park's "racist and repressive history [which is] . . . refracted in the impoverished conditions of those descendent communities forcibly removed" from the park.[18] The KNP certainly tried to mend fences.

In April 1991 the park hosted Nelson Mandela, only a year after his release from prison and three months before his election as president of the ANC. The two-day stay was the first formal visit by a representative of the ANC to South Africa's premier wildlife sanctuary. The visit made Mandela the first black nationalist not connected to the homeland system to stay in the park. Long a playground of Afrikaner intellectuals and white nationalist elites, the KNP sought to use Mandela's visit to build relations with the politically ascendant African nationalist elite in a bid to secure a postapartheid future for itself. When Mandela visited the Kruger, he had just spent two weeks at a game reserve near the park called Mthethomusha as a guest of the KaNgwane Parks Board, the conservation arm of the Swazi-speaking Bantustan of KaNgwane. Enos Mabuza, the chief minister of KaNgwane who hosted Mandela at Mthethomusha, would go on to become, in September 1991, the first black member of the twelve-person National Parks Board.[19]

Mandela's two-week stay at Mthethomusha became more famous than his visit to the KNP because that was when he killed an impala and a blesbok—the latter hunt immortalized in the photograph that adorns the cover of this book.[20] The photograph, taken shortly after Mandela killed the blesbok, shows him and Jeremy Anderson, director of the KaNgwane Parks Board, in a typical hunters' pose, the two men leaning over Mandela's kill (see fig. 7.1). Coming at a time when most blacks could still not hunt legally, let alone own guns, and three years before the formal end of apartheid, Mandela's hunt and visit to the KNP marked for some the moment that black nationalism (in the person of Mandela himself) began making its peace with conservation, long identified with the marginalization of blacks in South Africa. The visit signaled the instant the "national" in KNP started expanding its conceptual limits to include blacks.

In 1992 the park hosted ANC leaders Oliver Tambo, Albertina Sisulu, Walter Sisulu, and Gertrude Shope, as well as Stanley Mokgoba, later president of the Pan Africanist Congress (see fig. 7.2). That same year, the ANC unveiled policy proposals regarding conservation and national parks in postapartheid South Africa. The organization called for the democratization of park management and for the use of protected areas to aid economic development. In August 1993 the National Parks Board hosted an ANC delegation in the KNP.[21] Over three days, meeting attendees agreed on the need to make national parks an integral part of South Africa's economic development policies, to transform wildlife sanctuaries into places accessible to all South Africans, to promote an environmental ethic, and to integrate local communities in the management of conservation areas. However, no amount of *toenadering* (Afrikaans for "rapprochement") between the ANC and the KNP could hide the fact that, if the park had any accounts to settle, those accounts were with communities such as the Ngomanes. No amount of peacemaking with the ANC could hide the fact that the people to whom the National Parks Board needed to make amends were real people from real communities—not abstract black victims of apartheid.

THE WEEKLY MAIL

The paper for a changing South Africa

R2,20 (R1,95 + 25c GST) ★ Southern Africa: R2,20 excl. tax ★Volume 7, Number 13. April 5 to April 11 1991

Mandela goes Green

A hunting trip converts the ANC leader to conservation

Story: EDDIE KOCH
Photos: JEREMY ANDERSON
and TONY FERRAR

THE picture on the left shows Nelson Mandela proudly posing with a blesbok he shot while on safari with game wardens from kaNgwane's wildlife department.

The African National Congress leader has developed a passionate interest in environmental issues since spending a two-week holiday at a Lowveld nature reserve hunting and learning about innovative approaches to nature conservation.

The kaNgwane Parks Board is renowned for its methods — including hunting and culling of overpopulated species — that allow nature conservation to be combined with rural development.

Mandela told The Weekly Mail, after returning to his office in Johannesburg this week, that he believed it was vital to promote environmental conservation and to devise new methods to protect this country's fast-dwindling plant and animal species.

He spent his annual leave at the Mthethomusha Game Reserve in kaNgwane and used the opportunity to hold extensive and wide-ranging discussions with some of the country's top ecologists.

"It is important for conservation and rural development to be combined," he said. "Nature conservationists must take into account the needs of people around the reserves. They need to encourage education programmes about protecting wildlife and always act in co-operation with the local communities."

The ANC deputy president also developed a passionate interest in hunting as kaNgwane conservation officials took him on safaris into the bush.

● To PAGE 2

Crack shot: Mandela and his host, ranger Jeremy Anderson (top picture), pose proudly with a blesbok

WHY FW IS HANGING ON TO MAGNUS Page 16 ☆ WHOSE RESEARCH: SCIENCE OR INDUSTRY? Page 19

FIGURE 7.1. "Mandela Goes Green," says headline in the *Weekly Mail* after Mandela goes hunting in the lowveld. *Source: Mail and Guardian*

MEMORIES OF HISTORY

The story of Ngomane's descendants recounted in this chapter illustrates both continuities and changes in the way the park relates to its neighbors. The story of the Ngomanes is by no means the story of all blacks. It is the story of one community and its dealings with the

FIGURE 7.2. Black political leaders visiting the KNP in 1992. *Left to right*: unnamed woman, Walter Sisulu, Mrs. Mokgoba, KNP official Gert Erasmus, Pan Africanist Congress leader Stanley Mokgoba, unnamed man, Oliver Tambo, unnamed man, and Albertina Sisulu. *Source*: SANParks Archive

park under colonialism, apartheid, and, post-1994, democratic rule in South Africa. Ngomane is a common last name, especially in the Swazi-speaking areas to the southwest and southeast of the KNP. The Ngomanes whose stories fill up the following pages are not necessarily blood relations of Chief Lugedlana Ngomane. They are descendants only to the extent that they belong to the same community of which he was a leader and, to that end, share a history with him. Their stories help us understand some of the relationships between blacks and the KNP in the twentieth century. The stories also bring to light the mediums—conflict, labor, uneasy coexistence—through which the KNP continues to mediate relations with its neighbors.

These mediums include ongoing struggles over animal depredations and poaching, the use of labor to give the Ngomanes and other communities a stake in the KNP's commercial enterprise, and the management of conflict over history between the park and its neighbors. What does the KNP owe those whose land was taken away for its creation? At the heart of this question lie deeper concerns about the multiple histories of South Africa as a political entity and the KNP as a conservationist enterprise, as well as the relationship between democracy and conservation. What have been the changes and continuities between colonial and apartheid rule, on the one hand, and democratic rule, on the other? In other words, what does the political transformation of blacks from natives to citizens mean, and what compensatory claims has this transformation made possible?

Second, to what extent should the KNP be held responsible for the political sins (expulsions, racial marginalization, etc.) of the past? Can this be done without undermining the park's existence as a conservationist enterprise? Questions about the relationship between democracy and conservation stem from debates in South Africa between conservationists, scholars, and politicians over whether conservation can shed its authoritarian past—one informed by logics of exclusion and marginalization?[22] In other words, can conservation be democratized? In 1993, Derek Hanekom, a senior member of the African National Congress even suggested that the park be dismantled.[23]

Hanekom said that the park would be more useful to its neighbors if it were turned into grazing ground for local domestic herds. Howls of protest greeted Hanekom's proposal. But the protesters could not come up with solutions fair to both local communities and the park's denizens. The protesters took the virtue of conservation to be self-evident. They would not engage with the substance of Hanekom's argument about what the park had meant to its neighbors during the twentieth century. However, the stories that follow show that there are no clear answers to the questions above. South Africa has undergone such dramatic change over the course of the second half of the twentieth century that even though this book is about that century, it would be incomplete unless it considered the complex ways in which history makes the present.

An examination of the park's ethnographic present shows that past decisions and their effects are still being felt. More than that, however, an examination of the park's contemporary history brings to the fore Africans in their own voices as citizens. Looking at the park's ethnographic present means we can study the park from the point of view of its African neighbors. This is not to suggest that the neighbors' own versions of history are innocent. But, to borrow a phrase from Jane Carruthers, we need to look at the KNP from "the other side of the fence" in order to fully understand its social history.[24]

Sometime in the early 1990s, a pride of lions broke out of the south-western section of the KNP, near the Numbi Gate. The lions killed a number of cattle belonging to African farmers living near the park. This was a regular occurrence and local farmers were used to it. They were also used to the fact that the park did not pay compensation for crops or livestock destroyed by its animals. However, the early 1990s were a different time in South Africa. Nelson Mandela was out of prison, the ANC had been unbanned, and apartheid looked to be on its deathbed. Change was in the air. Even communities long used to being given short shrift wanted to experience that change.

So, instead of shrugging their shoulders as they had been doing for decades each time park animals destroyed their crops and livestock, the farmers decided to fight back. They loaded the carcasses of the cattle killed by the lions onto the back of a tractor and drove to the Numbi Gate, where they showed the remains to park officials and demanded compensation. Elmon Mthombothi, a local farmer who helped drive the tractor that day, said of the park officials he and his comrades met at the gate: "They would not listen to us. They told us: *Terug. Gaan weg. Dis nie ons sake nie. Gaan eet jou beeste.* (Back. Go away. This is not our business. Go and eat your cattle.)"[25] The farmers did indeed return home. But they had, in a sense, broken the spell. They had staged their first direct and public protest against the KNP. Recalling the attitude of the park's white officials, Mthombothi said: "They did not care." But the farmers had had enough. "We decided this couldn't go on."

Asked what emboldened the farmers to confront the park, Mthombothi pointed to the year 1990, when South Africa started on the difficult road to political freedom. "The year 1990 had an influence," he said. "I am quite sure about that. . . . [The year] had an influence because there was change. If the country was changing, the Kruger National Park also had to change." Park officials could also see that apartheid would soon become a thing of the past, meaning that the park had to find new ways of relating to its African neighbors and the new political order. According to Salomon Joubert, the KNP's last white warden and the man at the helm when apartheid began to unravel, the park accepted an invitation in 1993 to join the Community and Parks Liaison Committee, which brought together African farmers, officials from the black homelands adjacent to the park, conservationists, and the private sector. The committee sought to mend fences between the park and its neighbors.[26]

In Mthombothi's recollection, park officials went to the first meeting keen to discuss the future; African farmers went there to talk about the past. The farmers wanted to talk about the damage done to crops and livestock by park animals. Mthombothi, a small-scale farmer in an area called Makoko, said one practice particularly incensed the farmers: "If lions go outside the park, they are not the park's responsibility. But the funny thing is, snare the lions and you get arrested." Joubert also remembered this, as well as the necessity to share the park's economic riches with neighboring communities, as some of the issues raised at the meeting. Attendees resolved to form community forums to link the park and its neighbors. The body formed for Mthombothi's area, in the southwestern corner of the park, was called the Lubambiswano forum. It was launched in November 1993, with Mthombothi as chairman.

FROM SOCIAL ANTAGONISM TO SOCIAL ECOLOGY

According to Joubert, the idea of community forums came from the park and was part of its attempts to rebrand and reorient itself toward the communities it had spent the better part of the twentieth century neglecting.[27] However, Mthombothi remembered the origins of the idea differently: "It was a community initiative because we were experiencing problems with the Kruger National Park. . . . Farmers did not look at the Kruger National Park as something to be enjoyed— lions, elephants, hyenas" were breaking out of the park and destroying fields and livestock.[28] But in the 1990s, the park seemed determined to change.[29] It allowed local traders to sell their wares inside the park and created special educational programs whereby local schoolchildren could visit for free. It also gave local communities special permits to visit the park outside popular holiday times, such as winter and summer holidays.

The permits cost half of what South Africans living away from the park paid and a fraction of what it cost international tourists to enter. Local chiefs distributed the permits. Chiefs, their headmen, and executive members of forums such as Lubambiswano could enter for free. The park also allowed people with ancestral graves inside the park to visit the graves, mainly at Easter. People who wanted to visit graves had to inform the park in advance, and the park arranged for a ranger escort on the appointed day. The park also established a nursery to cultivate medicinal plants that traditional doctors could harvest. Additionally, the forums were invited to help interview the park's first head of the Social Ecology Unit, set up in 1994 to build positive relations between the park and its neighbors.[30] The creation of the unit marked a significant change in the KNP's conservation philosophy. It signaled an acceptance by park officials that the KNP was part of a wider social and political ecosystem in which humans—especially the African communities living adjacent to the park—were a key part. The unit's creation meant, at least on paper, that the park had finally accepted that its African neighbors were not a problem but instead potential partners in the conservation enterprise. However, this did not mean that the park had necessarily changed its attitude toward its neighbors. In fact, some park officials saw the unit's establishment as nothing more than a cosmetic sop to South Africa's new rulers.[31]

Described by South African National Parks (SANP) as a "strategy and process that conveys the philosophy and approach of the SANP to neighboring communities and establishes mutually beneficial dialogues and partnerships with these communities," the field of social ecology sought to give the park's neighbors a voice in park-related matters.[32] The strategy sought to ensure that the views of local communities were "taken into account to the largest extent possible . . . [and] that the Parks' existence is a direct benefit to neighboring communities."

Although the strategy did not democratize the management of the KNP—as the qualifying phrase "to the largest extent possible" quoted above shows—it did allow park officials to present themselves as good neighbors prepared to listen. However, some park officials worried that the strategy risked turning the park into a development agency. They worried that the park might be asked to do things it could not do. The biggest change for the farmers was the park's agreement to compensate them for livestock destroyed by animals from the park. The parties agreed on R500. But when the figure was first agreed to in the early 1990s, the going rate for a cow was R4,000 and for a sheep or goat, about R1,000. Why agree to a compensation figure that bore no relation to market prices? "It was a random decision," Mthombothi said. "But farmers were happy because it was better than nothing. This was a sensitive item on the agenda [of forum meetings with the park]. We would spend hours talking about it." It is not clear why the KNP or the

Lubambiswano forum thought that such an arbitrary and uneconomical arrangement could hold. As Mthombothi said, the farmers were only too grateful to get something. The park possibly saw the arrangement as something with which to mollify poor African farmers who had a list of grievances going back generations. The arrangement did not hold. It collapsed in the most dramatic way possible.

MAN EATS LIONS

On March 23, 1997, the *Sunday Times* carried a story headlined "Villagers Kill and Eat Four Kruger Park Lions." Reporter Mzilikazi wa Afrika wrote: "The villagers of Makoko Trust do not usually kill and eat lions. But they were desperate—and angry. They claimed that eight of their cattle had been killed by lions in two weeks and said that the man who put an end to the reign of terror was a hero." Samson Ngomane, a descendant of chief Lugedlana Ngomane, was the hero of the piece. KNP officials blamed the residents of Makoko for allowing the lions to leave the park. They accused the villagers of tearing down 500 meters of the reserve's fence to use for housing and to protect crops. Samson Ngomane told the *Sunday Times*, "We have no idea where the reserve fence went. It is the officials' fault that these animals were killed because they took so long to fix the fence. What are we supposed to do when lions and elephants come onto our land and destroy our livelihood?" Ngomane trapped the lions by creating a tunnel made up of barbed wire and logs, with goat meat, placed at the far end of the tunnel, as bait. As each lion went into the tunnel, in hopes of grabbing the meat, the logs would collapse on it, breaking its back and killing it. Ngomane killed four lions in this fashion. He told the *Sunday Times*, "When we heard the police were coming, we decided to eat the meat, in the hope that it would send a message to other lions that there was only death for them here." The lion meat was rancid and tasted awful.

The police did indeed come, courtesy of the park. A spokesman for the park said, "These people have only themselves to blame. Every year we lose thousands of rands because of damaged fences and poached game." About one hundred policemen in two armored trucks and police vans descended on Makoko, surrounded it, and searched every house. Police captain Barkies Barkhuizen told the *Sunday Times*, "We were armed because we were told the villagers had weapons and would resist our search. But we found no firearms or other dangerous weapons during the search." The confrontation between the police and the community ended without incident. The police captain's relief at finding no guns spoke to a history of official paranoia about Africans with guns that went back to the earliest days of colonial conquest. Colonial authorities and the apartheid state did not want Africans armed independently with guns. The idea of Africans with guns was threatening because it suggested something subversive and therefore a threat to the state. It spoke of freedom and agency, something that called into question the state's monopoly over the means of violence. In the case of the park, the fear of Africans with guns gained added urgency because of the role played by guns in the decimation of South Africa's fauna. In terms of the law, Africans could indeed do whatever it took to protect their livestock and crops. But they could not rely on that law to protect them or their property. Even though the law had been on the books for more than a century, Africans' recourse to it had always been limited. Africans who destroyed wildlife to protect their property ran the risk of being branded poachers. However, the changes that took place in the 1990s meant that Africans could take their chances with the law in bolder fashion than they had done before.

This entailed, in the case of Samson Ngomane and the residents of Makoko, a spectacular form of protest that not only destroyed park animals but also reduced them to food. Ngomane told the *Sunday Times* that he ate the lions to draw strength from them. He was also signaling a profound political change that would lead, at the close of the first decade of the twenty-first century, to the rejection of some of the decisions taken in the early 1990s as the park sought to mend fences with its neighbors. On April 29, 2009, the Lubambiswano forum told park officials it would no longer accept the R500 compensation policy. The forum said it would henceforth only accept R8,000 per cow, and R1,000 each per goat or pig. The forum threatened to lodge a lawsuit unless the park met its demands. The park rejected the forum's demands. In January 2010 the forum filed a lawsuit against the park, demanding R1.3 million for more than 115 cattle killed by park animals since 2006.

According to Enos Ngomane, a farmer in Makoko and younger brother of Samson Ngomane, the claim did not count the sheep, goats, pigs, chickens, and pets such as dogs killed by park animals since 2006.[33] Cases from the village of Makoko listed in the lawsuit included the following:

- On September 14, 2007, lions killed three cattle, one of which was about to calve, belonging to Ngomane.
- On September 18, 2007, lions killed a cow belonging to a Lekhuleni family.
- On September 26, 2007, lions killed a cow belonging to the Sambo family.
- On September 28, 2007, lions killed a cow belonging to a man named Lubisi.
- On March 18, 2008, lions killed two cattle belonging to Amos Lekhuleni.

Lekhuleni, a former mineworker, bore the brunt of the misfortune visited on Makoko by the park. In September 2001 he lost his wife Eslina Sithebe to a fire that killed twenty-four people and destroyed a huge section of the park. Sithebe was a seasonal temporary worker in the park hired to cut grass used to thatch the park's tourist facilities. The same fire cost Amos's younger brother Moses Lekhuleni, a ranger at the park, eight fingers. In October 2007 a lion attacked Amos while he was looking for his cattle outside the park. Amos was with a neighbor, Elliot Mgwenya, outside the park when a male lion hidden behind tall grass in the bush pounced on him. "It jumped at me, bit into my arm and looked at me as I fell back," Amos said. "It then let go of my arm, peed on the ground and left. I was scared."[34] People and cattle were not the only ones terrorized by the park's lions. Grace Leyane, a farmer and one of Ngomane's neighbors, said she had lost three dogs to leopard attacks.[35] The lions that terrorized Makoko in late 2007 and early 2008 were a pride of five that had escaped from the park through a hole in the park's fence created when severe floods in 2000 damaged the park's infrastructure. A train on a line that runs adjacent to the park killed one of the lions; park rangers shot another dead, and a third was caught and returned to the park, but two ran away.

Enos Ngomane, who lived 600 meters from the park's southwestern fence, said that although domestic livestock had always been attacked by park animals, the attacks in 2007 were the worst he had experienced. "The cause is the fence," he said. "The fence collapsed in 2000 with the floods but has not been fixed." Ngomane was critical of the park and its R500 compensation: "It does not even buy a goat. You can't even buy groceries." He objected to the way the park had dealt with

Africans over the years. "It's oppressing us. We love the Kruger but it's oppressing us." Mthombothi, however, also blamed neighboring communities for some of the problems between them and the park: "We have some problems coming from the community. Elephants felled the fence and people started looting it. The fence was completely destroyed. We tried as a forum to call the community where the fence was looted but the [local] chief was not supportive. People don't respect the fence."

But the park's relations with its neighbors were not limited to the other side of its fence. They also extended to an archaic and paternalistic labor relations regime that had survived the end of apartheid. The features of this system came to the fore through the worst human disaster in the park's history: the fire that killed Eslina Sithebe and twenty-three others.[36] The system—patriarchal and gendered in the extreme—assumed essentially that every nonmale African in the lowveld was a legal minor. This meant, for example, that men handled employment negotiations on behalf of "their" women, that the park recruited female laborers through local chiefs, and that female employees— whom the park started hiring in big numbers in 1977—had no standing independent of their chiefs, fathers, or uncles. The 2011 fire tragedy laid this bare.

FIRE AND CHANGE

On September 4, 2001, a fire—probably started by a cigarette discarded by a tourist—swept through the Pretoriuskop area, in the southwestern part of the park. The fire claimed twenty-four lives, killed thirty elephants and four rhinos, and destroyed a hiking trail. Among the dead were nineteen women and five men, including four field rangers. The fire raged for four days and burned 45,000 hectares of the park's 2-million-hectare land surface. But the fire did more than destroy life and scorch the environment. It also exposed a labor relations regime that had not changed much despite seven years of democracy. Once the charred bodies had been removed, the injured had been ferried to hospital, the smoke had cleared, and the last embers had died out, the public and park authorities were confronted with the fact that little had changed for the park's neighbors employed by the park. The advent of democracy in 1994 might have transformed the nineteen women killed in the fire from subjects to citizens. But it had not changed their material circumstances. The park had a rich research history on the use of fire as a management tool going back to 1954, when it initiated systematic experimental burns on four blocks carved out of the four main vegetation types of the park.[37] The park's rich research history, coupled with the natural prevalence of fire in the southern African savanna, meant that the park had one of the "most comprehensive fire records for any ecosystem in the world."[38] The park had a lot of experience in the study and handling of fires. But its bias toward tourists and its archaic labor relations regime meant that, when it was confronted with the worst fire in its history, it prioritized the protection of tourists over its staff. The park had dealt with fire disasters before. In 1954 a "series of disastrous conflagrations" destroyed 517,997 hectares, a fourth of the total area of the park.[39] The fires killed and injured forty animals, including six elephants, two lions, twelve impala, and ten kudu.

In fact, some of the animals had to be put down by park staff because of their injuries. On February 2, 1968, a dry thunderstorm led to seven fires inside the park. Only four of the seven could be put out in time. The rest caused serious damage. In total, the park experienced a record twenty-five fires, all caused by lightning, between April 1967 and March 1968. In 1972–73 the park experienced an "unprecedented number of accidental fires" that affected a third of the park.[40] In 1977, an electrical short caused a fire that destroyed the historic home of James Stevenson-Hamilton. In October 1996 the park experienced the worst fire in forty years. The fire, sparked by lightning, lasted five days and destroyed 200,000 hectares. In 2000 the park lost a field ranger to fire. Then came September 2001. The 2001 fire was the worst in terms of lives lost. The park had lost rangers to animals and poachers' bullets before; it had lost staff to predators and suffered numerous fires and other disasters throughout its history. In February 2000 the park suffered the worst floods on record, forcing it to shut down for more than a month for the first time in its history. The floods, caused by cyclone activity along Mozambique's coast, destroyed infrastructure and swept hundreds of animals along the park's rivers and into the Indian Ocean. But the park had not lost human lives on this scale before. Never before had it lost twenty-four employees, full-time or temporary, in one go. That is what made the disaster the worst in the history of the park. However, as journalists and a commission appointed by government to look into the causes of the disaster found, the tragedy could have been avoided. Chief Magistrate David Ngobeni, who chaired the government-appointed commission of inquiry into the tragedy, said there was more than one "atmosphere and climate" to explain the tragedy.[41]

The nineteen women who died on September 4, 2001, were among a group of thirty-seven in the park cutting thatching grass for use in the park's facilities, especially its African-style round-hut tourist chalets. The women were on three-month contracts and were paid 47 South African cents a bundle; on average each woman harvested 1,050 bundles a week. They had no benefits and were each subject to the different chiefs whose fiefdoms lie outside the park. Asked how they were recruited, one of the survivors of the fire, Linah Leyane, said, "The Kruger would tell the chief it was looking for people to cut grass; the chief would tell us."[42] The institution of cutting grass in the Kruger had been around for twenty-five years by 2001. Some of the grass cutters had been doing the job for five years or more. Linah Leyane inherited the job from her mother. Her mother had been cutting grass for years before she got too old and passed the job on to her daughter. Cutting grass was backbreaking work. The women used sickles and spent an entire day bent over double, cutting grass into the recommended bundles. The grass cutters had been working in the park that year since July 2001 and were about to leave when disaster struck.

They were staying in a tented camp, one of many temporary campsites used specifically once a year by grass cutters. In terms of precedent, the park was supposed to clear and grade an area of about 150 meters by 80 meters for the cutters' campsite. The women's tents were supposed to be pitched in two rows no closer than 5 meters to the perimeter of the graded area to protect them from wildfires. The park had to provide a 5,000-liter water tank, to be filled every second day. The park was also supposed to provide food rations, toiletries, and essential medicines such as antimalarial tablets, plus paraffin lamps and firewood. The thatching area, where the harvest was stocked, was meant to be away from the campsite, separated by a firebreak or a firebreak road. The park was supposed to station a ranger at the campsite to protect the women from dangerous animals.

However, an area only about 75 meters by 29 meters had been graded, and the firebreak road was less than the recommended 5 meters in width. The graded area was insufficient, such that some of the tents were pitched atop a grass patch. The space between the tents and where the harvested thatch was stored was not graded. The women told Shadrack Mhlanga, the headman watching over and supposedly protecting the women, that the campsite was unsafe. Mhlanga did not have a firearm or a two-way radio. "The reason why they felt unsafe was because of the fact that the place was not graded," said Ngobeni.[43] The women were also not provided with a first-aid kit, meaning that if they got injured during work they would have to wait until the following day for the truck that transported the harvested thatch to take them to the hospital or a doctor. The camp was situated deep in the bush and the women could hear wild animals roaring every night. This forced them "to do drum beating for their safety." As Ngobeni said in his report, "They were fortunate because there were no casualties ever experienced caused by wild animals."[44]

The Pretoriuskop area, where the women were stationed, is made up of savanna woodland, one of the major veld types of the park. Savanna woodland occurs mostly on sandy soils. The area enjoys a mean annual rainfall of about 706 millimeters and has been subjected to autumn burnings since the late 1800s. The dominant tree species are *Dichrostachys cinerea*, subspecies *nyassana*, and *Terminalia sericea*. There is minimal shrub cover, and sour grass, which many grazers dislike because they find it unpalatable, dominates. The park had had higher than average rainfall in 2000, and the place where the grass cutters and their camp were sited had had no fire, deliberate or natural, in the previous three years.

According to Ngobeni, "The evidence shows very clearly that the fire commenced in the vicinity of Napi Boulders which is one of the areas frequently visited by tourists."[45] Ngobeni said that although arson and negligence were likely the causes of the fire, "there is no evidence to identify who specifically set the fire alight." The commission might not have been able to identify the source of the fire, but it did know that September 4, 2001, was the second-worst, if not the worst, day on record for possible runaway veld fires.

However, Ngobeni said, the park did not have the capacity to fight fires. Park employees who knew how to fight fires had only received "on-the-job training," meaning that there was no formal training given to park employees to fight fires. Ngobeni found that even the rangers, the park's first responders, were ill-equipped to fight fires: "They have undergone military-style training with an emphasis on physical fitness, weapons handling, decision-making in the field and interpretation of natural phenomena, namely plants and animals."[46] Firefighting was not a part of their training. What training they had was on the job, just as it was for laborers hired by the park to help fight its perennial fires.

It did not help matters, on that day, that three of the four first field rangers to respond to the fire as it swept toward the grass cutters' campsite did not have adequate equipment. They did not have fireproof clothing, and they had between them one handheld radio whose battery died just as they were responding to the fire. They also did not have firefighting respirators, safety goggles, leather boots, or firefighting equipment such as rakes and fire beaters, first-aid kits, and sufficient water tanks.

The tragedy can be said to have really started, however, when four rangers were first mobilized to fight the fire. The rangers knew there were thirty-seven people in the middle of the bush cutting grass and that these people needed evacuation. But the rangers did not see this as their first priority. Their first priority was the Hlangweni Breeding Camp, a facility in the southwest of the park used to breed rare antelope. Their second priority was to evacuate the Napi Trails Camp, which had a group of tourists staying in it. The grass cutters were the last priority. Even though the breeding camp was a low-risk area because the surrounding area had already been burnt out, the rangers proceeded anyway to start back burns. These are fires set to deprive an oncoming fire of fuel material.

"The evacuation of the grass cutters," Ngobeni said, "was never an issue that was discussed as an alternative precautionary measure to be considered for its possible implementation."[47] By the time the rangers made it to the women, it was too late. The fire had got faster, stronger, and deadlier. Lorraine Khumalo, one of the survivors, told Ngobeni's commission:

> The wind was blowing very strongly immediately when it had changed from blowing from west to east to east to west. In some of their tents they [the women] could not open and in some tents they tried to fasten not to be taken by the wind. Some were blown away and rolling with the wind. The fire was coming towards their direction. The amount of the fire smoke increased,

that at one stage they could not see each other. They were screaming and they could feel the heat. The rangers arrived and ordered them out.[48]

Ngobeni noted that whereas the rangers went out of their way to evacuate tourists from the Napi Trail Camp and the bush *braai* (grilling) area, they did not seem anxious to get the women out: "The most surprising factor was that the very same thinking was not exercised when it came to the protection of the human lives of the grass cutters."[49] By the time the first four rangers made it to the women's camp, they had no choice but to enlist the women's support in fighting what had become a raging fire. The women had to fetch water in their buckets to try to help the rangers start a back burn. The only water available was from the tank used by the women for their cooking, drinking, and washing needs. Neither the rangers in their regular uniforms nor the women had any fireproof clothing.

There was also only one vehicle available to ferry the women out when the fire caught their camp at about 8:00 p.m. Ngobeni said the rangers should have immediately understood the danger posed by the fire and evacuated the women as soon as they could, instead of prioritizing sections that were not in danger. "The strength of the fire revealed from the outset that human force could not fight such fire. The only option was to give way and the probable accepted approach was to evacuate them," said Ngobeni.[50] Looking back at the events that led to the disaster, Ngobeni found that problems began with the confusion caused by whether or not the smoke that people started seeing at about 8:00 a.m. that morning was from a controlled burn or not.

Some people assumed it was and thus did not act, losing the park crucial time in its response. Ngobeni found that while there was a fire management policy in place, there was no fire security policy at the time of the disaster. The park was used to dealing with the controlled, natural, or anthropogenic fires endemic to the park, but there had "always been different procedures or practices in combating such fires."[51] The fire that swept through the park on September 4, 2001, was different from the fires the park was used to. As Ngobeni said:

> To manage fire, the park is divided into ±400 burning blocks, separated by graded fire breaks and tourists roads. A total of

890km for tarred roads, 1742km dirt roads and 5700km graded management roads which are used to facilitate fire management in the park. A total of 22 section rangers, 220 field rangers and 132 laborers are responsible to implement this adopted procedure which had become a policy. It must be noted that this human resource capacity covers the whole of the Kruger National Park which indeed is a vast area.[52]

For all its history with fire, the park proved incapable of dealing with a fire that threatened not its famous flora and fauna but the people who worked deep in the bush, behind the scenes, as it were, to help the park maintain its "pristine" wildlife status. But what of the women affected by the fire? How did they experience the disaster? What did they see? The women came from Shangaan- and Swazi-speaking villages, and they arranged themselves according to village and language. The Shangaans stayed with other Shangaans; Swazis shared tents with fellow Swazis. There was a simple logic to this.

A GENDERED LABOR REGIME

The Swazis tended to come from the same villages; likewise with the Shangaans. The women had a basic routine during their time in the bush. They would wake up at about 7:00 a.m. and make fires to heat up water for food. They were provided with maize meal, for the staple pap, and tinned vegetables. This is what they had for breakfast, lunch, and supper. They would then start cutting grass or tying their bundles at 8:00 a.m. and would go on until lunchtime, when they would stop for some more pap and vegetables. They would then continue until 4:00 p.m., when they would retire to their camp to cook supper. They were usually in their tents by 5:00 p.m. Linah Toropo Lekhuleni, one of the survivors, said: "It was a Tuesday. We saw fire in the distance. We never thought it would come to the camp. At sunset, it came for us. It burnt our friends. It destroyed them."[53] Lekhuleni had been cutting grass for four years. Asked whether she knew what caused the fire, Lekhuleni, seventy at the time, said: "We don't know what caused the fire. No one knows what caused the fire." She said chaos ensued when the fire swept through the camp at about 7:00 p.m.: "We tried running. There was fire everywhere. I tried to run back to the tent to get my pass (identity document). I got my pass but fell and the fire caught me. I had fire coming out of my mouth. I ran to the water tank. We were pouring water on each other." Lekhuleni said she did not know what made her decide, after first following some of her colleagues who ran into the bush, to turn back and return to her tent to retrieve her document. "I can't say what made me remember my pass. I had started to run into the bush but turned and the fire came with me. Maybe it's God, I can't tell. I can't say what saved me. I was about to follow the others but something told me to turn back." Lekhuleni said she saw some of her colleagues climbing up trees to escape the fire, "but the fire dragged them down."

For her, the disaster was connected to the political and staffing changes that had taken place at the park since the end of apartheid: "I don't know why this happened. It never used to happen under whites." Lekhuleni, who suffered second-degree burns on her arms, was offered R5,000 in compensation, the same amount given to every survivor (families who lost relatives in the fire were given R10,000). She said she and her fellow survivors had fought for a bigger compensation amount, to no avail. "We even went to the chief. We don't get a straight story. He is friends with Mabunda [the Kruger's director at the time of the fire]. We went after this thing. We have given up." Lekhuleni was not the only one who might have been saved by the fact that instead of running into the bush, she ran back to her tent to retrieve her identity document. Another cutter, Anisi Mashego, also survived possibly because she decided to try to save her identity document:

> When I saw the fire coming I just ran to my tent to fetch my ID book. Then I ran away. I didn't know what to do or where to go. Everybody was running around. I saw the toilet and tried to get in but the door wouldn't open. Then I saw the rangers' bakkie [truck] and I ran through the fire to get to it. I lay in the bakkie until the fire had passed.[54]

Here is how Asya Nkuna, another survivor, remembered the day of the disaster:

> · We woke up on a Tuesday and started fastening bundles. At about 8am we saw smoke rising from Napi. We could see it going up, going up but we continued fastening. By 4pm we saw

the wind turning in our direction and smoke coming towards us at speed. We asked the Kruger park's truck driver if the fire was not coming towards us. He said it was under control. By 5pm the smoke was coming towards us. We decided to cook quickly (pap and tinned beans), killed our cooking fires and got into our tents. We were woken up by sirens from a rangers' truck. We grabbed rakes and water containers. The fire was dancing. I tried to get into the rangers' truck but it was full of Shangaans. [I went to the water tank] and we were pouring water on each other. Our clothes had melted on our skins.[55]

Nkuna said she had never seen a fire like that before. She suffered severe burns on her arms and legs. She spent a month and a half in the hospital. "I could not eat. I had to be fed." Nkuna said park officials would not call ambulances to ferry the injured to the hospital. Instead, they were put in trucks. What's more, some of the victims' relatives could see the fire from beyond the park's boundaries, and as soon as word spread that people had died in the fire, locals started flocking to the park's Numbi Gate to see if they could get in. The park and its neighbors are so close to each other that outsiders could see what was going on. "The Kruger would not let people in," Nkuna said. "People had to force their way in. They found us hungry."

Among those who forced their way into the park was Amos Lekhuleni. His wife of twenty years, Eslina Sithebe, was among the grass cutters, and Lekhuleni wanted to know if she had survived. He was home when he saw smoke rising over the area that he knew his wife was cutting grass in: "I saw smoke at about noon. I saw the wind coming this way and then turning back that way."[56] Lekhuleni said he and a neighbor drove to the Numbi Gate. "The rangers would not let us in. They told us to wait at the gate. We saw ambulances taking people out. The rangers wanted to know who told us about the fire. They said they wanted to get the dead and injured out first before telling us."

It took Lekhuleni two weeks to identify his wife's remains. He had been going to the mortuary, looking at charred bodies, trying to identify his wife. He was about to give up when he noticed a melted piece of a rubber boot on one of the bodies. It was part of the boots his wife had been wearing when she cut grass. "Doctors were telling us to get used to our wives' teeth, saying that's how you identify them." Lekhuleni wanted to bury his wife in the village of Makoko, which lost eight women and one ranger to the fire. But park officials insisted on a mass burial. "I wanted to bury her here. The Kruger said there was to be one burial. They're making money with their graves. They benefitted. We did not."

Linah Leyane, another survivor, remembers the omen that preceded the big fire. She says that two weeks before the big fire, two lions attacked the grass cutters' camps. The women managed to chase the lions away by beating on pots and drums and shouting. "We thought we were dying. It's as if those lions knew that death was approaching." Leyane, for whom this was a third tour of cutting grass in the Kruger and who inherited the job from her mother, said the job made them a part of the landscape for some tourists: "We sing when we cut grass to keep the animals away. Tourists would come by and take pictures of us. They would ask us to load up the grass and take pictures. Whites would come and ask us to put loads together."[57] Moses Lekhuleni, another survivor, had been a ranger for six years at the park when he lost eight fingers in the fire. This is how he remembered the fire:

> The fire started between 9h00 and 10h00 by Napi Boulders. There were people conducting fire research. The fire got out of control because of the wind. It was our job to put in back burns. We started in Hlangweni. Four rangers split up along the Skukuza road, others joined us to start back burns. Four of us went to join up with the thatch cutters. But first we went to tell tourists having a bush braai to get out. There was a fire raging. At about 5pm or 6pm we were busy with back burns but the head wind jumped and the head fire was too close. We had nowhere to run. The place was not graded. We ran into the bush. Everyone was running in whichever direction. We could not see where we were running.[58]

Lekhuleni climbed atop a tree. Fortunately for him, there was no fuel load at the bottom of the tree. A white rhino had been grazing in the area and had eaten the grass cover. The fire passed him by. "There was no grass so the fire went past," he said. "I got down to help the women. I was wearing a green lumber jacket. I rolled up the jacket into a ball around my arm and tried to put out the fire by beating it.

But I fanned it." That is when he lost the eight fingers. He spent three weeks in an intensive care unit. Lekhuleni blamed the Kruger's failure to grade properly the site of the cutters' camp:

> The graded place was too small and it was not graded properly. Perhaps they did not want to disturb nature. If they had graded a bigger place, this would not have happened. If the fire had been reported earlier and the rangers told to get a truck to evacuate the women, this tragedy would not have happened. If the Kruger had called the firefighters from Nelspruit [the capital of Mpumalanga Province, where half of the Kruger lies], this would have been stopped.[59]

Lekhuleni was scathing about the way the Kruger treated the survivors and the families of the deceased. "The Kruger did not treat people well. It made promises that were not kept. It promised to give the children of the deceased work but there's no work. Some people have not received compensation." He said he had been denied his insurance payout. At first, the park, which kicked him off its payroll in June 2007, would not support his insurance claim. When it eventually did, the insurer, Old Mutual, said his claim was too old and could not be settled. Lekhuleni said it was not lack of experience that defeated the rangers who tried to deal with the fire of September 4, 2001: "We were used to big fires. The difference was the wind. The fire was too big to be fought by humans."

The question of experience raised by Lekhuleni goes to the heart of the political "atmosphere and climate" in which the fire occurred. The disaster came amid an unpopular corporate restructuring and retrenchment process at the Kruger. In fact, Solidarity, a union representing white workers at the park, was quick to blame the tragedy on affirmative action. The union said that experienced white workers had been let go and replaced with inexperienced black workers. It said this was a big contributing factor to the park's poor handling of the disaster. However, as Lekhuleni points out, experience was not at issue for the rangers who attended to the fire. They certainly made bad calls, but these were not due solely to their alleged lack of experience. They were also actors in a tragic historical drama—one with no clear ending, as the following chapter shows.

8 ⌒ The Road to the Kruger National Park

WHEN THE KNP celebrated its centenary on March 26, 1998, with South African president Nelson Mandela as the keynote speaker, South Africa was a different country from what it had been in 1898, when Paul Kruger's South African Republic proclaimed the Sabi Game Reserve into existence. The republic, whose constitution forbade equality between Africans and Europeans in matters of church and state, had long disappeared from the face of the earth. It had been replaced by the Union of South Africa in May 1910, following the amalgamation of the Transvaal, the Orange Free State, Natal, and the Cape Colony. That, too, had disappeared. It had been replaced by the Republic of South Africa, which quickly made itself an international pariah with its commitment to apartheid and, after the Sharpeville massacre on March 21, 1960, its use of violence to suppress political opposition.[1] But that republic had also disappeared from history on April 27, 1994, replaced by a nonracial democracy.

Mandela was aware of the changes that had taken place in twentieth-century South Africa. He had, after all, lived them. South Africa's first democratically elected president reminded guests at the celebrations of the complex history of the park, as well as the many threads that bound the park to local and global histories. He recalled these linkages not to bemoan the park's histories but to point out what and whom the park owed for its very existence.[2] Mandela said South Africans had to recall these threads in order to show their commitment to using the park to benefit its rural neighbors. He sought to show that, far from being a natural playground isolated from wider social and political struggles about citizenship and land ownership, the KNP was important as both player and site in these struggles. As Mandela said in his celebration of the centenary of the KNP:

> We recall these threads in our history not to decry the foresight of those who established the park, nor to diminish our enjoyment of it. We do so rather to reaffirm our commitment that the rural communities in and around our parks should also benefit from our natural heritage and find in it an opportunity for their development.[3]

Mandela insisted that we recall the threads in the park's history because South Africa's future depended on it. In some ways, the 1998 speech recalled the address that Mandela gave in 1994, upon taking the oath of office as South Africa's first democratically elected president. Mandela had said then:

> To my compatriots, I have no hesitation in saying that each one of us is as intimately attached to the soil of this beautiful country as are the famous jacaranda trees of Pretoria and the mimosa trees of the bushveld. Each time one of us touches the soil of this land, we feel a sense of personal renewal. . . . That spiritual and physical oneness we all share with this common homeland explains the depth of pain we all carried in our hearts as we saw our country tear itself apart in a terrible conflict.[4]

Commenting on Mandela's 1994 inauguration speech, Paul Gilroy said, "Mandela constructed an ecological account of the relationship between shared humanity, common citizenship, place and identity."[5] Mandela drew on the natural beauty of the South African landscape and on the link between that landscape and South Africa's inhabitants to cast apartheid as a "brutal violation of nature that could be repaired only if people were prepared to pay heed to the oneness established by their connection to the beautiful environment they share and hold in common stewardship."[6] Gilroy said that Mandela's strategic deployment of nature used the common ground "beneath the feet of his diverse, unified, and mutually suspicious audience" to lay, as it were, a new basis upon which a nonracial citizenry might be produced.[7] His speech worked with the "organicity that nature has bequeathed to modern ideas of culture."[8] But what if, Gilroy asked, instead of going along with Mandela's ecological account of citizenship for South Africa, we set aside the "powerful claims of soil, roots and territory"?[9] Mandela did not need to set apart the claims of soil, roots, and territory, however, because his ecological conception of citizenship was open-ended. It did not depend on the demarcation of insiders and outsiders. Mandela spoke of "compatriots" and "our people" but left unstated how those compatriots and people were constituted. For Mandela, one did not need to be a son or daughter of the soil to belong. The jacaranda did not need to be indigenous to anchor the attachment of individuals to South African soil. Ironically, Mandela chose the jacaranda as his symbol for a united South Africa at the very moment that South Africa's conservation officials were launching an all-out war against so-called invasive species.[10] This did not deter Mandela. He believed that the jacaranda had long earned the right to be called South African. This became his signature argument throughout his five years (1994–99) in office. He used nature to assert a common South Africanness.

He became an ardent conservationist, even serving on the first board of the Peace Parks Foundation (see fig. 8.1).[11] But he did not lose sight of the park's history. He did not forget that the park participated in and played host to some of the most pressing battles between blacks and the state, and between native administration and nature conservation in twentieth-century South Africa. Or that the park also provided important linkages between conservation and capitalism in South Africa, through its relationship with the country's mining industry. He understood also how the association between conservation and mining allowed the park and the Chamber of Mines to serve as extensions of the colonial and apartheid order.

However, if Mandela's move from prison to the presidency—his switch from incarceration to conservation—signaled South Africa's transition from apartheid to democracy, for millions of South Africans the advent of majority rule marked the beginning of yet more safaris toward an uncertain future. The end of apartheid marked not the end of the journeying so characteristic of the region's history but its intensification. This intensification spoke as much to the meaning of democracy in South Africa as it did to the transformation of the relationship between black South Africans and the KNP. Black South Africans who

FIGURE 8.1. Nelson Mandela at KNP ceremony marking the release of elephants to Mozambique as part of Great Limpopo transfrontier initiative. *Left to right:* Tourism minister Mohammed Valli Moosa, SANParks board chairman Murphy Morobe, Mandela, SANParks executive director Mavuso Msimang, and KNP director David Mabunda. KNP, October 4, 2001. *Source:* SANParks Archive

encounter the park in postapartheid South Africa do so as citizens and not subjects. They do so as people with greater means to make their voices heard and grievances attended to, even if the attention paid to their complaints might be no different from what blacks were exposed to in colonial and apartheid South Africa.

MELANCHOLY TRAVEL

In a short story from 1981 titled "The Haunting Melancholy of Klipvoordam," writer Miriam Tlali tells of a group of six Soweto residents (three adults and three children) who decide to spend the last day of 1979 and to bring in the New Year by camping at a holiday resort in the homeland of Bophuthatswana.[12] As the unnamed narrator tells the reader, her friends Donald and Pauline, a married couple, came up with the idea. Donald and Pauline are clearly old hands at the business of camping, as we can see from the camping paraphernalia that fills their Volkswagen van. Don and Paul are special beings, says the narrator:

The like of them in a place like Soweto should be protected from extinction; they should be honored and revered. They are like a rare and endangered species of God's creation. They are among the few who still strive to bring about order where there is only chaos and despair. In the jumbled shattered existence of the Soweto Ghetto, they hanker after the sustaining force of mother nature. For does nature's eternal seasonal cycle not offer the propagation of new life in place of the withering and dying and hence hope for the future?[13]

To get to the resort, the campers drive through Soweto, past the affluent and tree-lined white suburbs of northern Johannesburg, and through what the narrator calls a scantily populated countryside. As the campers approach Bophuthatswana, the narrator says:

One would have expected that we would arrive at some border post, some line; a river or a bridge, at the end of which would be stationed a pair of stern-looking uniformed guards. That these honorable gentlemen would be wearing labeled epaulettes over their proud shoulders, or even medals on their lapels. I had looked around expecting to see sign-posts along the road reading: "Welcome to the Sovereign State of Bophuthatswana."

Yet we knew that by . . . taking a turn away from the smoothly-tarred road onto the gravel one, we had in fact departed from the so-called "white" South Africa. We had left behind all the comfort that goes with that part of this land. We were now part of the so-called Bophuthatswana self-governing black state, having automatically relinquished all that was of merit. The whole transition had been as easy as taking candy from a child. Just like that. No lines of demarcation had been drawn, no signs, nothing.

It would have been redundant. We knew it; our bodies *felt* it. We were all aware that the one world had come to an end and a new one had begun. The dry dust, the thorny scrub on either side of the uneven road had warned us.[14]

Having made the transition from "white" to "black" South Africa, the party arrives at the resort, "the first time I had the honor of visiting a 'black' recreational area in a so-called independent state in my own country and naturally I was curious."[15] The narrator proceeds to examine the different trees and observe the birds and animals in the resort. She is clearly a fish out of water here. None of what she finds in the resort is known to her. She has no prior knowledge of the wild. She has to be schooled. "There was ever so much to learn," she says. But she also learns that the resort is an incomplete construction site dotted with "poor skeletal left-overs." The resort's previous white owners were on the verge of building an electricity plant but abandoned their plans when the government created Bophuthatswana in 1977. "The whole business of the poverty—the ever-present legacy always so readily bequeathed to the 'honorable' inheritors of the so-called free black states. Who bothers about freedom in a deprived desert anyway, I wondered."[16]

Despite her disappointment, the narrator is still able to enjoy herself. She had got away from the noise and the dancing of Soweto. Disturbed by the sounds of the wild, she plays the music of Brook Benton to calm her nerves. As the campers count the hours toward the dawn of the New Year, they talk about the death of loved ones and the imminent independence of Zimbabwe. Early the next morning, as the six campers enjoy the break of dawn—what the narrator chooses to call by the Sotho-Tswana name *mafube* "because to my mind, in the English medium in which I am writing, no word that I can think of describes adequately the whole mesmerizing excellence of the break of dawn than 'mafube,' especially when seen in the clear open emptiness of unspoilt nature"—a melancholy dark figure emerges from the thicket. The man looks like he is bearing the world's problems on his shoulders. "The man was very likely trying to escape from the helplessness of a lifetime of unfulfilled aspirations—an existence where hopes and dreams remain forever a receding mirage."[17] But the man is also there to enjoy *mafube*. He is there to witness the break of dawn. Oppression and thwarted aspiration are no bar to an appreciation of nature.

Distilled into this poignant four-page story are some of the key themes of this book—not to mention twentieth-century South African history—from the fraught mediation of the divide between the urban and the rural, to the black and the white worlds, to the negotiation of the apartheid atlas, to a material engagement with homelands, to an affective sense of place, to the politics of black life in apartheid Africa, to the meaning of Africa's decolonization for black South Africa, to the social distinctions and class divides within South Africa, and to the use of African languages to articulate black appreciations of nature. To be sure, Tlali's is a fictional account, but in that fiction lie contested histories and histories of presence.

If Tlali offers an imaginative account of the black middle-class experience of the wild, Njabulo Ndebele provides more critical—but not necessarily historically accurate—reflections on the existential state of black tourism in South Africa. These reflections are not, as I show above, beyond challenge, but they are good to think with. Reflecting on a visit to a game lodge, Ndebele says that black visits to game lodges amount to the "experience of cultural domination in a most intimate way."[18] This feeling is most acute during game viewing. He writes:

> It is difficult [for blacks] not to feel that, in the total scheme of things, perhaps they should be out there with the animals, being viewed. Caught in a conversation with their white fellow refugees, brought together with them by an increasingly similar, stressful lifestyle, they can engage in discussions which bring out both the artificiality and the reality of their similarity. The black tourist is conditioned to find the political sociology of the game lodge ontologically disturbing. It can be so offensive as to be obscene. He is a leisure colonialist torn up by excruciating ambiguities. He pays to be the viewer who has to be viewed.[19]

Ndebele says blacks are conditioned to find game lodges "ontologically disturbing." These lodges began life as extensions of white power in South Africa but had become, by the end of the twentieth century, places of white refuge from the stress of living in a black-ruled country. Everything is still in place in a lodge, from the amenities to the mute black workers. This is troubling to the black tourist:

> Until very recently, one of the distinguishing features of the game lodge was the marked absence of black tourists, but now they are beginning to show up in steadily increasing numbers. Being there, they experience the most damning ambiguities. They see the faceless black workers and instinctively see a reflection of themselves. They may be wealthy or politically powerful, but at that moment they are made aware of their special kind of powerlessness: they lack the backing of cultural power.[20]

Ndebele offers a powerful account of the black experience in post-apartheid South Africa, where affluence cannot protect members of the black elite from racist humiliation. But Ndebele's account also offers a powerful reminder of the cultural and political safaris, not to mention the class struggles going back at least a century, that sought to make South Africa a home for all: a home where pioneers of the black elite such as D. D. T. Jabavu worried about soil conservation, thinkers like Thema fretted over the meaning of the KNP, and theorists of black nationalism such as Anton Lembede thought about "trees and their value to human beings."[21] But elite blacks did not and do not have a monopoly on safari.

CONTINUITY AND CHANGE

There has been change. But there has also been continuity. Animals from the park continue to prey on livestock and crops belonging to the park's neighbors. Poaching remains a serious problem.[22] So-called illegal immigrants continue to travel to South Africa via the park, sometimes with fatal consequences.[23] So dire is the situation that *City Press* newspaper columnist Charles Mogale asked fellow South Africans, "Do we really have hearts of stone?"[24] The columnist recounted a harrowing tale of

> a woman with two little children who joined a group trying to walk the 200km or so across the breath [*sic*] of the Park. She was too slow for the rest of the group and they left her behind. As days passed and she ran out of food and water for the children, she broke their necks—apparently to save them from a worse death in the jaws of predators. The woman was picked up by tourists driving through the park—but it was too late for her offspring.[25]

The problem of immigrants getting killed by animals got so bad that park rangers started fearing for the immigrants' safety. In 1997, for example, rangers killed seven lions that "seemed to have developed a taste for the flesh of easy human prey."[26] As for the park's neighbors, living with the park means that making claims on the South African state works best when done through the park. The park might represent peril, but it also presents opportunities that they have been quick to exploit. The park's neighbors have discovered that they have more leverage when they make the park a key part of their political calculus.

On September 23, 2009, a month before the government announced that it would no longer settle land claims in the park by returning land to claimant communities, hundreds of residents of Shabalala township, about 20 kilometers southwest of the KNP, blockaded the R536, a tarred road leading to the Paul Kruger Gate, the main entrance to the park. The protesters, made up mostly of lower-middle-class and middle-class women and young men, used felled trees, rocks, and burning tires to shut down the road.

The revolt was part of a wave of so-called service delivery protests that swept South Africa with increasing force after the end of apartheid, as communities took to the streets to complain about the lack of or poor provision of water, electricity, roads, and housing and about the performance of their elected representatives.[27] In the case of Shabalala, situated on the edge of the Kruger Road, the community had not had decent services since the advent of democracy in 1994. A schoolteacher, who was one of the protest organizers, said: "For twelve years we have had no water, no roads and no electricity. That's what made us say 'enough is enough.'"[28] In theory, residents were supposed to get water from the municipality twice a week, on Tuesday and Saturday. But as one resident said, "Three months go by here without any water." Local entrepreneurs were taking advantage of the municipality's failure. A protest organizer said, "Water is on sale here: R4 for 25 liters and R300 for 5,000 liters." The community had been pleading with and protesting against the municipality for years to improve the delivery of services. Each time, the municipality would promise to deliver. But nothing would happen. In August 2009 community leaders even went to Nelspruit, the capital of both the province of Mpumalanga and the Mbombela Local Municipality, to plead with Lassy Chiwayo, the executive mayor. Chiwayo had asked them not to take to the streets, saying that their grievances would be addressed. In postapartheid South Africa, the park is divided in half between two provinces, Limpopo in the north and Mpumalanga in the south. Shabalala is in Mpumalanga. A protest organizer said:

> We were promised too many times that the water matter was going to be solved and that Eskom [the state-owned electricity utility] had a problem with generating capacity but that the problem was being attended to. Our argument was: if Eskom has

a capacity problem, how come you can pay its employees to put electricity in your house for four thousand rands? We were tired of unkept promises.[29]

The women said that by blockading the Kruger Road, they "were trying something that would shake government." One said: "We knew this was a national road going to the Kruger National Park. We knew that if we could turn back four or five busses, that that would be felt."[30] They certainly knew that while they could count on their protest drawing public attention (the protest made it into the national newspapers), they could not depend on the ANC—South Africa's ruling party, which controls both the Mpumalanga provincial government and the Mbombela municipality—for support. The organizers said that Sipho Mpangane, the chairman of the ANC branch in Shabalala, was opposed to the protest.

One organizer said: "The ANC chairman was walking around with the police and council officials on the day of the protest. He said going down the Kruger Road does not solve anything because the road does not have water and does not have electricity. It's a national road."[31] Mpangane might have been trying to downplay the importance of the protest because it was essentially against his organization. But he had no illusions about why the protesters targeted the Kruger Road:

> They wanted the attention of the national government. They wanted the national government to pay attention. They realize this road is a national road. This is the main road to the Kruger. They realize that if they block this road, the national government will pay attention. This road is important to the Kruger National Park. It's the main one. It leads to the main gate.[32]

Mpangane was not the only one who understood the strategic significance of shutting down the Kruger Road. Carriot Mthethwa, a headman in Shabalala suspected by the police of being the key organizer, said: "They know this is the Kruger Road and that South Africa benefits from it. This is a national road and the protesters wanted to call the mayor. They were trying to disturb traffic so the mayor would come."[33] Mthethwa was keen to prove he was not among the organizers. However, he said the protest succeeded in drawing attention to Shabalala. The mayor did come, as did a deputy government minister, executive members of the ANC, and teams of provincial and government experts.

Mpangane was not the only one who downplayed the importance of the protest. Sick Winlight Mdluli, also a headman in Shabalala, said the protesters were trying to draw government's attention to themselves — not to Shabalala:

> The protest was not against Skukuza [meaning the park]. People want positions. They want to become known in the community. The closing down of the road was just a strategy. Actually, they are fighting councilors. In fact, this is not about water it's about politics. Why did they close down the road when they can get water from the Sabie River [which transects the northern edge of Shabalala]? But people are like that. They always want more. You give them ten cents, they want more. People met somewhere and decided to protest. I am a resident and should have joined in. But I just saw this happening. It's possible they thought "let's close the road." But doing that hurt the wrong person. What have they achieved? They have achieved nothing.[34]

It is debatable whether the protest was indeed the failure Mdluli thought it was. After all, the protest made the national news and brought a whole army of ANC and state officials to Shabalala who promised to speed up the delivery of services and hold the local councilor to account. For her part, the local councilor, Mantombazana Khoza, was honest enough to admit that poor service delivery by her council was the cause of the protest:

> The Kruger Road was closed because of service delivery issues. As a municipality we failed to give the area electricity. People have been there for years but we have not given them electricity. That caused a lot of noise. We budgeted 3.2-million rands in the 2008/9 financial year for electricity but that was not used. Eskom said it could not produce transformers as it did not have sufficient capacity. That's what made the community angry. Eskom said it had no capacity.[35]

Shabalala's budget allocation was shifted to another township near Hazy View named Mbonisweni while Eskom was busy beefing up its capacity. Khoza said there would be another budgetary allocation for Shabalala once Eskom had increased its capacity. Khoza said protest leaders were arrested because they were threatening to burn down her house. She said that although political opportunists had taken advantage of community grievances to push their own agendas (she seemed to have in mind Carriot Mthethwa, a defector from the ANC), the community did have legitimate concerns about the municipality:

> The community started toyi-toying (protesting) in 2008. They threatened to blockade the Kruger Road because it is a busy road used by tourists. They knew that if they closed the road, the world would pay attention. It's very important. It's the only road that draws people to the Kruger. It has two gates. People use Malelane and other gates but Paul Kruger is the big one and you see more.[36]

PREMONITIONS OF INSURGENT CITIZENSHIP

In truth, the September 23, 2009, protest was not the first time that a community adjacent to the KNP had incorporated the park into its political calculus during confrontations with the state. It was also not the first time that the Kruger Road had been blockaded during a community protest. If anything, blocking the road and setting up barricades had become a part of the repertoire of protest for many of the communities on the margins of the park. In May 1997 residents of Bushbuckridge, a town to the west of the park, put trees and burnt tires across a road leading to the KNP.[37] They also hurled rocks at the police and passing motorists. According to the *Sunday Times* newspaper, "A German woman had to be treated for burns suffered in a petrol-bomb attack on a tourist bus."[38] The park was aware of the protests. In fact, the park knew that its history of exclusion and conflict with its surrounding communities placed it at risk. It also knew that the location of the roads leading to the park, all of which cut through communities not enamored of the park, made it vulnerable to the kinds of protest action it saw in the late 1990s and again in 2009. In September 1994, four months after the election of Mandela as South Africa's first democratic president, Chris van der Linde, a spokesman for the park, announced that the "old way of running the park has forever gone." The park could no longer afford to be seen as a "white man's playground." There were four million people living near the park, he said, and they were looking to the park to make the new South Africa a reality for them: "Most of them are totally unemployed. If these guys wanted to close down our roads, they could do it overnight. We are in a situation of mutual need and co-operation. Unless that [cooperation] happens, we could bleed to death here."[39]

Van der Linde was not the first park official to look into the past and the future and see a history that needed to change—fast. J. Fourie, an official of the National Parks Board, was warning as early as 1991 that the park needed to change the way it related to its neighbors. Using language peculiar to apartheid government officials at the time, Fourie said the park had "First World visitors" (meaning whites) and "Third World rural" neighbors, meaning the millions of black people whose townships and villages abutted the park. Writing in *Koedoe*, the National Parks Board's in-house scientific journal, Fourie said the park's first-world visitors and third-world neighbors had different needs:

> The typical First World visitor to an area such as the Kruger National Park experiences a set of needs that are strongly related to self-actualization. . . . The needs of this group center around relaxation, breaking away from the city routine, and fulfilling personally rewarding pastimes such as bird-watching, etc. In direct contrast with this the needs of the rural communities bordering on conservation areas such as the Kruger National Park [focus] on the use of natural resources essential for day-to-day survival, as well as jobs.[40]

Fourie wanted the park and, by extension, the board to take account of these different needs. This way, he reasoned, the park would be made relevant to both the first and third worlds, thus ensuring its protection and success under black majority rule, which even he could see, as early as 1991, was coming. Fourie refined his argument even further in 1994 in another article for *Koedoe*. He began by noting that South Africa boasted a "proud history of conservation."[41] It had rescued the white and black rhino, the bontebok antelope, and the Cape mountain zebra from certain extinction; its elephant and crocodile numbers were rising; and the country's coastline had a rich marine life.[42] "Why is it then," he asked, "that with such a success story we have failed to take with us the majority of the population of this country?"[43]

Fourie answered his own question by pointing to a "Eurocentric" conception of conservation. This approach "tends to display a paternalism, elitism and an attitude of supremacy that regards local people as ignorant and therefore of lesser importance." He suggested four strategies as a way of fixing the park's relationship with its neighbors: revamp the National Parks Board to make it more representative and sensitive to the history and African experiences of conservation; introduce corporate social responsibility into the board's operations; form partnerships with neighboring communities and create a "dialogic relationship"; and, finally, introduce affirmative action to draw Africans into the country's conservation management ranks. J. A. Loader, another National Parks Board official, joined Fourie's crusade. Writing in *Koedoe* in 1994, Loader said the need for change was not simply a political necessity but an ecological necessity as well.

Loader said the park's fidelity to ecological and ecosystem integrity compelled it to bring neighboring communities in from the margins, as it were:

> Even if the socio-economic realities of present-day South Africa had not forced us to pay serious attention to this matter, there would still have been scientific grounds for not only realizing that the inherent logic of ecology itself necessitates the acknowledgment of the interrelatedness of nature and culture, but also to take the social involvement of the National Parks Board seriously for ecological reasons.[44]

Loader's claims invite a question: if the connection between nature and culture was inherent to the logic of ecology and conservation, then why had it taken the park, with its rich and internationally acclaimed reputation for research, so many years to realize the folly of what Jacklyn Cock and Eddie Koch called an "authoritarian conservation perspective" that focused solely on nature and neglected human needs?[45] Why had it taken the National Parks Board more than fifty years to change its attitudes toward black South Africans? But Loader was focused on the future, not the past. He said the National Parks Board must give up on "old-style paternalistic negotiations of yesteryear":

> Ingenuous plans to facilitate neighboring communities to ben-
> efit from assets such as thatch, fuel, hides, cheap meat, a com-
> missioned curio trade and employment will need to be made.
> Social services, such as housing, schooling, medical care and
> general medical services, will have to be developed much fur-
> ther than they have. . . . This means that one basic error is to be
> avoided at all costs: The support of the bordering communities
> and the community at large should not be "bought" by social
> involvement in order to attain an implied more important goal.
> Another basic error should be studiously avoided: Talking down
> to communities is worse than not embarking on the undertaking
> of social involvement at all.[46]

There was a perfectly good reason why Fourie and Loader sounded so anxious to mend relations with the park's "third-world" neighbors. With the ANC about to take over in 1994 and with no guarantees that a black-led government would be as sympathetic toward conservation as its white predecessor had been, the National Parks Board was worried about the future of national parks. It had also not helped matters that a senior ANC member had suggested in 1993 that the park was useless to its neighbors and could be put to better use as pasture. However, there was a more immediate reason for the anxiety expressed by the likes of Fourie and Loader. The park and its neighbors were a study in contrasts. To look at the park in relation to its neighbors was to look at South Africa in miniature. Fourie might have been echoing apart-heid officialese with its grammar of a developed "white" South Africa separate from underdeveloped "black" Bantustans, when he spoke of "first world" visitors and "third world" neighbors. But he was not far off the mark. The park and its neighbors might have exhibited a simi-lar topography and even sat on the same geological foundation. But the two places were different in terms of their economic well-being. The contrasts were such that Jane Carruthers and others warned in 2003 that "Kruger's survival in its present form may be threatened by circumstances beyond its boundaries and outside its control."[47] Car-ruthers and colleagues pointed out that two million people lived within a 50-kilometer radius of the park's western boundary. The population density here was three hundred people per square kilometer, and the dominant "land-use activities . . . include small-scale cropping, limited commercial farming, and grazing."[48]

In contrast, the neighboring commercial farms, owned by whites, had population densities of between five and twenty people per square kilometer. The white-owned commercial farms were involved in cattle and game farming, private game reserves, and the growing of tropical crops such as oranges, mangoes, bananas, and papaws. White control of the land dated to the 1860s when Paul Kruger's South African Republic doled out farms, average size 1,500 hectares, to whites as military or civic rewards.[49] Land ownership patterns had not changed much by the end of apartheid, even if some of the white farms had gone down in size. Agriculture was a mainstay of the local economy until the 1930s, when the government introduced policies that made the economy dependent on migrant remittances and state pensions. By 1989, only 6 percent of the local cash economy came from agriculture.[50] Until the formal end of apartheid in April 1994, the estimated four million people who live adjacent to the park did not, properly speaking, belong to South Africa. They were, in fact, citizens of the four homelands bordering the park on its southern, western, and northern sides: KaNgwane for Swazi-speakers, Lebowa for Pedis, Gazankulu for the Tsonga, and Venda, in the north, for Venda-speakers. When the Bantustans, which included Transkei, Bophuthatswana, Ciskei, KwaZulu, KwaNdebele, and Qwaqwa, were abolished in 1994, they accounted for about seventeen million people, 48 percent of all black South Africans. The majority of those who lived in homelands were divided between eight hundred chieftaincies.[51] The homelands were economically poor, and their ecological systems were degraded from overcrowding and overuse. The homelands were mostly rural and also the home of most of South Africa's fauna. But, as H. Els and J. du Pisani, National Parks Board officials, wrote in *Koedoe*: "If people cannot realistically survive in the rural areas of South Africa, the country's wildlife will definitely also not do so."[52]

Conclusion

WHAT'S IN A NAME?

Speaking on May 31, 1926, during the second parliamentary reading of the bill that ushered in the KNP, Hebert B. Papenfus, a member of parliament and former chairman of the Transvaal Game Protection Association, said:

> I should like to express my unqualified delight that this park is to be named the Kruger National Park. There is no doubt that President Kruger . . . saved for posterity the fauna of this country, and I trust that in the near future some worthy memorial, some memorial will be erected in the park to commemorate this great act of President Kruger's . . . a monument which countless visitors from other lands will view with admiration and respect, and which future generations of South Africans will gaze on with feelings of gratitude and veneration.[1]

However, it was only after 1968 that the National Parks Board finally erected a granite bust to commemorate Kruger.[2] And the bust, intended to serve as a Mount Rushmore–style icon, was never popular.[3] The democratic state tried after the formal end of apartheid in 1994 to remove it and to change the park's name. But such is the park's place in South Africa's history—not to mention the imperatives of racial reconciliation—that postapartheid conservation authorities found it politically difficult to change even the park's name.[4] Asked in 1998 why the park had still not changed its name, Environment Minister Pallo Jordan answered, "The name could not be changed this year because of the [park's] centenary, and next year is the anniversary of the Boer War. But in 2000 there is nothing to suggest we can't drop the

'Kruger.'"[5] But 2000 came and went and the Paul Kruger monument was still where it had been; the park was still called the Kruger National Park (see fig. C.1).

In some ways, the difficulty of removing Kruger's statue and renaming the park reflected the park's own mobility, its own imaginative movement from one context to another. It showed the park's ability

FIGURE C.1. Author standing next to granite bust of Paul Kruger, outside the Paul Kruger Gate in the park. *Source*: Patricia McGaughey

to transform itself from a national asset into an international icon, a consumer brand known to the rest of the world simply as "the Kruger." But the park's imaginative movement was not natural. It was political. That is, the failure of the South African government to change the park's name and to move Kruger's statue from the main gate—thereby uncoupling the park, even if only symbolically, from a white segregationist past—was the result of political choices made and not made by a number of actors, especially the ruling ANC. There is nothing natural about its name.

Contrary to fears that tourists might not know the park were it to assume a new name, tourists who want to visit the park will still visit regardless of what name it goes by. Yet the idea has taken hold that one cannot change the name without losing the thousands of overseas tourists who travel thousands of miles each year to see "the Kruger." For those opposed to changing the name of the park, tinkering with the label Kruger National Park would be as misguided as changing the name Coca-Cola while still expecting consumers to go for the iconic brand. The trouble with that argument is that it seeks to insulate the park from the claims of history—not to mention the demands of justice—by arguing that consumer brands can be removed from their social and political contexts. But what of the black experience to which this book has borne witness? What of the black presence to which this book has testified? What of the names under which all these have gone? To answer those questions, let us conclude with two episodes, the first from 1949 and the second from 1977, to show both the continuities and changes in the ways different black actors have made their presence felt and have thought about nature and, by extension, about conservation over the course of the twentieth century. The first is a travelogue written by black educationalist and nationalist D. D. T. Jabavu following a four-month-long trip to East Africa and India; the second is a letter written by B. P. Kumalo, a seventeen-year-old schoolboy, following his participation in a nature trail organized by the Wilderness Leadership School.[6] Jabavu and Kumalo spoke across generations and social backgrounds, but each spoke to the richness of the black experience of nature conservation. Each testified to histories of presence that can be recuperated and understood only if historians learn not to grant the colonial and apartheid states a hegemony they did not have.

On November 1, 1949, Jabavu boarded a train in Middledrift, in the Cape, bound for Durban, from where he was to sail to India for a peace conference. As the train made its way to Durban via Mthatha, Kokstad, and Pietermaritzburg, Jabavu marked the different places the train tracks went through:

> This route goes through the Africans and their rivers: Kingwilliamstown amongst amaNgqika, Kei amongst amaMfengu, Butterworth amongst amaGcaleka, Bashee amongst abaThembu, Mthatha amongst amaMpondo of Ndamase, Gungululu amongst amaMpondomise of Mditshwa in Tsolo and Tsitsa amongst the Mhlonto people in Qumbu. The land was dry and in some parts green. When we passed Qumbu we crossed the Tina River and we arrived in Bhacaland in Mount Frere at Lugangeni at Wabana not faraway from the water of Mvuzi. Here is the place where the Jili clan is found (to which the author belongs) at Ntlangwini.[7]

This attractive train route, Jabavu tells the reader, goes through "Africans and their rivers." The train goes through landscapes of affect. It goes through places filled with history. Notice, however, that as Jabavu reads different African groups into their respective landscapes and rivers, he does so in ways alive to the present. These places not only bear African names; they also bear names that speak directly to the colonial encounter between African and European on the eastern Cape frontier. Jabavu uses African and European names interchangeably. In other words, Jabavu is not looking into these different landscapes—dry in parts and green in others—for the essence of some African identity. He is interested instead in presence and in location, in who is located where, who claims this or that river as his or her source? He makes no nativist claim on the lands he sees.

As we imagine the besuited Jabavu in his first-class compartment, looking out the window as the train shuttles by and over the different rivers, it is worth recalling that here routes—journeying—mattered more than roots. Travel mattered more than who came first to which location. For people of Jabavu's social background and class, the train provided the spine along which moved their aspirations, ideas, and (of course) bodies.[8] It was routes, not roots, that rooted them to South

Africa. As Jabavu tells the reader in the introduction to his travelogue, by the time he was sixty-four, he had traveled more than 400,000 miles. He had visited four continents. Here was a man whose standing and politics were connected intimately to his travels and to his presence in history. Through those travels he had met, for example, Booker T. Washington and Jawaharlal Nehru. Jabavu, then, was anything but a native stuck in place. As his daughter Noni Jabavu recounts in her memoir, the Jabavu household boasted a huge map of South African Railways that hung on his study wall, as well as a much-thumbed railway timetable. Noni Jabavu tells us that her father

> loved trains for long journeys. Connections, junctions, time-tables, the pros and cons of alternative routes; the European guards throughout the Cape were old friends to him, tested by thousands of miles of journeys together during which they always lingered at the door of his compartment to hail him, "Hello, Professor!" and he would sit pipe in mouth, hand on knee and call them "Baas So-and-so" and they would pass the time of day and talk about the drought and changing conditions in our country.[9]

But we also know from Jabavu's travelogue that he was more than a political actor. We know, in other words, that he did not live only in the mode of resistance. Among the things he did during his stay in India was visiting the zoo in Calcutta to see the tiger. He also saw Asian elephants but was disappointed to discover that their trunks are smaller than those of their African cousins. Jabavu also visited the River Ganges as well as the Himalayas. That was Jabavu, well traveled, interested, and connected. His experience spoke to that of the members of his class, which, although small, spoke loudly and eloquently about the need for democracy in South Africa.

Now for the second episode. In 1977, B. P. Kumalo, age seventeen, said the following in a letter to Sue Hart, a teacher and conservationist:

> For sixteen years I've walked with eyes closed whereas I thought they were wide open. I've been to places like Zululand, learnt how to look after cattle, look for wood and how to fetch water, but all this must have happened automatically because I benefited

nothing out of it. If I were to tell everything I saw, heard or learnt about in Umgeni valley, it would be very difficult because there are many things we came across. I will tell of some things which most struck me. We looked at trees in a different light. We were taught their names and adaptation and were told everything about them in terms of ecology. When our forefathers carried out their traditional customs, they used these trees. Some of us had already forgotten about them. I, for instance, was in Zulu-land in June. There would be an unveiling of a tombstone of my grandfather. I heard my father saying that they were going to fetch my grandfather's spirit. Somehow I did not understand because I was too ignorant to notice what they really did, but I learnt later that the tree, *umphafa*, was used. This visit has really increased my knowledge about nature and, above all, I've enjoyed myself. People like me who live in townships rarely have these opportunities of seeing and learning about these things. Thanks to the Wildlife Society and their good, patient teachers, now I enjoy sitting down and looking at grass, trees, or when the sun sets, I become worried if I see erosion.[10]

Kumalo had recently participated in a nature trail organized by the Wilderness Leadership School and wished to thank his hosts and teachers for educating him. Ian Player, a South African conservationist famous for his work on saving the rhino, founded the school in 1957 to connect people, especially urban dwellers. Although never acknowledged by Player, he founded the school in part as a response to the complaint raised by Thema in 1950 that the animals in the KNP were better cared for than blacks in South Africa. Player was active in conservation circles in Natal at the time of Thema's complaint and was among those who saw the complaint as a direct challenge to white conservationists to do more to involve blacks in conservation. So he founded the Wilderness School.[11] Seven years later the Natal Wildlife Society founded the African Wildlife Society to cater exclusively to blacks. The Natal Wildlife Society said that the new society would target both peasants and city dwellers, such as B. P. Kumalo. The young student is unlikely to have known this, but he was in fact the beneficiary not simply of white paternalism but also of black agitation. Kumalo was the beneficiary of a movement that sought to read blacks into nature, not as abject animals but as rights-bearing subjects with claims to South Africa. As Thema said in 1950, "Apartheid means putting us in zoos. Has the white man gone so far that after having put our animals into zoos he now wants to put us into zoos? Well, we are not animals, and we shall never agree to be put into zoos. We want to live in open spaces."[12] So blacks fought in different ways for both a place in these open spaces and access to them. This book recounts these struggles.

Although not necessarily political, such struggles could not help but assume a political dimension. They were not about natives and settlers; they were not about who, between black and white, came first to South Africa and who, therefore, had a greater claim to the country. They were about ways of being present in the world. By looking at this presence in the KNP, *Safari Nation* has challenged accounts of an absence that was in fact not there. People like Jabavu and Thema fought for democracy without reducing that fight to a struggle about autochthony. They insisted on their right to move about the country unmolested and to buy land wherever they desired. But they did not insist on that right on the grounds that they were native and, therefore, more deserving of said right. By recalling the struggles waged by people like Jabavu, Thema, and countless others, this book has tried to recuperate a much more cosmopolitan, democratic, and ultimately more hopeful history of approaches to the KNP, to conservation, and to the land question in South Africa.

By reminding the reader of struggles for justice that were not about creating nativist queues divided between native and settler, *Safari Nation* has tried to call to mind memories of a modern vision for South Africa with long antecedents. By recalling a time when black was a political and not an ethnic or racial category, this book has tried to show how a range of southern Africans and South Africans—elites and nonelites, nationalists and nonnationalists—contributed to the development of a country in which the welfare of whites did not have to come at the expense of blacks, and blacks did not have to bear the sole cost of the conservation of flora and fauna. As the book shows, the black actors who thought seriously about the KNP did not oppose conservation in principle. They opposed injustice.

Notes

INTRODUCTION

1. Even though the Kruger National Park is widely recognized as South Africa's premier national park, it was not, strictly speaking, the first to bear the label national park. That honor belongs to the Royal Natal National Park. See Jane Carruthers, "The Royal Natal National Park, KwaZulu-Natal: Mountaineering, Tourism and Nature Conservation in South Africa's First National Park, c. 1896 to c. 1947," *Environment and History* 19, no. 4 (November 2013): 459–85.

2. See Jane Carruthers, "'Why Celebrate a Controversy?': South Africa, the United States, and National Parks," in *National Parks beyond the Nation: Global Perspectives on "America's Best Idea,"* ed. Adrian Howkins, Jared Orsi, and Mark Fiege (Norman: University of Oklahoma Press, 2016), 145. For the claim by Hector Magome and James Murombedzi, see their essay "Sharing South African National Parks: Community Land and Conservation in a Democratic South Africa," in *Decolonizing Nature: Strategies for Conservation in a Post-colonial Era*, ed. William Adams and Martin Mulligan (London: Earthscan, 2003), 115. For Jacklyn Cock, see *The War against Ourselves: Nature, Power, and Justice* (Johannesburg: Wits University Press, 2007), 148. Lynn Meskell's claim is in her essay "The Nature of Culture in Kruger National Park," in *Cosmopolitan Archaeologies*, ed. Lynn Meskell (Durham, NC: Duke University Press, 2009), 97. See, for Lindisizwe Magi's claim, his essay "People, Recreation, and the Environment," in *The Geography of South Africa in a Changing World*, ed. Roddy Fox and Kate Rowntree (Oxford: Oxford University Press, 2000), 439.

3. The idea of Africans as either selfless servants (always working under the tutelage of a wise white master) or rapacious poachers is quite dominant in most academic and popular accounts of conservation in Africa. See, for a sample, Dian Fossey, *Gorillas in the Mist* (Boston: Houghton Mifflin, 1983), see especially chap. 11; Donna Haraway, *Primate Visions: Gender, Race, and Nature in the World of Modern Science* (New York: Routledge, 1989), see especially pt. 3; Craig Parker, *Into Africa* (Chicago: University of Chicago Press, 1994), see pts. 1 and 2; and David Western, *In the Dust of Kilimanjaro* (Washington, DC: Island Press, 1997), see pts. 1 and 4.

4. The burden of race placed on scholars of South Africa is such that no racial label can be considered innocent or purely descriptive. Whatever term is used is politically loaded and scarred by history. Still, needs must. In this book the term *African* is used to refer to those generally considered to be indigenous to Africa. When the term *black* is used, it refers jointly to Africans, Coloureds, and Indians—that is, the so-called nonwhite communities. The terms *white* and *European* are used interchangeably and refer to people of European descent. A lot of the archival material used in the preparation of this book uses terms such as *Asiatic, native,* and *Bantu.* I have tried to make clear in each instance that these are not my terms.

5. I borrow the formulation "living with—as opposed to living under—" from a remark that Daniel Magaziner made during a talk at Princeton University titled "Art, Education and Knowledge in Apartheid South Africa," March 1, 2018.

6. See *Unspoilt Africa* (Pretoria: National Parks Board of Trustees, 1938), 47.

7. See *Unspoilt Africa* (1938), 47.

8. The 1946 edition of *Unspoilt Africa* says: "Parties of Asiatics, Natives or Coloureds may visit the park but they should note that except at Skukuza, there is as yet no accommodation available for them. They are advised to provide for their own shelter by carrying tents, bedding, etc., when it is proposed to make a stay at any other camp." See *Unspoilt Africa* (Pretoria: National Parks Board of Trustees, 1946), 107.

9. See James Ferguson, *Give a Man a Fish: Reflections on the New Politics of Distribution* (Durham, NC: Duke University Press, 2015), 184, 214–15; Anne-Maria Makhulu, *Making Freedom: Apartheid, Squatter Politics, and the Struggle for Home* (Durham, NC: Duke University Press, 2015), 5. To be sure, other scholars have used the concept of politics of presence before. See political theorist Anne Phillips, *The Politics of Presence* (Oxford: Clarendon Press, 1995); and anthropologist Peter Pels, *A Politics of Presence: Contacts between Missionaries and Waluguru in Late Colonial Tanganyika* (Amsterdam: Harwood Academic, 1999).

10. See Makhulu, *Making Freedom,* 5.

11. "More Land for Animals," editorial, *Bantu World,* February 9, 1935.

12. Krishna Somers, email interview with author, March 13, 2015. It is possible that Somers misremembered the camp at which he stayed. Because of the Second World War, the KNP was closed to visitors, except at Pretoriuskop in the southwestern section of the park, between 1941 and 1945. So he probably stayed at Pretoriuskop and not at Skukuza. See Office of Census and Statistics, *Official Year Book of the Union of South Africa, Basutoland, Bechuanaland Protectorate and Swaziland* (Pretoria: Government Printing and Stationery Office, 1946), 35.

13. See, for another attempt to do more than tell stories of black victimization, Lily Saint, *Black Cultural Life in South Africa: Reception, Apartheid, and Ethics* (Ann Arbor: University of Michigan Press, 2018).

14. See David Bunn, "The Museum Outdoors: Heritage, Cattle, and Permeable Borders in the Southwestern Kruger National Park," in *Museum Frictions: Public Cultures/Global Transformations*, ed. Ivan Karp et al. (Durham, NC: Duke University Press, 2006), 374.

15. For more on the migrant labor system, see Patrick Harries, *Work, Culture, and Identity: Migrant Laborers in Mozambique and South Africa, c. 1860–1910* (Johannesburg: Wits University Press, 1994); see also Jonathan Crush, Alan Jeeves, and David Yudelman, *South Africa's Labor Empire: A History of Black Migrancy to the Gold Mines* (Boulder: Westview, 1991).

16. See Julia Adeney Thomas, *Reconfiguring Modernity: Concepts of Nature in Japanese Political Ideology* (Berkeley: University of California Press, 2001), 2–3.

17. See Floris A. van Jaarsveld, "Interpretations and Trends in South African Historical Writing," in *The Afrikaner's Interpretation of South African History* (Cape Town: Simondium, 1964), 125. Van Jaarsveld was a prolific Afrikaner historian and the father of Afrikaner nationalist historiography.

18. See Thomas, *Reconfiguring Modernity*, 2.

19. My argument for a deracialized understanding of blackness draws inspiration from the kind of critical tradition that Steve Biko sought to promote. See his essay "The Definition of Black Consciousness," in *I Write What I Like*, ed. Aelred Stubbs (Johannesburg: Heinemann, 1987), 48–53. By stripping blackness of its racial coating and asking that we see it instead as a political label or even a political condition that describes an individual's relative distance from power, I am also drawing on the work of Kopano Ratele, who argues for "intra-African strangeness" between people of color. As Ratele says: "In the face of intransigent stereotypes fostering exclusivity, Africans need to re-accept that we have always been strange to one another." See, for an elaboration of Ratele's argument, Antjie Krog, *Conditional Tense: Memory and Vocabulary after the South African Truth and Reconciliation Commission* (Calcutta: Seagull Books, 2013), 113.

20. I am, of course, aware that these were not stable categories of identity and that they, in fact, changed over time. See, for work on racial classification and its changes over time in South Africa, Gerhard Maré, *Declassified: Moving Beyond the Dead End of Race in South Africa* (Johannesburg: Jacana, 2014); and Yvonne Erasmus, "Racial (Re)classification during Apartheid South Africa: Regulations, Experiences and Meaning(s) of 'Race'" (PhD thesis, St. George's, University of London, 2007).

21. I borrow from Christopher Boyer the idea of political landscapes, by which he means geographies rent by political contestation over the meaning of conservation, as well as access and resource extraction. See Christopher Boyer, *Political Landscapes: Forests, Conservation, and Community in Mexico* (Durham, NC: Duke University Press, 2015).

22. In keeping with the work of scholars such as Fred Cooper, Mark Mazower, and Luise White, I do not see the transformation of southern Africa or indeed the continent as a whole into discrete nation-states as

either natural or inevitable. See Fred Cooper, *Citizenship between Empire and Nation: Remaking France and French Africa, 1945–1960* (Princeton: Princeton University Press, 2014); Mark Mazower, *No Enchanted Palace: The End of Empire and the Ideological Origins of the United Nations* (Princeton: Princeton University Press, 2009); and Luise White, *Unpopular Sovereignty: Rhodesian Independence and African Decolonization* (Chicago: University of Chicago Press, 2015).

23. "The Kruger National Park," *South African Railways and Harbours Magazine*, December 1926, https://railways.haarhoff.co.za/issue/314/page /153.

24. "Kruger National Park."

25. Annie Coombes, *History after Apartheid: Visual Culture and Public Memory in a Democratic South Africa* (Durham, NC: Duke University Press, 2003), 154.

26. Susan Sessions Rugh, *Are We There Yet? The Golden Age of American Family Vacations* (Lawrence: University Press of Kansas, 2008), 51.

27. Jan Smuts, speech at Paarden Island Motor Show, April 1934. H. J. Crocker, director of the Johannesburg Publicity Association, mentioned Smuts's speech at a meeting of the Standing Advisory Board of the South African National Publicity Association in Pretoria in September 1934. National Archives and Records Service of South Africa, SAS G4/13/2 608.

28. Lynn Meskell, "Archaeological Ethnography: Conversations around Kruger National Park," *Archaeologies* 1, no. 1 (August 2005): 81–100.

29. See Cock, *War against Ourselves*, 148; Njabulo Ndebele, *Fine Lines from the Box: Further Thoughts about Our Country* (Roggebaai, Cape Town: Umuzi, 2007), 101; Jane Carruthers, "Game Protection in the Transvaal, 1846 to 1926" (PhD thesis, University of Cape Town, 1988), 20, http:// hdl.handle.net/11427/23736; Stanley Trapido, "Poachers, Proletarians and Gentry in the Early Twentieth-Century Transvaal" (paper presentation, African Studies Seminar, Wits University, Johannesburg, South Africa, March 12, 1984), http://hdl.handle.net/10539/9906. I am grateful to William Beinart for bringing Trapido's important but unpublished text to my attention and for sharing his copy with me. See, for a good example of a book that offers a supposedly apolitical but misleading history of the KNP, Rudolph Bigalke, *Let's Visit the Kruger Park* (Johannesburg: Afrikaanse Pers-Boekhandel, 1961).

30. See Bram Büscher, *Transforming the Frontier: Peace Parks and the Politics of Neoliberal Conservation in Southern Africa* (Durham, NC: Duke University Press, 2013); Elizabeth Lunstrum, "Articulated Sovereignty: Extending Mozambican State Power through the Great Limpopo Transfrontier Park," *Political Geography*, no. 36 (September 2013): 1–11; Clapperton Mavhunga and Marja Spierenburg, "Transfrontier Talk, Cordon Politics: The Early History of the Great Limpopo Transfrontier Park in Southern Africa, 1925–1940," *Journal of Southern African Studies* 35, no. 3 (September 2009): 715–35; Maano Ramutsindela, *Transfrontier Conservation in Africa: At the Confluence of Capital, Politics, and Nature* (Wallingford, Eng.: CABI, 2007);

Marja Spierenburg and Harry Wels, "'Securing Space': Mapping and Fencing in Transfrontier Conservation in Southern Africa," *Space and Culture* 9, no. 3 (August 2006): 294–312.

31. See, especially for more on the mobility of women through the borderlands of South Africa and Mozambique, Angela Impey, *Song Walking: Women, Music, and Environmental Justice in an African Borderland* (Chicago: University of Chicago Press, 2018).

32. See, for a history of this corner of southern Africa, Martin J. Murray, "'Blackbirding' at 'Crooks' Corner': Illicit Labour Recruiting in the Northeastern Transvaal, 1910–1940," *Journal of Southern African Studies* 21, no. 3 (September 1995): 373–97.

33. See Leslie Dikeni, *Habitat and Struggle: The Case of the Kruger National Park in South Africa* (Johannesburg: Real African Publishers, 2016).

34. See Lynn Meskell, *The Nature of Heritage: The New South Africa* (Malden, MA: Wiley-Blackwell, 2012).

35. See David Bunn, "Museum Outdoors," 359.

36. See Salomon Joubert, *The Kruger National Park: A History* (Johannesburg: High Branching, 2007); and Uys de V. Pienaar, *A Cameo from the Past: The Prehistory and Early History of the Kruger National Park*, trans. Helena Bryden (Pretoria: Protea Book House, 2012).

37. See Jacklyn Cock and Eddie Koch, eds., *Going Green: People, Politics and the Environment in South Africa* (Cape Town: Oxford University Press, 1991); and Cock, *War against Ourselves.*

38. See Jane Carruthers, *The Kruger National Park: A Social and Political History* (Pietermaritzburg: University of Natal Press, 1995), 96

39. See, for a representative sample, Meskell, *Cosmopolitan Archaeologies*; Cock, *War against Ourselves*; Magome and Murombedzi, "Sharing South African National Parks"; Carruthers, *Kruger National Park.*

40. See Dan Brockington, *Fortress Conservation: The Preservation of the Mkomazi Game Reserve, Tanzania* (Bloomington: Indiana University Press, 2002); Roderick P. Neumann, *Imposing Wilderness: Struggles over Livelihood and Nature Preservation in Africa* (Berkeley: University of California Press, 2002).

41. Carruthers, *Kruger National Park*, 96.

42. Carruthers, 90.

43. Julius Nyerere quoted in Roderick Nash, *Wilderness and the American Mind* (New Haven: Yale University Press, 2014), 342.

44. Clark C. Gibson, *Politicians and Poachers: The Political Economy of Wildlife Policy in Africa* (Cambridge: Cambridge University Press, 1999), 67.

45. Nash, *Wilderness*, 342. This is not to say that Nyerere was not a conservationist or that he did not care about wildlife. He did. As he said, although he might not have cared personally to spend his holidays watching crocodiles, "nevertheless, I am entirely in favor of their survival. I believe that after diamonds and sisal, wild animals will provide Tanganyika with its greatest source of income." Martha Honey, *Ecotourism and Sustainable Development: Who Owns Paradise?* (Washington, DC: Island Press, 1999), 227. Nyerere

sought to instrumentalize Tanzania's wildlife in order to take advantage of the growing international interest in African wildlife.

46. To be fair, Julius Nyerere's attitude to conservation was much more complex than his own pronouncements made it sound. See G. Wesley Burnett and Richard Conover, "The Efficacy of Africa's National Parks: An Evaluation of Julius Nyerere's Arusha Manifesto of 1961," *Society and Natural Resources* 2, no. 1 (1989): 251–60.

47. Contrary to fears among white settlers and Western conservationists that political independence in Africa would lead to the destruction of the continent's natural heritage, conservation has in fact thrived in Africa, with many more game reserves and national parks than there were under colonial or white rule. See Raymond Bonner, *At the Hand of Man: Peril and Hope for Africa's Wildlife* (New York: Knopf, 1993), 195.

48. Clapperton Chakanetsa Mavhunga, *Transient Workspaces: Technologies of Everyday Innovation in Zimbabwe* (Cambridge, MA: MIT Press, 2014), 5.

49. See Nash, *Wilderness*, 344; and Gilson Kaweche, "The Dilemma of an African Conservationist: Reflections from the Past, Hope for the Future," in *Voices from Africa: Local Perspectives on Conservation*, ed. Dale Lewis and Nick Carter (Washington, DC: World Wildlife Fund, 1993), 10.

50. Roderick Nash quoted in Jonathan S. Adams and Thomas O. McShane, *The Myth of Wild Africa: Conservation without Illusion* (Berkeley: University of California Press, 1996), xviii.

51. The first claim comes from Moeketsi Mosola, CEO of South African Tourism, quoted in Christian M. Rogerson and Zoleka Lisa, "'Sho't Left': Changing Domestic Tourism in South Africa," in *Urban Tourism in the Developing World: The South African Experience*, ed. Christian M. Rogerson and Gustav Visser (New Brunswick, NJ: Transaction, 2007), 70; Njabulo Ndebele's claim comes from Ndebele, *Fine Lines from the Box*, 102. Mosola's claim must be an article of faith at South African Tourism because we see it repeated more than ten years later by Mosola's successor Sisa Ntshona in an interview with *Sawubona*, the in-flight magazine of South African Airways. Ntshona says that "mobility is not ingrained within the general population." Trevor Crighton, "Rethinking Tourism in South Africa," *Sawubona*, August 2017, 83.

52. See Carolyn Finney, *Black Faces, White Spaces: Reimagining the Relationship of African Americans to the Great Outdoors* (Chapel Hill: University of North Carolina Press, 2014).

53. See Nancy Jacobs, *Birders of Africa: History of a Network* (New Haven: Yale University Press, 2016). Jacobs offers a brilliant prosopographic study of ornithologists from Africa, Europe, and North America.

54. See Maitseo Bolaane, *Chiefs, Hunters and San in the Creation of the Moremi Game Reserve, Okavango Delta: Multiracial Interactions and Initiatives, 1956–1979* (Osaka: National Museum of Ethnology, 2013), 3.

55. See Bolaane, *Chiefs, Hunters and San*, 124.

56. Edward Teversham, "Representations and Perceptions of the Kruger National Park and the Manyeleti Game Reserve, 1926–2010" (PhD thesis, Oxford University, 2014), 15.

57. See Reuben Matheka, "Antecedents to the Community Wildlife Conservation Program in Kenya, 1946–1964," *Environment and History* 11, no. 3 (August 2005): 245.

58. Matheka, "Antecedents to the Community Wildlife Conservation Program," 263.

59. Adrian Browne, "Conservation Converts? Africanizing Wildlife Conservation, Uganda National Parks, c. 1950–1973" (master's thesis, University of Oxford, 2010), 2. For more on the fears that the onset of decolonization in Africa would lead to the end of wildlife on the continent, see Bonner, *At the Hand of Man*, 195.

60. Browne, "Conservation Converts?," 2.

61. See Daniel Brockington and James Igoe, "Eviction for Conservation: A Global Overview," *Conservation and Society* 4, no. 3 (2006): 424–70.

62. See Jane Carruthers, "'South Africa: A World in One Country': Land Restitution in National Parks and Protected Areas," *Conservation and Society* 5, no. 3 (2007): 292; Brockington and Igoe, "Eviction for Conservation," 424–70; and Mahesh Rangarajan and Ghazala Shahabuddin, "Displacement and Relocation from Protected Areas: Towards a Biological and Historical Synthesis," *Conservation and Society* 4, no. 3 (2006): 359–78.

63. See Kathleen McKeown, "Tracking Wildlife Conservation in Southern Africa: Histories of Protected Areas in Gorongosa and Maputaland" (PhD diss., University of Minnesota, 2015), 1.

64. Jimmy Mnisi, interview with author, Shabalala, Mpumalanga, South Africa, November 2009.

65. See Lynn Meskell, "The Nature of Culture in Kruger National Park," in Meskell, *Cosmopolitan Archaeologies*, 91.

66. In 1957 the National Parks Board put up a 15-mile fence along its boundary with the Numbi area, southwest of the KNP. The erection of the fence followed the exchange of land between the park and the Department of Native Affairs. By the mid-1980s, the entire park was fenced, with the fence along the border with Mozambique electrified. See National Parks Board, *Annual Report for the Period January 1, 1956, to March 31, 1957* (Pretoria: National Parks Board of Trustees, 1957), 12.

67. However, the fact that the area was malarial did not mean that local Africans did not use it. See Randall Packard, "'Malaria Blocks Development' Revisited: The Role of Disease in the History of Agricultural Development in the Eastern and Northern Transvaal Lowveld, 1890–1960," *Journal of Southern African Studies* 27, no. 3 (2001): 591–612.

68. Roger Wagner, "Zoutpansberg: The Dynamics of a Hunting Frontier, 1848–67," in *Economy and Society in Pre-industrial South Africa*, ed. Shula Marks and Anthony Atmore (London: Longman, 1980), 293–313. The lowveld has been the subject of excellent studies into the precolonial history

of southern Africa. See, for example, Peter Delius and Michelle Hay, eds., *Mpumalanga: An Illustrated History* (Johannesburg: Highveld, 2009); see also Natalie Swanepoel, Amanda Esterhuysen, and Philip Bonner, *Five Hundred Years Rediscovered: Southern African Precedents and Prospects* (Johannesburg: Wits University Press, 2008).

69. Patrick Harries, "Exclusion, Classification and Internal Colonialism: The Emergence of Ethnicity among the Tsonga-Speakers of South Africa," in *The Creation of Tribalism in Southern Africa*, ed. Leroy Vail (London: Currey, 1989), 93.

70. Peter Warwick, *Black People and the South African War, 1899–1902* (Cambridge: Cambridge University Press, 1983).

71. To be sure, the process by which African polities lost their land was long and complicated. See, for a treatment of this complicated process, Harvey Feinberg, *Our Land, Our Life, Our Future: Black South African Challenges to Territorial Segregation, 1913–1948* (Pretoria: UNISA, 2015).

72. See Phia Steyn, "A Greener Past? An Assessment of South African Environmental Historiography," *New Contree*, no. 46 (November 1999): 7–31.

73. See Carruthers, *Kruger National Park*.

74. See Jeanne van Eeden, "Surveying the 'Empty Land' in Selected South African Landscape Postcards," *International Journal of Tourism Research* 13, no. 6 (2011): 600–612.

75. Jane Carruthers, "Creating a National Park, 1910 to 1926," *Journal of Southern African Studies* 15, no. 2 (January 1989), 189

76. See Carruthers, "Creating a National Park," 189. This is not to suggest that "white South Africa" had a commonality of interests. It did not. See, for studies examining some of the fissures within white South Africa, Saul Dubow and Alan Jeeves, eds., *South Africa's 1940s: Worlds of Possibilities* (Cape Town: Double Storey Books, 2005). For a classic exploration of divisions within Afrikaner South Africa, see Dan O'Meara, *Volkskapitalisme: Class, Capital and Ideology in the Development of Afrikaner Nationalism, 1934–1948* (Johannesburg: Ravan, 1983).

77. Carruthers, "Creating a National Park," 189.

78. South African National Archives and Records Service, SNA NTS 92/400 and 95/400.

79. See, for the surveyors' account of the demarcation, W. P. Murray, "Definition of the Northern Section of the Transvaal-Portuguese Boundary Line," *South African Survey Journal* 2, no. 3 (1926–27): 125–31.

80. See Karl Jacoby, *Crimes against Nature: Squatters, Poachers, Thieves, and the Hidden History of American Conservation* (Berkeley: University of California Press, 2001), 29.

81. House of Assembly *Hansard* 31 May 1926 Col 4367 (S. Afr.).

82. Lynn Meskell, "The Nature of Culture in Kruger National Park," in Meskell, *Cosmopolitan Archaeologies*, 89–113.

83. House of Assembly *Hansard* 31 May 1926 Col 4369 (S. Afr.).

84. See, for an example of this kind of territorial swaps, the *National Parks Board Annual Report for the Period January 1, 1956, to March 31, 1957* (Pretoria: National Parks Board of Trustees, 1957), 12.

85. See James Stevenson-Hamilton's description in the National Parks Board's annual report for 1940, as well as Lynn Meskell's description in Meskell, "Archaeological Ethnography.": Conversations around Kruger National Park," *Archaeologies* 1, no. 1 (2005), 81–100.

86. See Lynda von den Steinen, "MK in the Frontline States and South Africa," in Department of Historical Studies, University of Cape Town, ed., *From Apartheid to Democracy: Localities and Liberation* (Cape Town: Department of Historical Studies, University of Cape Town, 2007), 69–104. MK refers to Umkhonto we Sizwe, the military wing of the ANC. As MK operative Garth Strachan says on pages 74–75, insurgents trying to infiltrate South Africa through the KNP suffered an almost 100 percent casualty rate. Strachan's account on this score is more sobering than the accounts offered by Lynn Meskell and Edward Teversham. See Meskell, *Nature of Heritage*, 75; and Teversham, "Representations and Perceptions," 15.

87. See, for more on land restitution in postapartheid South Africa, Ben Cousins and Cherryl Walker, eds., *Land Divided, Land Restored: Land Reform in South Africa for the 21st century* (Johannesburg: Jacana, 2015); Fred Hendricks, Lungisile Ntsebeza, and Kirk Helliker, eds., *The Promise of Land: Undoing a Century of Dispossession in South Africa* (Johannesburg: Jacana, 2013); Cherryl Walker et al., eds., *Land, Memory, Reconstruction, and Justice: Perspectives on Land Claims in South Africa* (Athens: Ohio University Press, 2010); and, for a classic treatment of land claims in South Africa, see Cherryl Walker, *Landmarked: Land Claims and Land Restitution in South Africa* (Johannesburg: Jacana, 2008). For more on Mandela's role in land restitution, see Colin Murray, preface to *Land Restitution in South Africa: A Long Way Home*, ed. Marj Brown et al. (Cape Town: IDASA, 1998).

88. See *39th Annual Report of the National Parks Board for the Year 1963 to October 1964* (Pretoria: National Parks Board of Trustees), 35.

89. I owe my conception of the idea of dissonance to historian Justin Willis. See his essay "Two Lives of Mpamizo: Understanding Dissonance in Oral History," *History in Africa*, no. 23 (January 1996): 319–32.

90. See Richard Drayton, "Where Does the World Historian Write From? Objectivity, Moral Conscience and the Past and Present of Imperialism," *Journal of Contemporary History* 46, no. 3 (July 2011): 672.

91. The Mahashi claim sought to emulate arguably the most successful challenge to the KNP to date, namely the Makuleke land claim of 1998. Like the Mahashi, the Makulekes (in the northern section of the park) were also forcibly expelled from the KNP in 1969. In 1998 the Makuleke won back control of their lands from the KNP. However, instead of returning to the restored lands, the Makuleke leased the land back to the KNP in return for a share of the proceeds. See, for more on the Makuleke, Steven Robins and Kees van der Waal, "'Model Tribes' and Iconic Conservationists? Tracking

the Makuleke Restitution Case in the Kruger National Park," in Walker et al., *Land, Memory, Reconstruction, and Justice*, 163–80. The Makuleke case has become something of a cause célèbre in debates about land claims in South Africa, and, for that reason, this book avoids a detailed discussion of it. But it certainly acknowledges its importance.

92. See Carruthers, "'South Africa: A World in One Country,'" 293.

93. I borrow the idea of social memories from Jan Bender Shetler, *Imagining Serengeti: A History of Landscape Memory in Tanzania from Earliest Times to the Present* (Athens: Ohio University Press, 2007), 6.

94. See, for a novel treatment of South Africa's unsettled pasts, Leslie Witz, Gary Minkley and Ciraj Rasool, *Unsettled History: Making South Africans Public Pasts* (Ann Arbor: University of Michigan Press, 2017).

CHAPTER 1: NATURAL ENEMIES

1. The South African War was key to the making of South Africa as a unitary state, as Stanley Trapido and Shula Marks show in two of the most cogent contributions to debates about the war. See Stanley Trapido, "Imperialism, Settler Identities and Colonial Capitalism: The Hundred-Year Origins of the 1899 South African War," in *The Cambridge History of South Africa*, vol. 2, *1885–1994*, ed. Robert Ross, Anne Kelk Mager, and Bill Nasson (New York: Cambridge University Press, 2011), 66–101; Shula Marks, "War and Union: 1899–1910," in Ross, Mager, and Nasson, *Cambridge History of South Africa*, 2:157–210. See, for insightful literature on the war, Bill Nasson, *The South African War, 1899–1902* (New York: Oxford University Press, 1999); Warwick, *Black People and the South African War*; John Comaroff and Brian Willan, *The Mafeking Diary of Sol T. Plaatje* (Cape Town: David Philip, 1999). For more on the regiment called Steinhecker's Horse, see Joubert, *Kruger National Park*.

2. South African National Archives and Records Service, *Transvaal Administration Reports for 1903*, Annexure H (Pretoria: Government Printers, 1904), D44, hereafter Transvaal Administration Reports.

3. Transvaal Administration Reports, D44. Jane Carruthers's biography of Stevenson-Hamilton remains the definitive account of this complicated but remarkable Scottish aristocrat. A beautiful writer, Stevenson-Hamilton was also possessed of political savvy and stamina. These two qualities helped him stamp his authority on the lowveld and on the park in particular. See Jane Carruthers, *Wildlife and Warfare: The Life of James Stevenson-Hamilton* (Pietermaritzburg: University of Natal Press, 2001). To this day, for many locals in the lowveld, the park is synonymous with Skukuza, the nickname by which Stevenson-Hamilton went. He ran the park for forty-four years.

4. Transvaal Administration Reports, D44.

5. Transvaal Administration Reports, D44. On the notion of exemplary violence as colonialism's favorite tool, see Allen Isaacman, *Cotton is the Mother of Poverty: Peasants, Work and Rural Struggle in Colonial Mozambique, 1938–1961* (London: Heinemann, 1995); and Isaacman, "Coercion, Paternalism

and the Labor Process: The Mozambique Cotton Regime, 1938–1961," *Journal of Southern African Studies* 18, no. 3 (September 1992): 487–526. See also Jeanne Penvenne, "João dos Santos Albasini (1876–1922): The Contradictions of Politics and Identity in Colonial Mozambique," *Journal of African History* 37, no. 3 (1996): 417–64.

6. George Steinmetz, "'The Devil's Handwriting': Precolonial Discourse, Ethnographic Acuity, and Cross-identification in German Colonialism," *Comparative Studies in Society and History* 45, no. 1 (January 2003): 53.

7. Carruthers, "Game Protection in the Transvaal, 1846 to 1926" (PhD thesis, University of Cape Town, 1988), 264, http://hdl.handle.net /11427/23736.

8. Jan Smuts, foreword to *The Lowveld: Its Wildlife and Its People*, by James Stevenson-Hamilton (London: Cassell, 1929).

9. See Jane Carruthers, "'Police Boys' and Poachers: Africans, Wildlife Protection and National Parks, the Transvaal 1902 to 1950," *Koedoe* 36, no. 2 (September 1993): 13. The fact that the game laws were being honored more in the breach than in practice is a useful illustration of a point made by a number of scholars: some writers are too quick to accord the colonial and apartheid state a bureaucratic consistency and intellectual coherence it simply did not have. One striking example of this concerns the 1913 Natives Land Act. It has become an article of faith that the act confined Africans to 13 percent of South Africa's land mass and that the act was the origin of the political sin of dispossession. However, as Harvey Feinberg shows, the state simply did not have the capacity to enforce the law, and it would not be until the second half of the twentieth century that the act was implemented in full. See Harvey Feinberg and André Horn, "South African Territorial Segregation: New Data on African Farm Purchases, 1913–1936," *Journal of African History* 50, no. 1 (March 2009): 41–60. Feinberg and Horn show that, despite the law's stated intention to prevent Africans from buying land outside so-called scheduled areas, meaning land identified by the state for sole African purchase and use, Africans continued to buy land. For studies that show the fragility of the colonial and apartheid state, see Charles van Onselen, *The Seed Is Mine: The Life of Kas Maine, A South African Sharecropper* (New York: Hill and Wang, 1996); Saul Dubow, *Racial Segregation and the Origins of Apartheid in South Africa, 1919–36* (London: Palgrave Macmillan, 1989); Ivan Evans, *Bureaucracy and Race: Native Administration in South Africa* (Berkeley: University of California Press, 1997); and Deborah Posel, *The Making of Apartheid: Conflict and Compromise, 1948–1961* (Oxford: Clarendon Press, 1992). What these scholars do, each in his or her own way, is show the ideological inconsistencies and bureaucratic incoherence of segregation and apartheid.

10. South African National Archives and Records Service, *Transvaal Native Affairs Department Report for the Years 1919 to 1921* (Pretoria: Government Printers), 6; Howard Rogers, *Native Administration in the Union of South Africa* (Johannesburg: University of Witwatersrand Press, 1933), 150. For the definitive and standard account of taxation in South Africa, see Sean

Redding, *Sovereignty and Sorcery: Taxation, Power, and Rebellion in South Africa, 1880–1963* (Athens: Ohio University Press, 2006).

11. Jane Carruthers, "'Police Boys' and Poachers," 13.

12. Carruthers, 14.

13. James Stevenson-Hamilton, *Animal Life in Africa* (London: Heinemann, 1912), 15–22.

14. John Knight, introduction to *Natural Enemies: People-Wildlife Conflicts in Anthropological Perspective* (London: Routledge, 2000).

15. Knight, *Natural Enemies*, 6–7.

16. For a different but illuminating case of struggles over natural resource control, see Ekaterina Pravilova, *A Public Empire: Property and the Quest for the Common Good in Imperial Russia* (Princeton: Princeton University Press, 2014). The key difference, as Pravilova shows so well in her rich monograph, is that in the case of Russia in the 1890s, it was the aristocracy and the landowning class that saw their customary hunting rights curtailed by the imperial state as it sought to protect nature as the patrimony of the nation. See especially pp. 70–72.

17. The Africans had to do this because colonial authorities would not allow them to keep dogs. Dogs were, after guns, one of the most important means of hunting for black South Africans. This made black-owned dogs, especially in the rural areas of South Africa, a special target of the colonial and apartheid state. See, for a general history of the dog in southern Africa, Sandra Swart and Lance von Sittert, eds., *Canis Africanis: A Dog History of Southern Africa* (Boston: Brill, 2008).

18. The Native Affairs Department has generated first-rate monographs. See, for example, Dubow, *Racial Segregation*; and Evans, *Bureaucracy and Race*.

19. This clash of mandates confirms the validity of a revisionist historiography that presents a more complex view of the South African state during both segregationist (1910–48) and apartheid (1948–94) eras. See, for a representative sample of this literature, Dubow, *Racial Segregation*; and Posel, *Making of Apartheid*.

20. See Carruthers, *Wildlife and Warfare*.

21. Carruthers, 90.

22. Transvaal Administration Reports, D47.

23. Transvaal Administration Reports, D47.

24. Transvaal Administration Reports, D47.

25. South African National Archives and Records Service, NTS 7612, 8/329.

26. South African National Archives and Records Service, NTS 7612, 8/329.

27. Guns, a symbol of power, resistance, and violence, have been an important part of the portmanteau of colonial rule in Africa. See, for a history of the gun in southern Africa, William K. Storey, *Guns, Race, and Power in Colonial South Africa* (New York: Cambridge University Press, 2008).

28. There is extensive literature on the social history of hunting, especially the fraught topic of who decides when a hunter is a poacher. Scholars working in this area have also done sterling work examining the links between hunting, criminalization, and racialization. See, for some of the best examples, Mavhunga, *Transient Workspaces*; and Edward Steinhart, *Black Poachers, White Hunters: A Social History of Hunting in Colonial Kenya* (Athens: Ohio University Press, 2006); for the U.S. case, see Louis S. Warren, *The Hunter's Game: Poachers and Conservationists in Twentieth-Century America* (New Haven: Yale University Press, 1997); for Imperial Russia, see Pravilova, *Public Empire*. For the use of the law in disputes over hunting/ poaching, see E. P. Thompson, *Whigs and Hunters: The Origin of the Black Act* (London: Breviary Stuff, 2013); and Douglas Hay et al., *Albion's Fatal Tree: Crime and Society in Eighteenth-Century England* (London: Verso, 2011). Jane Carruthers also offers a brilliant examination of this in her classic PhD dissertation. See Carruthers, "Game Protection in the Transvaal."

29. Transvaal Administration Reports.

30. Transvaal Administration Reports.

31. Borders in Africa have been the subject of intense scholarship, with some scholars looking mainly at their colonial origins and others questioning the idea that Africa owes its borders to colonialism. See, for a sample of this literature, Paul Nugent, *Smugglers, Secessionists and Loyal Citizens: On the Ghana-Togo Frontier* (Athens: Ohio University Press, 2003); Achille Mbembe, "At the Edge of the World: Boundaries, Territoriality and Sovereignty in Africa," in *Globalization*, ed. Arjun Appadurai (Durham, NC: Duke University Press, 2001), 22–51. Whereas Nugent and Mbembe are among those who question the idea that Africa owes its borders to European rule, Jeffrey Herbst counts among those scholars who not only date African borders to colonial rule but connect those borders to the economic and political problems of contemporary Africa. See Herbst, *States and Power in Africa: Comparative Lessons in Authority and Control* (Princeton: Princeton University Press, 2000).

32. South African National Archives and Records Service, NTS 7612, 8/329.

33. South African National Archives and Records Service, NTS 7612, 8/329.

34. South African National Archives and Records Service, NTS 7612, 8/329.

35. National Parks Board, *Annual Report for 1911* (Pretoria: National Parks Board of Trustees, 1912).

36. Stanley Trapido makes the telling remark that these men's names were "doubtless assigned to them in the manner of settler tradition." See Trapido, "Poachers, Proletarians and Gentry in the Early Twentieth-Century Transvaal" (paper presentation, African Studies Seminar, Wits University, Johannesburg, South Africa, March 12, 1984), http:// hdl.handle.net/10539/9906, 21. I am grateful to William Beinart for bringing Trapido's important text to my attention and for sharing his copy with me.

37. South African National Archives and Records Service, NTS 7612, 8/329.

38. South African National Archives and Records Service, NTS 7612, 8/329.

39. South African National Archives and Records Service, NTS 7612, 8/329.

40. South African National Archives and Records Service, NTS 7612, 8/329.

41. South African National Archives and Records Service, NTS 7612, 8/329.

42. South African National Archives and Records Service, NTS 7612, 8/329.

43. The story of female mobility is an important part of the overall story of black presence told in this book, even though the archival evidence is either thin or silent. See, for arguably the most important contribution to this topic, Teresa Barnes's priceless chapter "Virgin Territory? Travel and Migration by African Women in Twentieth-Century Southern Africa," in *Women in African Colonial Histories*, ed. Jean Allman, Susan Geiger, and Nakanyike Musisi (Bloomington: Indiana University Press, 2002), 164–90. As Barnes shows, men might have dominated the migrant labor system, but they certainly did not have a monopoly on migration and mobility. Women also moved around, to the utter chagrin of colonial officials who preferred to see African women rooted to the rural areas, away from the cities. See, for another insightful take on the role of women, mobility, and migrancy in southern Africa, Impey, *Song Walking*.

44. Mavhunga, *Transient Workspaces*, 20.

45. Mavhunga, 17.

46. Mavhunga, 20.

47. Mavhunga, 7.

48. Bunn, "Museum Outdoors," 376.

49. Bunn, 383.

50. Martin Chanock offers a cogent political history of the law in South Africa, showing the complex ways in which the law buttressed white rule in the country. See Chanock, *The Making of South African Legal Culture, 1902–1936: Fear, Favor and Prejudice* (Cambridge: Cambridge University Press, 2001).

51. South African National Archives and Records Service, NTS 7612, 7/329 and 9/329.

52. South African National Archives and Records Service, NTS 7612, 7/329 and 9/329.

53. E. P. Thompson, *Whigs and Hunters*, 107.

54. See Trapido "Poachers, Proletarians and Gentry," 20.

55. South African National Archives and Records Service, JUS 432, 3/702/27 and 3/1082/27.

56. South African National Archives and Records Service, JUS 432, 3/702/27 and 3/1082/27.

57. South African National Archives and Records Service, JUS 432, 3/702/27 and 3/1082/27.

58. South African National Archives and Records Service, JUS 432, 3/702/27 and 3/1082/27.

59. South African National Archives and Records Service, JUS 432, 3/702/27 and 3/1082/27.

60. South African National Archives and Records Service, JUS 432, 3/702/27 and 3/1082/27.

61. South African National Archives and Records Service, NTS 3589, 847/308 and 859/308.

62. South African National Archives and Records Service, NTS 3589, 847/308 and 859/308.

63. South African National Archives and Records Service, NTS 3589, 847/308 and 859/308.

64. South African National Archives and Records Service, NTS 3589, 853/308.

65. South African National Archives and Records Service, NTS 3589, 853/308.

66. South African National Archives and Records Service, NTS 3589, 847/308.

67. South African National Archives and Records Service, NTS 7618, 31/329.

68. South African National Archives and Records Service, NTS 7618.

69. See Carruthers, "'Police Boys' and Poachers," 14.

70. South African National Archives and Records Service, NTS 7612, 9/329.

71. South African National Archives and Records Service, NTS 7612, 9/329.

72. South African National Archives and Records Service, NTS 7612.

73. South African National Archives and Records Service, NTS 7612, 9/329.

74. South African National Archives and Records Service, NTS 7612.

75. South African National Archives and Records Service, NTS 7612.

76. South African National Archives and Records Service, NTS 7618.

77. South African National Archives and Records Service, NTS 7618.

78. South African National Archives and Records Service, NTS 7618, 28/329.

79. Carruthers, "'Police Boys' and Poachers," 12.

CHAPTER 2: STRAY BOYS

1. The migrant labor system in southern Africa is, arguably, one of the most researched topics in histories of the region. Scholars working on the topic have explored a number of its aspects, from what made Portuguese East Africa (especially Mozambique) such a key recruitment area, to how Africans responded to the challenges and opportunities presented by mining, and to

the history of mining itself. See, for example, Patrick Harries's classic *Work, Culture, and Identity*; Simon Katzenellenbogen, *South Africa and Southern Mozambique: Labour, Railways and Trade in the Making of a Relationship* (Manchester: Manchester University Press, 1982); Peter Delius, *The Land Belongs to Us: The Pedi Polity, the Boers and the British in the Nineteenth-Century Transvaal* (London: Heinemann, 1984); Peter Delius, Laura Phillips, and Fiona Rankin-Smith, eds., *A Long Way Home: Migrant Worker Worlds, 1800–2014* (Johannesburg: Wits University Press, 2014); William Beinart, *The Political Economy of Pondoland, 1860–1930* (Cape Town: Cambridge University Press, 1982); Jade Davenport, *Digging Deep: A History of Mining in South Africa, 1852–2002* (Johannesburg: Jonathan Ball, 2013). The definitive text on labor migrancy remains Jonathan Crush, Alan Jeeves, and David Yudelman, eds., *South Africa's Labor Empire: A History of Black Migrancy to the Gold Mines* (Boulder: Westview, 1991). Keith Breckenridge's pathbreaking work on the history of surveillance in South Africa shows the central role played by the mining industry in the development of everything from policing to modern surveillance technologies such as fingerprinting. See Breckenridge, *Biometric State: The Global Politics of Identification and Surveillance in South Africa, 1850 to the Present* (New York: Cambridge University Press, 2014).

2. See, for a history of Wenela and a detailed explanation of how the system worked, Katzenellenbogen, *South Africa and Southern Mozambique*.

3. University of Johannesburg, TEBA/Chamber of Mines Archives, WNLA 197/16.

4. University of Johannesburg, TEBA/Chamber of Mines Archives, WNLA 197/16.

5. University of Johannesburg, TEBA/Chamber of Mines Archives, WNLA 197/16.

6. University of Johannesburg, TEBA/Chamber of Mines Archives, WNLA 197/16.

7. University of Johannesburg, TEBA/Chamber of Mines Archives, WNLA 197/16.

8. Transvaal Administration Reports.

9. For an excellent general history of mining in South Africa, see Davenport, *Digging Deep*.

10. For an examination of these dynamics, see Harries, *Work, Culture, and Identity*.

11. University of Johannesburg, TEBA/Chamber of Mines Archives, file no. 45B.

12. See Peter Alexander, "Oscillating Migrants, 'Detribalized Families' and Militancy: Mozambicans on Witbank Collieries, 1918–1927," *Journal of Southern African Studies* 27, no. 3 (September 2001): 509.

13. For a classic treatment of the problem of forced labor in Mozambique, see Allen Isaacman, *Cotton is the Mother of Poverty: Peasants, Work, and Rural Struggle in Colonial Mozambique, 1938–1961* (London: James Currey, 1996).

See also Jeanne Penvenne, "Forced Labor and the Origins of an African Working Class: Lourenço Marques, 1870–1962" (working paper, African Studies Center, Boston University, 1979).

14. Alexander, "Oscillating Migrants," 509.

15. Peter Alexander disputes the claim by David Yudelman and Alan Jeeves that "by 1910, the mines had created a low wage system of oscillating migration which subjected blacks to quasi-servitude as unskilled workers in a rigidly hierarchical racial division of labor." Yudelman and Jeeves make the claim in "New Labour Frontiers for Old: Black Migrants to the South African Gold Mines, 1920–85," *Journal of Southern African Studies* 13, no. 1 (October 1986): 103.

16. Alexander, "Oscillating Migrants," 515.

17. See, for excellent scholarship on worker consciousness in southern Africa, Helen Bradford, *A Taste of Freedom: The ICU in Rural South Africa, 1924–1930* (Johannesburg: Ravan, 1987); P. L. Wickins, *The Industrial and Commercial Workers' Union of Africa* (Cape Town: Oxford University Press, 1978); and Charles van Onselen, "Worker Consciousness in Black Miners: Southern Rhodesia, 1900–1920," *Journal of African History* 14, no. 2 (April 1973): 237–55.

18. Alexander, "Oscillating Migrants," 524.

19. See Leonard Thompson, *A History of South Africa* (Johannesburg: Jonathan Ball, 2006), 163.

20. Peter Limb offers a sobering account of the criminally paltry pay that black miners received. See Limb, *The ANC's Early Years: Nation, Class and Place in South Africa before 1940* (Pretoria: UNISA, 2010).

21. Jeremy Krikler gives a detailed account of the violence to which black mineworkers were subjected by their white counterparts. See Krikler, *White Rising: The 1922 Insurrection and Racial Killing in South Africa* (Manchester: Manchester University Press, 2005).

22. Yudelman and Jeeves, "New Labour Frontiers for Old," 104.

23. See Katzenellenbogen, *South Africa and Southern Mozambique.*

24. University of Johannesburg, TEBA/Chamber of Mines Archives, unnumbered NRC pads, file no. 197/9.

25. David Yudelman and Alan Jeeves, "New Labour Frontiers for Old," 104.

26. William Beinart, *Twentieth-Century South Africa* (Oxford: Oxford University Press, 2001), 70.

27. Alan Jeeves, "The Control of Migratory Labor on the South African Gold Mines in the Era of Kruger and Milner," *Journal of Southern African Studies* 2, no. 1 (October 1975): 16. Jeeves is writing about the period before the South African War in 1898–1902. But his conclusions still hold for the first three decades of the twentieth century.

28. H. H. Mockford, who was a senior Wenela official stationed in the park, gives a fascinating account of his time in the park. See Mockford, "The Saga of the WNLA in the Kruger National Park," in Pienaar, *Cameo from*

the Past, 666–84. Such was the closeness of Mockford's relationship with park officials that he served as an honorary ranger in the park. This is not to downplay Mockford's own commitment to conservation.

29. University of Johannesburg, TEBA/Chamber of Mines Archives, WNLA 46B, Pad 1.

30. See Carruthers, *Kruger National Park*, 95.

31. Mockford, "Saga of the WNLA," 674.

32. University of Johannesburg, TEBA/Chamber of Mines Archives, WNLA 46B, Pad 1.

33. Mockford, "Saga of the WNLA," 674–75.

34. Mockford, 666–84.

35. University of Johannesburg, TEBA/Chamber of Mines Archives, unnumbered NRC pad, file no. 197.

36. University of Johannesburg, TEBA/Chamber of Mines Archives, W. Gemmill letter dated 9 June 1922, file no. 197.

37. Joubert, *Kruger National Park*, 1:87.

38. Joubert, 1:107.

39. Joubert, 1:257.

40. Joubert, 1:257.

41. Carruthers, *Kruger National Park*, 94.

42. Carruthers, "'Police Boys' and Poachers," 13.

43. To get a sense of the conditions in rural South Africa, see John Higginson's *Collective Violence and the Agrarian Origins of South African Apartheid, 1900–1948* (New York: Cambridge University Press, 2014); and Jeremy Krikler, *Revolution from Above, Rebellion from Below: The Agrarian Transvaal at the Turn of the Century* (Oxford: Clarendon Press, 1993).

44. A particularly important piece of territory was a strip of no-man's-land between Mozambique, Rhodesia, and South Africa called Crook's Corner. Here all sorts of characters sought refuge from the law. See Martin J. Murray, "'Blackbirding' at 'Crooks' Corner': Illicit Labour Recruiting in the Northeastern Transvaal, 1910–1940," *Journal of Southern African Studies* 21, no. 3 (September 1995): 373–97.

45. University of Johannesburg, TEBA/Chamber of Mines Archives, WNLA 46/B.

46. University of Johannesburg, TEBA/Chamber of Mines Archives, WNLA 46/B.

47. South African National Archives and Records Service, NTS 7618, 28/329.

48. University of Johannesburg, TEBA/Chamber of Mines Archives, WNLA 46/B.

49. University of Johannesburg, TEBA/Chamber of Mines Archives, WNLA 46/B.

50. National Parks Board, *Annual Report 1928* (Pretoria: National Parks Board of Trustees, 1929).

51. University of Johannesburg, TEBA/Chamber of Mines Archives, WNLA 46/B.

52. University of Johannesburg, TEBA/Chamber of Mines Archives, WNLA 46/B.

53. University of Johannesburg, TEBA/Chamber of Mines Archives, WNLA 46/B.

54. University of Johannesburg, TEBA/Chamber of Mines Archives, WNLA 46/B.

55. University of Johannesburg, TEBA/Chamber of Mines Archives, WNLA 46/B.

56. See chap. 1, n. 43.

57. University of Johannesburg, TEBA/Chamber of Mines Archives, WNLA 46/B.

58. Carruthers, *Kruger National Park*, 95.

59. University of Johannesburg, TEBA/Chamber of Mines Archives, WNLA 46/B.

60. See Carruthers, *Kruger National Park*, 92.

61. South African National Archives and Records Service, NTS 28/329.

62. Bunn, "Museum Outdoors," 361.

63. National Parks Board, *Annual Report 1928*.

64. Bunn, "Museum Outdoors," 361.

65. Bunn, 362.

66. Bunn, 370.

67. National Parks Board, *Annual Report 1928*.

68. National Parks Board, *Annual Report 1945*.

69. National Parks Board, *Annual Report 1932*.

70. Harvey Feinberg, arguably one of the best historians writing about the land question in South Africa, offers an informative explanation of the meaning of terms such as "scheduled" and "released" lands. See Feinberg, *Our Land, Our Life, Our Future*.

71. National Parks Board, *Annual Report 1937* (Pretoria: National Parks Board of Trustees, 1938).

72. The figures of 7 percent and 13 percent have acquired lives of their own, making it sound as if black South Africans literally occupied only 13 percent of South Africa's landmass. This is not true. As William Beinart says, "It may be more accurate to say that the 'homelands' came to cover perhaps 30 per cent of the land which the African chiefdoms had previously occupied, often in their old heartlands, most of it in the wetter parts of the country." See Beinart, "Beyond 'Homelands': Some Ideas about the History of African Rural Areas in South Africa," *South African Historical Journal* 64, no. 1 (2012): 8.

73. South African National Archives and Records Service, NTS 28/329.

74. South African National Archives and Records Service, NTS 28/329.

75. This point is well made by Carruthers, *Kruger National Park*, 92.

76. South African National Archives and Records Service, NTS 28/329.

77. James Stevenson-Hamilton, *South African Eden: From Sabi Game Reserve to Kruger National Park* (London: Cassell, 1937), 116.

78. The episode is recounted with some glee in the 1963 edition of *Our National Parks* (Pretoria: National Parks Board, 1963), 47.

79. For an account of epidemics in southern Africa, see Pule Phoofolo, "Epidemics and Revolutions: The Rinderpest Epidemic in Late Nineteenth-Century Southern Africa," *Past and Present*, no. 138 (1993): 112–43. See also Charles van Onselen, "Reactions to Rinderpest in Southern Africa, 1896–97," *Journal of African History* 13, no. 3 (1972): 473–88.

80. Joubert, *Kruger National Park*, 1:169.

81. Joubert, 1:70.

82. Joubert, 1:70.

83. Joubert, 1:71.

84. This was a common belief among farmers, who took it as an article of faith that wildlife was, by definition, bad for agriculture and livestock farming. See, for example, Shirley Brooks's account of the Hluhluwe-Umfolozi Game Reserve in Brooks, "Re-reading the Hluhluwe-Umfolozi Game Reserve: Constructions of a 'Natural' Space," *Transformation: Critical Perspectives on South Africa*, no. 44 (2000): 63–79.

85. National Parks Board, *Annual Report 1940*, 5.

86. National Parks Board, *Annual Report 1940*, 5.

87. National Parks Board, *Annual Report 1949*, 9.

88. National Parks Board, *Annual Report 1956/7*, 24.

89. The figures are drawn from National Parks Board annual reports from the 1930s to the 1950s.

CHAPTER 3: NEW AFRICANS

1. See, for a helpful study of struggles over mobility in South Africa, Jonathan Klaaren, "Migrating to Citizenship: Mobility, Law, and Nationality in South Africa, 1897–1937" (PhD diss., Yale University, 2004).

2. I would like to propose, after Paul Gilroy, that we think of what these actors were doing along two tracks—autonomy and mobility—and that we see the cultures of travel enacted in this chapter as instances of this marriage of freedom and movement. Gilroy calls this "automobility," an insightful and productive marriage of the drive for freedom and movement. See Gilroy's W. E. B. Du Bois Lectures, published as *Darker than Blue: On the Moral Economies of Black Atlantic Culture* (Cambridge, MA: Belknap, 2011), and his brilliant essay "Driving while Black," in *Car Cultures*, ed. Daniel Miller (Oxford: Berg, 2001), 81–104. Those interested in black automobility should also look forward with great interest to Allyson Hobbs's book project *Far from Sanctuary: African American Travel and the Road to Civil Rights* (Cambridge, MA: Harvard University Press, forthcoming).

3. See, for the importance of newspapers as invaluable historical sources for African history, Derek Peterson, Emma Hunter, and Stephanie Newell,

eds., *African Print Cultures: Newspapers and Their Publics in the Twentieth-Century* (Ann Arbor: University of Michigan Press, 2016); Lynn Thomas, "The Modern Girl and Racial Respectability in 1930s South Africa," in *The Modern Girl around the World: Consumption, Modernity, and Globalization*, ed. Alys Eve Weinbaum et al. (Durham, NC: Duke University Press, 2008), 96–119. See also Ntongela Masilela, *An Outline of the New African Movement in South Africa* (Trenton: African World Press, 2013). For an insightful look at the creative and subversive ways in which West Africans used newspapers, see Stephanie Newell, *The Power to Name: A History of Anonymity in Colonial West Africa* (Athens: Ohio University Press, 2013). Sol Plaatje was a pioneering member of the black elite in colonial South Africa. See, for an excellent study of Plaatje and his place in the colonial and imperial world, Brian Willan, *Sol Plaatje: A Life of Solomon Tshekiso Plaatje, 1876–1932* (Johannesburg: Jacana, 2018).

4. For the rich ways in which members of this class represented themselves through their leisure activities, see Tim Couzens, "'Moralizing Leisure Time': The Transatlantic Connection and Black Johannesburg, 1918–1936," in *Industrialization and Social Change in South Africa: African Class Formation, Culture, and Consciousness, 1870–1930*, ed. Shula Marks and Richard Rathbone (London: Longman, 1982), 314–37.

5. Thorstein Veblen's observations about the activities and motivations of classes with the means and the time for leisure remain the standard for any work interested in the class and social dimensions of leisure. See Veblen, *The Theory of the Leisure Class* (New York: Dover, 1994). Of course, as we know from Pierre Bourdieu, there is always more to leisure than what a class of people does when on holiday. There is always an assertion of status and difference. See Bourdieu, *Distinction: A Social Critique of the Judgment of Taste* (London: Routledge, 2010).

6. The use of the Swiss Alps was a common trope in South African writing about Lesotho. See Eric Rosenthal's travelogue *African Switzerland: An Account of the Country and People of Basutoland* (Johannesburg: Juta, 1948).

7. The writer likely had in mind Ray Phillips, a U.S. missionary based in Johannesburg who believed that so-called empty leisure bred laziness, which, in turn, bred indolence and led Africans away from God. For a distillation of Phillips's philosophy, see Phillips, *Bantu in the City: A Study of Cultural Adjustment on the Witwatersrand* (Alice, S. Africa: Lovedale, 1938). For a critical analysis of Phillips and his ideas, see Couzens, "'Moralizing Leisure Time.'"

8. *Umteteli wa Bantu*, August 9, 1924.

9. See, for a brilliant examination of the ways in which members of this elite encountered Romanticism in mission schools and then repurposed its ideas in their writings, Bhekizizwe Peterson, *Monarchs, Missionaries and African Intellectuals: African Theatre and the Unmaking of Colonial Marginality* (Johannesburg: Wits University Press, 2000).

10. *Umteteli wa Bantu*, July 21, 1928.

11. The best way to think of what it meant for these actors to see themselves as modern is to draw on the definition of modernity provided by C. A. Bayly and Peter Wagner. Bayly says that to be modern is to be "up with the times." See Bayly, *The Birth of the Modern World, 1780–1914: Global Connections and Comparisons* (Oxford: Blackwell, 2004), 10. Wagner says that to be modern is "to be in one's own time." See Wagner, *Modernity: Understanding the Present* (London: Polity, 2012), 152.

12. *Umteteli wa Bantu*, July 26, 1930. See Tim Couzens's excellent biography of Dhlomo, *The New African: A Study of the Life and Work of H.I.E. Dhlomo* (Johannesburg: Ravan, 1985); see also Nick Visser and Tim Couzens, eds., *H.I.E. Dhlomo: Collected Works* (Johannesburg: Ravan, 1985).

13. *Umteteli wa Bantu*, July 26, 1930.

14. *Umteteli wa Bantu*, July 26, 1930.

15. However, this does not mean the existence of a huge income gap between Dhlomo and members of the African working class. Dhlomo's class might have been vocal and aspirational, but it was also, as Peter Limb points out, deformed. See Limb, *ANC's Early Years*.

16. Herbert Dhlomo, "The Bantu and Leisure," *Umteteli wa Bantu*, August 15, 1931.

17. See, for a good economic history of South Africa, Charles Feinstein, *An Economic History of South Africa: Conquest, Discrimination and Development* (Cambridge: Cambridge University Press, 2005). For a sophisticated study of the history of inequality in South Africa, see Nicoli Nattrass and Jeremy Seekings, *Class, Race and Inequality in South Africa* (New Haven: Yale University Press, 2005). This book has the added virtue of offering the most sober account of historiographic trends in South African studies.

18. R. V. Selope Thema, "The Duty of Bantu Intellectuals," *Umteteli wa Bantu*, August 3, 1929.

19. For example, an advertisement placed by Haak's Garage, a Johannesburg car dealership, in the October 12, 1929, edition of *Umteteli wa Bantu* showed that a Fiat Touring cost £160, a Buick Touring £260, an Overland Four £60, a Ford Tourer £45, and a Studebaker Light Six £110.

20. Ronald Ellsworth, " 'The Simplicity of the Native Mind': Black Passengers on the South African Railways in the Early Twentieth-Century," in *Resistance and Ideology in Settler Societies*, ed. Tom Lodge (Johannesburg: Ravan, 1986), 88.

21. *Verbatim Report of the Proceedings of the Natives Representative Council*, December 6, 1937 (Pretoria: Government Printers, 1937), 180–81.

22. See *Verbatim Report of Natives Representative Council*, 181.

23. See, for an excellent history of consumerism in southern Africa, Timothy Bourke, *Lifebuoy Men, Lux Women: Commodification, Consumption and Cleanliness in Modern Zimbabwe* (Durham, NC: Duke University Press, 1996). See, for some of the latest research on consumerism in South Africa, Deborah Posel, "Getting Inside the Skin of the Consumer: Race,

Market Research and the Consumerist Project in Apartheid South Africa," *Itinerario* 42, no. 1 (April 2018): 120–38; see also Posel, "Races to Consume: Revisiting South Africa's History of Race, Consumption and the Struggle for Freedom," *Ethnic and Racial Studies* 33, no. 2 (2010): 157–75. The classic treatment of the changing consumer habits of colonized Africans comes from Jean Comaroff and John Comaroff, *Of Revelation and Revolution*, vol. 1, *Christianity, Colonialism and Consciousness in South Africa* (Chicago: Chicago University Press, 1991).

24. For a critical reading of the commission, see Adam Ashforth, *The Politics of Official Discourse in Twentieth-Century South Africa* (Oxford: Clarendon Press, 1990), 69–114.

25. See T. D. Mweli Skota, ed., *The African Who's Who: An Illustrated Classified Register and National Biographical Dictionary of the Africans in the Transvaal* (Johannesburg: R. L. Esson, 1930). For an analysis of the register, see Tim Couzens's biography of Dhlomo, *New African*.

26. Allyson Hobbs promises to offer a rereading and retracing of Green's footsteps in her next book project, *Far from Sanctuary*.

27. Victor H. Green, *The Negro Motorist Green Book* (New York: Victor H. Green, 1936).

28. Rugh, *Are We There Yet?*, 69.

29. T. D. Mweli Skota, ed., *The African Yearly Register* (Johannesburg: R. L. Esson, 1930).

30. Skota, *African Yearly Register* (1930). Indeed, as Harvey Feinberg and Tembeka Ngcukaitobi point out, that is exactly what members of this class sought to do. See Feinberg, *Our Land*; see also Ngcukaitobi, *The Land Is Ours: South Africa's First Black Lawyers and the Birth of Constitutionalism* (Cape Town: Penguin, 2018).

31. Wits University Historical Papers, A951, C3-D1. The Hertzog bills became the 1936 Native Trust and Land Act. The Hertzog bills were an especially egregious assault on the few political rights that the African elite had in colonial South Africa. For a detailed study of the bills, eventually passed in 1936, and what they represented, see C. M. Tatz's classic *Shadow and Substance in South Africa: A Study in Land and Franchise Policies Affecting Africans, 1910–1960* (Pietermaritzburg: University of Natal Press, 1962).

32. See, for a solid study of one of the families that made up this black elite, Khumisho Moguerane, "A History of the Molemas, African Notables in South Africa, 1880s–1920s" (PhD thesis, University of Oxford, 2014).

33. It is instructive to read these struggles along similar strivings in other parts of the world and to pay close attention to the complex ways in which formerly oppressed and marginalized groups turned places of their oppression and marginalization into places of freedom, however relative that freedom might have been. See, for example, Sonya Postmentier's recuperation of black environmental writing within the Black Atlantic world. Postmentier challenges the assumption that black modernity was purely an urban phenomenon by showing how a range of black thinkers and writers engaged with nature, the

land, and landscapes, many of which were rural. See Postmeinter, *Cultivation and Catastrophe: The Lyric Ecology of Modern Black Literature* (Baltimore: Johns Hopkins University Press, 2017); see also Sydney Nathans, *A Mind to Stay: White Plantation, Black Homeland* (Cambridge, MA: Harvard University Press, 2017). Nathans offers a compelling and gripping account of how former slaves in the U.S. South bought the plantation on which they had been enslaved and kept it, against all odds, within the family.

34. The literature on sports in South Africa is quite extensive and rich. See, for a sample, Tyler Fleming, "'Now the African Reigns Supreme': The Rise of African Boxing on the Witwatersrand, 1924–1959," in *Sport Past and Present in South Africa: Transforming the Nation*, ed. Scarlet Cornelissen and Albert Grundlingh (London: Routledge, 2012), 31–45; Albert Grundlingh, *Potent Pastimes: Sport and Leisure Practices in Modern Afrikaner History* (Pretoria: Protea Book House, 2013); Couzens, "'Moralizing Leisure Time'"; David B. Coplan, *In Township Tonight! South Africa's Black City Music and Theatre*, 2nd ed. (Auckland Park, S. Africa: Jacana, 2007); Peter Alegi, *Laduma! Soccer, Politics and Society in South Africa: From Its Origins to 2010* (Pietermaritzburg: University of KwaZulu-Natal Press, 2010); Alan Cobley, *The Rules of the Game: Struggles in Black Recreation and Social Welfare Policy in South Africa* (Westport, CT: Greenwood, 1997); and André Odendaal, *The Story of an African Game: Black Cricketers and the Unmasking of One of Cricket's Greatest Myths, South Africa, 1850–2003* (Cape Town: David Philip, 2003). For the history of soccer in Mozambique, see Nuno Domingos, *Football and Colonialism: Body and Popular Culture in Urban Mozambique* (Athens: Ohio University Press, 2017).

35. See Phyllis M. Martin, *Leisure and Society in Colonial Brazzaville* (Cambridge: Cambridge University Press, 1995).

36. See, for a study of the role of black newspapers in the cultivation of a consumer culture, Brian Rutledge, "South African Readers and Consumer Capitalism, 1932–1962" (PhD diss., Cornell University, 2018).

37. *Bantu World*, December 23, 1933.

38. "Visiting friends and relatives" is a popular phrase in the literature on tourism and it is used to designate the most common form of tourism in the world.

39. South African National Archives and Records Service, NTS 2363, 8/284.

40. South African National Archives and Records Service, NTS 2363, 8/284.

41. There is perhaps no better evidence than this of the fact that hunting, and the kinds of hunting that one is involved in, is essentially a class project. See, for elaborations of this observation, Thompson, *Whigs and Hunters*; Pravilova, *Public Empire*, especially pp. 70–72; see also Charles Trench, *The Poacher and the Squire: A History of Poaching and Game Preservation in England* (London: Longmans, 1967); Douglas Hay et al., *Albion's Fatal Tree: Crime and Society in Eighteenth-Century England* (London: Verso, 2011);

and Angela Thompsell, *Hunting Africa: British Sport, African Knowledge and the Nature of Empire* (London: Palgrave Macmillan, 2015).

42. South African National Archives and Records Service, NTS 2363, 8/284.

43. South African National Archives and Records Service, NTS 2363, 8/284.

44. *Umteteli wa Bantu*, October 15, 1921.

45. See, for another good study of the black elite, especially its occupational dimensions, Leo Kuper, *An African Bourgeoisie: Race, Class and Politics in South Africa* (New Haven: Yale University Press, 1965).

46. The term is borrowed from James Ferguson, "Formalities of Poverty: Thinking about Social Assistance in Neoliberal South Africa," *African Studies Review* 50, no. 2 (2007): 71–86.

47. *Umteteli wa Bantu*, May 14, 1921.

48. R. V. Selope Thema, "Let the African Dance and Sing," *Umteteli wa Bantu*, January 18, 1930.

49. "Preservation of Native Life," *Bantu World*, April 6, 1935.

50. Carruthers, "'Police Boys' and Poachers," 12.

51. Ndebele, *Fine Lines from the Box*, 102.

52. "More Land for Animals," editorial, *Bantu World*, February 9, 1935.

53. Carruthers, *Kruger National Park*, 98.

CHAPTER 4: FROM ROOTS TO ROUTES

1. See *Tsala ea Becoana*, April 6, 1912.

2. The history of the SANNC, renamed the African National Congress in 1923, has been covered extensively by a number of scholars. See, for a sample, André Odendaal, *The Founders: The Origins of the ANC and the Struggle for Democracy in South Africa* (Lexington: University Press of Kentucky, 2013); Arianna Lissoni et al., eds., *One Hundred Years of the ANC: Debating Liberation Histories Today* (Johannesburg: Wits University Press, 2012); Bongani Ngqulunga, *The Man Who Founded the ANC: A Biography of Pixley ka Isaka Seme* (Cape Town: Penguin, 2017); Busani Ngcaweni, ed., *The Future We Chose: Emerging Perspectives on the Centenary of the ANC* (Pretoria: Africa Institute of South Africa, 2013). For some of the older but still fresh perspectives on the ANC, see Limb, *ANC's Early Years*; and, for an absolute classic, Peter Walshe, *The Rise of African Nationalism: The African National Congress, 1912–1952* (London: Hurst, 1970).

3. See, for a history of the railways in South Africa, Gordon Pirie, "Railways and Labour Migration to the Rand Mines: Constraints and Significance," *Journal of Southern African Studies* 19, no. 4 (1993): 713–30; for much older literature, see Jean van der Poel, *Railway and Customs Policies in South Africa, 1885–1910* (London: Longmans, Green, 1933). Manu Goswami provides arguably the best monograph on the relationship between railways and state-formation in a former colony. See Goswami, *Producing India: From Colonial Economy to National Space* (Chicago:

University of Chicago Press, 2004). For a challenge to the idea that railways were colonialism's greatest gift to the colonies, see Shashi Tharoor, *Inglorious Empire: What the British Did to India* (London: Hurst, 2017).

4. See James Clifford, *Routes: Travel and Translation in the Late Twentieth Century* (Cambridge, MA: Harvard University Press, 1997). Clifford challenges the tendency, both academic and popular, to privilege dwelling over movement. He calls attention to the price we pay by putting roots ahead of routes. See, especially, the first part of the book, appropriately titled "Travels." Clifford's argument offers a powerful rejoinder to the kinds of patronizing nonsense peddled, for example, by Simone Weil in her programmatic *The Need for Roots: Prelude to a Declaration of Duties towards Mankind*, trans. Arthur Wills (London: Routledge, 2002). Weil claims that Africa did not know the "disease" of rootlessness until the advent of European rule in Africa (p. 81).

5. The exception is Gordon Pirie, who has studied extensively South Africa's railways and transport history. Although I draw a great deal from Pirie's insightful work for this chapter, it is not concerned with questions such as land.

6. Jeremy Foster offers an illuminating analysis of the role of the railways in the making of South Africa but his concern is limited to white South Africans. See Foster, *Washed with Sun: Landscape and the Making of White South Africa* (Pittsburgh: University of Pittsburgh Press, 2008).

7. See, for an account of the relationship between train travel and modernity, Wolfgang Schivelbusch, *The Railway Journey: Trains and Travel in the Nineteenth Century*, trans. Anselm Hollo (New York: Urizen Books, 1979). For excellent accounts of the changes wrought by railways and train travel, see On Barak's *On Time: Technology and Temporality in Modern Egypt* (Berkeley: University of California Press, 2013); Tony Judt's elegiac *The Memory Chalet* (London: Penguin Books, 2010); and Andreas Killen, *Berlin Electropolis: Shock, Nerves, and German Modernity* (Berkeley: University of California Press, 2006).

8. Tony Judt, "The Glory of the Rails," *New York Review of Books*, December 23, 2010.

9. Judt, "Glory of the Rails."

10. See William G. Thomas, *The Iron Way: Railroads, the Civil War and the Making of Modern America* (New Haven: Yale University Press, 2011).

11. Jeremy Foster, "'Land of Contrasts' or 'Home We Have Always Known'? The SAR&H and the Imaginary Geography of White Nationhood, 1910–1930," *Journal of Southern African Studies* 29, no. 3 (September 2003): 657–80.

12. Foster, "'Land of Contrasts,'" 657–80.

13. The corporation began as South African Railways. Harbours was added later.

14. Foster, "'Land of Contrasts,'" 657–80.

15. Foster, 657–80.

16. Andre Odendaal gives a detailed but depressing account of this betrayal in *Vukani Bantu! The Beginnings of Black Protest Politics in South Africa to 1912* (Cape Town: David Philip, 1984).

17. R. V. Selope Thema, *Umteteli wa Bantu,* January 18, 1930.

18. For an account of the pass system and the way it worked, see Martin Chanock, *The Making of South African Legal Culture, 1902–1936: Fear, Favor and Prejudice* (Cambridge: Cambridge University Press, 2001); and Doug Hindson, *Pass Controls and the Urban African Proletariat in South Africa* (Johannesburg: Ravan, 1987). For a microhistory of the importance of documents to black freedom struggles in the Black Atlantic, see Rebecca Scott and Jean Hébrard, *Freedom Papers: An Atlantic Odyssey in the Age of Emancipation* (Cambridge, MA: Harvard University Press, 2012).

19. *Tsala ea Becoana,* April 6, 1912. The meeting and its contents are reconstructed from a report of the meeting published in this edition.

20. *Koranta ea Becoana,* August 12, 1903.

21. *Koranta ea Becoana,* December 2, 1903. James T. Campbell offers a moving account of Charlotte Maxeke, an exceptional member of the black elite educated in the United States, traveling by goods train. See Campbell, *Songs of Zion: The African Methodist Episcopal Church in the United States and South Africa* (New York: Oxford University Press, 1995), especially pp. 284–85.

22. Pirie, "Railways and Labour Migration," 716.

23. Pirie, 713.

24. Pirie, 716.

25. See, for histories of tourism in South Africa, Berendien Lubbe, *Tourism Distribution: Managing the Travel Intermediary* (Kenwyn: Juta, 2000), 26.

26. See Foster, *Washed with Sun,* 116, 211.

27. Although separate initiatives, these ventures were all united by an imperial project that imagined the British empire as that vast geographic real on which the sun never set. See, for an elaboration of this, James Ryan, *Picturing Empire: Photography and the Visualization of the British Empire* (Chicago: University of Chicago Press, 1997).

28. Foster, *Washed with Sun,* 202.

29. Foster, 201.

30. William Waldegrave Palmer Selborne, *The Selborne Memorandum* (London: Oxford University Press, 1925), 50–51, 68.

31. Mark Mazower provides an account of the white supremacist and segregationist beliefs that animated people like Jan Smuts. See Mazower, *No Enchanted Palace.* Mahmood Mamdani also offers a revealing account of Smuts's thinking in *Citizen and Subject: Contemporary Africa and the Legacy of Late Colonialism* (Princeton: Princeton University Press, 1996), 1–8.

32. Ciraj Rassool and Leslie Witz offer a sophisticated reading of attempts by Afrikaner nationalists to resolve some of these contradictions by naturalizing Africans and Coloureds. See Rassool and Witz, "The 1952 Jan

Van Riebeeck Tercentenary Festival: Constructing and Contesting Public National History in South Africa," *Journal of African History* 34, no. 3 (1993): 447–68. For a book-length elaboration of the argument first explicated in this essay, see Leslie Witz, *Apartheid's Festival: Contesting South Africa's National Pasts* (Bloomington: Indiana University Press, 2003).

33. See Papers of the South African National Publicity Association, National Archives and Records Service of South Africa, SAS G4/13/2, 1933-1935.

34. See Minutes of SAPA meeting, East London, October 3–5, 1925, National Archives and Records Service, SAS G4/13/2, 608.

35. See Minutes of meeting, South African Publicity Conference, Cape Town, November 7, 1929, National Archives and Records Service, SAS G4/13/1, 607, p. 7.

36. See Minutes of meeting, South African Publicity Conference, Cape Town, November 7, 1929, National Archives and Records Service, SAS G4/13/1, 607, p. 13.

37. SAPA policy statement, National Archives and Records Service, SAS G4/13/2.

38. Minutes of meeting, South African Publicity Conference, Cape Town, November 7, 1929, National Archives and Records Service, SAS G4/13/1, 607, p. 23.

39. See Minutes of meeting, South African Publicity Conference, Cape Town, November 7, 1929, National Archives and Records Service, SAS G4/13/1, 607, p. 7.

40. SAPA policy statement, National Archives and Records Service, SAS G4/13/2.

41. SAPA policy statement, National Archives and Records Service, SAS G4/13/2.

42. Hannah Arendt, *The Origins of Totalitarianism* (New York: Harcourt, 1968), 193–94. I am aware of the trenchant criticism to which Arendt's secondary reading of South Africa has been subjected. I am aware also of the criticism of the anti-Semitic undertones of her claims about mining in South Africa. See, for example, Ron Rosenbaum, "The Evil of Banality," *Slate*, October 30, 2009.

43. Minutes of meeting of the South African Publicity Advisory Committee, Cape Town, May 16–17, 1927, National Archives and Records Service, SAS G4/13/2.

44. Minutes of the South African Publicity Conference meeting, Durban, January 6–7, 1927, National Archives and Records Service, SAS G4/13/2.

45. A. J. Christopher comments on South Africa's failure to compete with countries such as Australia, Canada, and New Zealand for white settlers. See Christopher, *The Atlas of Apartheid* (London: Routledge, 1994). Hannah Arendt makes a similar comment in *The Origins of Totalitarianism*, pt. 2.

46. Minutes of the South African Publicity Advisory Committee meeting, Cape Town, June 15–16, 1926, National Archives and Records Service, SAS G4/13/2.

47. Minutes of the Standing Advisory Committee meeting, October 29, 1923, National Archives and Records Service, SAS G4/13/2.

48. See Minutes of the South African Publicity Advisory Committee meeting, Cape Town, June 15–16, 1926, National Archives and Records Service, SAS G4/13/2.

49. See Minutes of the South African Publicity Conference meeting, Port Elizabeth, November 2–3, 1927, National Archives and Records Service, SAS G4/13/2.

50. Minutes of the Standing Advisory Committee meeting, October 29, 1923, National Archives and Records Service, SAS G4/13/2.

51. Minutes of the South African Publicity Conference meeting, Cape Town, February 11, 1925, National Archives and Records Service, SAS G4/13/1.

52. See Minutes of meeting of South African Publicity Conference, Durban, January 6–7, 1927, National Archives and Records Service.

53. *Graaff-Reinet Advertiser*, editorial, January 7, 1929, National Archives and Records Service, SAS G4/13/1.

54. Minutes of the Standing Advisory Committee meeting, October 29, 1923, National Archives and Records Service, SAS G4/13/2.

55. Minutes of the South African Publicity Conference meeting, Port Elizabeth, November 2–3, 1927, National Archives and Records Service, SAS G4/13/2.

56. Cape Times report from Minutes of National Publicity meeting in Cape Town, February 11, 1925, National Archives and Records Service, SAS G4/13/1.

57. Minutes of National Publicity meeting in Cape Town, February 11, 1925, National Archives and Records Service, SAS G4/13/1.

58. This should not surprise us because, as we know from a number of scholars, colonialism and imperialism were by definition immodest projects. See, for example, JoAnn McGregor, "The Victoria Falls 1900–1940: Landscape, Tourism and the Geographical Imagination," *Journal of Southern African Studies* 29, no. 3 (September 2003): 717–37; see also Andrea Arrington-Sirois, *Victoria Falls and the Colonial Imagination in British Southern Africa: Turning Water into Gold* (London: Palgrave Macmillan, 2017). However, as McGregor points out, Africans—who had their own histories of the Victoria Falls—challenged this geographical imagination that sought to push them imaginatively and politically off the land.

59. Minutes of South African Publicity Conference meeting in Lourenço Marques, August 16–18, 1932, National Archives and Records Service, SAS G4/13/1.

60. Minutes of South African Publicity Conference meeting Pietermaritzburg, August 22–23, 1932, National Archives and Records Service, SAS G4/13/1.

61. Minutes of the South African Publicity Advisory Committee meeting, Cape Town, May 16–17, 1927, National Archives and Records Service, SAS G4/13/2.

62. Minutes of the South African Publicity Conference meeting, Durban, January 6–7, 1927, National Archives and Records Service, SAS G4/13/2.

63. Minutes of the South African Publicity Advisory Committee meeting, Johannesburg, November 20, 1925, National Archives and Records Service, SAS G4/13/2.

64. See Minutes of the South African Publicity Conference meeting, Durban, January 6–7, 1927, National Archives and Records Service, SAS G4/13/2.

65. Minutes of South African National Publicity Conference meeting, Oudtshoorn, October 7, 1931, National Archives and Records Service, SAS G4/13/2.

66. My observation here complicates Annie Coombes's claims about the place of blacks in the marketing of South Africa's landscapes. See her wonderful book *History after Apartheid: Visual Culture and Public Memory in a Democratic South Africa* (Durham, NC: Duke University Press, 2003).

67. South African Publicity Advisory Committee meeting, Johannesburg, June 17, 1935, National Archives and Records Service, SAS G4/13/2.

68. South African Publicity Advisory Committee meeting, Johannesburg, June 17, 1935, National Archives and Records Service, SAS G4/13/2.

69. South African Publicity Advisory Committee meeting, Johannesburg, June 17, 1935, National Archives and Records Service, SAS G4/13/2.

70. South African Publicity Advisory Committee meeting, Johannesburg, June 17, 1935, National Archives and Records Service, SAS G4/13/2. See the introduction for my explication of the genealogy of Crocker's idea.

71. South African Publicity Advisory Committee meeting, Johannesburg, June 17, 1935, National Archives and Records Service, SAS G4/13/2.

72. South African Publicity Advisory Committee meeting, Johannesburg, June 17, 1935, National Archives and Records Service, SAS G4/13/2.

73. Bantu World, editorial, "Preservation of Native Life," April 6, 1935.

74. C. J. Uys, *Native Life in South Africa* (Pretoria: Government Printers, 1936), 5.

75. Uys, *Native Life in South Africa*, 5.

76. South African Transnet Heritage Museum, SAR&H Publicity and Travel Department, undated document, publication no. 329.1.11 PUB.

77. "The Kruger National Park," *South African Railways and Harbours Magazine*, December 1926, https://railways.haarhoff.co.za/issue/314/page/153.

78. See Carruthers, *Kruger National Park*, 96

79. Bunn, "Museum Outdoors," 365.

80. Bunn, 371.

81. Bunn, 370.

82. Alfred Norval, *The Tourist Industry: A National and International Survey* (London: Sir Isaac Pitman and Sons, 1935), 181.

83. Norval, *Tourist Industry*, 182.

84. James B. Wolf, "A Grand Tour: South Africa and American Tourists between the Wars," *Journal of Popular Culture* 25, no. 2 (1991): 103, 106.

85. See Wolf, "Grand Tour," 99–116.

86. See Gordon Pirie, "Elite Exoticism: Sea-Rail Cruise Tourism to South Africa, 1926–1939," *African Historical Review* 43, no. 1 (2011): 88.

87. Minutes of the South African Publicity Advisory Committee meeting, Johannesburg, June 4, 1929, National Archives and Records Service, SAS G4/13/2.

88. Minutes of the South African Publicity Advisory Committee meeting, Cape Town, May 16–17, 1927, National Archives and Records Service, SAS G4/13/2.

89. For a study of colonial attempts to marry recreation to tribal identity, see the article by Cecile Badenhorst and Charlie Mather, "Tribal Recreation and Recreating Tribalism: Culture, Leisure and Social Control on South Africa's Gold Mines, 1940–1950," *Journal of Southern African Studies* 23, no. 3 (September 1997): 473–89.

90. See Minutes of the South African Publicity Advisory Committee meeting, Cape Town, May 16–17, 1927, National Archives and Records Service, SAS G4/13/2.

91. Pirie, "Elite Exoticism," 91.

92. Pirie, 73–99.

93. Memorandum from G. O. Lovett, Acting General Manager of N.R.C., August 19, 1942, University of Johannesburg/TEBA archive, file no. 23, pad 1, folder 1-4, 28/08/24 to 28/02/48.

94. See Memorandum from Chamber of Mines to WNLA Kazungula, January 18, 1938, University of Johannesburg/TEBA archive, file no. 23, pad 1, folder 1-4, 28/08/24 to 28/02/48.

95. Memorandum from S.H. Davies to WNLA head office, January 29, 1938, University of Johannesburg/TEBA archive, file no. 23, pad 1, folder 1-4, 28/08/24 to 28/02/48.

96. Memorandum from F. N. Balme to the General Manger of WNLA, November 10, 1937, University of Johannesburg/TEBA archive, file no. 23, pad 1, folder 1-4, 28/08/24 to 28/02/48. *Kgotla* is a Tswana word that means "council."

97. See University of Johannesburg/TEBA archive, file no. 23, pad 1, folder 1-4, 28/08/24 to 28/02/48.

98. Memorandum from G. O. Lovett, Acting General Manager of N.R.C., August 19, 1942, University of Johannesburg/TEBA archive, file no. 23, pad 1, folder 1-4, 28/08/24 to 28/02/48.

99. Letter from A. J. Limebeer, June 10, 1943, University of Johannesburg/TEBA archive, file no. 23, pad 1, folder 1-4, 28/08/24 to 28/02/48.

100. Letter regarding Gluckman's request, University of Johannesburg/ TEBA archive, file no. 23, pad 1, folder 1-4, 28/08/24 to 28/02/48.

101. Letter from Ray Phillips to Gold Producers' Committee, July 21, 1954, University of Johannesburg/TEBA archive.

102. Letter from Ray Phillips to Gold Producers' Committee, July 21, 1954, University of Johannesburg/TEBA archive.

103. Saul Dubow, *Apartheid, 1948–1994* (Oxford: Oxford University Press, 2014), 276.

104. "Mr. Macmillan's Visit to South Africa," *South African Scope* 3, no. 2 (February 1960).

105. Albert Grundlingh, "Revisiting the 'Old' South Africa: Excursions into South Africa's Tourist History under Apartheid, 1948–1990," *South African Historical Journal* 56, no. 1 (January 2006): 111.

106. Grundlingh, "Revisiting the 'Old' South Africa," 111.

107. Van Eeden, "Surveying the 'Empty Land,'" 600–612.

108. Pirie, "Elite Exoticism," 73–99.

CHAPTER 5: CIVILIZED NATIVES

1. Wits University Historical Papers, South African Institute of Race Relations papers (hereafter SAIRR papers), AD 843/RJ/Aa 3.1.7, file 6. The use of white politicians to serve as so-called native senators was one of the compromises struck when Afrikaner nationalists under the leadership of Prime Minister J. B. Hertzog finally succeeded in removing African voters from the common voters' roll. See, for background on how Hertzog's compromise worked, Mia Roth, *The Rhetorical Origins of Apartheid: How the Debates of the Natives Representative Council, 1937–1950, Shaped South African Racial Policy* (Jefferson, NC: McFarland, 2016); for an account of J. D. Rheinhallt-Jones's election in 1937, see Roth's "Domination by Consent: Elections under the Representation of Natives Act, 1937–1948," in *Resistance and Ideology in Settler Societies, Southern African Studies*, vol. 4, ed. Tom Lodge (Johannesburg: Ravan, 1986), 144–67.

2. Lest we be tempted to see the park's employees living in the compound at Skukuza as mute subjects of colonial rule, a letter in the SAIRR archive suggests that these employees were anything but mute. On October 3, 1937, a man from the Skukuza area named R. G. Kondowe sent Rheinhallt-Jones a postal order worth four pounds "and ask you to pay it as subscription of *The Bantu World* which I wish to get every week. I beg pardon, Sir, to send this money to you because I don't know the address of *Bantu World*." See SAIRR papers, file 3, Aa3.1.6a. Kondowe asked that the newspaper be delivered care of James Stevenson-Hamilton, the warden of the Kruger National Park.

3. Carruthers, "'Why Celebrate a Controversy?,'" 145. See Magome and Murombedzi, "Sharing South African National Parks," 115. See Jacklyn Cock, *War against Ourselves*, 148. See Lynn Meskell, "The Nature of Culture in Kruger National Park," in Meskell, *Cosmopolitan Archaeologies*, 97. See Lindisizwe Magi, "People, Recreation, and the Environment," 439. None of

their claims is true, as this book shows. It would appear that these scholars took the presence of apartheid in the KNP to mean that black people could not go there. While the National Parks Board certainly restricted access to its restaurants, it did not bar black people from visiting the park itself.

4. Lynn Meskell, "The Nature of Culture in Kruger National Park," in Meskell, *Cosmopolitan Archaeologies*, 97.

5. Cock, *War against Ourselves*, 151.

6. See, for insight into the world of leisure-making among black South Africans, Cobley, *Rules of the Game*. For an excellent study of colonial attempts to marry recreation to tribal identity, see the article by Cecile Badenhorst and Charlie Mather, "Tribal Recreation and Recreating Tribalism: Culture, Leisure and Social Control on South Africa's Gold Mines, 1940–1950," *Journal of Southern African Studies* 23, no. 3 (September 1997): 473–89.

7. See Peter Alegi, *Laduma! Soccer, Politics and Society in South Africa: From Its Origins to 2010* (Pietermaritzburg: University of Kwazulu-Natal Press, 2010); Coplan, *In Township Tonight!*; Couzens, "'Moralizing Leisure Time,'" 314–38; Bhekizizwe Peterson, *Monarchs, Missionaries and African Intellectuals*. See also Paul La House, *Brewers, Beer Halls and Boycotts: A History of Liquor in South Africa* (Johannesburg: Ravan, 1988). For a West African perspective on the connection between alcohol and leisure, see Emmanuel Akyeampong, *Drink, Power and Cultural Change: A Social History of Alcohol in Ghana, c. 1800 to Recent Times* (Portsmouth, NH: Heinemann, 1996).

8. See O. Zachariah, *Travel in South Africa* (Johannesburg: South African Railways and Harbours, 1921), 178–79.

9. Martin, *Leisure and Society*, 1.

10. I borrow the idea of coevalness from Johannes Fabian, *Time and the Other: How Anthropology Makes Its Object* (New York: Columbia University Press, 1983).

11. Native Affairs Department, *Annual Report for Year Ended June 30th, 1909* (Pretoria: Government Printing and Stationery Office, 1910), 35.

12. Native Affairs Department, *Annual Report 1909*, 35.

13. Native Affairs Department, 36.

14. Native Affairs Department, 36. See also South African Transnet Heritage Museum, SAR&H Publicity and Travel Department, file no. 329.1.11. PUB, and Transvaal Native Affairs Department annual report for 1909.

15. Leon de Kock makes a particularly powerful point regarding assumptions about colonial mimicry. See de Kock, "'Sitting for the Civilization Test:' The Making(s) of a Civil Imaginary in Colonial South Africa," in *South Africa in the Global Imaginary*, ed. Leon de Kock, Louise Bethlehem, and Sonja Laden (Durham, NC: Duke University Press, 2004), 117–35, see especially pp. 117–27. De Kock is, of course, going against Homi Bhabha's argument for colonial mimicry and sly civility as modes of resistance in the colonial world. See, for articulations of Bhabha's claims,

Bhabha, *The Location of Culture* (London: Routledge, 1994). See especially chaps. 4 and 5.

16. Alan Cobley, *Class and Consciousness: The Black Petty Bourgeoisie in South Africa, 1924 to 1950* (New York: Greenwood, 1990), 106.

17. See Cooper, *Citizenship between Empire and Nation*.

18. R. V. Selope Thema, "Let the African Sing and Dance," *Umteteli wa Bantu*, January 18, 1930.

19. See Thema's essay, written under the pen name Scrutator, "Along the Color Line," November 18, 1933, in *From Cattle-Herding to Editor's Chair: The Unfinished Autobiography and Writings of Richard Victor Selope Thema*, ed. Alan Cobley (Cape Town: Van Riebeeck Society, 2016), 114.

20. Thema made his comments in November 1941 during the session of the Natives' Representative Council, of which he was a member. See the *Verbatim Report of the Proceedings of the Natives' Representative Council*, November 27, 1941 (Pretoria: Government Printers, 1941), 237. For more on the council, see Mia Roth, *The Rhetorical Origins of Apartheid: How the Debates of the Natives Representative Council, 1937–1950, Shaped South African Racial Policy* (Jefferson, NC: McFarland, 2016).

21. Thema made these comments in December 1950 during a session of the Natives' Representative Council. Thema was an elected member of the council. See the *Verbatim Report of the Proceedings of the Natives' Representative Council*, December 5, 1950 (Pretoria: Government Printers, 1950), 28.

22. The society published its response in its journal, "A New Challenge to the Principle of Wildlife Protection," *African Wildlife* 5, no. 1 (March 1951): 67.

23. See " "Role of Africans in Conservation," *Natal Wildlife* 4, no. 4 (November 1963): 6; and "African Wildlife Society Formed," *Natal Wildlife* 5, no. 4 (May 1964): 19. I am grateful to the Wildlife and Environment Society of South Africa, especially Nikki Veenstra and Jenny Duvenage, for tracking down these archival materials for me. See, for more on the history of the African Wildlife Society, Farieda Khan, "Towards Environmentalism: A Sociopolitical Evaluation of Trends in South African Conservation History, 1910–1976, with a Specific Focus on the Role of Black Conservation Organizations" (PhD diss., University of Cape Town, 2001).

24. See Thema's comments in *Verbatim Report of the Proceedings of the Natives' Representative Council*, December 9, 1938 (Pretoria: Government Printers, 1938), 164. See, for the history of the council, Roth, *Rhetorical Origins of Apartheid*.

25. See Thema's comments in *Verbatim Report of the Proceedings of the Natives' Representative Council*, January 4 and 5, 1949 (Pretoria: Government Printers, 1949), 28.

26. See Bheki Peterson, "*The Bantu World* and the World of the Book: Reading, Writing, and 'Enlightenment,'" in *Africa's Hidden Histories:*

Everyday Literacy and Making the Self, ed. Karin Barber (Bloomington: Indiana University Press, 2006), 236–57.

27. See A. Minnaar and Uys de V. Pienaar, "The Eastern and Selati Railway Lines," in Pienaar, *Cameo from the Past,* 363. See also Joubert, *Kruger National Park,* 1:36. Edward Teversham claims that the park only began accepting tourists in 1926. See Teversham, "Representations and Perceptions," vi, 49. In fact, the reserve began accepting visitors three years before it became a national park.

28. Foster, "'Land of Contrasts,'" 657–80.

29. Trollope's words are found in his biography by Barbara Matthews, *The Man They Called "Vukani": The Life and Times of Harold Trollope* (Port Elizabeth: Bluecliff, 2005).

30. Matthews, *Man They Called "Vukani."*

31. See Carruthers, *Kruger National Park,* 64.

32. Carruthers, 99.

33. See Carruthers, 99.

34. See Carruthers, 99.

35. See Joubert, *Kruger National Park,* 1:95.

36. National Parks Board, *Unspoilt Africa* (1938), 47.

37. Limb, *ANC's Early Years,* 12.

38. Limb, 41–49. Basner quoted on p. 48.

39. Limb, 46–48.

40. Limb, 48.

41. See Michael O. West, *The Rise of an African Middle Class: Colonial Zimbabwe, 1898–1965* (Bloomington: Indiana University Press, 2002), 36–40.

42. West, *Rise of an African Middle Class,* 1.

43. West, 1.

44. See Partha Chatterjee, *The Nation and Its Fragments: Colonial and Postcolonial Histories* (Princeton: Princeton University Press, 1993). See also Derek Peterson's rejoinder to Chatterjee, *Ethnic Patriotism and the East African Revival: A History of Dissent, c. 1935–1972* (Cambridge: Cambridge University Press, 2012), 26.

45. James T. Campbell, *Songs of Zion: The African Methodist Episcopal Church in the United States and South Africa* (New York: Oxford University Press, 1995), 253.

46. James Stevenson-Hamilton, *Our South African National Parks* (1940), 51.

47. For details of the fares and related charges, see National Parks Board, *Unspoilt Africa* (1938), 25–31.

48. *Padkos* is an Afrikaans term meaning "food for the road."

49. See the 1938 edition of *Unspoilt Africa* for these details.

50. See Joubert, *Kruger National Park,* 1:95.

51. National Parks Board, *Unspoilt Africa* (1938).

52. See the 1938 edition of *Unspoilt Africa* for these details.

53. National Parks Board annual reports for years 1946–58.

54. National Parks Board annual reports for the years 1962–78.

55. Jacklyn Cock, *Maids and Madams: Domestic Workers under Apartheid* (London: Women's Press, 1989), 34. The quotation captions one of the photographs used in the book.

56. See Cock, *Maids and Madams*, 112.

57. Paul Gilroy, *The Black Atlantic: Modernity and Double Consciousness* (Cambridge, MA: Harvard University Press, 1993), 85.

58. See Jeremy Seekings and Nicoli Nattrass, "The Economy and Poverty in the Twentieth-Century in South Africa" (working paper no. 276, Centre for Social Science Research, July 2010), http://www.cssr.uct.ac.za/cssr/publications/working-paper/2010/economy-and-poverty-twentieth-century-south, 14–19.

59. See Minutes of meeting of South African Publicity Conference, Kimberley, November 22–23, 1928, National Archives and Records Service, SAS G4/13/1.

60. Rudolph Bigalke, *Let's Visit the Kruger Park* (Johannesburg: Afrikaanse Pers-Boekhandel, 1961), 96. For an account of Bigalke's career, see Jane Carruthers, *National Park Science: A Century of Research in South Africa* (Cambridge: Cambridge University Press, 2017).

61. Bigalke, *Let's Visit the Kruger Park*, 100.

62. Bunn, "Museum Outdoors," 371.

63. Shireen Ally, *From Servants to Workers: South African Domestic Workers and the Democratic State* (Ithaca: Cornell University Press, 2009), 24.

64. See Ally, *From Servants to Workers*, 24–30.

65. See Ally, 24–30.

66. Barnes, "Virgin Territory?," 164–91.

67. See Luise White, *The Comforts of Home: Prostitution in Colonial Kenya* (Chicago: University of Chicago Press, 1990).

68. *Report of the South African Native Affairs Commission, 1903–1905* (Cape Town: Government Printers, 1905), 1:83.

69. Ally, *From Servants to Workers*, 28–29.

70. Barnes, "Virgin Territory?," 164.

71. Barnes, 167, 165.

72. Barnes, 167.

73. Barnes, 167.

74. Barnes, 170.

75. Pirie, "Railways and Labour Migration," 729. Pirie's quote refers to migrant laborers to the mines but it is as apt for domestic servants.

76. National Parks Board annual report for 1928.

77. National Parks Board annual reports for 1949 and 1951.

78. The following reconstruction is based on an email exchange with Krishna Somers, March 13 and March 17, 2015.

79. Krishna Somers, email exchange, March 13, 2015.

80. Krishna Somers, email exchange, March 17, 2015.

81. Zuleikha Mayat, interview by author, Durban, South Africa, March 16, 2015.

82. Zuleikha Mayat, interview.

83. Zuleikha Mayat, interview.

84. Krishna Somers, email exchange, March 17, 2015.

85. Zuleikha Mayat, interview.

86. Krishna Somers, email exchange, March 17, 2015.

87. Zuleikha Mayat, interview.

88. Zuleikha Mayat, interview.

89. Zuleikha Mayat, interview. Mayat also recounts this story in Goolam Vahed and Thembisa Waetjen's delightful book *Indian Delights: Gender, Modernity and the Women's Cultural Group of Durban, 1954–2010* (Cape Town: HSRC Press, 2010), 54.

90. Mohamed Gardee, telephone interview by author, March 17, 2015.

91. Mohamed Gardee, interview.

92. It is instructive to think in this context of Antoinette Burton's insightful argument about the place of Africa in the postcolonial Indian imagination. Burton calls into quesiton easy and uncritical appreciations of relations between Africa and India that tend to gloss the tensions in this relationship. Burton's argument is good to think with, even though I am concerned here with South Africans classified as Indian and not Indian subjects/citizens as such. See Burton, *Africa in the Indian Imagination: Race and the Politics of Postcolonial Citation* (Durham, NC: Duke University Press, 2016).

93. Nasima Coovadia, telephone interview by author, April 6, 2015.

94. Nasima Coovadia, interview.

95. Nasima Coovadia, interview.

96. Ahmed Essop and Coco Cachalia, interview by author, Johannesburg, South Africa, July 26, 2016.

97. Ahmed Essop and Coco Cachalia, interview.

98. Ahmed Essop and Coco Cachalia, interview.

99. Vahed and Waetjen, *Indian Delights*, 38.

100. Nasima Coovadia, interview.

101. For an illuminating study of Indian South Africans in the intellectual and political history of South Africa, see Jon Soske, *Internal Frontiers: African Nationalism and the Indian Diaspora in Twentieth-Century South Africa* (Athens: Ohio University Press, 2017).

102. See Soske, *Internal Frontiers*, especially the introduction.

103. Zuleikha Mayat, interview.

104. Ed February, interview by author, Cape Town, South Africa, July 25, 2017.

105. Ed February, interview.

106. Ed February, interview.

107. Ed February, interview.

108. Joubert, *Kruger National Park*, 2:231.

109. Justin Willis, "Two Lives of Mpamizo: Understanding Dissonance in Oral History," *History in Africa*, no. 23 (January 1996): 320. For some of the most illuminating work on oral history, see Luise White, Stephan Miescher, and David William Cohen, eds., *African Words, African Voices: Critical Practices in Oral History* (Bloomington: Indiana University Press, 2001).

110. Willis, "Two Lives of Mpamizo," 327.

111. See Willis, 327.

112. Willis, 329.

113. Willis, 329.

CHAPTER 6: BLACK MOBILITY

1. *Holiday and Travel Facilities for Non-Whites in South Africa* (Johannesburg: South African Institute of Race Relations, 1962).

2. For insight into the connection between homelands and the black elite, see Roger Southall, *The New Black Middle Class in South Africa* (Johannesburg: Jacana, 2016); and Timothy Gibbs, *Mandela's Kinsmen: Nationalist Elites and Apartheid's First Bantustan* (Johannesburg: Jacana, 2014). For a comparative perspective on postcolonial subjects engaging with nature in nonnativist ways, see Anna Lowenhaupt Tsing, *Friction: An Ethnography of Global Connection* (Princeton: Princeton University Press, 2005).

3. This process of reconfiguring space and time in the light of European conquest was, of course, not unique to southern Africa. See, for a sample of examples from around the world, Richard Grove, *Green Imperialism: Colonial Expansion, Tropical Island Edens and the Origins of Environmentalism, 1600–1860* (Cambridge: Cambridge University Press, 1995); John M. MacKenzie, ed., *Imperialism and the Natural World* (Manchester: Manchester University Press, 1990); see, for East Africa, Steinhart, *Black Poachers, White Hunters*. For southern Africa, see William Beinart, *The Rise of Conservation in South Africa: Settlers, Livestock, and the Environment, 1770–1950* (Oxford: Oxford University Press, 2003). For a sense of how this process of reconfiguration sought to work in practice in South Africa, see Evans, *Bureaucracy and Race*. For an excellent examination of some of the ways in which blacks tried to fight the colonial reconfiguration of time and space, see Ngcukaitobi, *Land Is Ours*.

4. Deborah Posel, "Modernity and Measurement: Further Thoughts on the Apartheid State" (paper presentation, Wits University, Johannesburg, South Africa, August 19, 1996), 12. For insight into apartheid logics and thinking, see Lindie Koorts's wonderful *DF Malan and the Rise of Afrikaner Nationalism* (Cape Town: Tafelberg, 2014).

5. See, for a magisterial examination of what apartheid was and what it wanted to be, Dubow, *Apartheid*. See, for another brilliant survey of apartheid, Deborah Posel, "The Apartheid Project, 1948-1970," in *The Cambridge*

History of South Africa, vol. 2, *1885–1994*, ed. Robert Ross, Anne Kelk Mager, and Bill Nasson (Cambridge: Cambridge University Press, 2011), 319–68.

6. Scholars have worked on the histories of these laws. On the Population Registration Act of 1950, see Keith Breckenridge, "The Book of Life: The South African Population Register and the Invention of Racial Descent, 1950–1980," *Kronos*, no. 40 (2014): 225–40; on the Group Areas Act, see Brij Maharaj, "Apartheid, Urban Segregation and the Local State: Durban and the Group Areas Act in South Africa," *Urban Geography* 18, no. 2 (1997): 135–54.

7. *Holiday and Travel Facilities for Non-Whites in South Africa*, 58.

8. Carruthers, *Kruger National Park*, 99.

9. Carruthers, 100.

10. South African National Parks Board annual report for 1953.

11. See, for example, Edith L. Prance, *Three Weeks in Wonderland: The Kruger National Park* (Johannesburg: Juta, 1935).

12. See Carruthers, *Kruger National Park*, 2, 90, 101.

13. The first claim comes from Moeketsi Mosola, CEO of South African Tourism, quoted in Christian M. Rogerson and Zoleka Lisa, "'Sho't Left': Changing Domestic Tourism in South Africa," in *Urban Tourism in the Developing World: The South African Experience*, ed. Christian M. Rogerson and Gustav Visser (New Brunswick, NJ: Transaction, 2007), 70; Njabulo Ndebele's claim comes from Ndebele, *Fine Lines from the Box*, 102.

14. South African National Parks Board annual report for 1947.

15. National Parks Board, *Unspoilt Africa* (1946), 93.

16. South African National Parks Board annual reports for the 1950s.

17. National Parks Board annual reports for the years 1962–78.

18. See Jamie Miller, *An African Volk: The Apartheid Regime and Its Search for Survival* (Oxford: Oxford University Press, 2016).

19. Verwoerd quoted in Patrick Laurence, *The Transkei: South Africa's Politics of Partition* (Johannesburg: Ravan, 1976), 27.

20. Laurence, *Transkei*, 28.

21. Verwoerd quoted in Laurence, *Transkei*, 28.

22. Long the subject of ridicule and dismissal, homelands have come in for some innovative and much-needed reexamination. See, for example, Steffen Jensen and Olaf Zenker, eds., "Homelands as Frontiers: Apartheid's Loose Ends," special issue, *Journal of Southern African Studies* 41, no. 5 (2015). See also Arianna Lissoni and Shireen Ally, eds., "Let's Talk about Bantustans," special issue, *South African Historical Journal* 64, no. 1 (2012). Timothy Gibbs has also penned an illuminating study about the complicated relationship between the Transkei, South Africa's first Bantustan, and the black nationalist movement. See Gibbs, *Mandela's Kinsmen*. For insight into how the apartheid regime understood its position in relation to the Bantustans and to postcolonial Africa, see Miller, *African Volk*. For some of the scholarship on the environmental history of homelands, see Nancy Jacobs, *Environment, Power, and Injustice: A South African History* (Cambridge:

Cambridge University Press, 2003); and Isak Niehaus, *Witchcraft, Power, and Politics: Exploring the Occult in the South African Lowveld* (London: Pluto Press, 2001).

23. See, for more on the relationship between Mandela and Matanzima, Gibbs, *Mandela's Kinsmen*.

24. See Laurence, *Transkei*, 7.

25. See Joubert, *Kruger National Park*, 2:229–32.

26. Joubert, 2:232.

27. Joubert, 1:95.

28. Joubert, 2:229.

29. Joubert, 2:231.

30. Joubert, 2:232.

31. Joubert, 2:229.

32. Roger Southall, *South Africa's Transkei: The Political Economy of an "Independent" Bantustan* (London: Heinemann Educational Books, 1977), xii.

33. See, for the case of Bophuthatswana, Jane Carruthers, "Designing a Wilderness for Wildlife: The Case of the Pilanesberg National Park, South Africa," in *Designing Wildlife Habitats*, ed. John Beardsley (Washington, DC: Dumbarton Oaks Research Library and Collection, 2013), 107–30. See, for the case of KwaZulu, Shirley Brooks, "Planning for Leisure in 1940s Natal: Postwar Reconstruction and Parks as 'Public' Amenities," in *South Africa's 1940s: Worlds of Possibilities*, ed. Saul Dubow and Alan Jeeves, 129–48; and Malcolm Draper and Gerhard Maré, "The Garden of England's Gaming Zookeeper and Zululand," *Journal of Southern African Studies* 29, no. 2 (June 2003): 551–69.

34. Mangosuthu Buthelezi, "KwaZulu and Wildlife," in *Voices of the Wilderness*, ed. Ian Player (Johannesburg: Jonathan Ball, 1979), 106.

35. Enos Mabuza, "The Need for Wilderness Conservation in the KaNgwane Homeland," in *Voices of the Wilderness*, ed. Ian Player (Johannesburg: Jonathan Ball, 1979), 170.

36. Mabuza, "Need for Wilderness Conservation," 170.

37. Enos Mabuza, "The African and Wilderness," in *Wilderness*, ed. Vance Martin (Moray, Scotland: Findhorn Press, 1982), 44.

38. Buthelezi, "KwaZulu and Wildlife," 107.

39. Mabuza, "African and Wilderness," 44.

40. Buthelezi, "KwaZulu and Wildlife," 107.

41. Paige West, James Igoe, and Dan Brockington, "Parks and People: The Social Impact of Protected Areas," *Annual Review of Anthropology*, no. 35 (2006): 251–77.

42. It is important to point out that no two homelands were the same. KaNgwane, for example, refused to accept independence, and its leader, Enos Mabuza, was close to the exiled ANC. For more on the life of Mabuza, see Ashley Sarimana, "Trials and Triumphs in Public Office: The Life and Work of E.J.N. Mabuza" (PhD diss., Rhodes University, 2011).

43. See Cock, *War against Ourselves*, 148; Jacoby, *Crimes against Nature*, 190.

44. See, for a particularly dominant but flat rendering of homelands, Harold Wolpe's influential essay "Capitalism and Cheap Labor-Power in South Africa: From Segregation to Apartheid," *Economy and Society* 1, no. 4 (December 1972): 425–56. For a biography of Wolpe, see Steven Friedman, *Race, Class and Power: Harold Wolpe and the Radical Critique of Apartheid* (Pietermaritzburg: University of KwaZulu-Natal Press, 2015).

45. Audie Klotz, *Migration and National Identity in South Africa, 1860– 2010* (Cambridge: Cambridge University Press, 2013), 40.

46. Sick Winlight Mdluli, interview by author, Shabalala, Mpumalanga, South Africa, November 2009.

47. Simon Fakude, interview by author, Shabalala, South Africa, November 2009.

48. Jimmy Mnisi, interview by author, Shabalala, South Africa, November 2009.

49. Group interview, Shabalala, South Africa, November 2009.

50. See Harry Cooper and Mona Cooper, eds., "The Chief Minister Is a Man of Action," *Co-op Press*, July 7, 1985, Gazankulu archives, box CM/ NC/230.

51. See, for more on the Swiss missionaries in the lowveld, Patrick Harries, *Butterflies and Barbarians: Swiss Missionaries and Systems of Knowledge in South-East Africa* (Athens: Ohio University Press, 2007).

52. See Patrick Harries, "Exclusion, Classification and Internal Colonialism: The Emergence of Ethnicity among the Tsonga-Speakers of South Africa," in Vail, *Creation of Tribalism*, 82.

53. Van Warmelo quoted in South African Institute of Race Relations, "First Interim Report on the Establishment of Bantu Authorities," March 18, 1959, SAIRR papers, AD 1947/52.2.

54. Van Warmelo quoted in Harries, "Exclusion, Classification and Internal Colonialism," 85.

55. Harries, 103.

56. Harries, 103.

57. See Harries, 104.

58. Audie Klotz, *Migration and National Identity in South Africa*, 40.

59. See Harries, "Exclusion, Classification and Internal Colonialism," 108.

60. See Shireen Ally, "Material Remains: Artifice versus Artefact(s) in the Archive of Bantustan Rule," *Journal of Southern African Studies* 41, no. 5 (2015): 969–89.

61. See, for example, the anonymous letter dated April 6, 1989, sent to Ntsanwisi's office by a "Gazankulu citizen" who complained about "what is happening to your people and the Whiteman running businesses at Manyeleti Game Reserve. He is exploiting people" by charging high prices for food, making his staff work long and unpaid hours, forcing his staff to take unpaid leave, and cutting their salaries. Ntsanwisi ordered his office to probe the

allegations. It turned out the business was doing badly and the owner, a Mr. Swan, had asked his staff to agree to pay cuts in order to save the business. Correspondence in Gazankulu archives, box CM/NC/230.

62. Hudson Ntsanwisi to Gazankulu's Secretary of Education, January 17, 1985, Gazankulu archives, box CM/NC/230.

63. Report from Gazankulu's Secretary of Education to Hudson Ntsanwisi, January 16, 1985, Gazankulu archives, box CM/NC/230.

64. Report from Gazankulu's Secretary of Education to Hudson Ntsanwisi, January 16, 1985, Gazankulu archives, box CM/NC/230.

65. Report from Gazankulu's Secretary of Education to Hudson Ntsanwisi, January 16, 1985, Gazankulu archives, box CM/NC/230.

66. Hudson Ntsanwisi, "On the Occasion of the Handing Over of Manyeleti to Gazankulu," speech, March 26, 1985, Gazankulu archives, box CM/NC/230.

67. Ntsanwisi, "On the Occasion."

68. Ntsanwisi, "On the Occasion."

69. Ntsanwisi, "On the Occasion."

70. Ntsanwisi, "On the Occasion."

71. Ntsanwisi, "On the Occasion."

72. Ntsanwisi, "On the Occasion."

73. Ntsanwisi, "On the Occasion."

74. Steve Biko, "Let's Talk about Homelands," in *I Write What I Like*, ed. Aelred Stubbs (Oxford: Heinemann, 1987), 83.

75. See Joubert, *Kruger National Park*, 2:278. Professor C. J. Leonard became a board member in September 1992, bringing to two the number of blacks on the board.

76. Ntsanwisi, "On the Occasion."

77. For a history of Manyeleti, see Teversham, "Representations and Perceptions"; and Teversham, "The Nature of Leisure in the Manyeleti Game Reserve for Africans, South Africa, 1967–1985," *International Journal of the History of Sport* 30, no. 16 (2013): 1877–88.

78. Ntsanwisi, "On the Occasion."

79. Teversham, "Nature of Leisure," 1878.

80. Ntsanwisi, "On the Occasion."

81. Ntsanwisi, "On the Occasion."

82. Ntsanwisi, "On the Occasion."

83. See Teversham, "Nature of Leisure."

84. Progress Report on Letaba Ranch Hunting Project, 1981, Gazankulu archives, box CM/NC/230.

85. Stephen Ellis, "Of Elephants and Men: Politics and Nature Conservation in South Africa," *Journal of Southern African Studies* 20, no. 1 (March 1994): 53–69.

86. Chief S. D. Nxumalo to Hudson Ntsanwisi, April 9, 1985, Gazankulu archives, box CM/NC/230.

87. Chief S. D. Nxumalo to Hudson Ntsanwisi, April 9, 1985, Gazankulu archives, box CM/NC/230.

88. Chief S. D. Nxumalo to Hudson Ntsanwisi, April 9, 1985, Gazankulu archives, box CM/NC/230.

89. Secretary of Planning, "Relationships between Gazankulu and the Kruger National Park," report to Hudson Ntsanwisi, March 13, 1985, Gazankulu archives, box CM/NC/230.

90. Minutes of meeting of the Gazankulu/Kruger National Park Liaison Committee, held in Giyani, Gazankulu, July 13, 1988, Gazankulu archives, box CM/NC/230.

91. Secretary of Planning "Relationships between Gazankulu and the Kruger National Park."

92. Secretary of Planning "Relationships between Gazankulu and the Kruger National Park."

93. Kruger National Park warden Uys de V. Pienaar to Ian MacFadyen, October 8, 1984, Gazankulu archives, box CM/NC/230.

94. National Parks Board, "Proposed Co-operative Educational Project," report, October 7, 1987, Gazankulu archives, box CM/NC/230.

95. National Parks Board, "Proposed Co-operative Educational Project."

96. Minutes of meeting of the Gazankulu/Kruger National Park Liaison Committee, held in Giyani, Gazankulu, July 13, 1988, Gazankulu archives, box CM/NC/230.

97. Committee for Environmental and Nature Conservation, "Proposals for the Establishment of a Joint Authority," December 2, 1991, in the Gazankulu archives, box CM/NC/230.

98. Ian MacFadyen to Hudson Ntsanwisi's office, June 14, 1990, Gazankulu archives, box CM/NC/230.

99. Ian MacFadyen to Hudson Ntsanwisi's office, June 14, 1990, Gazankulu archives, box CM/NC/230.

100. John Comaroff and Jean Comaroff, *Ethnicity, Inc.* (Chicago: University of Chicago Press, 2009).

CHAPTER 7: BEGGAR THY NEIGHBOR

1. SAIRR papers, AD 1947/51.1.

2. See Cherryl Walker and Laurine Platzky, *The Surplus People: Forced Removals in South Africa* (Johannesburg: Ravan, 1985). Removal worked in a number of ways, including as a tool for repression. See Saleem Badat, *The Forgotten People: Political Banishment under Apartheid* (Johannesburg: Jacana, 2012). For a classic statement on the problem of removals, see Cosmas Desmond, *The Discarded People: An Account of African Resettlement in South Africa* (London: Penguin, 1971).

3. *Advance*'s reference to Meadowlands connected Ngomane's struggles to wider opposition by Africans to removals. Meadowlands was a new township in Soweto founded after forced removals from Sophiatown in 1955.

4. SAIRR Papers, AD 1947/51.1.

5. See, for insight into the workings of the trust, Feinberg, *Our Land*.

6. SAIRR Papers, AD 1947/51.1.

7. SAIRR Papers, AD 1947/51.1.

8. SAIRR Papers, AD 1947/51.1.

9. SAIRR Papers, AD 1947/51.1.

10. SAIRR Papers, AD 1947/51.1.

11. SAIRR Papers, AD 1947/51.1.

12. Charlie Mather, "Forced Removal and the Struggle for Land and Labor in South Africa: The Ngomane of Tenbosch, 1926–1924," *Journal of Historical Geography* 21, no. 2 (1995): 169–83.

13. Mather, "Forced Removal," 169.

14. Mather, 180.

15. Mather, 180.

16. Mather, 180.

17. Carruthers, *Kruger National Park*, 1.

18. Meskell, *Nature of Heritage*, 9.

19. See Joubert, *Kruger National Park*, 2:278.

20. Mandela's hunt actually took place at another KaNgwane sanctuary, the Songimvelo Game Reserve, south of Mthethomusha. At 49,000 hectares, Songimvelo, west of KaNgwane's border with Swaziland, was five times bigger than Mthethomusha and better stocked with wild animals.

21. See Joubert, *Kruger National Park*, 2:557.

22. See Cock and Koch, *Going Green*, 1; and Cock, *War against Ourselves*, 148.

23. See Jane Carruthers, "Dissecting the Myth: Paul Kruger and the Kruger National Park," *Journal of Southern African Studies* 20, no. 2 (June 1994): 263–83.

24. Carruthers, *Kruger National Park*, 89.

25. Elmon Mthombothi, interview by author, Mpumalanga, South Africa, November 2009.

26. Joubert, *Kruger National Park*, 2:548–51.

27. Joubert, 2:550.

28. Elmon Mthombothi, interview.

29. See, for an account of some of the first formal interactions between the ANC and the National Parks Board, Dikeni, *Habitat and Struggle*.

30. The unit has been renamed People and Conservation and was elevated to a directorate in 2003, giving it the status of a fully fledged department within the organization.

31. See Meskell, *Nature of Heritage*.

32. *Visions of Change: Social Ecology and South African National Parks* (Pretoria: SANParks, 2000), 20.

33. Enos Ngomane, interview by author, Mpumalanga, South Africa, November 2009.

34. Amos Lekhuleni, interview by author, Mpumalanga, South Africa, November 2009.

35. Grace Leyane, interview by author, Mpumalanga, South Africa, November 2009.

36. The reconstruction of the disaster is based in part on a government report on the disaster, D. D. Ngobeni, *Commission of Inquiry into the Fire at the Pretoriuskop Area in the Kruger National Park That Broke Out on 4 September 2001* (Pretoria, September 2, 2005), https://www.gov.za/sites/default/files/gcis_document/201409/2001ngobenikrugerparkcommisionofenquiry-20.pdf (hereafter *Ngobeni Commission Report*).

37. See, for a detailed study of the history of fire as a management tool in South Africa, Simon Pooley, *Burning Table Mountain: An Environmental History of Fire on the Cape Peninsula* (New York: Palgrave Macmillan, 2014). Pooley's book grew out of an Oxford PhD dissertation, which included an excellent chapter on the use of fire in the KNP. I am grateful to Dr. Pooley for sharing his chapter with me.

38. B. W. van Wilgen, Harry C. Biggs, and A. L. F. Potgieter, "Fire Management and Research in the Kruger National Park, with Suggestions on the Detection of Thresholds of Potential Concern," *Koedoe* 41, no. 1 (1998): 69–87.

39. A. M. Brynard, "Control Burning in the Kruger National Park: History and Development of the Range Burning Policy," *Proceedings: Tall Timbers Fire Ecology Conference*, no. 11 (1971): 219–31.

40. National Parks Board annual report for 1973.

41. *Ngobeni Commission Report.*

42. Linah Leyane, interview by author, Mpumalanga, South Africa, November 2009.

43. *Ngobeni Commission Report*, 75.

44. *Ngobeni Commission Report*, 76.

45. *Ngobeni Commission Report*, 22–23.

46. *Ngobeni Commission Report*, 33.

47. *Ngobeni Commission Report*, 58.

48. *Ngobeni Commission Report*, 59.

49. *Ngobeni Commission Report*, 57–59.

50. *Ngobeni Commission Report*, 62.

51. *Ngobeni Commission Report*, 72.

52. *Ngobeni Commission Report*, 73.

53. Linah Toropo Lekhuleni, interview by author, Mpumalanga, South Africa, November 2009.

54. Jeremy Lawrence, "Haunted by Their Screams," April 9, 2001.

55. Asya Nkuna, interview by author, Mpumalanga, South Africa, November 2009.

56. Amos Lekhuleni, interview.

57. Linah Leyane, interview.

58. Moses Lekhuleni, interview by author, Mpumalanga, South Africa, November 2009.

59. Moses Lekhuleni, interview.

CHPATER 8: THE ROAD TO THE
KRUGER NATIONAL PARK

1. The Sharpeville massacre was truly foundational to twentieth-century South African history. It effectively divided the country's history into a before and after. See, for work on the massacre, Tom Lodge, *Sharpeville: An Apartheid Massacre and Its Consequences* (New York: Oxford University Press, 2011); Phillip Frankel, *An Ordinary Atrocity: Sharpeville and Its Massacre* (Johannesburg: Wits University Press, 2001).

2. See Melanie-Ann Feris, "Remember the Poor," *Star*, March 27, 1998.

3. Nelson Mandela's speech on the centenary of the KNP. See *Visions of Change: Social Ecology and South African National Parks* (Pretoria: SANParks, 2000), 1.

4. Nelson Mandela's inaugural address, quoted in Paul Gilroy, *Between Camps: Nations, Cultures and the Allure of Race* (London: Routledge, 2004), 111.

5. Gilroy, *Between Camps*, 111. To be sure, Gilroy is trying to take us past the dead end of nationalism and nationalist thought. He is trying to encourage us to envision a world in which political membership and the very existence of the human as a human do not depend on the demarcation of nationalist camps. I agree fully with Gilroy's argument and support the ethical, intellectual, and political project behind his argument. However, I am reluctant to dispense with Mandela's own argument as I think it offers—in a world still defined by nationalist camps—a useful halfway house. This house is necessarily imperfect and impermanent, but it provides space to work out conceptions of belonging and citizenship that are more promising than the nativism that has given the world nothing but danger and populism.

6. Gilroy, *Between Camps*, 111.

7. Gilroy, 110.

8. Gilroy, 111.

9. Gilroy, 111.

10. I am indebted to Emmanuel Kreike for pointing this out to me.

11. See, for more on the Peace Parks Foundation, Bram Büscher and Marloes van Amerom, "Peace Parks in Southern Africa: Bringers of an African Renaissance?," *Journal of Modern African Studies* 43, no. 2 (2005): 159–82; Rosaleen Duffy, "Peace Parks: The Paradox of Globalization," *Geopolitics* 6, no. 2 (2001): 1–26.

12. See Miriam Tlali, "The Haunting Melancholy of Klipvoordam," *Staffrider*, April/May, 1981, 13–16. I am grateful to Pumla Gqola for bringing this wonderful, complicated gem of a story to my attention.

13. Tlali, 13.

14. Tlali, 13.

15. Tlali, 13.

16. Tlali, 14.

17. Tlali, 16.

18. Ndebele, *Fine Lines from the Box*, 102. Even though Ndebele's argument is about game lodges, it also holds for places such as the KNP.

19. Ndebele, 102.

20. Ndebele, 102.

21. See D. D. T. Jabavu, *The Black Problem* (New York: Negro Universities Press, 1920); R. V. Selope Thema, *From Cattle-Herding to Editor's Chair: The Unfinished Autobiography and Writings of Richard Victor Selope Thema*, ed. Alan Cobley (Cape Town: Van Riebeeck Society, 2016); see also Thema's writings cited throughout this book as well as his interventions in the Natives Representative Council, for example, *Verbatim Reports of the Proceedings of the Natives Representative Council*, December 5, 1950 (Pretoria: Government Printers, 1950), 1:28. For Lembede's writings about agriculture and trees, see Robert Edgar and Luyanda ka Msumza, eds., *Anton Lembede: Freedom in Our Lifetime* (Cape Town: Kwela Books, 2015), 69–71, 84–88.

22. The scale of the poaching problem is such that the KNP has become remilitarized. See John Hanks, *Operation Lock and the War on Rhino Poaching* (Cape Town: Penguin, 2015); see Julian Rademeyer, *Killing for Profit: Exposing the Illegal Rhino Horn Trade* (Cape Town: Zebra Press, 2014); Richard Leakey and Virginia Morell, *Wildlife Wars: My Fight to Save Africa's Natural Treasures* (New York: St. Martin's Griffin, 2001). For more scholarly treatments of the poaching problem, see Rosaleen Duffy, "Waging a War to Save Biodiversity: The Rise of Militarized Conservation," *International Affairs* 90, no. 4 (2014): 819–34. See also Elizabeth Lunstrum, "Green Militarization: Anti-poaching Efforts and the Spatial Contours of Kruger National Park," *Annals of the Association of American Geographers* 104, no. 4 (2014): 816–32; Bram Büscher and Maano Ramutsindela, "Green Violence: Rhino Poaching and the War to Save Southern Africa's Peace Parks," *African Affairs* 115, no. 458 (January 2016): 1–22. Then there is Stephen Ellis's classic essay "Of Elephants and Men: Politics and Nature Conservation in South Africa," *Journal of Southern African Studies* 20, no. 1 (1994): 53–69. The academic work on poaching represents collectively sophisticated attempts to strip conservation of its innocence and to show the violence that defines it in many parts of the world.

23. As pointed out earlier, borders in Africa have been the subject of intense scholarship, some scholars looking mainly at their colonial origins and others questioning the idea that Africa owes its borders to colonialism.

24. Charles Mogale, "Do We Really Have Hearts of Stone?," *City Press*, November 1, 1998. Mogale's story is uncannily similar to Nadine Gordimer's short story "The Ultimate Safari," in *Jump and Other Stories* (New York: Penguin, 1991), 33–49.

25. Mogale, "Do We Really Have Hearts of Stone?"

26. Sharon Hammond, "Game Park's Man-Eaters," *Star*, August 6, 1998.

27. These protests have been a remarkable and persistent feature of postapartheid South Africa. Not surprisingly, while the ruling ANC has tended to be dismissive of them, scholars have taken a more sober view. Drawing on the notion of insurgent citizenship developed by James Holston in his work on Brazil, some scholars have tried to understand these protests on their own terms. See Julian Brown, *South Africa's Insurgent Citizens: On Dissent and the Possibility of Politics* (London: Zed Books, 2015); James Holsten, *Insurgent Citizenship: Disjunctions of Democracy and Modernity in Brazil* (Princeton: Princeton University Press, 2008); Richard Pithouse, *Writing the Decline: On the Struggle for South Africa's Democracy* (Johannesburg: Jacana, 2016).

28. Protest organizer, interview by author, Shabalala, South Africa, September 2009. On the relationship between democracy and violence in South Africa, see Karl von Holdt, "On Violent Democracy," *Sociological Review* 62, no. 2 (2014): 129–51; and von Holdt, "South Africa: The Transition to Violent Democracy," *Review of African Political Economy* 40, no. 138 (2013): 589–604.

29. Protest organizer two, interview by author, Shabalala, South Africa, November 2009.

30. Protest organizer three, interview by author, Shabalala, South Africa, November 2009.

31. Protest organizer four, interview by author, Shabalala, South Africa, November 2009.

32. Sipho Mpangane, interview by author, Shabalala, South Africa, November 2009.

33. Carriot Mthethwa, interview by author, Shabalala, South Africa, November 2009.

34. Sick Winlight Mdluli, interview by author, Shabalala, South Africa, November 2009.

35. Mantombazana Khoza, interview by author, Shabalala, South Africa, November 2009.

36. Mantombazana Khoza, interview.

37. See, for more on the history of land struggles in Bushbuckridge, James Cockfield, "Land, Settlement and Narratives of History in Northern Bushbuckridge, c. 1890–1970" (PhD diss., University of Oxford, 2015). I am grateful to William Beinart for bringing this important study to my attention and for sharing his copy with me.

38. Graeme Eddison, "Going Mad for Mpumalanga," *Sunday Times*, May 25, 1997.

39. David Tucker, *Citizen*, September 3, 1994.

40. J. Fourie, "The Concept of Life: On the Social Role of Conservation Areas," *Koedoe* 34, no. 2 (1991): 158.

41. J. Fourie, "Comments on National Parks and Future Relations with Neighboring Communities," *Koedoe* 37, no. 1 (1994): 123.

42. See, for a magisterial history of the park's achievements in the field of science, Carruthers, *National Park Science*.

43. Fourie, "Comments on National Parks," 123–24.

44. J. A. Loader, "National Parks and Social Involvement," *Koedoe* 37, no. 1 (1994): 137–48.

45. Cock and Koch, *Going Green*, 1.

46. Loader, "National Parks and Social Involvement," 147.

47. Jane Carruthers, Sharon Pollard, and Charlie Shackleton, "Beyond the Fence: People and the Lowveld Landscape," in *The Kruger Experience: Ecology and Management of Savannah Heterogeneity*, ed. Johan T. du Toit, Kevin H. Rogers, and Harry C. Biggs (Washington, DC: Island Press, 2003), 422–47.

48. Carruthers, Pollard, and Shackleton, *Kruger Experience*, 429–32.

49. Carruthers, Pollard, and Shackleton, *Kruger Experience*, 432.

50. Carruthers, Pollard, and Shackleton, *Kruger Experience*, 429.

51. H. Els and J. du Bothma, "Developing Partnerships in a Paradigm Shift to Achieve Conservation Reality in South Africa," *Koedoe* 43, no. 1 (2000): 19–26.

52. Els and du Bothma, "Developing Partnerships," 19–26.

CONCLUSION

1. See debates in House of Assembly *Hansard* 31 May 1926 Col. 4374 (S. Afr.).

2. David Bunn offers a wonderful account of the controversy surrounding the erection of the Paul Kruger monument. See Bunn, "Whited Sepulchres: On the Reluctance of Monuments," in *Blank: Architecture, Apartheid and After*, ed. Hilton Judin and Ivan Vladislavi (Rotterdam: NAI, 1998), C4.

3. The monument and plans for it were sources of controversy right from the start. See, for an example of the media coverage of the controversy, "Administration Backs Bust of Kruger in Park," *Rand Daily Mail*, November 5, 1968. Among those opposed to the Kruger bust was the Transvaal Institute of Architects. See *Rand Daily Mail*, August 15, 1968.

4. See, for insight into the controversy surrounding Paul Kruger and his relationship with the KNP, Carruthers, "Dissecting the Myth"; see also Carruthers, "Defending Kruger's Honor? A Reply to Professor Hennie Grobler," *Journal of Southern African Studies* 22, no. 3 (September 1996): 473–80.

5. See Katrina Tweedie, *Sunday Independent*, April 5, 1998.

6. See, for a biography of Jabavu, Catherine Higgs, *Ghost of Equality: The Public Lives of D.D.T. Jabavu of South Africa, 1885–1959* (Athens: Ohio University Press, 1996).

7. See D. D. T. Jabavu, *In India and East Africa* (Lovedale: Lovedale Mission Press, 1951), 3. See Jacklyn Cock's wonderful memoir for a poignant examination of the connection between rivers and identity in the Eastern

Cape, *Writing the Ancestral River: A Biography of the Kowie* (Johannesburg: Wits University Press, 2018).

8. André Odendaal makes this point eloquently in *Founders*, 211: "The new railway line from the Cape to the new metropolis of Johannesburg, along which people and ideas started moving forwards and backwards, provided the spine for the new national movement."

9. See Noni Jabavu, *Drawn in Color: African Contrasts* (London: John Murray, 1960), 52–53.

10. See Sue Hart, "Wilderness and Black Education," in *Voices of the Wilderness*, ed. Ian Player (Johannesburg: Jonathan Ball, 1979), 127.

11. See, for a history of the school, Ian Player, "Wilderness Leadership School," in Player ed., *Voices of the Wilderness*, 24–28. See, for an institutional history of the Wildlife Society of Southern Africa, John Pringle, *The Conservationists and the Killers: The Story of Game Protection and the Wildlife Society of Southern Africa* (Cape Town: Books of Africa, 1982).

12. Thema made his comments in December 1950 during a session of the Natives' Representative Council. Thema was an elected member of the council. See the *Verbatim Report of the Proceedings of the Natives' Representative Council*, December 5, 1950 (Pretoria: Government Printers, 1950), 28.

Selected Bibliography

Ally, Shireen. *From Servants to Workers: South African Domestic Workers and the Democratic State*. Ithaca: Cornell University Press, 2009.

Barnes, Teresa. "Virgin Territory? Travel and Migration by African Women in Twentieth-Century Southern Africa." In *Women in African Colonial Histories*, edited by Jean Allman, Susan Geiger, and Nakanyike Musisi, 164–90. Bloomington: Indiana University Press, 2002.

Beinart, William. *The Rise of Conservation in South Africa: Settlers, Livestock, and the Environment, 1770–1950*. Oxford: Oxford University Press, 2003.

Beinart, William, and JoAnn McGregor, eds. *Social History and African Environments*, Oxford: James Currey, 2003.

Benningfield, Jennifer. *The Frightened Land: Land, Landscape and Politics in South Africa in the Twentieth Century*. London: Routledge, 2006.

Bolaane, Maitseo. *Chiefs, Hunters and San in the Creation of the Moremi Game Reserve, Okavango Delta: Multiracial Interactions and Initiatives, 1956–1979*. Osaka: National Museum of Ethnology, 2013.

———. "Wildlife Conservation and Local Management: The Establishment of Moremi Park, Okavango, Botswana in the 1950s–1960s." PhD diss., Oxford University, 2004.

Bonner, Raymond. *At the Hand of Man: Peril and Hope for Africa's Wildlife*. New York: Knopf, 1993.

Boyer, Christopher R. *Political Landscapes: Forests, Conservation, and Community in Mexico*. Durham, NC: Duke University Press, 2015.

Braun, Lindsay Frederick. *Colonial Survey and Native Landscapes in Rural South Africa, 1850–1913: The Politics of Divided Space in the Cape and Transvaal*. Boston: Brill, 2014.

Brooks, Shirley. "Planning for Leisure in 1940s Natal: Postwar Reconstruction and Parks as 'Public' Amenities." In *South Africa's 1940s: Worlds of Possibilities*, edited by Saul Dubow and Alan Jeeves, 129–48. Cape Town: Double Storey Books, 2005.

Browne, Adrian. "Conservation Converts? Africanizing Wildlife Conservation, Uganda National Parks, c. 1950–1973." Master's thesis, Oxford University, 2010.

Bunn, David. "The Museum Outdoors: Heritage, Cattle, and Permeable Borders in the Southwestern Kruger National Park." In *Museum Frictions:*

Public Cultures/Global Transformations, edited by Ivan Karp, Corinne A. Kratz, Lynn Szwaja, and Tomás Ybarra-Frausto, 357–97. Durham, NC: Duke University Press, 2006.

———. "Whited Sepulchres: On the Reluctance of Monuments." In *Blank: Architecture, Apartheid and After*, edited by Hilton Judin and Ivan Vladislavic. Rotterdam: NAi, 1999.

Burton, Antoinette. *Africa in the Indian Imagination: Race and the Politics of Postcolonial Citation*. Durham, NC: Duke University Press, 2016.

Büscher, Bram. *Transforming the Frontier: Peace Parks and the Politics of Neoliberal Conservation in Southern Africa*. Durham, NC: Duke University Press, 2013.

Candiani, Vera. *Dreaming of Dry Land: Environmental Transformation in Colonial Mexico City*. Stanford: Stanford University Press, 2014.

Carruthers, Jane. "Creating a National Park, 1910 to 1926." *Journal of Southern African Studies* 15, no. 2 (January 1989): 188–216.

———. "Defending Kruger's Honor? A Reply to Professor Hennie Grobler." *Journal of Southern African Studies* 22, no. 3 (September 1996): 473–80.

———. "Dissecting the Myth: Paul Kruger and the Kruger National Park." *Journal of Southern African Studies* 20, no. 2 (June 1994): 263–83.

———. "Game Protection in the Transvaal, 1846 to 1926." PhD thesis, University of Cape Town, 1988. http://hdl.handle.net/11427/23736.

———. *The Kruger National Park: A Social and Political History*. Pietermaritzburg: University of Natal Press, 1995.

———. *National Park Science: A Century of Research in South Africa*. Cambridge: Cambridge University Press, 2017.

———. "'Police Boys' and Poachers: Africans, Wildlife Protection and National Parks, the Transvaal 1902 to 1950." *Koedoe* 36, no. 2 (September 1993): 11–22.

———. "'Why Celebrate a Controversy?': South Africa, the United States, and National Parks." In *National Parks beyond the Nation: Global Perspectives on "America's Best Idea,"* edited by Adrian Howkins, Jared Orsi, and Mark Fiege, 135–56. Norman: University of Oklahoma Press, 2016.

———. *Wildlife and Warfare: The Life of James Stevenson-Hamilton*. Pietermaritzburg: University of Natal Press, 2001.

Clifford, James. *Routes: Travel and Translation in the Late Twentieth Century*. Cambridge, MA: Harvard University Press, 1997.

Cock, Jacklyn. *The War against Ourselves: Nature, Power, and Justice*. Johannesburg: Wits University Press, 2007.

———. *Writing the Ancestral River: A Biography of the Kowie*. Johannesburg: Wits University Press, 2018.

Cock, Jacklyn, and Eddie Koch, eds. *Going Green: People, Politics and the Environment in South Africa*. Cape Town: Oxford University Press, 1991.

Cockfield, James. "Land, Settlement and Narratives of History in Northern Bushbuckridge, c. 1890–1970." PhD diss., Oxford University, 2015.

Coombes, Annie E. *History after Apartheid: Visual Culture and Public Memory in a Democratic South Africa*. Durham, NC: Duke University Press, 2003.

Cooper, Frederick. *Citizenship between Empire and Nation: Remaking France and French Africa, 1945–1960*. Princeton: Princeton University Press, 2014.

Coplan, David B. *In Township Tonight! South Africa's Black City Music and Theatre*. 2nd ed. Auckland Park, S. Africa: Jacana, 2007.

Cousins, Ben, and Cherryl Walker, eds. *Land Divided, Land Restored: Land Reform in South Africa for the 21st Century*. Johannesburg: Jacana, 2015.

Couzens, Tim. "'Moralizing Leisure Time': The Transatlantic Connection and Black Johannesburg, 1918–1936." In *Industrialization and Social Change in South Africa: African Class Formation, Culture, and Consciousness, 1870–1930*, edited by Shula Marks and Richard Rathbone, 314–38. London: Longman, 1982.

Delius, Peter, and Michelle Hay, eds. *Mpumalanga: An Illustrated History*. Johannesburg: Highveld, 2009.

Delius, Peter, Laura Phillips, and Fiona Rankin-Smith, eds. *A Long Way Home: Migrant Worker Worlds, 1800–2014*. Johannesburg: Wits University Press, 2014.

Dikeni, Leslie. *Habitat and Struggle: The Case of the Kruger National Park in South Africa*. Johannesburg: Real African Publishers, 2016.

Domingos, Nuno. *Football and Colonialism: Body and Popular Culture in Urban Mozambique*. Athens: Ohio University Press, 2017.

Dubow, Saul. *Apartheid, 1948–1994*. Oxford: Oxford University Press, 2014.

———. "Imagining the New South Africa in the Era of Reconstruction." In *The Impact of the South African War*, edited by David Omissi and Andrew Thompson, 76–99. New York: Palgrave, 2002.

———. *Racial Segregation and the Origins of Apartheid in South Africa, 1919–36*. London: Palgrave Macmillan, 1989.

du Toit, Johan T., Kevin H. Rogers, and Harry C. Biggs, eds. *The Kruger Experience: Ecology and Management of Savanna Heterogeneity*. Washington, DC: Island Press, 2003.

Edgar, Robert, and Luyanda ka Msumza, eds. *Anton Lembede: Freedom in Our Lifetime*. Cape Town: Kwela Books, 2015.

Evans, Ivan. *Bureaucracy and Race: Native Administration in South Africa*. Berkeley: University of California Press, 1997.

Feinberg, Harvey. *Our Land, Our Life, Our Future: Black South African Challenges to Territorial Segregation, 1913–1948*. Pretoria: UNISA, 2015.

Ferguson, James. *Give a Man a Fish: Reflections on the New Politics of Distribution*. Durham, NC: Duke University Press, 2015.

Finney, Carolyn. *Black Faces, White Spaces: Reimagining the Relationship of African Americans to the Great Outdoors*. Chapel Hill: University of North Carolina Press, 2014.

Foster, Jeremy. "'Land of Contrasts' or 'Home We Have Always Known'? The SAR&H and the Imaginary Geography of White South African Nationhood, 1910–1930." *Journal of Southern African Studies* 29, no. 3 (September 2003): 657–80.

———. *Washed with Sun: Landscape and the Making of White South Africa.* Pittsburgh: University of Pittsburgh Press, 2008.

Fourie, J. "Comments on National Parks and Future Relations with Neighboring Communities." *Koedoe* 37, no. 1 (1994): 123–36.

Fox, Roddy, and Kate Rowntree, eds. *The Geography of South Africa in a Changing World.* Oxford: Oxford University Press, 2000.

Gibson, Clark C. *Politicians and Poachers: The Political Economy of Wildlife Policy in Africa.* Cambridge: Cambridge University Press, 1999.

Green, Victor H. *The Negro Motorist Green Book.* New York: Victor H. Green, 1936.

Grundlingh, Albert. *Potent Pastimes: Sport and Leisure Practices in Modern Afrikaner History.* Pretoria: Protea Book House, 2013.

———. "Revisiting the 'Old' South Africa: Excursions into South Africa's Tourist History under Apartheid, 1948–1990." *South African Historical Journal* 56, no. 1 (January 2006): 103–22.

Hanks, John. *Operation Lock and the War on Rhino Poaching.* Cape Town: Penguin, 2015.

Harries, Patrick. *Butterflies and Barbarians: Swiss Missionaries and Systems of Knowledge in South-East Africa.* Athens: Ohio University Press, 2007.

———. *Work, Culture, and Identity: Migrant Laborers in Mozambique and South Africa, c. 1860–1910.* Johannesburg: Wits University Press, 1994.

Hendricks, Fred, Lungisile Ntsebeza, and Kirk Helliker, eds. *The Promise of Land: Undoing a Century of Dispossession in South Africa.* Johannesburg: Jacana, 2013.

Hughes, Heather. "Doubly Elite: Exploring the Life of John Langalibalele Dube." *Journal of Southern African Studies* 27, no. 3 (September 2001): 445–58.

———. *First President: A Life of John L. Dube, Founding President of the ANC.* Johannesburg: Jacana, 2011.

Impey, Angela. *Song Walking: Women, Music, and Environmental Justice in an African Borderland.* Chicago: University of Chicago Press, 2018.

Jacobs, Nancy. *Birders of Africa: History of a Network.* New Haven: Yale University Press, 2016.

———. *Environment, Power, and Injustice: A South African History.* Cambridge: Cambridge University Press, 2003.

Jacoby, Karl. *Crimes against Nature: Squatters, Poachers, Thieves, and the Hidden History of American Conservation.* Berkeley: University of California Press, 2001.

Joubert, Salomon. *The Kruger National Park: A History.* 3 vols. Johannesburg: High Branching, 2007.

Khan, Farieda. "Rewriting South Africa's Conservation History: The Role of the Native Farmers' Association." *Journal of Southern African Studies* 20, no. 4 (December 1994): 499–516.

———. "Towards Environmentalism: A Socio-political Evaluation of Trends in South African Conservation History, 1910–1976, with a Specific Focus on the Role of Black Conservation Organizations." PhD diss., University of Cape Town, 2001.

Knight, John, ed. *Natural Enemies: People-Wildlife Conflicts in Anthropological Perspective*. London: Routledge, 2000.

Kreike, Emmanuel. *Environmental Infrastructure in African History: Examining the Myth of Natural Resource Management in Namibia*. Cambridge: Cambridge University Press, 2013.

———. *Recreating Eden: Land Use, Environment, and Society in Southern Angola and Northern Namibia*. Portsmouth, NH: Heinemann, 2004.

Krikler, Jeremy. *Revolution from Above, Rebellion from Below: The Agrarian Transvaal at the Turn of the Century*. Oxford: Clarendon Press, 1993.

Kuper, Leo. *An African Bourgeoisie: Race, Class and Politics in South Africa*. New Haven: Yale University Press, 1965.

Kupper, Patrick. *Creating Wilderness: A Transnational History of the Swiss National Park*. Translated by Gisselle Weiss. New York: Berghahn Books, 2014.

Lawrence, Benjamin, Emily Osborn, and Richard Roberts, eds. *Intermediaries, Interpreters and Clerks: African Employees in the Making of Colonial Africa*. Madison: University of Wisconsin Press, 2007.

Limb, Peter. *The ANC's Early Years: Nation, Class and Place in South Africa before 1940*. Pretoria: UNISA, 2010.

———, ed. *The People's Paper: A Centenary History and Anthology of Abantu-Batho*. Johannesburg: Wits University Press, 2012.

Loader, J. A. "National Parks and Social Involvement." *Koedoe* 37, no. 1 (1994): 137–48.

MacArthur, Julie. *Cartography and the Political Imagination: Mapping Community in Colonial Kenya*. Athens: Ohio University Press, 2016.

Magome, Hector, and James Murombedzi. "Sharing South African National Parks: Community Land and Conservation in a Democratic South Africa." In *Decolonizing Nature: Strategies for Conservation in a Post-colonial Era*, edited by William M. Adams and Martin Mulligan, 108–35. London: Earthscan, 2003.

Makhulu, Anne-Maria. *Making Freedom: Apartheid, Squatter Politics, and the Struggle for Home*. Durham, NC: Duke University Press, 2015.

MapStudio. *Kruger National Park Souvenir Map*. 3rd ed. Cape Town: MapStudio, 2003.

Martin, Phyllis M. *Leisure and Society in Colonial Brazzaville*. Cambridge: Cambridge University Press, 1995.

Matthews, Barbara. *The Man They Called "Vukani": The Life and Times of Harold Trollope*. Port Elizabeth: Bluecliff, 2005.

Mavhunga, Clapperton Chakanetsa. "The Mobile Workshop: Mobility, Technology, and Human-Animal Interaction in Gonarezhou (National Park), 1850–present." PhD diss., University of Michigan, 2008. http://hdl.handle.net/2027.42/61738.

———. *Transient Workspaces: Technologies of Everyday Innovation in Zimbabwe.* Cambridge, MA: MIT Press, 2014.

Mazower, Mark. *No Enchanted Palace: The End of Empire and the Ideological Origins of the United Nations.* Princeton: Princeton University Press, 2009.

McGregor, JoAnn. "Landscape, Politics and the Historical Geography of Southern Africa." *Journal of Historical Geography* 31, no. 2 (April 2005): 205–19.

———. "The Social Life of Ruins: Sites of Memory and the Politics of a Zimbabwean Periphery." *Journal of Historical Geography*, no. 31 (2005): 316–37.

McKeown, Kathleen. "Tracking Wildlife Conservation in Southern Africa: Histories of Protected Areas in Gorongosa and Maputaland." PhD diss., University of Minnesota, 2015.

Meskell, Lynn. "Archaeological Ethnography: Conversations around Kruger National Park." *Archaeologies* 1, no. 1 (August 2005): 81–100.

———, ed. *Cosmopolitan Archaeologies.* Durham, NC: Duke University Press, 2009.

———. *The Nature of Heritage: The New South Africa.* Malden, MA: Wiley-Blackwell, 2012.

Moguerane, Khumisho. "A History of the Molemas, African Notables in South Africa, 1880s to 1920s." PhD thesis, Oxford University, 2014.

National Parks Board. *Unspoilt Africa.* Pretoria: National Parks Board, 1938.

———. *Unspoilt Africa.* Pretoria: National Parks Board, 1939.

———. *Unspoilt Africa.* Pretoria: National Parks Board, 1946.

———. *Our National Parks.* Pretoria: National Parks Board, 1958.

———. *Our National Parks.* Pretoria: National Parks Board, 1963.

Ndebele, Njabulo. *Fine Lines from the Box: Further Thoughts about Our Country.* Roggebaai, Cape Town: Umuzi, 2007.

Neumann, Roderick P. "Africa's 'Last Wilderness': Reordering Space for Political and Economic Control in Colonial Tanzania." *Africa*, no. 17 (November 2001): 641–65.

———. *Imposing Wilderness: Struggles over Livelihood and Nature Preservation in Africa.* Berkeley: University of California Press, 1998.

Ngcukaitobi, Tembeka. *The Land Is Ours: South Africa's First Black Lawyers and the Birth of Constitutionalism.* Cape Town: Penguin, 2018.

Niehaus, Isak. *Witchcraft, Power, and Politics: Exploring the Occult in the South African Lowveld.* London: Pluto Press, 2001.

Nixon, Rob. *Slow Violence and the Environmentalism of the Poor.* Cambridge, MA: Harvard University Press, 2011.

Norval, Alfred. *The Tourist Industry: A National and International Survey.* London: Sir Isaac Pitman and Sons, 1936.

Ntsebeza, Lungisile. *Land Tenure Reform, Traditional Authorities and Rural Local Government in Post-apartheid South Africa: Case Studies from the Eastern Cape.* Belville: PLAAS, 1999.

Nyquist, T. E. *African Middle Class Elite.* Occasional Paper 28. Grahamstown: Institute of Social and Economic Research, Rhodes University, 1983.

Odendaal, André. *The Founders: The Origins of the ANC and the Struggle for Democracy in South Africa.* Lexington: University Press of Kentucky, 2013.

———. *Vukani Bantu! The Beginnings of Black Protest Politics in South Africa to 1912.* Cape Town: David Phillip, 1984.

Packard, Randall. "'Malaria Blocks Development' Revisited: The Role of Disease in the History of Agricultural Development in the Eastern and Northern Transvaal Lowveld, 1890–1960." *Journal of Southern African Studies* 27, no. 3 (2001): 591–612.

Pels, Peter. *A Politics of Presence: Contacts between Missionaries and Waluguru in Late Colonial Tanganyika.* Amsterdam: Harwood Academic, 1999.

Peterson, Bhekizizwe. *Monarchs, Missionaries and African Intellectuals: African Theatre and the Unmaking of Colonial Marginality.* Johannesburg: Wits University Press, 2000.

Peterson, Derek. *Ethnic Patriotism and the East African Revival: A History of Dissent, c. 1935–1972.* Cambridge: Cambridge University Press, 2012.

Peterson, Derek, Kodzo Gavua, and Ciraj Rassool, eds. *The Politics of Heritage in Africa: Economies, Histories and Infrastructures.* Cambridge: Cambridge University Press, 2015.

Phillips, Anne. *The Politics of Presence.* Oxford: Clarendon Press, 1995.

Phillips, Ray E. *The Bantu Are Coming: Phases of South Africa's Race Problem.* London: Student Christian Movement Press, 1930.

Pienaar, Uys de V. *A Cameo from the Past: The Prehistory and Early History of the Kruger National Park.* Translated by Helena Bryden. Pretoria: Protea Book House, 2012.

Pirie, Gordon. "Elite Exoticism: Sea-Rail Cruise Tourism to South Africa, 1926–1939." *African Historical Review* 43, no. 1 (2011): 73–99.

———. "Railways and Labour Migration to the Rand Mines: Constraints and Significance." *Journal of Southern African Studies* 19, no. 4 (1993): 713–30.

Pooley, Simon. *Burning Table Mountain: An Environmental History of Fire on the Cape Peninsula.* New York: Palgrave Macmillan, 2014.

Posmentier, Sonya. *Cultivation and Catastrophe: The Lyric Ecology of Modern Black Literature.* Baltimore: Johns Hopkins University Press, 2017.

Powell, Miles. *Vanishing America: Species Extinction, Racial Peril, and the Origins of Conservation.* Cambridge, MA: Harvard University Press, 2016.

Pravilova, Ekaterina. *A Public Empire: Property and the Quest for the Common Good in Imperial Russia*. Princeton: Princeton University Press, 2014.

Pringle, John. *The Conservationists and the Killers: The Story of Game Protection and the Wildlife Society of Southern Africa*. Cape Town: Books of Africa, 1982.

Rademeyer, Julian. *Killing for Profit: Exposing the Illegal Rhino Horn Trade*. Cape Town: Zebra Books, 2012.

Ramutsindela, Maano. *Transfrontier Conservation in Africa: At the Confluence of Capital, Politics, and Nature*. Wallingford, Eng.: CABI, 2007.

Ranger, Terence. *Are We Not Also Men? The Samkange Family and African Politics in Zimbabwe, 1920–64*. London: James Currey, 1995.

———. *Voices from the Rocks: Nature, Culture and History in the Matopos Hills of Zimbabwe*. Oxford: James Currey, 1999.

Rassool, Ciraj, and Leslie Witz. "The 1952 Jan Van Riebeek Tercentenary Festival: Constructing and Contesting Public National History in South Africa." *Journal of African History* 34, no. 3 (1993): 447–68.

Ritchken, Edwin. "Leadership and Conflict in Bushbuckridge: Struggles to Define Moral Economics within the Context of Rapidly Transforming Political Economies." PhD diss., Wits University, 1995.

Rogers, Howard. *Native Administration in the Union of South Africa*. Johannesburg: University of the Witwatersrand Press, 1933.

Roth, Mia. *The Rhetorical Origins of Apartheid*. Jefferson, NC: McFarland, 2016.

Rugh, Susan Sessions. *Are We There Yet? The Golden Age of American Family Vacations*. Lawrence: University Press of Kansas, 2008.

Rutledge, Brian. "South African Readers and Consumer Capitalism, 1932–1962." PhD diss., Cornell University, 2018.

Saint, Lily. *Black Cultural Life in South Africa: Reception, Apartheid, and Ethics*. Ann Arbor: University of Michigan Press, 2018.

Sarimana, Ashley. "Trials and Triumphs in Public Office: The Life and Work of E.J.N. Mabuza." PhD diss., Rhodes University, 2011.

Schirmer, Stefan. "The Struggle for Land in Lydenburg: African Resistance in a White Farming District, 1930–1970." PhD diss., Wits University, 1994.

Scott, Rebecca, and Jean Hébrard. *Freedom Papers: An Atlantic Odyssey in the Age of Emancipation*. Cambridge, MA: Harvard University Press, 2012.

Sellars, Richard West. *Preserving Nature in the National Parks: A History*. New Haven: Yale University Press, 1997.

Shetler, Jan Bender. *Imagining Serengeti: A History of Landscape Memory in Tanzania from Earliest Times to the Present*. Athens: Ohio University Press, 2007.

Skota, T. D. Mweli, ed. *The African Who's Who: An Illustrated Classified Register and National Biographical Dictionary of the Africans in the Transvaal*. Johannesburg: R. L. Esson, 1930.

Soske, Jon. *Internal Frontiers: African Nationalism and the Indian Diaspora in Twentieth-Century South Africa*. Athens: Ohio University Press, 2017.

Southall, Roger. *The New Black Middle Class in South Africa*. Johannesburg: Jacana, 2016.

———. *South Africa's Transkei: The Political Economy of an "Independent" Bantustan*. London: Heinemann Educational Books, 1982.

Spence, Mark David. *Dispossessing the Wilderness: Indian Removal and the Making of National Parks*. New York: Oxford University Press, 2000.

Spierenburg, Marja, and Harry Wels. "'Securing Space': Mapping and Fencing in Transfrontier Conservation in Southern Africa." *Space and Culture* 9, no. 3 (August 2006): 294–312.

Steinhart, Edward. *Black Poachers, White Hunters: A Social History of Hunting in Colonial Kenya*. Athens: Ohio University Press, 2006.

Stevenson-Hamilton, James. *Animal Life in Africa*. London: Heinemann, 1912.

———. *The Lowveld: Its Wildlife and Its People*. London: Cassell, 1929.

———. *Wildlife in South Africa*. London: Hamilton, 1957.

Steyn, Phia. "A Greener Past? An Assessment of South African Environmental Historiography." *New Contree*, no. 46 (November 1999): 7–31.

Suzuki, Yuka. *The Nature of Whiteness: Race, Animals, and Nation in Zimbabwe*. Seattle: University of Washington Press, 2017.

Swanepoel, Natalie, Amanda Esterhuysen, and Philip Bonner, eds. *Five Hundred Years Rediscovered: Southern African Precedents and Prospects*. Johannesburg: Wits University Press, 2008.

Teversham, Edward. "Representations and Perceptions of the Kruger National Park and the Manyeleti Game Reserve, 1926–2010." PhD thesis, Oxford University, 2014.

Thema, R. V. Selope. *From Cattle-Herding to Editor's Chair: The Unfinished Autobiography and Writings of Richard Victor Selope Thema*, edited by Alan Cobley. Cape Town: Van Riebeeck Society, 2016.

Thompsell, Angela. *Hunting Africa: British Sport, African Knowledge and the Nature of Empire*. New York: Palgrave Macmillan, 2015.

Thompson, E. P. *Whigs and Hunters: The Origin of the Black Act*. London: Breviary Stuff Publications, 2013.

Vahed, Goolam, and Thembisa Waetjen. *Indian Delights: Gender, Modernity and the Women's Cultural Group of Durban, 1954–2010*. Cape Town: HSRC Press, 2010.

Vail, Leroy, ed. *The Creation of Tribalism in Southern Africa*. London: James Currey, 1989.

van Eeden, Jeanne. "Surveying the 'Empty Land' in Selected South African Landscape Postcards." *International Journal of Tourism Research* 13, no. 6 (2011), 600–612.

Vinson, Robert Trent. *The Americans Are Coming: Dreams of African American Liberation in Segregationist South Africa*. Athens: Ohio University Press, 2012.

Wagner, Roger. "Zoutpansberg: The Dynamics of a Hunting Frontier, 1848–67." In Marks and Atmore, eds, *Economy and Society in Pre-industrial South Africa*, 313–50.

Wakild, Emily. *Revolutionary Parks: Conservation, Social Justice, and Mexico's National Parks, 1910–1940*. Tucson: University of Arizona Press, 2011.

Walker, Cherryl. *Landmarked: Land Claims and Land Restitution in South Africa*. Johannesburg: Jacana, 2008.

Walker, Cherryl, Anna Bohlin, Ruth Hall, and Thembela Kepe, eds. *Land, Memory, Reconstruction, and Justice: Perspectives on Land Claims in South Africa*. Athens: Ohio University Press, 2010.

Warren, Louis S. *The Hunter's Game: Poachers and Conservationists in Twentieth-Century America*. New Haven: Yale University Press, 1997.

Warwick, Peter. *Black People and the South African War, 1899–1902*. Cambridge: Cambridge University Press, 1983.

West, Paige, James Igoe, and Dan Brockington. "Parks and Peoples: The Social Impact of Protected Areas." *Annual Review of Anthropology*, no. 35 (2006): 251–77.

White, Luise. *Unpopular Sovereignty: Rhodesian Independence and African Decolonization*. Chicago: University of Chicago Press, 2015.

White, Luise, Stephan Miescher, and David William Cohen, eds. *African Words, African Voices: Critical Practices in Oral History*. Bloomington: Indiana University Press, 2001.

Willan, Brian. "An African in Kimberley: Sol T. Plaatje, 1894–1898." In *Industrialization and Social Change in South Africa: African Class Formation, Culture, and Consciousness, 1870–1930*, edited by Shula Marks and Richard Rathbone, 238–59. London: Longman, 1982.

———. *Sol Plaatje: A Life of Solomon Tshekiso Plaatje, 1876–1932*. Johannesburg: Jacana, 2018.

Witz, Leslie, Gary Minkley, and Ciraj Rassool. *Unsettled History: Making South African Public Pasts*. Ann Arbor: University of Michigan Press, 2017.

Wolmer, William. *From Wilderness Vision to Farm Invasions: Conservation and Development in Zimbabwe's South-East Lowveld*. Oxford: James Currey, 2007.

———. "Transboundary Conservation: The Politics of Ecological Integrity in the Great Limpopo Transfrontier Park." *Journal of Southern African Studies* 29, no. 1 (March 2003): 261–78.

———. "Wilderness Gained, Wilderness Lost: Wildlife Management and Land Occupations in Zimbabwe's Southeast Lowveld." *Journal of Historical Geography*, no. 31 (2005): 260–80.

Index

Judt, Tony, 109

KaNgwane Parks Board, 217
Kidger, Cecil E., 52
Kimberley, 37
Knight, John, 38
KNP (Kruger National Park), 1, 148;
    1913 Natives Land Act, 55; access
    to, 3; accommodations in, 3, 6,
    141, 187, 191; advertisement of,
    123; apartheid and, 153, 184, 189,
    192; black visitors to, 1, 142, 196;
    camps, 12; casualties in, 228–29;
    Coloureds and, 175–77; conserva-
    tion, 224; disease in, 84; domestic
    workers in, 159, 160; fire in, 228–
    30; Gazankulu and, 202, 204–6;
    harassment in, 207; illegal im-
    migration, 78; Indians and, 153,
    158, 168; labor, 14; Manyeleti
    Game Reserve and, 205; map, 69;
    mining and, 68; name, changes
    to, 255; neighbors of, 246, 251;
    poaching in, 51; protests and, 222;
    territorial integrity, 61; travel and,
    70, 104–7, 152, 156–58; trespass-
    ing in, 49; white visitors and,
    129, 158; women in, 197; zone of
    movement, 65. *See also* National
    Parks Act of 1926
Koedoe, 251
Komatipoort, 53
Koranta ea Becoana, 88, 113, 150
Kruger National Park (KNP). *See* KNP
Kumalo, B. P., 259–61

labor, 12, 146, 190, 228; domestic,
    165; mobilization of, 115, 189;
    recruits, 71
Lagden, Godfrey, 93
land: allocation, 213; connection to,
    90, 94, 240; natives and, 10, 25,
    144–45; ownership, 173, 254;
    trains and, 110, 258
lawful game-killing, 57–58
laws and ordinances, 48; pass laws, 113.
    See also acts
lawsuit, Makoko, 226
Lebombo Hills, 43
Legislative Assembly of the Machangana
    Territorial Authority, 198
leisure, 90–101, 142, 144, 181
Letaba Ranch, 206, 208, 209

Limebeer, A. J., 72
lions, damage from, 28, 227
livestock, 224
living, independent, 37
Lorgat, Moosa, 165
Louis Trichardt, 63, 70
lowveld, 48, 57, 172, 199; British
    rule, 6; conservation, 153; fu-
    ture of, 209; labor in, 228; new
    order, 35–36, 40
luxury goods, 91–92

Mabuza, Befula, 49
Mabuza, Enos, 193
MacFadyen, Ian, 209
MacMillan, Harold, 135, 136
Makabene, 46
Makgatho, Sefako, 108
Makoko lawsuit, 226
Maksin, 41
Makuleke, Longone, 62
Malafene, 46
malaria, 131–32
Maluleke, James, 44
mandates, clash of, 38
Mandela, Nelson, 217, 222, 239
Manyeleti Game Reserve, 202–3, 205;
    education, 210
Maori, 125
Mapikela, Thomas, 108
marginalization, 14, 104, 218, 221
marketing, 116–17, 120, 123; Indi-
    ans and, 168
Mastulela, 25–26
Matanzima, Kaizer, 188
Matebula, Mahashi, 53
Mathlabi, Cement, 51, 53
Mavhunga, Clapperton, 47
Mayet, Ismail, 165
Mdluli, Sick Winlight, 196
Mehlwana, 43
Mgvemana, Johannes, 53
Mhlangana tribe, 55
Mia, Mohammed, 165
migrant labor, 65, 66, 116, 189; motivat-
    ing factors, 66; railways and, 116
migration, urban, 92
military occupation of Gazankulu, 209
military presence, 207, 209
mining, 37, 164, 241; conservation
    and, 68–72
missionaries, 134–35, 145, 150,
    156, 197, 198

poaching (*continued*)
    political implications of, 12, 47,
        48; women and, 47
police, South African, 52
political recognition, African, 9, 111,
    115, 148, 150, 221
political resistance, African, 48, 150, 261
political tourism, 133
Population Registration Act of 1950, 183
Portugal, 53
Portuguese Territory, 36, 43, 208
possession, 16
Potgieter, J. S., 54
predjudice: anti-African, 37;
    anti-Boer, 122
premodern subjects, 10
preservation, 4, 107, 150, 205; KNP and,
    35, 56. *See also* conservation
professional hunters, 208
profitable citizens, 93
progress, 146. *See also* modernization
Prohibition of Mixed Marriages Act
    of 1949, 183
Promotion of Bantu Self-Government
    Act of 1959, 188, 198
protests: public, 222; service deliv-
    ery, 247–50
Publicity Advisory Committee, 118
Publicity and Travel Department,
    118, 123, 128
publicity fund, overseas, 118
public protests, 222
Punda Maria, 62; Gate, 44
pursuits of leisure, 144

race, role of, 109; homelands, 189;
    Olifants, 181
racialized paternalism, 130
racism, 167, 192; anti-African prejudices,
    37; anti-Boer prejudices, 122;
    freedom from, 158, 166; KNP
    and, 184; parallels in, 93; struggle
    against, 96; trains and, 114–15
railways, 146; migrant labor and, 116; or-
    ganization of, 116–17; purpose of,
    116; role of, 109, 111; segregation
    on, 110; territory and identity, 109
rangers, 35; arming of, 43, 51 (*see
    also* firearms); firefighting, 231–
    32; Gazankulu and, 207; poach-
    ing and, 45; responsibilities of, 71;
    squatters as, 82
raw materials, Africans as, 118

recognition, political, 150
recreation, 92, 142. *See also* leisure
recruits, labor, 71
Regional Authorities, 188
reintegration, 211
released lands, 54, 216
religion, 169
removal, 212. *See also* displacement
Rennie, John Thompson, 116
rent payment, 79
Reservation of Separate Amenities Act
    of 1953, 183
resident natives, 128–29
Rex v. Befula Mabuza, 49
*Rex v. Befula Mabuza and Mgono
    Mabuza*, 49
*Rex v. Chevalo, Falasa and Mu-
    nyonwse*, 49
Rhodesia, 65
roads: apartheid and, 184; in the
    KNP, 68–71; protests and,
    247–48, 250–51
Roos, J. C. V., 46
roots and routes, 108, 135, 258
Round in Nine tours, 151, 157

Sabi Bridge, 39
Sabi Game Reserve. *See* KNP (Kruger
    National Park)
Sajine, 41
SANNC (South African Native National
    Congress), 108
SANP (South African National
    Parks), 224
SAR (South African Railways and
    Harbours corporation), 71, 108,
    111, 144, 146, 151; Publicity and
    Travel Department, 118
scheduled lands, 54
Second World War, 134
segregation, 2, 4, 12, 81, 150, 158,
    181, 199; apartheid and, 182,
    196; shift in, 200; transportation
    and, 92, 110
self-government, 200; Gazankulu, 200
self-preservation, 58
service delivery protests, 247
settlement, 216
Shiluvane Mission Station, 197
Sibasa, 41, 62
Sigodo, 45, 51
Singwitsi, 40; Game Reserve, 40, 79
Sitoye, Mafuta, 62